The Caribbean Blue Economy

The Blue Economy is emerging on the global scene as a powerful and persuasive new concept for sustainable development based on economic activities associated with the ocean. Several regions globally have adopted this concept at national and regional levels, including the Caribbean. Given the complex, multisectoral and multilevel nature of the Blue Economy, it is clear that different approaches will be needed for different regions. Hence, this volume explores the opportunities, threats and risks involved in operationalising the Blue Economy in the Wider Caribbean Region, defined as northern Brazil to the USA and all mainland and island countries and territories in-between.

The first part of the book looks at where the region stands in the global picture regarding adoption of the Blue Economy and what is planned. The second set of chapters examines key crosscutting issues such as ecosystem services, climate change and governance at national and regional levels that could make or break the Blue Economy initiative. The book then goes on to explore the main sectoral activities that will constitute the Blue Economies in the region: fisheries, tourism, shipping and transport, renewable energy, oil and gas, seabed mining and waste management are all considered. The book ends with a synthesis of the political and technical requirements to overcome threats and take advantage of opportunities in the Blue Economy.

Peter Clegg, Department of Health and Social Sciences, University of the West of England, Bristol, UK.

Robin Mahon, Centre for Resource Management and Environmental Studies (CERMES), University of the West Indies, Cave Hill Campus, St Michael, Barbados.

Patrick McConney, Centre for Resource Management and Environmental Studies (CERMES), University of the West Indies, Cave Hill Campus, St Michael, Barbados.

Hazel A. Oxenford, Centre for Resource Management and Environmental Studies (CERMES), University of the West Indies, Cave Hill Campus, St Michael, Barbados.

Europa Regional Perspectives

Providing in-depth analysis with a global reach, this series from Europa examines a wide range of contemporary political, economic, developmental and social issues in regional perspective. Intended to complement the Europa Regional Surveys of the World series, Europa Regional Perspectives will be a valuable resource for academics, students, researchers, policymakers, business people and anyone with an interest in current world affairs with an emphasis on regional issues.

While the Europa World Year Book and its associated Regional Surveys inform on and analyse contemporary economic, political and social developments, the Editors considered the need for more in-depth volumes written and/or edited by specialists in their field, in order to delve into particular regional situations. Volumes in the series are not constrained by any particular template, but may explore recent political, economic, international relations, social, defence, or other issues in order to increase knowledge. Regions are thus not specifically defined, and volumes may focus on small or large group of countries, regions or blocs.

Parliamentary Institutions in Regional and International Governance
Functions and Powers
Andrea Cofelice

Youth at the Margins
Perspectives on Arab Mediterranean Youth
Elena Sánchez-Montijano and José Sánchez García

Terrorism and Insurgency in Asia
A contemporary examination of terrorist and separatist movements
Edited by Benjamin Schreer and Andrew T. H. Tan

Russia in the Middle East and North Africa
Continuity and Change
Chiara Lovotti, Eleonora Tafuro Ambrosetti, Christopher A. Hartwell and Aleksandra Chmielewska

The Caribbean Blue Economy
Edited by Peter Clegg, Robin Mahon, Patrick McConney and Hazel A. Oxenford

For more information about this series, please visit: www.routledge.com/Europa-Regional-Perspectives/book-series/ERP

The Caribbean Blue Economy

Edited by
Peter Clegg, Robin Mahon,
Patrick McConney and Hazel A. Oxenford

LONDON AND NEW YORK

First published 2021
by Routledge
2 Park Square, Milton Park, Abingdon, Oxon OX14 4RN

and by Routledge
52 Vanderbilt Avenue, New York, NY 10017

Routledge is an imprint of the Taylor & Francis Group, an informa business

© 2021 selection and editorial matter, Peter Clegg, Robin Mahon, Patrick McConney and Hazel A. Oxenford; individual chapters, the contributors

The right of Peter Clegg, Robin Mahon, Patrick McConney and Hazel A. Oxenford to be identified as the authors of the editorial material, and of the authors for their individual chapters, has been asserted in accordance with sections 77 and 78 of the Copyright, Designs and Patents Act 1988.

All rights reserved. No part of this book may be reprinted or reproduced or utilised in any form or by any electronic, mechanical, or other means, now known or hereafter invented, including photocopying and recording, or in any information storage or retrieval system, without permission in writing from the publishers.

Trademark notice: Product or corporate names may be trademarks or registered trademarks, and are used only for identification and explanation without intent to infringe.

British Library Cataloguing in Publication Data
A catalogue record for this book is available from the British Library

Library of Congress Cataloging-in-Publication Data
A catalog record has been requested for this book

ISBN: 978-0-367-26367-6 (hbk)
ISBN: 978-0-429-34223-3 (ebk)

Typeset in Times New Roman
by Taylor & Francis Books

Contents

List of illustrations	vii
List of contributors	ix
Abbreviations	xi

1 The Blue Economy as a global initiative   1
PAWAN G. PATIL, JOHN VIRDIN AND CHARLES S. COLGAN

2 Blue Economy opportunities and challenges for the
Wider Caribbean   9
PETER CLEGG, ROBIN MAHON, PATRICK MCCONNEY AND
HAZEL A. OXENFORD

3 The Blue Economy winners and losers in the Wider Caribbean   21
NICOLE LEOTAUD, ALEXANDER GIRVAN AND SASHA JATTANSINGH

4 The state of marine ecosystems that support Blue Economies in
the Wider Caribbean   35
HAZEL A. OXENFORD AND ROBIN MAHON

5 Implications of climate change for Blue Economies in the
Wider Caribbean   49
MICHAEL A. TAYLOR, MONA K. WEBBER, TANNECIA S. STEPHENSON AND
FELICIA S. WHYTE

6 The role of coastal and marine planning in achieving
Blue Economies   63
LORNA INNISS, LUCIA FANNING, ROBIN MAHON AND MARGAUX REMOND

7 Valuation of ecosystem services as a basis for investment in
Blue Economies   78
PETER W. SCHUHMANN

vi *Contents*

8 National ocean governance as a foundation for Blue
Economic development   92
PATRICK MCCONNEY AND SANYA COMPTON

9 Regional ocean governance: An imperative for addressing Blue
Economy challenges and opportunities in the Wider Caribbean   104
LUCIA FANNING AND ROBIN MAHON

10 Fisheries as a key component of Blue Economies in the
Wider Caribbean   118
HAZEL A. OXENFORD AND PATRICK MCCONNEY

11 Tourism in the Caribbean and the Blue Economy: Can the two
be aligned?   131
PETER CLEGG, JANICE CUMBERBATCH AND KARIMA DEGIA

12 The role of shipping and marine transport in developing
Blue Economies   143
DAVID JEAN-MARIE

13 Renewable energy: An emerging Blue Economy sector   156
INDRA HARAKSINGH

14 Is there a future for the oil and gas sector within the Caribbean's
Blue Economy?   169
ANTHONY T. BRYAN

15 The future of deep-seabed minerals and marine genetic resources
in Blue Economies   182
LALETA DAVIS-MATTIS

16 The role of waste management in underpinning the Blue Economy   195
CHRISTOPHER CORBIN

17 Financing the Blue Economy in the Wider Caribbean   210
JUSTIN RAM AND DONNA KAIDOU-JEFFREY

18 Limits and opportunities in supporting the Blue Economy:
A diplomat's view   226
SIR RONALD SANDERS

19 The Blue Economy in the Wider Caribbean: Opportunities,
limitations and considerations   236
PETER CLEGG, ROBIN MAHON, PATRICK MCCONNEY AND HAZEL A.OXENFORD

Index   243

Illustrations

Figures

5.1 A summary of likely threats from climate change to Caribbean fisheries. 55
6.1 Sea defences at Holetown on the west coast of Barbados. 68
6.2 Planning process for ICZM in Belize. 70
8.1 The relative importance and effectiveness of good governance principles will vary with the nature and complexity of the situation. 98
9.1 The Wider Caribbean Regional ocean governance cluster. 107
9.2 Graphical representation of the Large Marine Ecosystem Governance Framework showing (left) the need for process at multiple levels, lateral and vertical linkages among them, and (right) the stages of the policy process that are required for effective governance. 111
9.3 A diagram of the nested, multi-scale level nature of the proposed operational Regional Governance Framework for living marine resources in the WCR 112
17.1 Selected Caribbean countries' debt to GDP Ratios (2018). 211

Tables

1.1 Examples of estimates of the size of the ocean economy 3
4.1 Examples of valuable ecosystem services provided by selected coastal and marine ecosystems in the WCR 39
5.1 Historical and future change in marine climate variables for the Caribbean region 50
5.2 Impacts of climate induced stressors on living resources of the Caribbean Sea 52
5.3 Response measures for advancing the Blue Economy in the Caribbean 58
6.1 Barbados ICZM planning: main tasks in technical feasibility study (Caribbean Environment Programme, 1996) 69

viii *List of illustrations*

6.2 Some examples of Caribbean CBOs that have taken on
responsibility for aspects of ICZM — 74
7.1 Coastal and marine ecosystems, assets, services, benefits and
measures of economic value — 84
12.1 Caribbean Blue Economy activities, industries and
growth drivers — 144
16.1 Waste management challenges and needs — 204

Boxes

3.1 Caribbean definition of a Green Economy — 22
3.2 Delivering triple-bottom-line co-benefits — 27
3.3 Inclusive local Blue Economy in action — 28
3.4 Innovative insurance for fisherfolk — 29
3.5 People managing oceans — 29

Contributors

Anthony T. Bryan, Senior Associate of the Center for Strategic and International Studies (CSIS) in Washington, DC, USA.

Peter Clegg, Department of Health and Social Sciences, University of the West of England, Bristol, UK.

Charles S. Colgan, Center for the Blue Economy, Middlebury Institute of International Studies at Monterey, Monterey, CA, USA.

Sanya Compton, Centre for Resource Management and Environmental Studies (CERMES), University of the West Indies, Cave Hill Campus, Barbados.

Christopher Corbin, Caribbean Environment Programme, Regional Coordinating Unit, United Nations Environment, Kingston, Jamaica.

Janice Cumberbatch, Centre for Resource Management and Environmental Studies (CERMES), University of the West Indies, Cave Hill, Barbados.

Laleta Davis-Mattis, Faculty of Law, University of the West Indies, Mona, Jamaica.

Karima Degia, AKD Environmental Solutions, Barbados.

Lucia Fanning, Marine Affairs Program, Dalhousie University, Halifax, Canada.

Alexander Girvan, Caribbean Natural Resources Institute (CANARI), Barataria, Trinidad and Tobago.

Indra Haraksingh, University of the West Indies, St Augustine Campus, Trinidad and Tobago.

Lorna Inniss, Caribbean Environment Programme, Regional Coordinating Unit, United Nations Environment, Kingston, Jamaica.

Sasha Jattansingh, Caribbean Natural Resources Institute (CANARI), Barataria, Trinidad and Tobago.

x *List of contributors*

David Jean-Marie, Barbados Port Inc., Bridgetown, Barbados.

Donna Kaidou-Jeffrey, Caribbean Development Bank, Wildey, St Michael, Barbados.

Nicole Leotaud, Caribbean Natural Resources Institute (CANARI), Barataria, Trinidad and Tobago.

Robin Mahon, Centre for Resource Management and Environmental Studies (CERMES), University of the West Indies, Cave Hill Campus, St Michael, Barbados.

Patrick McConney, Centre for Resource Management and Environmental Studies (CERMES), University of the West Indies, Cave Hill Campus, St Michael, Barbados.

Hazel A. Oxenford, Centre for Resource Management and Environmental Studies (CERMES), University of the West Indies, Cave Hill Campus, St Michael, Barbados.

Pawan G. Patil, World Bank Group, Washington, DC, USA.

Justin Ram, Caribbean Development Bank, Wildey, St Michael, Barbados.

Margaux Remond, Caribbean Environment Programme, Regional Coordinating Unit, United Nations Environment, Kingston, Jamaica.

Sir Ronald Sanders, Antigua and Barbuda's Ambassador to the US and the Organisation of American States. He also served as Ambassador to the World Trade Organization.

Peter W. Schuhmann, Department of Economics and Finance, The University of North Carolina at Wilmington, Wilmington, North Carolina, USA.

Tannecia S. Stephenson, Department of Physics, University of the West Indies, Mona, Jamaica.

Michael A. Taylor, Department of Physics, University of the West Indies, Mona, Jamaica.

John Virdin, Nicholas Institute for Environmental Policy Solutions, Duke University, Durham, NC, USA.

Mona K. Webber, Department of Life Sciences, University of the West Indies, Mona, Jamaica.

Felicia S. Whyte, Department of Physics, University of the West Indies, Mona, Jamaica.

Abbreviations

ABNJ	Areas Beyond National Jurisdiction
ACS	Association of Caribbean States
BBNJ	Biodiversity Beyond National Jurisdiction
BODS	Big ocean developing states
CANARI	Caribbean Natural Resources Institute
CARICOM	Caribbean Community
CCRIF	Caribbean Catastrophe Risk Insurance Facility
CDB	Caribbean Development Bank
CHM	Common heritage of mankind
CLIA	Cruise Line International Association
CLME	Caribbean Large Marine Ecosystem
COAST	Caribbean Oceans and Aquaculture Sustainability Facility
CRFM	Caribbean Regional Fisheries Mechanism
CSA	Caribbean Shipping Association
CSC	Caribbean Sea Commission
CZMP	Coastal zone management planning
EBM	Ecosystem based management
ECLAC	Economic Commission for Latin America and the Caribbean
ECROP	Eastern Caribbean Regional Ocean Policy
EEZ	Exclusive Economic Zone
FAO	Food and Agriculture Organisation
FCCA	Florida Caribbean Cruise Association
GEF	Global Environment Facility
IMO	International Maritime Organization
IPCC	Intergovernmental Panel on Climate Change
IUCN	International Union for Conservation of Nature
ISA	International Seabed Authority
IUU	Illegal, unreported, unregulated fishing
LBS	Land-based sources of pollution
LME	Large Marine Ecosystem
MARPOL	International Convention for the Prevention of Pollution from Ships
MPA	Marine protected area

xii *Abbreviations*

MSP	Marine spatial planning
OECD	Organisation for Economic Cooperation and Development
OECS	Organisation of Eastern Caribbean States
OGC	Ocean governance committee
OSPESCA	Fisheries and Aquaculture Organisation for Central America
PSC	Port State Control
SAP	Strategic Action Programme
SDGS	Sustainable Development Goals
SICA	Central American Integration System
SIDS	Small island developing states
SPAW	Specially Protected Areas and Wildlife
SSF	Small-scale fisheries
SST	Sea surface temperatures
UNCLOS	United Nations Convention on the Law of the Sea
UNDP	United Nations Development Programme
UNEP	United Nations Environment Programme
WCR	Wider Caribbean Region
WECAFC	Western Central Atlantic Fisheries Commission
WWF	World Wide Fund for Nature

1 The Blue Economy as a global initiative

Pawan G. Patil, John Virdin and
Charles S. Colgan

Introduction

Within the last five years, the concept of the Blue Economy has entered into widespread use around the world (Colgan, 2017). The list of countries whose governments have promoted this concept in various forms as a strategy for economic development has grown long, and examples include: Australia, China, the European Union, India, Indonesia and a number of small island developing states such as Grenada and Mauritius (European Commission, 2012; Surís-Regueiro et al., 2013; Salim, 2014; Sunoto, 2014; Zhao et al., 2014; Conathan and Moore, 2015; ANI, 2017; Cervigni and Scandizzo, 2017; Voyer et al., 2017). Across these countries the concept has been defined and applied very differently (Voyer et al., 2018; Colgan 2017), and as a result has been characterised at times as a "buzzword" that has general agreement in the abstract but not in practice (Bueger, 2015; Voyer et al., 2017).

In some cases, the Blue Economy concept has been promoted as a response to a vision of rapidly increasing human activity in the ocean, labelled an "economic frontier" for an expanding population searching for new sources of growth, equipped with emerging technologies that make the global ocean and its resources more accessible (Jouffray et al., 2020; Economist Intelligence Unit, 2015). To some extent, the concept has evolved from the earlier idea of an "ocean economy", which aimed to link a diverse set of economic activities and industries under one label, because they all in some way shared the ocean as a physical context (OECD, 2016). For this reason, the concept of the ocean economy first needs some description, and to be distinguished from the concept of a Blue Economy.

Defining ocean economy

As a precursor to the term Blue Economy, the term ocean economy was used by economists to collectively describe the diverse ocean-linked economic activity in a given space, and define this activity as a unique segment of the broader economy. The aim of the ocean economy concept was often to provide the basis for more integrated ocean policies that could capture economies

2 *Pawan G. Patil et al.*

of scale and reduce negative externalities by regulating together the various competing and overlapping uses of a given ocean space, rather than industry-by-industry or sector-by-sector (Colgan, 2017). The ocean economy concept is analogous to other segments of an economy where industries are interlinked by some common feature (in this case the ocean environment), such that they collectively function as a system rather than a fragmented list of individual sectors, e.g. the "bioeconomy" or the "information economy" (Park and Kildow, 2014; OECD, 2016).

For many years the term ocean economy was not consistently applied around the world, reportedly defined 14 different ways by 14 different countries in 2014 (Park and Kildow, 2014). However, in 2016 the OECD provided what has become a more universal definition for the ocean economy concept, as a term referring to "the sum of the economic activities of ocean-based industries, and the assets, goods and services of marine ecosystems", including direct and indirect supporting activities necessary for the functioning of ocean-based industries (OECD, 2016).

Despite differences in definition, many countries have been working to measure the size of their ocean economy since the United States first attempted to estimate the contribution of ocean-related economic activity to Gross Domestic Product (GDP) in 1974, for example in Australia, Canada, France and the United Kingdom (Colgan, 2016). As these efforts have expanded over the years, countries have begun to formalise them as part of their national economic accounting systems, by establishing dedicated ocean accounts that derive from and add to their national income and product accounts (Colgan, 2017). The activities and industries that countries have categorised as part of their ocean economy have varied by context, but have often included a core group of traditional marine industries: fisheries and aquaculture, marine construction, tourism and recreation, boat building and repair, marine transportation and minerals including oil and gas (Colgan, 2017). More recently, offshore wind can be added to this list, along with emerging industries such as offshore aquaculture (OECD, 2016).

Global estimates of the size of the ocean economy have varied (as have the estimation methods used), including the estimates shown in Table 1.1. Perhaps the most extensive effort to measure the size of the global ocean economy was by the OECD in 2016, estimating a gross value added of US$1.5 trillion in 2010 (2.5% of the global total) and 31 million direct full-time jobs (though small-scale fisheries were not included) (OECD, 2016). By this measure, the ocean economy would have ranked in the world's top 12 national economies in 2010 (Patil et al., 2018).

Such measures of the ocean economy have rarely accounted for sustainability, often capturing only the economic output. However, over time the concept has evolved to reflect environmental and social considerations, coinciding with wider recognition of human-driven changes in the status of the ecosystems underpinning the ocean economy. As countries tried to adjust to the twin trends of accelerating growth in the ocean economy and the decline

Table 1.1 Examples of estimates of the size of the ocean economy

Estimation method	Estimated size of ocean economy (US$ trillion/year)	Source
Gross marine product	2.5	Hoegh-Guldberg et al. (2015)
Market value of marine and coastal resources	3.0	Global Ocean Commission (2014)
Annual gross revenues of ocean-linked industries	2.6	Golden et al. (2017)

of the underlying ecosystems, in the last decade many began to use the perspective of a "Green Economy" as a lens for trying to decouple economic growth and environmental degradation in the ocean (Patil et al., 2016). The term "Green Economy" was broadly applied to the ocean at the 2012 Rio +20 Summit, and subsequently the term "Blue Economy" became a more prominent feature in international policy dialogue on the ocean.

At the time of Rio+20 and soon after, the term Blue Economy was not universally defined, but rather reflected multiple and competing discourses on human–ocean relations, including: (i) the oceans as natural capital, (ii) the oceans as "good business", (iii) the oceans as integral to small island developing states (SIDS) and (iv) the oceans as a source of small-scale fishing livelihoods (Silver et al., 2015). The concept was the subject of a number of international summits held in the years following Rio+20 (e.g. the global ocean action summit for food security and blue growth hosted by the Government of the Netherlands in 2014,[1] the world ocean summit on financing the sustainable ocean economy organised by the Economist Intelligence Unit in 2017[2] and the global sustainable Blue Economy conference hosted by the Government of Kenya in 2018,[3] to name a few), and was reflected in FAO's 2014 State of World Fisheries and Aquaculture report (Patil et al., 2016). Yet among all of these discussions, the concept remained broadly and poorly defined.

Perhaps most commonly in the years after Rio+20, the Blue Economy concept has *de facto* been defined as a shorthand for sustainable development of the ocean. A widely cited white paper by the Economist Intelligence Unit in 2015 characterised the concept as a "sustainable ocean economy", which "emerges when economic activity is in balance with the long-term capacity of ocean ecosystems to support this activity and remain resilient and healthy" (Economist Intelligence Unit, 2015). In 2017 the World Bank and United Nations defined the Blue Economy as "comprising the range of economic sectors and related policies that together determine whether the use of oceanic resources is sustainable". These definitions essentially introduced the multi-dimensional concept of sustainable development (World Bank and

4 *Pawan G. Patil et al.*

UNDESA, 2017) to the economic concept of an ocean economy, similar in a number of ways to the older concept of a Green Economy. This is the essential feature of the Blue Economy concept often used today: an objective to balance both the economic opportunities and environmental limitations of using the ocean to generate wealth, in what is both a "bold vision and an excruciatingly delicate balancing act" (Colgan, 2017).

Creating a Blue Economy

As the term Blue Economy has increasingly been used to reflect the sustainability of an ocean economy, some organisations have emphasised its social dimensions (Patil et al., 2018). FAO for example included "social protection of coastal communities" in its description of the concept (FAO, 2014). Given that the largest source of employment in the ocean economy is likely to be small-scale fisheries, experts have recently cautioned that the concerns of these communities and stakeholders are at risk of being forgotten or ignored in the pursuit of a Blue Economy, particularly as their activities are often informal and harder to count than many ocean industries (Basurto et al., 2017; World Bank, 2012; Cohen et al., 2019).

If the Blue Economy concept is defined essentially as the pursuit or achievement of a sustainable ocean economy, relatively few frameworks yet exist for identifying (and/or encouraging) activities in the ocean that would fit in all three dimensions of sustainable development: social, environmental and economic. In 2015 the WWF proposed a set of Blue Economy principles to help fill this void, which are useful to repeat:

> A blue economy is a marine-based economy that …
> - Provides social and economic benefits for current and future generations by contributing to food security, poverty eradication, livelihoods, income, employment, health, safety, equity and political stability.
> - Restores, protects and maintains the diversity, productivity, resilience, core functions and intrinsic value of marine ecosystems – the natural capital upon which its prosperity depends.
> - Is based on clean technologies, renewable energy and circular material flows to secure economic and social stability over time, while keeping within the limits of one planet.
> - Is governed by public and private processes that are: inclusive; well-informed, precautionary and adaptive; accountable and transparent; holistic, cross-sectoral and long-term; and innovative and proactive.
>
> (World Bank and UNDESA, 2017)

Of course, examples of the application of these principles to ocean policy at a large scale, or preferably empirical observations of the development of a Blue Economy at a large spatial scale that is consistent with these principles, are still relatively scarce. The development of policy frameworks to guide a Blue

Economy is still nascent and few examples exist at the country level, much less the regional level such as applicable for the Caribbean.

Conclusion

This overview perhaps suggests a dose of realism. Despite the emphasis on sustainability, the terms "ocean economy" and "Blue Economy" have still been used interchangeably in many instances in recent years, as synonyms. For many countries, the focus has been largely on increasing economic growth from their ocean space and resources (Bennett et al., 2019), i.e. the development of an ocean-based economic growth model, promoted under the label of the Blue Economy (Voyer et al., 2018; Voyer and van Leeuwen, 2019).

In practice, the concept of a Blue Economy or a "sustainable ocean economy" more often remains an aspiration, whose recent prominence could perhaps rest upon two implicit assumptions: (i) that the ocean will actually be an economic frontier in the coming decades and century, particularly as terrestrial-based growth reaches limits in many countries and new technologies allow for more far-reaching and industrialised use of the ocean; and (ii) different or more sustainable models of economic development can be introduced to guide such growth, to avoid repeating mistakes made on land over the last century. For the first assumption, OECD has predicted that the global ocean economy will grow at a faster rate than the global economy between 2010 and 2030 (OECD, 2016). However, the second assumption remains largely untested.

In the end, for many governments the Blue Economy concept may simply translate into ocean-based research and development policies, essentially acting as an industrial policy for the ocean space under a state's jurisdiction. How fast and what kind of ocean-based economic growth emerges, and whether states can put guardrails on it to ensure sustainability, by and large remain open questions. Perhaps the aspiration of a Blue Economy will become a self-perpetuating goal rather than a passing fad, if it boosts attention, policy and investment to levels that yield socially and environmentally sustainable economic returns for coastal and island states. Indeed, the Economist Intelligence Unit (2019) suggests that a new wave of investment in the Blue Economy is rising, and that ocean industrialisation is upon us. Can the pursuit of new sources of wealth be decoupled from continued environmental degradation in the ocean, and marginalisation of coastal fishing communities? What policy frameworks would be required now to ensure this decoupling occurs? As a first step to carrying out the balancing act between the social, environmental and economic dimensions of ocean-based development, policymakers have been recommended to understand the full range of assets upon which output from the ocean economy rests, in order to monitor and measure trade-offs between them, including the: (i) natural capital (stocks of natural assets and resources, such as soil, water and biodiversity); (ii) produced

6 *Pawan G. Patil et al.*

capital (machinery, buildings, equipment, etc.); (iii) human capital (the value of skills, experience and effort by the working population); and (iv) financial capital (Lange et al., 2018; Patil et al., 2018). In carrying out the balancing act implied by Blue Economy aspirations, the Caribbean may provide a large laboratory for the world, and indeed many island states in the region have already begun.

Notes

1 http://www.fao.org/3/a-bl007e.pdf. Accessed 28 July 2019.
2 https://events.economist.com/events-conferences/asia/ocean-summit-2017/. Accessed 28 July 2019.
3 http://www.blueeconomyconference.go.ke/. Accessed 28 July 2019.

References

ANI. 2017. Blue economy can improve India's progress: PM Modi. Available at: http://www.abplive.in/india-news/blue-economy-can-improve-india-s-progress-pm-m odi-589488.
Basurto, X., Virdin, J., Smith, H. and Juskus, R. 2017. *Strengthening Governance of Small-Scale Fisheries*. Oak Foundation. Available at: https://nicholasinstitute.duke. edu/publications/strengthening-governance-small-scale-fisheries-initial-assessment-th eory-and-practice.
Bennett, N. J. *et al.* 2019. Toward a sustainable and equitable blue economy. *Nature Sustainability*, 2: 991–993.
Bueger, C. 2015. What is maritime security? *Marine Policy*, 53: 159–164.
Cervigni R. and Scandizzo, P. L. 2017. *The Ocean Economy in Mauritius: Making it Happen, Making it Last*. Washington, DC: The World Bank.
Cohen, P. J. *et al.* 2019. Securing a just space for small-scale fisheries in the blue economy. *Frontiers in Marine Science*. https://doi.org/10.3389/fmars.2019.00171.
Colgan, C. S. 2016. Measurement of the ocean economy from national income accounts to the sustainable blue economy. *Journal of Ocean and Coastal Economics*, 2(2): Article 12.
Colgan, C. S. 2017. The blue economy of the Indian Ocean: Context and challenge. *Journal of Indian Ocean Rim Studies*, 1: 7–37.
Conathan M. and Moore, S. 2015. *Developing a Blue Economy in China and the United States*. Center for American Progress. Available at: https://cdn.americanp rogress.org/wp-content/uploads/2015/05/ChinaBlueEcon-report-final.pdf.
Economist Intelligence Unit. 2015. *The Blue Economy: Growth, Opportunity, and a Sustainable Ocean Economy*. London: EIU. Available at: http://perspectives.eiu.com/ sustainability/blue-economy/white-paper/blue-economy.
Economist Intelligence Unit. 2019. World Ocean Summit 2020: The gap between intention and reality. Available at: https://www.woi.economist.com/world-ocea n-summit/.
European Commission (EC). 2012. Blue growth: Opportunities for marine and maritime sustainable growth. Available at http://eur-lex.europa.eu/legal-content/EN/ ALL/?uri=CELEX:52012DC0494.
FAO. 2014. *State of World Fisheries and Aquaculture*. Rome: FAO.

Global Ocean Commission (GOC). 2014. *From Decline to Recovery: A Rescue Package for the Global Ocean.* Oxford: Global Ocean Commission.

Golden J. S., Virdin, J., Nowacek, D., Halpin, P., Bennear, L. and Patil, P. G. 2017. Making sure the blue economy is green. *Nature Ecology & Evolution*, 1: Article 17.

Hoegh-Guldberg, O., Beal, D., Chaudhry, T., Elhaj, H., Abdullat, A., Etessy, P. and Smits, M. 2015. *Reviving the Ocean Economy: The Case for Action.* Gland and Geneva, Switzerland: WWF.

Jouffray, J. B., Blasiak, R., Norstrom, A. V., Osterblom, H. and Nystrom, M. 2020. The blue acceleration: The trajectory of human expansion into the ocean. *One Earth*, 2(1): 43–54.

Lange, G. M., Wodon, Q. and Carey, K. (eds). 2018. *The Changing Wealth of Nations 2018: Building a Sustainable Future.* Washington, DC: The World Bank.

OECD. 2016. *The Ocean Economy in 2030.* Paris: OECD.

Park, K. S. and Kildow, J. T. 2014. Rebuilding the classification system of the ocean economy. *Journal of Ocean and Coastal Economics*, 2014(1): Article 4.

Patil, P. G., Virdin, J., Diez, S. M., Roberts, J. and Singh, A. 2016. *Toward a Blue Economy: A Promise for Sustainable Growth in the Caribbean.* Washington, DC: The World Bank Group.

Patil, P. G., Virdin J., Colgan, C. S., Hussain, M. G., Failler, P. and Vegh, T. 2018. *Toward a Blue Economy: A Pathway for Sustainable Growth in Bangladesh.* Washington, DC: The World Bank Group.

Salim, T. 2014. Maritime-axis development to boost RI's GDP. *The Jakarta Post.* Available at: http://www.thejakartapost.com/news/2014/12/30/maritime-axis-development-boost-ri-s-gdp.html.

Silver, J. J., Gray, N. J., Campbell, L. M., Fairbanks, L. W. and Gruby, R. L. 2015. Blue economy and competing discourses in international oceans governance. *The Journal of Environment & Development*, 24: 135–160.

Sunoto, M. 2014. *Blue Economy: Promoting sustainable marine and fisheries development in Indonesia (A policy framework).* Presentation, Third APEC Blue Economy Forum, Xiamen, 25 August. Available at: https://www.slideshare.net/sunotomes/blue-economy-policy-frameworks

Surís-Regueiro J. C., Garza-Gil, M. D. and Varela-Lafuente, M. M. 2013. Marine economy: A proposal for its definition in the European Union. *Marine Policy*, 42: 111–124.

Voyer, M. and Leeuwen, J.van. 2019. 'Social license to operate' in the blue economy. *Resources Policy*, 62: 102–113.

Voyer, M., Quirk, G., McIlgorm, A., Kamal, A., Kaye, S. and McArthur, M. 2017. *The Blue Economy in Australia: Conceptualizing the Blue Economy, its Relationship with Maritime Security, and its Role in Australian Ocean Governance.* Canberra: Sea Power Centre. Available at: http://www.navy.gov.au/media-room/publications/sea-power-series-blue-economy-australia.

Voyer, M, Quirk, G., McIlgorm, A. and Azmi, K. 2018. Shades of blue: What do competing interpretations of the blue economy mean for ocean governance? *Journal of Environmental Policy & Planning*, 20 (5): 595–616.

Voyer, M., Schofield, C., Azmi, K., Warner, R., McIlgorm, A. and Quirk, G. 2018. Maritime security and blue economy: Intersections and interdependencies in the Indian Ocean. *Journal of the Indian Ocean Region*, 14 (1): 28–48.

World Bank. 2012. *Hidden Harvests: The Global Contribution of Capture Fisheries.* Washington, DC: The World Bank Group.

8 Pawan G. Patil et al.

World Bank and United Nations Department of Economic and Social Affairs (UNDESA). 2017. *The Potential of the Blue Economy: Increasing Long-Term Benefits of the Sustainable Use of Marine Resources for Small Island Developing States and Coastal Least Developed Countries.* Washington, DC: The World Bank.

Zhao, R., Hynes, S. and He, G. S. 2014. Defining and quantifying China's ocean economy. *Marine Policy*, 43: 164–173.

2 Blue Economy opportunities and challenges for the Wider Caribbean

Peter Clegg, Robin Mahon, Patrick McConney and Hazel A. Oxenford

Introduction

The Caribbean is a geopolitically diverse region with over 40 states and countries. It is also ecologically diverse with wide productive continental shelves, coastal lagoons and mangrove forests, coral reefs and associated seagrass beds, and areas of open ocean. Across the region, all the sectors relevant to a Blue Economy are important in varying degrees depending on the sub-region and the country. Tourism is the primary economic activity, but fisheries, energy, oil and gas and marine transportation are all prominent components of at least some national economies. Seabed mining for minerals and prospecting for genetic resources are activities that have been little explored. This chapter provides an overview of the sectoral diversity, as well as the challenges and opportunities that lie ahead as countries of the region seek to take advantage of their considerable ocean space and resources.

The lead-up to Rio+20, 2012, found many Caribbean states focused on transitioning to a Green Economy (UNEP, 2011; Smith et al., 2014). An important initial activity was the Regional Dialogue facilitated by the Caribbean Natural Resources Institute (CANARI), from 2009 to 2012, to develop a regional perspective. A key conclusion was that while consensus was possible in general terms, the countries were so diverse that each would have to define its own approach to a Green Economy. Barbados (2012) and Jamaica (2016) completed Green Economy Scoping Studies (Moore et al., 2012; UNEP, 2016). Following a Caribbean Community (CARICOM) decision in 2012 to pursue Green Economies, two Caribbean Green Economy Conferences (CGEC) were held, the first in St. Lucia in 2013 and the second in Jamaica in 2015.[1] These built on the Rio+20 outcome document "The future we want", which considered the Green Economy to be an important tool for achieving sustainable development and poverty eradication. In the immediate aftermath of Rio+20 many Caribbean states also took note of the increased emphasis on oceans, especially in Sustainable Development Goal SDG 14, "Conserve and sustainably use the oceans, seas and marine resources for sustainable development",[2] but also, in several other SDGs (Fanning and Mahon, 2017). The new idea of Blue Economies struck a chord with

10 *Peter Clegg et al.*

small Caribbean states that have large ocean spaces and high dependency on ocean services.

Despite the concept of Blue Economic Growth being a relatively new one, as Patil highlighted in Chapter 1, Caribbean states expressed the desire to explore Blue Economy policies in numerous high-level fora. Notable was the inaugural Caribbean Region Dialogue with the G20 Development Working Group that took place in April 2015.[3] Finance ministers and central bank governors focused on the development of Blue Economies and on the resources needed. Caribbean countries noted that transitioning to a Blue Economy would support several broader policy objectives captured in the SDGs, including poverty reduction, food security, energy security, disaster risk reduction, climate change mitigation and adaptation and ocean conservation.

There has been steady progress towards incorporating Blue Economy policies into regional and national development agendas. The extensive Caribbean presence at the Sustainable Blue Economy Conference held in Nairobi, in November 2018, underscored the interest of a broad cross section of countries in the region (IISD, 2018). In 2016, Grenada developed its Blue Growth Coastal Master Plan and the associated Integrated Coastal Zone Management Policy (Patil et al., 2016). In 2018 Barbados established the first ministry focused on the Blue Economy (The Ministry of the Blue Economy and Maritimes Affairs). In June 2019 UN Environment Caribbean Environment Programme and the Government of Honduras hosted the Blue Economy Summit in Roatán, Honduras aimed at advancing a regional Sustainable Blue Economy Strategy for the Caribbean. In August 2019 Mexico reaffirmed its commitment to a Sustainable Ocean Economy at the High-Level Panel for a Sustainable Ocean Economy.[4] Costa Rica has developed its Oceans Economy and Trade Strategies.[5] Many other countries are explicitly pursuing Blue Economic policies. A full review of related national activities is beyond the scope of this chapter, but the key point is that national pursuit of Blue Economies continues unabated.

Regional organisations have also been active in promoting Blue Economies. In 2014, countries urged the Association of Caribbean States (ACS) to use its Caribbean Sea Commission, then chaired by Costa Rica, to jumpstart a wider discussion on the Blue Economy. The Caribbean Development Bank launched Blue Economy Caribbean in November 2018 as a call for the region to prioritise coastal and marine economies that are sustainable, scalable, inclusive and environmentally sound.[6] At the launch the focus was on financing the transition to Blue Economies. The second Blue Economy Caribbean conference and exposition took place in October 2019.[7] It reviewed progress and programme development since the first conference and explored related issues such as technology, partnerships and gender equality.

The Organisation of Eastern Caribbean States (OECS) is also committed to transitioning its member states to Blue Economies. In October 2017 it obtained a US$6.3 million grant from the World Bank for its Caribbean

Regional Oceanscape Project (CROP). Specifically, CROP will support the implementation of regional policies, including mapping ocean assets, developing coastal and marine spatial plans and national ocean policies and strategies through active citizen engagement; collaborating with private sector technology companies and education platforms to advance ocean education; and improving OECS ocean data coverage and access through collaborative public–private platforms. Most recently, in October 2019, the CARICOM Caribbean Regional Fisheries Mechanism (CRFM) and the Central American Integration System (SICA) Fisheries and Aquaculture Organisation (OSPESCA) signed a joint declaration for cooperation on Blue Economic Growth in their 24 Member States. Despite these advances neither CARICOM, SICA nor the ACS appear to have well-articulated strategies for supporting Blue Economies in their member states.

UN agency programmes such as the FAO's Blue Growth Initiative, UN Environment's Blue Economy support programme and UNDP's Accelerator Labs can be expected to positively affect Blue Economy efforts in the region either directly or through their regional bodies. UNDP in December 2019 established its Blue Accelerator Lab in Barbados for the Eastern Caribbean to "promote out-of-the-box thinking and experimentation" in Small Island Developing States (SIDS)".[8] This initiative has a special focus on supporting sustainable development of ocean-based economies. Many projects and initiatives around the region are already oriented to Blue Economies or are rebranding with it in mind. For example, the region wide Caribbean Large Marine Ecosystem Project (Debels et al., 2017) is emphasising the critical importance of its activities, especially the proposed regional ocean coordination mechanism, for supporting Blue Economies.

Cross-cutting issues

As the Caribbean transitions towards a Blue Economy, consideration of cross-cutting issues will be critical to its foundation and long-term sustainability in a changing world. These will include the health and diversity of the marine ecosystems; the future impacts of, and responses to, climate change; recognition of the true value of marine ecosystem services; integrated coastal and marine planning; and sound ocean governance at all levels from national to international.

The Wider Caribbean is considered one of the most biodiverse areas of the world's oceans, exhibiting a broad range of oceanographic and hydrographic features and highly diverse tropical and subtropical seascapes, including a vast area of open ocean influenced by water masses from both the equatorial North and South Atlantic Oceans, transported by major ocean currents that link marine areas and populations across the region. Some of the most important habitats, considering their supporting and provisioning services, such as beaches, coral reefs, seagrass meadows, mangrove forests and saltmarshes, are also among the most vulnerable to anthropogenic stressors,

12 Peter Clegg et al.

including global climate change, and have suffered significant degradation across the region from overfishing, coastal development and land-based pollution (Rice et al., 2016). A key issue of concern therefore, is the maintenance, and in many cases rehabilitation, of the health and thus resilience of coastal and ocean habitats to protect the ecosystem services that underpin Caribbean economies and are critical for a Blue Economy. This issue is considered in more detail by Oxenford and Mahon in Chapter 4.

Of concern must be the many aspects of climate change and climate variability that pose a threat to the Caribbean's critical coastal and ocean ecosystems and related economic sectors (Oxenford and Monnereau, 2018; Taylor et al., Chapter 5 this volume). Increasing sea surface temperatures have already caused significant damage to coral reef ecosystems across the entire region, affecting the tourism and fisheries sectors by reducing the aesthetic value, fishery productivity and coastal protection services of reefs. Increasing temperatures will ultimately cause fishery stocks to become less productive and/or move out of the region to higher latitudes. Shifts in temperature and expected alterations in currents are likely to cause mismatches between peak spawning and best conditions for survival of larval stages of many marine species with wide-ranging implications for population sizes and genetic connectivity of commercially important stocks. Ocean acidification is expected to further negatively affect survival of planktonic larval stages and interfere with ocean food webs. Increasing sea level and more frequent dangerous Category 4 and 5 hurricanes are already wreaking havoc in coastal ecosystems and impacting coastal infrastructure critical to the fisheries, tourism and marine transport sectors, with serious implications for national economies.

More recently, mass influxes of sargassum seaweed, another symptom of climate change and ocean eutrophication are causing significant challenges to the fishery and marine transport sectors and damaging tourism across the region. However, some aspects of climate change may also present opportunities for innovation and improvements that should be explored in diversifying a Blue Economy such as using new raw materials (e.g. sargassum) or "building back better" after major hurricanes. This underscores the need for mainstreaming climate change into national policies to ensure adequate adaption, innovation opportunity and disaster risk reduction to support a Blue Economy in this vulnerable region.

The coastal and ocean resources of the Caribbean serve as the natural capital asset base, providing direct and indirect contributions to economic activity and human wellbeing (Schuhmann and Mahon, 2015). Benefits include the provision of oxygen, food and water, aesthetic appeal, cultural value and attraction to tourists, risk reduction from storm damage and climate change, opportunities for recreation, energy creation and carbon storage. Despite their obvious importance, however, values derived from environmental goods and services are often overlooked by policy makers, in part because people and governments most often respond to monetary price signals which may differ from economic values. Economic valuation estimates

Blue Economy opportunities and challenges 13

what something is worth to society at large. When applied to natural resources and ecosystem services, economic valuation can provide the information needed to estimate the costs associated with development and species and habitat loss; the benefits of conservation, restoration or risk-reduction efforts; or a nation's economic dependence on natural systems. The foundation of the Blue Economy concept is managing coastal and ocean resources in a way that maximises their economic value and benefits to society whilst at the same time ensuring the long-term health of ocean and coastal ecosystems. This requires measurement of ecosystem service stocks, flows and economic values in order to design policies that maintain and/or improve that value, and how this can be achieved is considered by Schuhmann in Chapter 7.

Inappropriate disposal of waste of all kinds poses a severe threat to Caribbean marine ecosystems (Burke and Maidens, 2004; Diez et al., 2019; Corbin, Chapter 16 this volume). Land-based marine pollution is caused by both solid and liquid waste entering the marine environment through direct dumping or littering along shorelines or via natural river systems, underground seepage, or man-made drains and outfalls. Solid waste includes the pervasive discarded plastics in particular, whilst liquid wastes include nutrients, suspended sediments, pesticides, pharmaceutical drugs, hydrocarbons, heavy metals and many other chemical contaminants that may enter the sea. Ship-based pollution is also a major concern, especially regarding petroleum products, discarded fishing gear and plastics. The Cartagena Convention, together with its Land Based Sources and Oil Spills Protocols, provides a legal structure under which members are required to take action aimed at preventing, controlling and reducing marine pollution in the Wider Caribbean. Furthermore, regional programmes such as the Caribbean Regional Fund for Wastewater Management have been supported by several donors.

A Blue Economy must be supported by coastal and marine planning that recognises the linkages between the land and the sea, and thus integrates both "Green" and "Blue" economic activities. For Small Island Developing States (SIDS) especially, this warrants an "island systems" type of approach to land use and coastal planning, extending seaward through marine spatial planning. Although Caribbean countries have been on this path for some time, the emergence of a Blue Economy as a driving force could be an important catalyst for accelerating action and adaptation in the anticipated era of increasing climate change and variability, and Chapter 6 by Inniss et al. evaluates how this can be done. A Blue Economy can also become a unifying element to improve the policy, planning and practical coherence among the typically highly fragmented institutional arrangements for coastal and marine planning. With prospects of more coastal, nearshore and offshore development associated with fisheries, aquaculture, tourism, transport, oil and gas, renewable energy and other economic arenas, this requirement is urgent. Planning at the geographic scale of whole-island system or continental coastal seascape is becoming more accepted, as is the need to involve both place-based communities and communities of interest and practice in planning and management.

14 *Peter Clegg et al.*

Determining how national and sub-regional intersectoral ocean governance can take place under the thrust towards a Blue Economy is one of the first steps in this new direction.

The notion of a Blue Economy has quickly become globalised. However, as McConney argues in Chapter 8, its successful implementation will largely require national-level ocean governance with sectoral integration across civil society, the public sector and the private sector as the basis for engaging at regional and global governance levels. Through the Caribbean and other Large Marine Ecosystem initiatives the region has become increasingly familiar with visualising multi-level marine governance as occurring through polycentric vertical and horizontal networks and linked policy cycles. Many regional and sub-regional projects are geared to operationalising these concepts. National intersectoral coordination mechanisms are at the heart of many of these governance arrangements, but currently more in theory than in practice. A Blue Economy approach has the potential to be truly transformative in these circumstances, tipping the levels of interest and effort towards more sustainable governance structures with functions that are well aligned with their parent policies. Developing both good and effective governance at the national level is fundamental to progress given the adjacent maritime jurisdictions in the Caribbean with high mobility of both living marine resources and human stakeholders.

It is also clear that regional ocean governance demonstrating strong linkages to both national and global levels, will be key to successful Blue Economies in the Wider Caribbean, especially given the transboundary nature of ocean issues and geopolitical complexities of this region. With 44 states, most of which are developing countries and 16 which are SIDS, it is well recognised that international collaboration is essential to building collective capacity and taking the transboundary action necessary for achieving the 2030 Sustainable Development Goals, particularly SDG 14. This is fundamental for the development of Blue Economies. This challenge is explored further in Chapter 9 by Fanning and Mahon. Around 25 regional organisations currently have mandates for various aspects of sustainable use of marine ecosystems. There have been efforts to promote region-wide approaches, most notably the ACS Caribbean Sea Initiative and the Caribbean Sea Large Marine Ecosystem (CLME) Project (Debels et al., 2017). The ACS and CARICOM have promoted a regional agenda through a United Nations General Assembly resolution, and the CLME Project is rationalising roles and responsibilities among regional organisations at a more technical level. Also notable is the OECS sub-regional ocean governance initiative.[9]

Key sectors influencing the Blue Economy

As well as the cross-cutting issues that are shaping, and will continue, to shape the Blue Economy in the Caribbean, there are a number of sectors that will likely play an important role in driving forward its development. These include fisheries, tourism, shipping and transport, renewable energy, offshore oil and gas, and deep seabed minerals and genetic resources. These sectors are at different stages in their development, but all have a role to play. However, due to intrinsic vulnerabilities and capacity constraints that face the countries of the Caribbean, including natural disasters and relatively weak regulatory capacity, these sectors have still some way to go before they are fully consolidated. This section of the chapter considers their position within the region's Blue Economy, and what challenges lie ahead.

Fisheries are critical to successful Blue Economy development. The Wider Caribbean is characterised by multi-species, multi-gear, small-scale fisheries. These fisheries employ hundreds of thousands of fisherfolk in the harvest and post-harvest sectors and associated industries across the region. Thus, as Oxenford and McConney argue in Chapter 10, they are critical to the livelihoods and food security of populations in the many SIDS within the Caribbean, where productive agricultural land and alternative employment opportunities may be extremely limited, and national economies are vulnerable to external shocks, and to climate variability and change. Additionally, export earnings of some high-value species (conch, lobster and shrimp) are significant to national economies (e.g. Belize, Jamaica, Suriname, Guyana and Mexico). Further development of the fisheries sector as a key component of the Blue Economy is essential, particularly as it remains poorly recognised for its substantial contribution to human health and welfare. However, this will require significant efforts in three areas. The first must address the reasons for the general lack of acknowledged value of the sector, which include poor fishery landings and socio-economic data collection. Second, the current issues threatening the sustainability of fishery resources themselves must be tackled. These include the common practice of allowing open access and severe resource depletion; habitat damage from land-based activities (particularly in the case of shallow-shelf, coral-associated resources); and poor capacity and lack of political will to implement existing fisheries legislation. The paucity of regional governance arrangements that are needed for managing transboundary species and tackling regional issues such as illegal unreported and unregulated (IUU) fishing and mainstreaming adaptation to climate change exacerbate these problems. The third is to invest in the development of value-added fishery products and the reduction of waste.

Another crucial sector is tourism. The tourism industry is a vital component for Caribbean economies. According to the World Travel and Tourism Council the total contribution of tourism to GDP in 2018 was over US\$62 billion, or 15.5% (WTTC, 2019). This means that tourism is more important to the Caribbean than any other region of the world. More specifically, the industry provided almost 14% of all employment, both directly and indirectly. So, for the majority of Caribbean countries, tourism is seen as the primary engine of economic growth, now and in the future. Of course, much of the tourism product is linked to nature, and a large part of that is framed around the coastal and marine environment, as Chapter 11 by Clegg et al. shows.

16 Peter Clegg et al.

This contribution is only likely to grow, and coastal and marine tourism is projected to be the largest part of the global ocean economy by 2030. The Caribbean is very likely to benefit from this trend, but of course managing it effectively and sustainably will be key challenges. The region must be responsive and think creatively in matters such as marine spatial planning, properly managing and resourcing marine areas, and empowering local communities to make decisions and defend their interests. Unfortunately, the region is presently some way off meeting these challenges.

Shipping and transport, which has close links to tourism, is a further important sector to consider, as detailed in Chapter 12 by Jean-Marie. The role of transport and shipping is of course crucial for the region because of its high dependence on imports and exports, whether one is talking about the trade in goods or services. However, as an industry in itself the Caribbean is only a very minor player globally, despite the intensity of traffic that passes through the region. It accounts for only 1% of global port throughput, despite its advantageous geographical location. Major shipping and transhipment ports are limited to Kingston, Jamaica; Freeport, The Bahamas; San Juan, Puerto Rico; Port-of-Spain, Trinidad and Tobago; and the Dominican Republic. Cruise ship tourism is growing fast in the Caribbean, but in the smaller islands, in particular, ports are located in urban areas, which causes problems of congestion and challenges well-managed coastal development that takes climate change into account. As the Caribbean Development Bank (2018) has noted, "the Region's connectivity to the global networks is rather low despite its closeness to major trans-shipment ports". However, regional gateway container demand is expected to increase, supported by the expansion of the Panama Canal. Some countries in the region, including The Bahamas and Jamaica are investing in new infrastructure, but there are challenges in relation to resourcing and getting the balance right between further exploiting the benefits of being maritime nations and managing issues around sustainability, including oil spills, greenhouse emissions, ballast waters and port expansion and construction.

The issue of sustainability is also very important in driving forward growth of the renewable energy sector. For many years, energy security has been a significant concern for the Caribbean. The PetroCaribe arrangement with Venezuela, which provides discounted oil, was an important source of assistance, particularly when prices were high. However, with the collapse of the Venezuelan economy and the retrenchment of PetroCaribe, plus the growing threat of climate change, greater efforts are now being made by countries in the region to use their natural (marine) environment to establish viable renewable energy sectors. However, investments in renewables are low. Nevertheless, many countries have set themselves ambitious targets for diversifying the energy mix, as detailed in Chapter 13 by Haraksingh. For example, Barbados has set a target of achieving 65% of its power from renewable sources by 2030. Similar targets have been set by St Vincent and the Grenadines and the Cayman Islands. The Caribbean Sea is a key component in any strategy to meet targets for the use of renewable energies, with huge solar, wind, geothermal and marine energy potential. Some external funding is being provided via such programmes as the US-backed Caribbean Energy Security Initiative and the Caribbean Hotel Energy Efficiency and Renewables initiative, but the foundations are not yet in place for a significant step-change in the future development of the sector.

So, while the renewables sector is still finding its feet, there is still significant interest in the offshore oil and gas industry, and Bryan in Chapter 14 evaluates this in more detail. A key question is to what extent oil and natural gas production and consumption can be accommodated within, and responsive to the needs, of a Blue Economy. In 2012, the US Geological Survey estimated that the Caribbean held up to 126 billion barrels of oil and 679 trillion cubic feet of undiscovered natural gases in 31 geological provinces. After several false starts offshore fossil fuel exploration was reinvigorated following a major oil discovery in Guyanese waters by ExxonMobil in 2015. Deep water drilling is also taking place in Jamaica, The Bahamas and elsewhere, and more technologically advanced exploration may further extend production in the region. However, there are concerns over the broader impact of these developments. There are increasingly influential voices, not just within the environmental community, that question whether hydrocarbon exploration and extraction fit well with the region's fragile ecosystem, biodiversity and dependence on tourism. This opposition has had some success with Belize's recent moratorium on oil exploration and mineral extraction in its offshore waters. Meanwhile in Barbados, the government has stated that if oil or gas is found, extraction should be undertaken in a way that does not damage tourism or fisheries, and that revenues should be used to finance renewable energy. However, the attraction of encouraging a lightly regulated expansion of offshore oil and gas exploration might be too hard to resist, which in turn would seriously undermine the broader Blue Economy agenda for at least a generation.

Another sector to consider is deep seabed minerals and genetic resources, which presents a special case for the development of a Blue Economy. While the Caribbean is not known to have significant deep-sea mineral resources within their Exclusive Economic Zones (EEZs), there may be benefits to be derived from engaging with the mining of such minerals in the Areas Beyond National Jurisdiction (ABNJ). The matter of sharing the benefits from these common property resources based on the Common Heritage of Mankind principle is currently being developed by the International Seabed Authority, which is located in Jamaica. However, as detailed by Davis-Mattis in Chapter 15, SIDS are experiencing challenges in getting their fair share of the resources of the deep seabed recognised in the draft Mining Code, which is attempting to set out the rules, regulations and procedures to regulate prospecting, exploration and exploitation of marine minerals in international waters. A similar situation prevails in relation to genetic resources. The extent to which these are present within Caribbean EEZs is unknown, but the region

18 *Peter Clegg et al.*

has also an interest in what is happening in international waters. In particular, the development of the international agreement on Biodiversity Beyond National Jurisdiction (BBNJ) expected to be concluded in 2020. Here the benefits from BBNJ are to be derived from bio-prospecting for genetic resources for medical purposes. In this case also, application of the Common Heritage of Mankind principle is being debated, and the outcome is uncertain. If the nascent framework of ocean governance mirrors shortcomings in global governance that marginalise SIDS, then there may be doubts as to whether the Caribbean can obtain the full benefits that might accrue from any agreement.

The way ahead

In considering the way ahead for the Caribbean one has to focus beyond the outlook for the key socio-economic sectors and envisage how a Blue Economy may or may not fit into sustainable development in a region characterised mainly by SIDS. Conceptually, the movement towards Blue Economies seems to be an appropriate expression of Caribbean sustainable development given the high ratio of sea space to land in this area. Yet, as was seen with other interplays of the ocean environment with the economy, such as the Caribbean Sea Initiative, institutional, policy and practical obstacles may occur. A critical aspect of this is the financing of the transition to Blue Economies, and this theme is taken up by Ram and Kaidou-Jeffrey in Chapter 17. So, in short, the conceptualisation and operationalisation of the Blue Economy in the Wider Caribbean is the central theme of this volume. The Blue Economy involves a wide diversity of sectors and actors that do not often interact. Many aspects of the Blue Economy require revisiting issues of ecosystem degradation and overexploitation that have been of concern for decades. Hopefully, a new focus on Blue Economies will provide the incentive to address these that has hitherto been lacking. Other aspects appear to offer new, if sometimes hazy, opportunities to derive economic benefits. The book's aim is to identify and analyse the nature of the Blue Economy in the Wider Caribbean; how established it already is within the region; the key cross-cutting issues that require consideration; the key sectors involved; and how the future of the Blue Economy can best be secured. The book offers a wide-ranging and comprehensive assessment of the opportunities and challenges linked to the concept and application of the Blue Economy.

Notes

1 https://www.unenvironment.org/news-and-stories/news/caribbean-region-lead-way-green-economy-0.
2 https://sustainabledevelopment.un.org/sdg14.
3 http://g20.org.tr/wp-content/uploads/2015/04/Outcome-Statement-CRD-DWG-Meeting-13-April-2015-Final.pdf.

4 https://www.gob.mx/sre/prensa/mexico-reaffirms-commitment-to-a-sustainable-ocean-economy.
5 https://www.oceanactionhub.org/costa-rica-course-vibrant-and-inclusive-blue-economy.
6 https://www.caribank.org/newsroom/news-and-events/blue-economy-caribbean.
7 http://newenergyevents.com/blue-economy-caribbean/.
8 https://www.bb.undp.org/content/barbados/en/home/presscenter/articles/2019/introducing-the-barbados—oecs-blue-economy-accelerator-lab.html.
9 https://pressroom.oecs.org/oecs-discuss-ocean-governance-and-policy#.

References

Burke, L. and Maidens, J. 2004. *Reefs at Risk in the Caribbean*. September. World Resources Institute, Washington, DC. Available at: https://www.wri.org/publication/reefs-risk-caribbean.

Caribbean Development Bank. 2018. *The Blue Economy: A Caribbean Development Opportunity*, p. 54. Available at: https://www.caribank.org/sites/default/files/publication-resources/Financing%20the%20Blue%20Economy-%20A%20Caribbean%20development%20opportunity.pdf.

Debels P., Fanning, L., Mahon, R. *et al.* 2017. The CLME+ Strategic Action Programme: An ecosystems approach for assessing and managing the Caribbean Sea and North Brazil Shelf Large Marine Ecosystems. *Environmental Development*, 22: 191–205.

Diez, S. M., Patil, P., Morton, J. *et al.* 2019. *Marine Pollution in the Caribbean: Not a Minute to Waste*. World Bank Group, Washington, DC, 100 pp.

Fanning, L. and Mahon, R. 2017. *Implementing the Ocean SDG in the Wider Caribbean: state of play and possible ways forward*, IASS, IDDRI, TMG, Potsdam, Germany, 53 pp.

IISD. 2018. The Sustainable Blue Economy Conference Bulletin 26–28 November 2018. International Institute for Sustainable Development, *Sustainable Blue Economy Bulletin*, 208 (31), 16 pp. Available at: http://enb.iisd.org/oceans/blueeconomy/2018/.

Moore, W., Alleyne, F., Alleyne, Y. *et al.* 2012. *Barbados Green Economy Scoping Study – Synthesis Report*, Government of Barbados, University of West Indies – Cave Hill Campus. United Nations Environment Programme, 55 pp.

Oxenford, H. A. and Monnereau, I. 2018. Chapter 9: Climate change impacts, vulnerabilities and adaptations: Western Central Atlantic marine fisheries. In: Barange, M., Bahri, T., Beveridge, M., Cochrane, K., Funge-Smith, S., and Poulain, F. (Eds), *Impacts of Climate Change on Fisheries and Aquaculture: Synthesis of Current Knowledge, Adaptation and Mitigation Options*. FAO Fisheries Technical Paper 627, pp. 147–168.

Patil, P. G., Virdin, J., Diez, S. M. *et al.* 2016. *Toward A Blue Economy: A Promise for Sustainable Growth in the Caribbean; An Overview*. The World Bank, Washington, DC, 91 pp.

Rice, J., Arvanitidis, C., Boicenco, L., Kasapidis, P. *et al.* 2016. Chapter 36A. North Atlantic Ocean. In: Inniss, L.*et al.* (Eds), *The First Global Integrated Marine Assessment (World Ocean Assessment 1)*, pp. 1–86. United Nations, New York. Available at: http://www.un.org/depts/los/global_reporting/WOA_RegProcess.htm.

Schuhmann, P. and Mahon, R. 2015. The valuation of marine ecosystem goods and services in the Caribbean: A literature review and framework for future valuation efforts. *Ecosystem Services*, 11: 56–66. https://doi.org/10.1016/j.ecoser.2014.07.013.

20 *Peter Clegg et al.*

Smith, N., A. Halton and J. Strachan. 2014. *Transitioning to a Green Economy: Political Economy of Approaches in Small States.* Commonwealth Secretariat, London, 213 pp. Available at: https://read.thecommonwealth-ilibrary.org/commonwealth/economics/transitioning-to-a-green-economy_9781848599178-en#page234.

UNEP. 2011. *Towards a Green Economy: Pathways to Sustainable Development and Poverty Eradication – A Synthesis for Policy Makers.* Available at: www.unep.org/greeneconomy.

UNEP. 2016. *Green Economy Scoping Study for Jamaica.* United Nations Environment Programme, 64 pp.

World Travel and Tourism Council. 2019. *Caribbean – 2019 Annual Research: Key Highlights.* https://www.wttc.org/economic-impact/country-analysis/region-data/.

3 The Blue Economy winners and losers in the Wider Caribbean

Nicole Leotaud, Alexander Girvan and Sasha Jattansingh

Introduction

The Blue Economy has emerged as a rallying point for many recent global and regional high-level policy discussions and emerging initiatives on ocean and coastal sustainable development.

> The sea is currently a subsistence resource for coastal villagers ... these are the real people who are the human focus of our blue economy work ... We want to help them move from subsistence to prosperity.
> (Didacus Jules, Director General of the Organisation of Eastern Caribbean States (OECS) Commission)[1]

Unfortunately, these place disproportionate emphasis on large-scale resource-based economic opportunities (e.g. major capture fisheries, seabed mining) and physical development projects (e.g. ports, marinas, mega-tourism developments) that are attractive opportunities for large trans-national corporate investments. Recent reports (e.g. Caribbean Development Bank, 2018; Patil et al., 2016) articulate the need for fairness, yet they place emphasis on initiatives that will only be available to big business (e.g. marine renewable energy, shipping) rather than on equitable engagement in and sharing of Blue Economy gains. Similarly, national Blue Economy plans (e.g. Government of Grenada, 2016) are focused on large coastal development projects which threaten to displace existing livelihoods and fail to convincingly show how they improve equitable outcomes in micro-, small and medium enterprises (MSMEs) and the informal economy to improve resilience of coastal communities. Current Blue Economy initiatives generally pay limited attention to spreading economic opportunities and benefits to the poor and vulnerable, and ensuring reskilling and social protection for fairness and well-being.

Indeed, large-scale economic initiatives have historically been proven to have significant negative impacts on coastal communities, small-scale fisherfolk and other resource users, and local formal and informal MSMEs, who are all highly dependent on resources from the oceans and on linking coastal ecosystem services to the wider economy. Furthermore, conversations on Blue

Economy in the Caribbean have thus far largely excluded the voices of coastal communities, MSMEs, small-scale fisherfolk and other resource users, who will be the most affected by these developments.

We must thus question the poverty alleviation and livelihood outcomes the Blue Economy promises. This link seems to be elusive and the concept of what is meant by Blue Economy remains unclear (Voyer et al., 2018), perhaps deliberately in the Caribbean, as it has the potential to act as a Trojan horse through which powerful interests and unsustainable activities persist. Even if this is not the intent, there is a significant risk of ignoring those traditionally disenfranchised in the economic opportunities being promoted in current Blue Economy approaches.

Although the Blue Economy idea seems attractive for the Caribbean, we need to beware of misconceptions or misapplication in ways that harm the people who are most dependent on marine and coastal resources. One of the problems is a lack of clarity on the specific development principles or objectives that must underlie Blue Economy. The past 10 years of dialogues to elucidate principles underlying Green Economy in the Caribbean should form a logical basis for developing parallel definitions and principles focusing on the use of coastal and ocean resources. Multi-stakeholder dialogues facilitated by the Caribbean Natural Resources Institute (CANARI) since 2010 created an early understanding of what Green Economy means in the Caribbean context (see Box 3.1). There is also growing consensus on fundamental principles underlying a Blue Economy and the need for transformation to economies that are more environmentally sustainable, inclusive and resilient (e.g. Caribbean Development Bank, 2018). These principles must underlie whatever monikers are used – blue, green or circular economies (for example see Partners for Inclusive Green Economy, 2019). The 11 Member States of the Organisation of Eastern Caribbean States (OECS) are developing a regional Green-Blue Strategy and Action Plan which seeks to integrate key principles into a coherent approach to transforming economic development in the sub-region.

Box 3.1 Caribbean definition of a Green Economy

"A Green Economy is one that aims for long-term prosperity, rather than solely for growth, through equitable distribution of economic benefits and effective management of ecological resources. It is economically viable and resilient to both external and internal shocks; self-directed and not driven by external agendas or funding opportunities, and self-reliant by being based predominantly on domestic production and investment. A Caribbean Green Economy is pro-poor and generates decent jobs and working conditions that offer opportunities for self-advancement for local people" (CANARI, 2012).

The Blue Economy winners and losers   23

Considering the increasing attention being paid to Blue Economy in the Caribbean and recognising the risks that inappropriate marine and coastal investments present to coastal peoples, this chapter aims to:

1   clearly articulate the risks presented by inappropriate Blue Economy initiatives to the region's most vulnerable;
2   present key principles that can be used to guide the direction of Blue Economy to support fair and inclusive approaches; and
3   identify how a focus on MSMEs provides opportunities for making the potential losers the winners in Blue Economy initiatives.

The risk of transferring the brown to the blue

Coastal and ocean natural capital has and continues to form a critical part of Caribbean economies; in a sense a very robust economy based on these already exists (Caribbean Development Bank, 2018). Gross revenues generated by the ocean economy in the Caribbean were estimated at US$407 million (as of 2012) (Patil et al., 2016). Yet the existence of this significant Blue Economy has not resulted in widespread poverty alleviation or sustainable development outcomes. This can be attributed to a combination of poor governance, a focus on unsustainable resource extraction practices (e.g. mining and marine fossil fuel extraction), an overemphasis on capturing large foreign direct investment, and inadequate attention to local livelihoods and well-being of the poor and vulnerable.

This section will outline the main risks presented by the current iteration of Blue Economy, which will be characterised as risks to: (1) environmental sustainability; (2) economic and social development; and (3) governance.

Risks to environmental sustainability

Coastal and marine ecosystems are recognised as the natural capital that drives the Blue Economy (see Chapter 4 Oxenford & Mahon; Patil et al., 2016). If the development models practised on land are not modified significantly, there is a large risk that Blue Economy approaches will degrade marine and coastal ecosystems goods and services that are the base for livelihoods and economic opportunities for coastal communities, small-scale fisherfolk and other resource users, and local formal and informal MSMEs who become the losers to powerful economic interests.

Blue economy initiatives are promoting opportunities based on fisheries, tourism, shipping and transport, renewable energy and deep seabed minerals and genetic resources (e.g. Caribbean Development Bank, 2018) (see Chapters 10–15). Unfortunately, brown economy modalities used in these sectors have already produced significant environmental impacts to marine ecosystems, and an expansion under a Blue Economy would likely increase threats. These

24   Nicole Leotaud et al.

activities are currently contributing to ecosystem destruction and degradation, ocean warming, decreased ocean oxygenation, increased ocean acidification and shifting phytoplankton productivity, and other impacts which are severely impacting natural capital. For example, 24% of mangrove area has been lost in the last quarter century in the Caribbean (Polidoro et al., 2010; FAO, 2007) and live coral cover declined from 34% to 16% between 1970 to 2011 (Jackson et al., 2014; see also Chapter 4).

Blue Economy advocates must also acknowledge the inherent risk of large-scale environmental problems on oceans that are slow to observe. Oceans have significant "inertia" in that they can absorb large amounts of energy or pollutants without observable short-term changes (UNESCO, 2017). There can be a long delay between a pressure and an observable change in state. Plastics and microplastic pollution, ocean acidification and ocean warming are all problems which were recognised well after they were created. Thus, new extractive industries present a major risk to environmental sustainability if the precautionary principle is not applied to every stage of their development.

Further, risks to natural capital from activities in the high seas or within national waters that will have an impact on the waters of other countries and the high seas must be considered. For example, what are the risks from spills from oil exploration in Guyana (Bitto, 2019) to other Caribbean countries that are up current? How can deep-sea mining in the Atlantic threaten Caribbean marine ecosystems and species? How does industrial fishing in the high seas impact on small-scale fisheries in the Caribbean? Losers may be Caribbean people and countries whose natural capital is degraded by the economic activities of other sectors, large corporations or countries.

Risks to economic and social development

Since its emergence in the 1960s (Sezgin & Yolal, 2012), large-scale tourism in the Caribbean has not contributed to poverty alleviation and has failed to reduced wealth inequality (Oviedo-García et al., 2018). In fact, tourism has been shown to increase inequality (Alam & Paramati, 2016) as those with the ability to capitalise on emerging opportunities extend their power over suppliers of labour and raw materials and do not adequately support local social development. Tourism is further linked to underinvestment in local food production in the Caribbean (Bélisle, 1983; Rhiney, 2011) and worsening Caribbean food security, where more than half of Caribbean countries import more than 80% of their total food consumption (CARICOM, 2011).

The ability of aquaculture to alleviate poverty, improve food security and nutrition in developing and emergent countries is at best described as inconsistent (Abu Nasar et al., 2016) with most studies focusing on global and national level benefits (Béné et al., 2016) in terms of trade and foreign exchange earnings (Allison, 2011). Large-scale aquaculture in fact can increase local inequality, as it worsens power imbalances between producers and buyers, factory owners and exporters, and between men and women who play varying roles in the value chain (Allison, 2011). Additionally, global growth in aquaculture is largely to satisfy growing demand from growing middle-income populations in domestic cities and international markets with little positive benefits to the rural and vulnerable in terms of local markets, food security and nutrition (Thilsted et al., 2016).

Ocean-based mining and extractive industries have existed in the region now for well over one hundred years. They have brought significant income to petrochemical-based economies such as Trinidad and Tobago, but the impact in terms of poverty alleviation and improved welfare requires further research. In other developing regions, countries with high dependence on oil and mineral exports have shown lower growth rates, higher corruption, violence and lower living standards when compared to resource poor countries (Pegg, 2003). Mining and extractive industries are well connected to global value chains, and thus heavily reliant on external expertise and technology, resulting in the repatriation of incomes and profits by the involved multinational corporations in the Caribbean and globally (Girvan, 1970). The Caribbean must thus question the ability of emergent Blue Economy initiatives on seabed mining and mineral extraction from the water column to deliver significant and equitable economic and social benefits. Research from the Extractive Industries Transparency Initiative suggests that such extractive activities may not deliver the envisioned economic benefits to those most at need and may increase income inequality (Ocheje, 2006).

These existing industries in the Blue Economy, such as tourism, fisheries and aquaculture and extractive industries, have demonstrated ability to support the rapid accumulation of material wealth. However, value chain analysis of these industries indicates that with globalisation of their value chain comes increased income inequality (Kaplinsky, 2000). However, as discussed above, the increased livelihood and job opportunities in these sectors should not be viewed as an automatic poverty alleviation solution.

If economic diversification through the Blue Economy focuses on large-scale industrial developments in a few sectors, advantages for foreign investment and big business will exacerbate existing inequities in capacity development, skills and technology transfer. The losers will continue to be the poor and vulnerable in our societies as they are even further marginalised from economic opportunities. Regional and national development strategies will need to utilise a holistic and balanced approach, which recognises the risks in narrow pursuit of a few large-scale projects.

Finally, the Blue Economy conversation has not justified how increasing Caribbean economic activities in its most physically vulnerable zones (i.e. coasts) will enhance economic resilience. We cannot ignore the risk of deriving a more significant portion of our economic earnings from a geographic space which faces the largest risk of damage from sea level rise, coastal flooding, storm surge and coastal erosion. The Caribbean has faced severe damage to coastal infrastructure such as ports, airports, resorts, roads and fish landing sites in recent years due to more intense weather events as a result of climate change.

26 Nicole Leotaud et al.

Risk to governance

Governance, understood as the process of decision-making and the process by which decisions are implemented (or not), presents a persistent challenge in Caribbean states due to our history, high economic inequality and small comparative role in global economies. Already in the Caribbean, our ability to govern terrestrial ecological assets has proven to be limited, as evidenced by the declining health of many ecosystems in the face of potentially avoidable human pressures.

Governance of the Caribbean Sea is more challenging simply in scale (the total land area of all Caribbean island states is less than 10% of the area of the Caribbean Sea) and complexity (with interconnected ecological systems and multiple socio-political systems). Significant efforts are being made to enhance governance of the Caribbean Sea (see Chapters 8 and 9). However, this has not yet been fully translated into concrete mechanisms at national and regional levels to guide shared decision-making on economic development opportunities to ensure sustainability and fairness. Civil society and associations representing resource users or MSMEs are usually excluded from engaging in these complex governance arrangements, which lack practical and meaningful mechanisms to support their participation. Blue economy initiatives can further increase disparities if they do not explicitly focus on engagement of and ensuring benefits to those most marginalised.

When the risks to governance and cost of enforcement are extended beyond the exclusive economic zone (EEZ) of states into international waters, all the above risks are amplified. The impending growth in Blue Economy initiatives in international waters presents inherent risks for the Caribbean. The ability of international instruments to manage these issues has a significant bearing on how the Caribbean will benefit (or be impacted by) the Blue Economy. If new treaties, such as the legally binding instrument under the United Nations Convention on the Law of the Sea on the conservation and sustainable use of marine biological diversity of areas beyond national jurisdiction (the BBNJ Agreement) currently being negotiated, are unable to effectively guarantee sustainable and equitable outcomes, the strong economic interests of individual countries and operators makes unequitable and unsustainable outcomes likely. The capacity of Caribbean states to effectively negotiate in these spaces is limited and, in this case, the losers will not only be the Caribbean's coastal peoples but also the Caribbean states themselves.

Key principles to guide a more inclusive and equitable Blue Economy

Despite the risks outlined above, a renewed focus on sustainable use of the Caribbean's marine and coastal resources can bring equitable economic benefits if this is done with a deliberate people-centred and pro-poor focus.

The global alliance of Partners for Inclusive Green Economy (2019) has identified five key principles, three of which are particularly useful for a

The Blue Economy winners and losers 27

people-centred approach. These focus on well-being, justice and good governance and can be used to frame how Blue Economy approaches in the Caribbean can be more inclusive. An additional principle on resilience is recommended given the vulnerability of ocean ecosystems and the associated economies and livelihoods.

1 The well-being principle: The economy enables all people to create and enjoy prosperity

In order to create well-being of Caribbean people, a Blue Economy would need to not only create financial wealth, but also contribute to strengthening the full range of human, social, physical and natural capitals that are part of livelihood assets. This would increase attention on human development through education, particularly reforming educational systems and providing options which offer young people knowledge, disciplines and skills that are relevant to their lives and potential career opportunities. Local people would have access to information and tools to enable them to develop sustainable livelihoods and business opportunities. Their traditional and local knowledge would be valued and utilised in management of our marine and coastal resources. A more holistic approach to business development would emphasise the delivery of triple-bottom-line benefits, i.e. economic, social and environmental co-benefits (see Box 3.2).

> **Box 3.2 Delivering triple-bottom-line co-benefits**
>
> CANARI has been working with local community micro-enterprises based on the use of ecosystem goods and services, for example in small-scale fisheries, eco-tourism, craft, natural pharmaceuticals, food and cosmetics. Entrepreneurs are using an innovative tool called the Local Green-Blue Enterprise (LGE) Radar that CANARI has developed to explore how they are delivering economic, social and environmental co-benefits alongside good governance. The LGE Radar is helping entrepreneurs to identify areas where they can improve their business practices to enhance these benefits.

Development support would focus on building and rebuilding local communities and community organisations. Investment would focus on development of appropriate infrastructure, technology and skills development to support local development. Natural capital assets would be protected, including from threats from externally driven and controlled economic activities, to ensure a sustainable resource base to support local enterprises and bottom-up economic development.

28   *Nicole Leotaud et al.*

2 The justice principle: The economy promotes equity within and between generations

A fair Blue Economy is inclusive and non-discriminatory. This would require focusing on those who are marginalised from or at the margins of current economic systems, especially local people, vulnerable and highly ocean-dependent coastal communities, and women.

Local economic development models need to be supported in coastal communities whose livelihoods are highly dependent on coastal and marine resources. Work by the Laborie Development Foundation in Saint Lucia can provide inspiration (see Box 3.3). Benefits and costs of a Blue Economy need to be shared fairly while respecting the rights and interests of local communities and transferring costs of degradation of natural blue capital to industries that are doing the damage, as well as mandating mitigation. Capture of economic benefits by foreign and elite interests needs to be avoided to promote the equitable distribution of opportunity and outcome, reducing disparities between people. The costs of the transition should not be borne by the poor and vulnerable and instead explicitly pro-poor policies are needed in the Caribbean Blue Economy.

Box 3.3 Inclusive local Blue Economy in action

In the tiny fishing village of Laborie on the south-west coast of Saint Lucia, the Laborie Development Foundation works with the community to promote social and economic development that will contribute to a "culturally vibrant community where there is continuous improvement in the quality of life and where people are able to enjoy all the basic necessities and to participate fully in the process of development". Work has involved development of tourism, agriculture and fishing, youth and sports, education and the human resources, and health care and social services. (See www.ilovelaborie.com.)

Transformation of current financing, labour and welfare policies and practices and development of new innovative models are required to address the needs and constraints of specific groups. Women, including single female heads of households, are largely excluded from current maritime industries (except in fisheries postharvest) and appropriate opportunities need to be identified to allow them to be part of the new Blue Economy. Small-scale fisherfolk and other resource users have difficulty accessing financing, insurance and other support (see Box 3.4). Current Caribbean legal, regulatory, fiscal and funding frameworks do not effectively recognise or support informal enterprises, social enterprises, green enterprises or micro-enterprises and a much more enabling environment is needed for empowerment of entrepreneurs. Social protection and reskilling will also be needed.

Box 3.4 Innovative insurance for fisherfolk

The Caribbean Oceans and Aquaculture Sustainability FaciliTy (COAST) fisheries parametric insurance was developed by the Caribbean Catastrophe Risk Insurance Facility (CCRIF) SPC and the World Bank to address the needs of small-scale fisherfolk facing devastation from intense storms, which are expected to increase due to the impacts of climate change.

A just Blue Economy shares economic decision-making. It leaves no-one behind and rather enables vulnerable groups to self-organise and be agents of transition. Blue Justice for small-scale fisheries is one commendable initiative.[2] A long-term perspective is needed to ensure that economic development will serve the interests of future citizens, while also acting urgently to tackle today's multi-dimensional poverty and injustice.

3 The good governance principle: The economy is guided by integrated, accountable and resilient institutions

Appropriate governance models must underpin an inclusive Blue Economy. Participatory governance approaches will be needed to effectively engage stakeholders with interests, rights and responsibilities – particularly local communities and resource users, women and other vulnerable groups which are highly dependent on ocean resources – in economic decision-making. Civil society efforts to engage in governance and management of the Caribbean Sea demonstrate the willingness of these stakeholders to be real partners in a Blue Economy (see Box 3.5).

Box 3.5 People managing oceans

Civil society is already playing a key role in conservation of the marine environment and development of sustainable livelihoods. Civil society organisations (including fisherfolk organisations) and community micro-enterprises developed the *Civil Society Action Programme for the Sustainable Management of the Shared Living Marine Resource of the Caribbean and North Brazil Shelf Large Marine Ecosystems* (CLME+ C-SAP), popularly known as *People Managing Oceans* (CANARI, 2018). This aims to strengthen the role, participation and ownership of civil society actors in the implementation of the politically endorsed 10-year Strategic Action Programme, which has a long-term vision of "a healthy marine environment that provides benefits and livelihoods for the well-being of the people of the region". The C-SAP includes a strategy on enhancing the role of civil society in governance, including through preparing local management and community-based development plans, inputting in policy development, conducting advocacy and playing a watchdog role.

30   *Nicole Leotaud et al.*

Strengthening transparency and accountability of public and private interests through strengthening national legal, regulatory and policy frameworks and their implementation is needed, including considering prior informed consent and social and environmental safeguards. This can be catalysed and supported by regional and global commitments, for example linked with Sustainable Development Goal 16 on peace, justice and strong institutions or with the Regional Agreement on Access to Information, Public Participation and Justice in Environmental Matters in Latin America and the Caribbean (the Escazú Agreement).[3] The process of strengthening governance will need to be inclusive and engage civil society and other actors in the transformation.

4 The resilience principle: Economic development enhances adaptation and reduces vulnerability to internal and external environmental, social and economic risks

Current and future Blue Economies in the Caribbean will not exist if our ecosystems and coastlines have not adapted to the inevitable impacts of climate change. Investments in the Blue Economy must be used to enhance our resilience to climate change by directly supporting adaptation actions. If not, by placing increasing proportions of our economy into the firing line of impacts such as coastal flooding, ocean acidification, ocean warming and sea level rise, we will be increasing the vulnerability of our economy to these inevitable impacts. Marine-based activities must support (financially or technologically) the physical adaptations of our coasts and enhance resilience of our macro-economies. Where Blue Economy activities cannot directly support adaptation, Caribbean governments should look towards the creation of funds which direct revenues from these activities towards adaptation initiatives. The poor and marginalised will require special support to build their adaptive capacity and ensure that they do not become losers in the short term.

Additionally, Blue Economy plans must consider pre-existing climate change vulnerabilities and be built on scenarios and models of how ecosystems will be disrupted by sea level rise, ocean warming, oxygenation, acidification, storm surge and extreme events. A precautionary approach is essential given the poorly understood feedback loops and knock-on effects. For example, limited information currently exists on how ocean acidification will affect the productivity of Caribbean reef fisheries, conch and lobster fisheries, and how impacts on these sectors will influence the productivity of pelagic fisheries. A deeper understanding of the extent of these impacts and their knock-on effects is critical to enable sound investments.

"Climate proofing" sectors and businesses must be part of a resilient economy. Climate variability and change, and associated intense natural hazards, threaten natural ecosystems which are the foundation of many rural nature-based enterprises in the Caribbean. Work has been underway to analyse the impacts of climate change and build resilience of Caribbean small-scale fisheries sector.[4] CANARI's tool to "climate proof" nature-based micro- and small enterprises, using a value chain approach, can also help to build resilience of the most vulnerable informal micro-enterprises in poor coastal communities (Sandy and Dardaine-Edwards, 2017).

MSMEs as a pathway to an inclusive Blue Economy

A common thread in the discussion above has been the need, and the opportunity, to support MSMEs as a key pathway to an inclusive and more equitable Blue Economy. Focusing on supporting informal local micro-enterprises will best target the needs of the most poor and vulnerable, who are marginalised from economic sectors and opportunities.

Nature-based micro-enterprises are the foundation of livelihoods and local economies in Caribbean coastal communities but are also the most vulnerable to the impacts of climate change. These enterprises often deliver social and/or environmental benefits to the surrounding community, as well as providing incomes. The form these take is highly variable, ranging from for-profit businesses that are legally registered or informal, formal or informal associations of resource users, cooperatives, to non-profit organisations with objectives centred on providing employment and economic opportunities to local communities. The legal, regulatory, fiscal, funding and technical support mechanisms in the Caribbean are generally not adequate to meet the needs of these social/green/blue enterprises. Existing entrepreneurship and innovation support programmes are targeted at higher-capacity businesses and exclude those most in need. A more enabling environment is needed to support coastal community entrepreneurs, across various sectors, to strengthen their businesses and take advantage of emerging opportunities. This can be a concrete pathway to an inclusive and more equitable Blue Economy.

Conclusion

The reality is that not only do Caribbean states and territories have opportunities to gain from an enhanced focus on utilisation of ocean resources, they sadly also have the most to lose from failed Blue Economy initiatives due to the risks it poses to environmental sustainability, economic and social development and governance. These risks necessitate the application of a clear framework of principles for the Blue Economy to reduce poverty and inequality, protect and restore critical natural capital, and enhance climate change resilience. The current top-down and high-level Blue Economy discourse pays lip service to concepts of equity and fairness but fails to articulate clearly how these will be achieved.

Key to achieving inclusive, sustainable and resilient economic development based on the use of coastal and marine resources will be a strong focus on supporting current users of these resources and rural coastal communities, whose

32 *Nicole Leotaud et al.*

livelihoods centre around the goods and services provided by these ecosystems but who are generally marginalised from economic opportunities, have limited access to social safety nets, are highly vulnerable to climate change and have little voice in economic decision-making. The current trend of Blue Economy development focused on shipping, mining, large-scale tourism, renewable energy and large-scale fishing excludes these stakeholders who most deserve our attention if we are to "leave no one behind" in our pursuit of the 2030 Sustainable Development Agenda. Enhancing support for development of a vibrant MSME sector, including informal enterprises, that is better integrated within the economy, will be critical in making potential losers the winners.

Using a global lens, another concern is that if the principle of freedom of the high seas alone continues to prevail, the opportunity to access and exploit ocean resources (including deep-sea minerals and marine genetic resources) will continue to lie only in the hands of developed countries which have advanced technological capacity. In negotiations of the BBNJ Agreement, Caribbean countries and others are advocating that resources in international waters should be the common heritage of mankind, and thus all countries and peoples should equitably benefit. Including this principle is an attempt to bring more equity into sharing benefits from the oceans and ensuring that Caribbean people and countries are not the losers while others reap rewards from the ocean. While the focus is on bringing this principle into international law, it needs to also remain at the heart of regional and national Blue Economy initiatives.

Since Blue Economy is a fast-moving global conversation, the possibility of tools and approaches being imposed on the region is high. We must have a clear concept of what Blue Economy means and the pathways to achieve a truly inclusive, sustainable and resilient Blue Economy in the Caribbean. There must be Caribbean ownership of the conversation and development process. Certainly, Caribbean stakeholders will need time for dialogue, experimentation, learning, debate, changing views, and adapting policy and practice.

Notes

1 Statement made at the UN Trade Forum's 5th BioTrade Congress.
2 http://toobigtoignore.net/blue-justice-for-ssf/.
3 https://www.cepal.org/en/escazuagreement.
4 For example, under the Climate Change Adaptation in the Fisheries Sector project (CC4Fish) being implemented by the Food and Agriculture Organisation (FAO) with support from the Global Environment Facility (http://www.fao.org/in-action/climate-change-adaptation-eastern-caribbean-fisheries/en/).

References

Abu Nasar, A., Myers, B., Natasha, S., Zander, K. and Garrett, S. 2016. The impact of the expansion of shrimp aquaculture on livelihoods in coastal Bangladesh. *Environment, Development and Sustainability*, 19: 2093–2114.

Alam, M. S. and Paramati, S. R. 2016. The impact of tourism on income inequality in developing economies: Does Kuznets curve hypothesis exist? *Annals of Tourism Research*, 61: 111–126.

Allison, E. H. 2011. *Aquaculture, Fisheries, Poverty and Food Security.* Seattle: University of Washington. Available at: https://www.researchgate.net/publication/227642907_Aquaculture_Fisheries_Poverty_and_Food_Security.

Bélisle, F. J. 1983. Tourism and food production in the Caribbean. *Annals of Tourism Research*, 10 (4): 497–513.

Béné, C., Arthur, R., Norbury, H., Allison, E. *et al.* 2016. Contribution of fisheries and aquaculture to food security and poverty reduction: Assessing the current evidence. *World Development*, 79: 177–196.

Birdlife International. 2010. *The Caribbean Islands Biodiversity Hotspot: Ecosystem Profile.* Washington, DC: Critical Ecosystem Partnership Fund. Available at: https://www.cepf.net/sites/default/files/final_caribbean_ep.pdf.

Bitto, R. 2019. Guyana to become a major oil producer. *World Oil*, 240 (9). Available at: https://www.worldoil.com/magazine/2019/september-2019/features/guyana-to-become-a-major-oil-producer.

CANARI. 2012. *Towards a Green and Resilient Economy for the Caribbean.* CANARI Policy Brief 13. Port of Spain: CANARI. Available at: http://www.canari.org/wp-content/uploads/2014/09/13-Towards-a-green-and-resilient-economy-for-the-Caribbean-English.pdf.

CANARI. 2018. *Civil Society Action Programme for the Sustainable Management of the Shared Living Marine Resources of the Caribbean and North Brazil Shelf Large Marine Ecosystems (2018–2030).* Port of Spain: CANARI. Available at: https://www.canari.org/wp-content/uploads/2017/08/csapbookletenglishfinal.pdf.

Caribbean Development Bank. 2018. *Financing the Blue Economy: A CDB Report.* Bridgetown: CDB. Available at: https://www.caribank.org/publications-and-resources/resource-library/thematic-papers/financing-blue-economy-caribbean-development-opportunity.

CARICOM. 2011. *CARICOM View – Food Security in CARICOM.* Georgetown: CARICOM.

Food and Agriculture Organisation of the United Nations. 2007. The world's mangroves 1980–2005. FAO Forestry Paper 153. Rome: FAO. Available at: http://www.fao.org/3/a1427e/a1427e00.htm.

Girvan, N. 1970. *Multinational Corporations and Dependent.* New Haven: Economic Growth Center, Yale University.

Government of Grenada. 2016. *Blue Growth Coastal Master Plan.* Washington, DC: World Bank Group. Available at: http://documents.worldbank.org/curated/en/358651480931239134/Grenada-Blue-growth-coastal-master-plan.

Jackson, J., Donovan, M., Cramer, K. and Lam, V. (Eds). 2014. *Status and Trends of Caribbean Coral Reefs 1970–2012.* Washington, DC: Global Coral Reef Monitoring Network.

Kaplinsky, R. 2000. Globalisation and unequalisation: What can be learned from value chain analysis? *Journal of Development Studies*, 37 (2): 117–146.

Ocheje, P. D. 2006. The Extractive Industries Transparency Initiative (EITI): Voluntary codes of conduct, poverty and accountability in Africa. *Journal of Sustainable Development in Africa*, 8 (3), 222–239.

Oviedo-García, M. Á., González-Rodríguez, M. R. and Vega-Vázquez, M. 2018. Does sun-and-sea all-inclusive tourism contribute to poverty alleviation and/or income inequality reduction? The case of the Dominican Republic. *Journal of Travel Research*, 58 (6): 995–1013.

Partners for Inclusive Green Economy. 2019. *Principles, Priorities and Pathways for Inclusive Green Economies: Economic Transformation to Deliver the SDGs.* London: Green Economy Coalition, International Institute of Environment & Development. Available at: https://www.greeneconomycoalition.org/assets/reports/GEC-Reports/Principles-priorities-pathways-inclusive-green-economies-web.pdf.

Patil, P. G., Virdin, J., Roberts, J., Singh A. and Diez, S. M. 2016. *Toward a Blue Economy: A Promise for Sustainable Growth in the Caribbean.* Washington, DC: World Bank.

Pegg, S. 2003. *Poverty Reduction or Poverty Exacerbation?: World Bank Group Support for Extractive Industries in Africa.* Environmental Defense.

Polidoro, B. A., Carpenter, K. E., Collins, L., Duke, N. C. *et al.* 2010. The loss of species: Mangrove extinction risk and geographic areas of global concern. *PLoS ONE*, 5 (4). https://doi.org/10.1371/journal.pone.0010095.

Rhiney, K. 2011. Agri-tourism linkages in Jamaica: Case study of the Negril all-inclusive hotel sub-sector. In Momsen, R. T. *Tourism and Agriculture: New Geographies of Consumption, Production and Rural Restructuring.* pp 117–138. London & New York: Routledge.

Sandy, K. and Dardaine-Edwards, A. 2017. *Building Resilience and Adding Value to Local Green Enterprises: Developing a 'Climate-Proofing' Methodology.* Technical Report No. 403. Port of Spain: CANARI.

Sezgin E. and Yolal, M. 2012. Golden age of mass tourism: Its history and development. In Kasimogla, M. (ed.) *Visions for Global Tourism Industry – Creating and Sustaining Competitive Strategies.* IntechOpen.

Thilsted, S.-H., Thorne-Lymana, A., Webb, P., Bogard, J. R., Subasinghe, R., Phillips, M. J. and Allison, E. H. 2016. Sustaining healthy diets: The role of capture fisheries and aquaculture for improving nutrition in the post-2015 era. *Food Policy*, 61: 126–131.

UNESCO. 2017. *Global Ocean Science Report: The Current Status of Ocean.* Available at: https://sustainabledevelopment.un.org/content/documents/2449249373e.pdf.

Voyer, M., Quirk, G., McIlgorm, A. and Azmi, K. 2018. Shades of blue: What do competing interpretations of the Blue Economy mean for oceans governance? *Journal of Environmental Policy & Planning*, 20: 595–616.

4 The state of marine ecosystems that support Blue Economies in the Wider Caribbean

Hazel A. Oxenford and Robin Mahon

Introduction

The Wider Caribbean region (WCR) hosts a large array of marine ecosystems and is considered one of the most biodiverse marine areas in the world. This rich natural ocean capital underpins the region's major economic sectors including coastal tourism and fisheries, as well as many other economic activities and potential. The ecosystem services provided by these natural assets currently support an ocean economy conservatively estimated to exceed US$407 billion a year for the Caribbean alone (Patil et al., 2016). These services currently support livelihoods, human wellbeing and the continued socioeconomic development of the region. However, some of the most important ecosystems, such as coral reefs, seagrasses and mangroves are also among the most vulnerable to anthropogenic stressors including land-based sources of pollution, over-exploitation, marine construction and global climate change and their true economic worth remains undervalued in national accounting. As a consequence, they have suffered substantial degradation and destruction over recent decades (Jackson et al., 2014). The on-going erosion of the region's natural ocean capital is a significant threat to sustaining and further developing Caribbean Blue Economies and will need urgent action beyond current efforts to address both local and external stressors. This chapter reviews the region's marine ecosystems, the vital services they provide, the current threats they face, and some urgently needed actions.

Marine ecosystem diversity and connectivity

The WCR encompasses more than 14 million km^2 of tropical and sub-tropical ocean space overlaying three tectonic plates (North American, Caribbean and South American), and includes two of the world's largest semi-enclosed seas (Caribbean Sea, Gulf of Mexico). This represents a marine area many times that of the land and includes four biophysically distinct Large Marine Ecosystems (LMEs): Caribbean Sea, Gulf of Mexico, North Brazil Shelf and Southeast US Continental Shelf LMEs (Fanning et al., 2009). Seven marine ecoregions (Sullivan-Sealy and Bustamante 1999) and 16 distinct

36   Hazel A. Oxenford and Robin Mahon

physiochemical provinces (Chollett et al., 2012) have been described in the WCR, illustrating the heterogeneity of marine ecosystems in this region.

The diverse coastal and marine habitats include thousands of kilometres of coastline, estuaries of some of the world's largest rivers (e.g. Amazon, Orinoco, Mississippi and Magdalena), coastal lagoons and wetlands, shallow-shelf areas, steep continental shelf slopes, offshore shallow banks and remote atolls. There are also sea mounts, underwater volcanoes and deep-sea hydrothermal vents, ocean trenches and a deep ocean floor dissected by ridges to form a complex set of sub-basins (Smith et al. 2002). The deep-sea ecosystems include diverse but under-studied communities living in the dark and at extreme pressures on the ocean floor, as well as those around hot vents and cold seeps that uniquely rely on chemosynthesis for energy. Better-known valuable ecosystems include mangrove forests, seagrass meadows and coral reefs that are among the world's most biologically productive and species-rich communities. The Wider Caribbean hosts approximately 14% of the world's mangrove forests and 8% of the world's shallow coral reefs, including the second largest barrier reef (MesoAmerican Barrier Reef) extending approximately 1000 km along Honduras, Guatemala, Belize and Mexico. There are also largely uncharted, deep, cold-water coral communities.

The extensive open ocean supports diverse pelagic communities, including those living at or near the surface (epipelagic communities) that are supported by phytoplankton primary production (through photosynthesis). This feeds a large biomass of zooplankton which in turn supports many commercially important finfishes (e.g. sardines, pilchards, menhaden, mackerels, dolphin-fish, tunas and billfishes) as well as sea turtles and marine mammals. Further below the surface are mesopelagic communities (e.g. finfishes, shrimps, squids) living in mid-depths with little light and no primary productivity. As such, many come to the surface at night to feed. Deeper still, and living in permanent darkness, at low temperatures and intense pressure, are much less well-known bathypelagic and abyssopelagic communities, supported by the rain of dead and decaying matter falling from the surface.

In summary, this heterogeneous marine space is one of the most biodiverse areas of the world's oceans, supporting extremely high species diversity and a surprisingly high number of marine species that are found nowhere else in the world (Linardich et al., 2017). It includes 19 recognised Ecologically or Biologically Significant Marine Areas (EBSAs), regarded as critical for supporting the healthy functioning of the oceans and its ecosystem services (CBD, 2014). The WCR is also the main breeding area for several highly migratory Atlantic populations of globally endangered species (e.g. five species of sea turtles, humpbacked whale and whale shark).

Despite the heterogeneity of WCR marine ecosystems, there is considerable connectivity (Cowen and Sponaugle, 2009). Major equatorial ocean currents link surface waters and marine populations across the region, albeit with considerable seasonal and inter-annual variability and a complex system of meanders and eddies. Furthermore, many marine species are highly migratory

The state of marine ecosystems 37

as adults, travelling through the region and beyond. Home ranges of others straddle the mosaic of Exclusive Economic Zones (EEZs) within the region. Adding to this, most marine species have free-floating planktonic early life-stages that may disperse broadly, resulting in mixing of species' gene pools across wide areas, even for species that are bottom-dwelling in fixed habitats as adults (e.g. queen conch, spiny lobster). This results in considerable genetic connectivity among many marine populations and could allow connectivity among geographically separated marine protected areas (MPAs) with some acting as key sources, whilst others act as sinks, primarily receiving larvae from elsewhere.

Ecosystem value

With the coastal population in the WCR exceeding 148 million, millions of people currently benefit from, or depend on, ocean ecosystem services. These include seafood, oxygen, desalinated water, income and employment, recreation, cultural and spiritual enrichment, coastal protection, transport, carbon sequestration, climate regulation and biodiversity, *inter alia*. However, attributing a monetary value to many of these ecosystem services is extraordinarily hard and there are major gaps in knowledge of the true value of natural marine assets (Schuhmann and Mahon, 2015; Schuhmann, Chapter 7). Nevertheless, it is clear that several key economic sectors in the WCR (e.g. tourism and fisheries) are highly dependent on marine ecosystem services, and these industries can be valued in monetary terms. Therefore, the cost of failing to protect these marine ecosystems can be estimated through lost earnings, although this does not provide the real cost of lost natural capital.

Economic data for sectors of the ocean economy, aggregated at the level of the WCR as described here, are few, but several recent studies have focused on the 37 coastal and small island states of the Caribbean Sea and Bahamas. Using 2012 data, Patil et al. (2016) estimated the ocean economy for this area to be worth about US$407 billion/year. Tourism sectors in particular, which are critical to national economies of this region and attract 6% of global tourists (WTTC, 2018), rely on healthy marine ecosystems. Clear water and white sand beaches (reliant on healthy coral reefs, mangroves and seagrasses) have enormous aesthetic value and are the selling feature for Caribbean holidays. The estimated 2012 value for coastal tourism and recreation in the Caribbean was US$47.1 billion/year with a projected increase to US$70 billion by 2024 (Patil et al., 2016). More recent estimates support these predictions with gross revenues from marine and coastal tourism in the Caribbean of approximately US$57 billion, with tourism accounting for 15% of the region's GDP (WTTC, 2018, Diez et al., 2019). Fisheries and aquaculture in the Caribbean were valued at approximately US$6.9 billion in 2012 (Patil et al., 2016) and employ 4.3% of the CARICOM workforce (CRFM, 2015).

Tourism and fisheries in this region are underpinned by marine ecosystems. Key natural assets are healthy coral reefs, mangroves and seagrasses that

38   Hazel A. Oxenford and Robin Mahon

provide a wide array of ecosystems services (Table 4.1). They create and protect beautiful white sand beaches, attenuating wave energy and storm surges, thus mitigating coastal erosion and seawater flooding, and provide protection for coastal infrastructure. They help maintain water clarity and high biodiversity, providing excellent underwater viewing and opportunities to see iconic marine species (turtles, large groupers, sharks and rays, marine mammals). They also provide the seascapes sought after by coastal tourists, yachters and cruise ship passengers. Furthermore, their high fish abundance supports recreational and commercial fishing and provides seafood for tourism, domestic consumption and export (Table 4.1) (Oxenford and McConney, Chapter 10).

The marine ecosystems of this region also hold enormous value and potential value beyond the tourism and fisheries sectors such as in renewable energy (e.g. biogas from seaweeds and marine phytoplankton); carbon sequestration (e.g. by saltmarshes, mangrove forests and seagrass meadows) and bioprospecting for unique biochemicals (Table 4.1).

Significant concerns

Trends in ecosystem health

With a population of 45 million people living within 30 km of the coast and 90 million within 100 km, there is significant pressure on the coastal and marine resources in the WCR and it is considered to be among the world's marine areas most at risk from pollution and over-exploitation (Burke et al., 2011; Diez et al. 2019). Regional and global assessments show that many marine ecosystems in the WCR have been deteriorating for decades (Debels et al., 2017; IOC-UNESCO and UNEP, 2016a; 2016b). For example, live coral cover on shallow reefs has declined drastically, averaging just 14.3% in 2012, which represents almost 50% loss since the 1970s (Jackson et al., 2014). Coral reef accretion rates are also declining across the WCR, with the carbonate framework of more than a third (37%) of reefs now eroding (Perry et al., 2013). Caribbean coral reefs have already lost reef architectural complexity (Alvarez-Filip et al., 2011) and associated species diversity of reef communities (Newman et al., 2015), representing massive losses in coral reef fish biomass and resilience (Mumby et al., 2014). Mangrove ecosystems across the WCR are also being lost at an alarming rate, with an estimated 24% reduction between 1980 and 2005, the second highest regional loss-rate in the world (Polidoro et al., 2010) and a loss that is several-fold greater than any other forest type. Complete removal of mangrove forests is still common in this region for coastal development (urban and tourism, golf courses, marinas) and aquaculture (Wilson, 2017). Seagrass ecosystems, although less well studied, also show widespread environmental degradation with significant declines at 43% of study sites across the WCR (van Tussenbroek et al., 2014).

Table 4.1 Examples of valuable ecosystem services provided by selected coastal and marine ecosystems in the WCR

Ecosystem feature	Ecosystem services	Coral reef	Mangrove	Seagrass	Coastal wetlands	Continental shelf	Open ocean	Deep ocean
Biophysical structure	• Attenuates waves, protecting coasts, infrastructure and communities against erosion and flooding	×××	××	×	×			
	• Produces white sand, creating beaches and protecting coastlines – white sand beaches have high value for tourism and local culture	×××		××				
	• Recreational opportunity for tourism and local use	×××	××	×	×	×	××	
	• Creates land mass, e.g. atolls, barrier islands, coral islands, overwash islands and deltas	×××	××		××			
	• Provides building material, e.g. lime, rubble, blocks, timber and thatch	×	×					
	• Vegetation slows discharge of freshwater into the sea and removes pollutants, e.g. nutrients, heavy metals		×××		××			
	• Vegetation slows water movement causing sediments to settle out of the water column and prevent resuspension, thus maintaining clear water		××	×××	××			
	• Source of water, e.g. for desalination	×	×	×	×	×	×	
	• Rhizomes and roots bind sand and silt, protecting beaches from erosion		×	××	×			
	• Space for aquaculture and mariculture		××		××	×	×	
	• Living space for enormous diversity and biomass of marine and terrestrial species	×××	××	×	××	××	×	?

Ecosystem feature	Ecosystem services	Coral reef	Mangrove	Seagrass	Coastal wetlands	Continental shelf	Open ocean	Deep ocean
High biodiversity	• High biological productivity (with low nutrient input in reefs), unique symbiotic relationships, nutrient recycling	×××	××	××	××	××	×	?
	• Bioprospecting value, e.g. biomedical drugs from marine species are already being used to treat cancer, HIV, cardiovascular diseases, ulcers	×××	××	×	×	×	×	×?
	• Supports tourism-based livelihoods and revenue generation, e.g. SCUBA diving, snorkelling and other underwater viewing activities, especially for iconic species	×××	×	×	×			
	• Includes endangered species, e.g. sea turtles, manatees, sharks, rays, Nassau grouper	×××	××	××	××	××	×	?
	• Supports eco-tourism livelihoods and revenue generation, e.g. bird watching, nature tours, boardwalks, kayaking, boat tours		×××		××			

Key stressors

The key stressors are anthropogenic (caused by humans) and can be grouped into (1) marine pollution, (2) over-harvesting, (3) physical destruction, and (4) climate change.

Marine pollution

Marine pollution issues are fully addressed in Corbin, Chapter 16, and are only briefly reviewed here. Marine pollutants of particular concern to marine ecosystems of the WCR include: nutrients (mostly nitrates and phosphates), sediments (mostly terrigenous), chemicals (e.g. chlorine, pesticides, pharmaceutical drugs and personal care products, caffeine, oil, heavy metals, microbes) and solid waste, especially plastics. These pollutants are mainly from wastewater and sewage (85% of which enters the ocean untreated in the WCR), and runoff from agricultural and urban areas (including golf courses and hotel gardens) (Diez et al., 2019). Thousands of tons of plastic waste remain uncollected each year in the WCR, and much of this ends up in the sea (Diez et al., 2019). Industrial effluents and solid waste are also discharged or dumped in water courses or directly into the sea. The abundance of floating plastics in the ocean is considered to be high in the WCR (IOC-UNESCO and UNEP, 2016a).

Nutrients lead to algal blooms in the water column, reduced light and low oxygen to benthic communities, and changes in biological community composition. This is particularly damaging to corals and seagrasses that need good sunlight to survive. Furthermore, they can easily be taken over by the accelerated growth of seaweeds, cyanobacteria and sponges that do well in high nutrient conditions. Increasingly, Caribbean coral reefs are changing to algal- and sponge-dominated communities, due to nutrient pollution exacerbated by over-harvesting of herbivores (Mumby et al., 2014). High nutrient loading, together with increasing water temperatures create critically low oxygen conditions which cause mass fish kills and seasonal "dead zones". These are increasing in size and duration, especially off rivers in the WCR. Toxic algal blooms also develop in high-nutrient warm waters, causing significant mortality of shellfish and other marine organisms, and posing a health threat to marine mammals and humans (IOC-UNESCO and UNEP, 2016a).

Sediments, largely from poor watershed management, cause turbidity, reduce light and smother benthic communities. This again is particularly damaging to coral reefs and seagrasses and significantly affects the aesthetic value of nearshore waters.

Many chemicals found in wastewater, sewage, runoff, industrial effluent and solid waste are either directly toxic or have sub-lethal effects (e.g. endocrine disrupters) on marine organisms. Marine invertebrates and fishes are exceptionally vulnerable even to very low concentrations of these chemicals because they are so easily absorbed through the porous surfaces of these water-breathing organisms. Sub-lethal effects can damage reproduction and cause populations to decline. Some pollutants, such as heavy metals, bio-accumulate up the food chain, and become toxic to humans consuming higher predators (e.g. tunas, billfishes).

High bacterial loads (especially from untreated sewage) threaten many marine species. For example, the Caribbean is considered a global "hot spot" for coral diseases, some of which have been linked to pathogens in sewage (Sutherland et al., 2011). Humans who swim in coastal waters may also experience ear, skin and gastrointestinal infections.

Solid waste including discarded fishing gear, especially from plastics that last for hundreds of years, damages marine ecosystems and organisms through smothering, entanglement, choking, abrasion and damage to the digestive tract that impacts feeding. Furthermore, microplastics (small particles of degraded plastic) may adsorb toxins and bacteria, potentially making their consumption by marine organisms lethal. Plastic waste has also been implicated in increased incidences of coral disease (Lamb et al., 2018). Accumulations of marine litter at sea, along shorelines and in harbours and marinas, has a high aesthetic cost, and microplastics and their associated toxins and microbes that end up in the flesh of marine organisms may be consumed by humans.

Over-harvesting

Heavy fishing and inadequate management of fishing effort has led to the over-exploitation of many of the WCR's commercially important fishery resources (Singh Renton and McIvor, 2015; Oxenford and McConney, Chapter 10). Consequently, many exploited fish populations have become depleted or even collapsed with consequent loss of fisheries yield and ecosystem function. For example, removal of top predators has disrupted marine food webs and predator–prey relationships and has altered community species composition and function. This is particularly evident in Caribbean coral reefs where sequential removal of turtles, sharks, snappers, groupers and ultimately herbivores has resulted in loss of biodiversity and ecosystem resilience, as well as aesthetic value (Schuhmann et al., 2013).

Over-harvesting of timber (e.g. for lumber and charcoal) continues to degrade the mangrove forests of the WCR, destroying their many valuable ecosystem functions (Table 4.1).

Physical destruction

Coastal and marine construction, land reclamation and dredging (e.g. for coastal infrastructure including tourism, port facilities, marinas, piers, ship channels, runways, coastal protection structures, aquaculture ponds) all of which will likely increase under a Blue Economy, continue to pose a

The state of marine ecosystems   43

significant threat to mangroves, saltmarshes, seagrasses and coral reefs in the WCR, often resulting in wholesale removal of the ecosystem and complete loss of the ecosystem function and services. Negative impacts for adjacent ecosystems include lack of supporting ecosystem services, reduced biodiversity, and both acute and chronic increases in nutrient and sediment loading. Other sources of physical damage especially to coral reefs and seagrasses include anchoring, propeller damage and vessel groundings.

Climate change

Extreme climate variability and long-term change induced by global warming, causes serious environmental stress. Especially damaging to marine ecosystems are: (1) heating stress from increasing sea surface temperatures (SSTs) and repeated anomalously high temperature events; (2) decreasing carbonate saturation levels from increasing ocean acidity (OA); (3) sea level rise (SLR); and (4) increased frequency of extreme weather events (Taylor et al., Chapter 5). These stresses significantly impact coastal and marine ecosystems across the WCR and exacerbate the impacts of marine pollution and over-harvesting (Oxenford and Monnereau, 2018).

Since the late 1990s coral reef ecosystems in the WCR have experienced repeated heat-induced mass bleaching, and the associated high mortality of corals was especially severe in 1998, 2005 and 2010 (Eakin et al., 2010). Corals have also suffered from increased incidences of disease outbreaks linked to increased temperature (Ruiz-Moreno et al., 2012). Increasing temperature also has far-reaching effects on the physiologies and behaviours of marine organisms in general. As most are "cold blooded", their metabolism will speed up and behaviours with strong temperature cues (such as reproduction) will be disrupted. Impacts will include increased mortality from low oxygen levels, shorter larval development times and mismatches in availability of food and suitable settlement areas for larvae, resulting in increased incidences of recruitment failure, especially for those species with specific benthic habitat requirements such as coral reef species. Climate-induced changes in SST and global winds are also affecting surface currents and upwelling events with implications for biological productivity, larval transport and connectivity across marine ecosystems. Changes in SST, winds and currents, together with increased ocean nutrient loading, have also been linked to the recent mass influxes of pelagic sargassum into the Caribbean Sea that are causing further long-term damage to coastal habitats, especially seagrasses (van Tussenbroek et al., 2017).

Increasing OA is constraining carbonate production and many coral reefs in the region are now experiencing net erosion of their reef framework; putting them at a disadvantage in keeping up with SLR (Perry et al., 2018). OA is also having more insidious impacts on the physiologies of marine organisms through impairment of a diverse suite of sensory and behavioural abilities, especially in the early life history stages, which is likely to reduce recruitment success (Oxenford and Monnereau, 2017).

44   Hazel A. Oxenford and Robin Mahon

Mangrove, seagrass and saltmarsh ecosystems are being damaged by SLR inundation, while coastal development constrains them from retreating inland. Placement of coastal protection structures in response to SLR are also causing physical damage to corals reefs and seagrasses.

Major hurricanes in the WCR have caused massive physical damage to coral reefs, and an increase in their frequency is reducing the time available for recovery (Gardner et al., 2005). Seagrasses and mangroves are also being increasingly damaged by these larger, stronger storms. For example, the WCR has experienced five Category 5 and three Category 4 hurricanes in 2017, 2018 and 2019 alone.

Over the long term, expected impacts are reduced biodiversity, decreasing biological productivity, declining populations and loss of ecosystem services and function across marine ecosystems, especially coral reef ecosystems.

Action for securing the foundation of a Blue Economy

There has been a great deal of effort within the last few decades to research, monitor, document and diagnose the deterioration of marine ecosystems across the WCR. Clearly, significant and urgent action at local, national, regional and international levels is needed to address this chronic deterioration; otherwise, these ecosystems will no longer be able to support even current ocean economies, far less the aspirations for blue growth expressed throughout the region. It is also clear that complementary action at all levels is needed to mitigate and adapt to the increasing severity of global climate change impacts on these ecosystems. The needed actions for sectoral issues such as overfishing, tourism and pollution have been fully addressed in chapters in this volume and will not be revisited here. Likewise, regional and national governance needs are addressed in other chapters. As such, this chapter only considers selected specific actions that are needed to ensure sustainability of biodiversity and ecosystem function of the marine ecosystems of the WCR.

MPAs

Primary among the actions needed for habitat and biodiversity conservation is the establishment of a network of effective marine protected areas (MPAs) that safeguard representative marine ecosystems (Cowen and Sponaugle, 2009). Foundational to MPAs, and indeed orderly use of marine space overall, is marine spatial planning (as discussed in Inniss et al., Chapter 6). The Specially Protected Areas and Wildlife (SPAW) Protocol of the Cartagena Convention (Protection and Development of the Marine Environment in the WCR) is aimed at addressing this need. Although it came into force in 2000, only 17 countries have endorsed SPAW to date. The Aichi Target for MPAs, reaffirmed in SDG14, is 10% of ocean space to be applied globally. Many consider this level inadequate, and several initiatives within the WCR have adopted higher targets (e.g. Caribbean Challenge Initiative goal is 20% by 2020). However, there is still a long way to go to meet these targets in most countries in the region, and to reverse the tendency to establish parks that are ineffective due to inadequate management and resources (Linardich et al., 2017). Considerable capacity development, investment and stakeholder involvement will be required for targets to be met effectively.

Endangered species

Attention to the status and protection of endangered marine species is also needed. The SPAW Protocol lists species that are considered to be at risk, using IUCN Red List criteria. However, these assessments are science-based and availability of information is a serious limiting factor. Here again, MPAs have a key role to play in securing critical adult and breeding habitat, as do harvesting regulations or even complete bans for these species.

Habitat restoration

Restoration or at least rehabilitation of ecosystem function in degraded coastal and marine ecosystems is gaining prominence in the WCR, especially for mangroves and coral reefs. These generally involve transplanting propagules or fragments from healthier ecosystems to degraded sites, and some also involve much higher-cost nursery facilities for grow-out or rearing. However, efforts to date are mainly small-scale, costly and too new to evaluate effectiveness. Valid concerns include transplanting corals in waters that remain polluted.

Conclusion

The current poor status of some of the most critical marine ecosystems in this region is clear, and multiple solutions have been well articulated. The current enthusiasm for transitioning to a Blue Economy should catalyse action at all levels to secure the sustainability of the region's marine ecosystems underpinning Blue Economies. Caribbean nations can also use the SDG framework to realign and strengthen national efforts to protect the environment and achieve inclusive economic prosperity. Paradoxically, the economic sectors dependent on marine ecosystems in the WCR are also some of the main stressors. Projected increases in coastal urban populations and tourism in particular, the development of new industries and continued global warming will increase these stressors under a business as usual scenario. Further, there are other marine ecosystems, much less well-known, that will likely be important as new Blue Economy avenues are explored. Attention to biodiversity conservation measures, including research and monitoring, and enhanced governance will be key in ensuring sustainability of currently used and hitherto underused living resources and ecosystems.

46   Hazel A. Oxenford and Robin Mahon

References

Alvarez-Filip, L., Perry, A. L., Gill, J. A. *et al.* 2011. Drivers of region-wide declines in architectural complexity on Caribbean reefs. *Coral Reefs*, 30: 1051–1060.

Burke, L., Reytar, K., Spalding, M. *et al.* 2011. *Reefs at Risk Revisited.* World Resources Institute, Washington, DC. 114 pp.

CBD. 2014. *Ecologically or Biologically Significant Marine Areas (EBSAs): Special Places in the World's Oceans.* Volume 2: *Wider Caribbean and Western Mid-Atlantic Region.* Secretariat of the Convention on Biological Diversity, Montreal. 86 pp.

Chollett, I., Mumby, P. J. and Muller-Karger, F. E. *et al.* 2012. Physical environments of the Caribbean Sea. *Limnology and Oceanography*, 57: 1233–1244.

Cowen, R. K. and Sponaugle, S. 2009. Larval dispersal and marine population connectivity. *Annual Review of Marine Science*, 1: 443–466.

CRFM. 2015. *CRFM Statistics and Information Report – 2014.* 82 pp.

Debels, P., Fanning, L., Mahon, R., *et al.* 2017. The CLME+ Strategic Action Programme: an ecosystems approach for assessing and managing the Caribbean Sea and North Brazil Shelf Large Marine Ecosystems. *Environmental Development*, 22: 191–205.

Diez, S. M., Patil, P. G., Morton, J. *et al.* 2019. *Marine Pollution in the Caribbean: Not a Minute to Waste.* World Bank Group, Washington, DC. 100 pp.

Eakin, C. M., Morgan, J. A., Heron, S. F. *et al.* 2010. Caribbean corals in crisis: Record thermal stress, bleaching, and mortality in 2005. *PLoS ONE*, 5: e13969.

Fanning, L., Mahon, R. and McConney, P. 2009. Focusing on living marine resource governance: The Caribbean Large Marine Ecosystem and Adjacent Areas Project. *Coastal Management*, 37: 219–234.

Gardner, T. A., Cote, I. M., Gill, J. A. *et al.* 2005. Hurricanes and Caribbean coral reefs: Impacts, recovery patterns, and role in long-term decline. *Ecology*, 86: 174–184.

IOC-UNESCO and UNEP. 2016a. *Large Marine Ecosystems: Status and Trends. Transboundary Waters Assessment Programme (TWAP)*, Vol. 4. United Nations Environment Programme (UNEP), Nairobi. 299 pp.

IOC-UNESCO and UNEP. 2016b. *The Open Ocean: Status and Trends. Transboundary Waters Assessment Programme (TWAP)*, Vol. 5. United Nations Environment Programme (UNEP), Nairobi. 331 pp.

Jackson, J. B. C, Donovan, M. K. and Cramer, K. L. *et al.* (Eds). 2014. *Status and Trends of Caribbean Coral Reefs: 1970–2012.* Global Coral Reef Monitoring Network, IUCN, Gland, Switzerland. 304 pp.

Lamb, J. B., Willis, B. L. Fiorenza, E. A. *et al.* 2018. Plastic waste associated with disease on coral reefs. *Science*, 359: 460–462.

Linardich, C., Ralph, G., Carpenter, K. *et al.* 2017. *The Conservation Status of Marine Bony Shorefishes of the Greater Caribbean.* IUCN, Gland, Switzerland. 75 pp.

Mumby, P. J., Flower, J., Chollett, I. *et al.* 2014. *Towards Reef Resilience and Sustainable Livelihoods: A Handbook for Caribbean Coral Reef Managers.* University of Exeter, UK. 172 pp. Available at: http://www.force-project.eu/.

Newman, S. P., Meesters, E. H., Dryden, C. S. *et al.* 2015. Reef flattening effects on total richness and species responses in the Caribbean. *Journal of Animal Ecology*, 84: 1678–1689.

Oxenford, H. A. and Monnereau, I. 2017. Impacts of climate change on fish and shellfish in the coastal and marine environments of Caribbean small island developing states (SIDS). *Caribbean Marine Climate Change Report Card: Science Review*, 2017: 83–114. Available at: https://www.gov.uk/government/publications/commonwealth-marine-economies-cme-programme-caribbean-marine-climate-change-report-card-scientific-reviews.

Oxenford, H. A. and Monnereau, I. 2018. Chapter 9: Climate change impacts, vulnerabilities and adaptations: Western Central Atlantic marine fisheries, In: Barange, M., Bahri, T., Beveridge, M.*et al.* (Eds), *Impacts of Climate Change on Fisheries and Aquaculture: Synthesis of Current Knowledge, Adaptation and Mitigation Options*, pp. 147–168. FAO Fisheries Technical Paper 627.

Patil, P. G., Virdin, J., Diez, S. M. *et al.* 2016. *Toward A Blue Economy: A Promise for Sustainable Growth in the Caribbean: An Overview.* The World Bank, Washington DC. 91 pp.

Perry, C. T., Murphy, G. N., Kench, P. S. *et al.* 2013. Caribbean-wide decline in carbonate production threatens coral reef growth. *Nature Communications*, 4: 1402.

Perry, C. T., Alvarez-Filip, L., Graham, N. A. J., *et al.* 2018. Loss of coral reef growth capacity to track future increases in sea level. *Nature*, 558: 396–400.

Polidoro, B. A., Carpenter, K. E., Collins, L. *et al.* 2010. The loss of species: mangrove extinction risk and geographic areas of global concern. *PLoS ONE*, 5: e10095.

Ruiz-Moreno, D., Willis, B. L., Page, A. C. *et al.* 2012. Global coral disease prevalence associated with sea temperature anomalies and local factors. *Diseases of Aquatic Organisms*, 100: 249–261.

Schuhmann, P. W. and Mahon, R. 2015. The valuation of marine ecosystem goods and services in the Caribbean: A literature review and framework for future valuation efforts. *Ecosystem Services*, 11: 56–66.

Schuhmann, P. W., Casey, J. F., Horrocks, J. A. *et al.* 2013. Recreational SCUBA divers' willingness to pay for marine biodiversity in Barbados. *Journal of Environmental Management*, 121: 29–36.

Singh Renton, S. and McIvor, I. 2015. *Review of Current Fisheries Management Performance and Conservation Measures in the WECAFC Area.* FAO Fisheries and Aquaculture Technical Paper 587, 293 pp.

Smith, M. L., Carpenter, K. E. and Waller, R. W. 2002. An introduction to the oceanography, geology, biogeography, and fisheries of the tropical and subtropical Western Central Atlantic, In: Carpenter, K. E. (Ed.) *The Living Marine Resources of the Western Central Atlantic*, pp. 1–23. Food and Agriculture Organisation of the United Nations, Rome.

Sullivan-Sealy, K. and Bustamante, G. 1999. *Setting Geographic Priorities for Marine Conservation in Latin America and the Caribbean.* The Nature Conservancy, Arlington, VA. 125 pp.

Sutherland, K. P., Shaban, S., Joyner, J. L.*et al.* 2011. Human pathogen shown to cause disease in the threatened elkhorn coral Acropora palmata. *PLoS ONE*, 6: e23468.

van Tussenbroek, B. I., Hernández Arana, H. A., Rodríguez-Martínez, R. E.*et al.*2017. Severe impacts of brown tides caused by *Sargassum* spp. on near-shore Caribbean seagrass communities. *Marine Pollution Bulletin*, 122: 272–281.

Wilson, R. 2017. Impacts of climate change on mangrove ecosystems in the coastal and marine environments of Caribbean Small Island Developing States (SIDS). *Caribbean Marine Climate Change Report Card: Science Review* 2017: 60–82. Available at: https://www.gov.uk/government/publications/commonwealth-marine-e

conomies-cme-programme-caribbean-marine-climate-change-report-card-scientific-reviews.

WTTC. 2018. *Travel and Tourism Economic Impact 2018: Caribbean*. World Travel and Tourism Council. Available at: https://www.wttc.org/-/media/files/reports/economic-impact-research/regions-2018/caribbean2018.pdf.

5 Implications of climate change for Blue Economies in the Wider Caribbean

Michael A. Taylor, Mona K. Webber, Tannecia S. Stephenson and Felicia S. Whyte

Introduction

Developing countries, including those constituting the Wider Caribbean, will be among the most disadvantaged under future global warming. This is due to multiple interrelated climate risks they already face from climatic variations and extreme weather events, which are further magnified at higher levels of future warming (IPCC, 2018). Especially for the small island developing states of the Wider Caribbean basin, the economic cost of climate change is projected to significantly increase in the future as a result of greater damage to critical infrastructure which support human settlements and the high cost of the damages in comparison to their small economies (Burgess et al., 2018).

The region's strong climate vulnerability arises in part from the strong linkages between Caribbean economies and way of life and the ocean, i.e. the resources it encompasses and supports. This chapter explores the implications of present and future climate change for the sustainability and viability of critical regional marine ecosystems (e.g. seas, reefs and coasts) and key sectors of the ocean economy (tourism, fisheries, shipping and trade and energy). Specifically, the chapter examines, in the context of how the region's climate is changing, the impact of the change on living and non-living marine resources, the need to respond to the challenges posed, and the possible nature of that response.

The Caribbean's climate is changing

The climate of the Caribbean has already changed in significant ways and is projected to continue changing through the end of the current century due to further global warming. Some of the changes to key marine climate variables are summarised in Table 5.1. The overall picture is of a Caribbean already characterised by increases in storm intensity, drought risk, ocean temperatures, acidity, sea levels and wave heights. The future climate will likely see more intense storms, even higher sea levels, smaller wave heights, and warmer, more acidic oceans.

50   *Michael A. Taylor et al.*

Table 5.1 Historical and future change in marine climate variables for the Caribbean region

Marine climate variables	Historical changes	Projected changes
Tropical cyclones	• Increase in potential destructiveness since 1980s • Increase in intensity and storm duration since 1970s • Increase in average number of Category 4 and 5 hurricanes per year over the past 30 years	• Increase in most intense storms • Increase in rainfall amounts and maximum hurricane wind speed (by up to 11%, depending on warming scenario) by end of century
Extreme rainfall	• Small increase in heavy rainfall associated with rain events in some parts of the Caribbean • Increase in drought risk since 1950s	• Increase in heavy rainfall by 2100 with regional variations • Significant drying after 2050 with up to 10% of Caribbean land masses under drought
Sea surface temperatures	• Increase over the Wider Caribbean (~1°C per century) and the Antilles (~1.3°C per century)	• For business-as-usual, further increase in sea surface temperatures in the Antilles (1.39–2.21°C per century) and for the Wider Caribbean (1.37–2.15°C per century), with Intensification towards the end of century
Ocean acidification	• Increase in surface ocean acidity (by ~12%) over past three decades • Decrease in surface aragonite saturation state (by ~8%) over past three decades	• Increase in acidity by 58% by 2100s • Decrease in sea surface saturation state by 32% by 2100s
Sea level rise	• Increase in Caribbean sea levels around global mean values (~ 0.19 ± 0.02 m) for 1901 to 2010	• For business-as-usual, increase in Caribbean sea levels by ~ 1 m by end of century • Southernmost Caribbean show marginally higher rates of increase
Sea wave heights	• Positive trends in significant wave height since 1948	• Negative trend in significant wave heights ~1–2% by the end of century

Source: Information taken from the State of the Caribbean Climate (CSGM, 2020) and supplemented with data from Bates et al. (2012), Guinotte et al. (2003), Reguero et al. (2013) and IPCC (2013).

Climate impacts on marine systems

Impact on living resources

Regional changes in climate directly and through compounding effects impact the living resources of the Caribbean Sea. The climate-induced stressors that have greatest impact on each of the living resources of the Caribbean are summarised in Table 5.2. The effect of climate change will be most critical for the major coastal ecosystems (coral reefs, seagrasses and mangroves) as well as their associated organisms (fish and shellfish). Corals have received the greatest attention due to the severe decline in live coral cover over the last 30 years (Jackson et al., 2014) and the alarming bleaching events that have occurred after periods of extremely high sea surface temperatures. Corals offer an example of impact due to climate stressors originating from both land and sea (Table 5.2). Seagrasses and mangroves have similar responses to variables like sea level rise and intense storms. Seagrasses, more so than mangroves, are also threatened by increased turbidity from land derived sediments and high sea surface temperatures.

Ecosystem impacts from climate can also emerge indirectly. The sargassum inundation that has been affecting the Wider Caribbean and West Africa since 2011 (Schell et al., 2015) is theorised to be triggered by climate variability and anthropogenic nutrient enrichment (Wang et al., 2019; Oviatt et al., 2019). Unprecedented sargassum blooms have had devastating consequences for Caribbean marine resources and especially for Blue Economy sectors like fishing and tourism (Burrowes et al., 2019; Franks et al., 2016). Sargassum mats on shores quickly rot to produce hydrogen sulphide gas, which has adverse effects on seagrasses and mangroves. Beaches are exposed to erosion due to the increased weight of the swash, and further damage is inflicted by use of heavy machinery to remove the tonnes of algal biomass (UNEP, 2018).

Other stressors, including eutrophication and plastic and microplastic contamination, along with unregulated coastal development and use of limited coastal resources, threaten the Caribbean's natural marine resources. Eutrophication is considered the most common form of marine pollution affecting the Caribbean (Siung-Chang, 1997). Approximately "85% of wastewater entering the Caribbean Sea remains untreated" (Cashman, 2014) as sewerage infrastructure struggles to keep pace with economic development (Nurse et al., 2012). Solid waste and plastic marine debris also threaten regional marine resources. Plastic pollution, in particular, is not only conspicuous but persistent, especially since the largely non-biodegradable material, weathers, fragments and becomes microplastics (Au et al., 2017). Concentrations of microplastics in Caribbean environments and species are only just being assessed with only a few Caribbean territories reporting baselines (e.g. Rose and Webber, 2019). Though non-climatic, the extent and frequency of impact of these other stressors can be modulated by climate e.g. increased garbage outflows following heavy rain events. These stressors also compromise the ability of habitats and species to cope with climate induced stresses.

Impact on non-living resources

Key sectors of the regional ocean economy, in particular tourism, fisheries and shipping and trade, are extremely vulnerable to climate change.

Table 5.2 Impacts of climate induced stressors on living resources of the Caribbean Sea

Living resource	Climate stressor				
	Intense rainfall periods with increased sedimentation and nutrient inputs	*Increased sea surface temperatures*	*Ocean acidification*	*Increased storminess*	*Sea level rise*
Coral reefs	Blanketing reefs in sediments, which reduces light for photosynthesis; nutrient-fed macroalgal growth smothering corals	Bleaching, which kills or weakens corals making them more susceptible to disease (Jackson et al., 2014)	Reduced calcification rates (already 15% lower; predicted to decline to 30% by 2050) (Friedrich et al., 2012); weakened skeletal structures (Pulwarty et al., 2010)	Breaking, rolling, tossing; reduction in structural complexity of reefs; called flattening of Caribbean reefs (Alvarez-Filip et al., 2009)	
Seagrasses	Reduced light penetration leading to lower productivity, shoot biomass and density (Green and Webber, 2003)	Death due to "heatwaves" (IPCC, 2014)		Uprooting and erosion of seagrass beds	"Drowning" of seagrasses by reduction in optimal depth and effective light intensity (Hogarth, 2015)
Mangroves				Uprooting and toppling of trees	Coastal "squeeze" or lack of space for upland migration (IPCC, 2014)
Associated fish and shellfish		Increased sensitivity to acidification (Kroeker et al., 2013)	Reduced fecundity and recruitment (Ross et al., 2011)		

Tourism

The tourism sector is a significant employer and contributes millions to the Caribbean economy. Climate extremes and in particular hurricanes pose a direct threat in the form of damages incurred to coastal structures (e.g. hotels, marinas) and supporting infrastructure (e.g. roads, communication networks, airports, etc.) from strong winds, intense rainfall and significant inland flooding exacerbated by higher sea levels. It was estimated that the 2017 hurricane season, which saw three category 5 hurricanes traverse the Caribbean Sea, set back the region's tourism sector by up to four years (provided there were no further serious impacts from hurricanes for a few years thereafter) (WTTC, 2017). The vulnerability of the sector to direct impact damages will only likely increase given the future projections of increased frequency of the most intense storms (see Table 5.1).

The degradation of marine-based environmental destination assets, including biodiversity (e.g. coral reef attractions) and beaches, through repeated storm events and from slow onset change (e.g. rising temperatures and sea levels) also represents a challenge. There are, for example, direct linkages between the loss of corals due to rising ocean temperatures, the vulnerability of the beach to erosion during strong wave events (as coral reefs break wave action), and the attractiveness of dive tourism. Approximately 30% of 900 coastal resorts in 19 Caribbean countries could be partially or fully inundated under 1 m sea level rise, while a substantially higher proportion (49–60%) would be vulnerable due to the associated coastal erosion (Scott and Verkoeyen, 2017).

Further challenges to the Caribbean tourism sector will come from: (i) increased operational costs, e.g. due to greater energy demand for cooling; costs associated with acquiring water, or from the loss of property value and higher insurance costs; (ii) diminished worker productivity due to climate-induced health impacts on sector employees or their dependants; and (iii) changes in tourism demand patterns linked to either increased favourable climates of nearer destinations, increased visitor environmental consciousness, and/or the diminished attractiveness of destinations due to perceived or actual impact or degradation or increased incidence of vector borne diseases (e.g. dengue). In 2017, even islands not directly hit were impacted due to "public misconception that the entire Caribbean was struck by the storms" (WTTC, 2017). When the other impacts such as operational and transportation costs, tourist demand patterns and the relative contribution to the national economy are considered, many of the tourism-dependent countries within the Wider Caribbean emerge as amongst those with highest sector risk from climate change.

Fisheries

The Caribbean fisheries sector employs hundreds of thousands of people, earns in excess of US$6 billion annually and provides about 10% of the region's protein intake (Nurse, 2011: Patil et al., 2016). Climate variations and

54 *Michael A. Taylor et al.*

the resulting impacts are already posing significant risk to the Caribbean Sea's fish stocks and fisheries, especially when combined with other threats including developments, pollution of coastal waters and overfishing (Monnereau and Oxenford, 2017). Changes in environmental conditions impact abundance, distribution and availability of fish populations, while the increasing frequency of extreme climate events affect fish habitat, productivity and distribution, and have direct impacts on coastal communities dependent on the fishing industry. Many of these communities are already vulnerable due to poverty and the lack of social services and essential infrastructure.

CFRM (2019) note that for a business-as-usual future, more than 70% of 106 commercially important fishery species will be at very high risk to climate impacts. They also note the likelihood of a shift in the distribution of Caribbean marine species by tens to hundreds of kilometres in response to changing ocean conditions, resulting in reduced species richness, changing community composition and substantially reduced maximum fisheries catch potential (5–15% by the 2030s and 0–30% by the 2050s relative to 1970–2000 values under low-warming scenarios). More intense storms and hurricanes will also lead to changes in supply and demand and ultimately changes in household fish consumption, due to smaller catches and supply disruptions.

The materialisation of the above risks will have significant socio-economic impacts on those working in the harvest and post-harvest sectors as well as their dependants. Implications at the level of national governments are also anticipated for: domestic productivity in the fishing sector; food security and food sovereignty (and by implication the food import bill); export trade and foreign currency earnings. Figure 5.1 summarises some of the specific livelihood and economic related threats for Caribbean fisheries due to climate change impacts.

Shipping and trade

Caribbean territories rely on international transportation to support trade with external markets, for tourism and for accessibility to the wider global community. Coastal airports or their access roads sited on low-lying lands are vulnerable to coastal flooding from extreme rain events and storms. Increased risk from heatwaves can impact worker safety, drive up operational costs, cause heat buckling of runways, as well as resulting in payload restrictions and disruptions through impact on aircraft lift (Coffel et al., 2017). In the future, relocation and/or extension of some existing runways (within topographical limitations) may be necessary due to the multi-hazard risks from flooding and heatwaves. Sea level rise and storm events may also necessitate reinforcing and/or redesign of seaport infrastructure, or the need for more dredging, thereby increasing operational costs (Asariotis et al., 2017).

For 1 m sea level rise, it is projected that 3108 km^2 of Caribbean coastal land will be lost, 21 out of 64 (32%) of CARICOM airports inundated, and 80% of CARICOM ports will have adjacent lands inundated if no protective measures are undertaken (Simpson et al., 2010). Monioudi et al. (2018) show

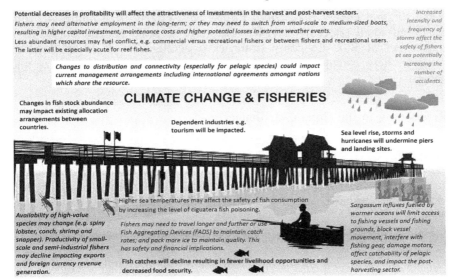

Figure 5.1 A summary of likely threats from climate change to Caribbean fisheries. Information adapted from Monnereau and Oxenford (2017)

that for a further half-degree global warming the critical international transportation assets in Jamaica and Saint Lucia are vulnerable to operational disruptions and increased costs, mostly due to increasing temperatures and exceedance of high temperature thresholds, and increasing coastal inundation of the airport and seaport assets. The port cities of Port of Spain (Trinidad), Kingston (Jamaica), Georgetown (Guyana), Nassau (Bahamas) and Paramaribo (Suriname) are identified as examples of those already affected by sea level rise and flooding which may worsen at higher global temperatures (Mycoo, 2018). Hallegatte et al. (2013) identify Santo Domingo (Dominican Republic) as among the leading port cities globally with the greatest increase in risk due to future climatic changes.

Notably, none of the studies above explicitly consider increased vulnerability of the airport and seaport facilities and supporting infrastructure due to changing hurricane characteristics, or the potential impact on international trade due to increased storminess along trading routes, including those outside Caribbean waters. Additionally, the contribution of regional shipping and trade to greenhouse gas emissions and ultimately climate change is yet to be comprehensively examined.

Energy

Some Caribbean territories are beginning to explore the potential of harvesting renewable energy from the ocean via wind, tides, waves, biomass and

56 Michael A. Taylor et al.

ocean thermal energy conversion. Efforts have largely been limited to concepts and small pilots to date, but the move to scale up and pursue as a component of Blue Economy strategies is accelerating. It is still unclear, however, how climate change may impact marine energy prospects and potential.

Responding to the climate challenge

A raft of adaptation strategies and interventions will be needed in the Wider Caribbean to respond to climate's threats to the Blue Economy and to tackle the integrated nature of the threat. A part of the challenge of responding is determining which adaptation actions and strategies are most feasible, when are they best applied, and if the capacity and resources exist to undertake them.

Some or all of the following must be factored into the region's response:

1   *Reducing non-climatic stresses.* Adaptation responses must support and/or target reducing known non-climatic stresses on the region's marine environment in an attempt to ameliorate climate's exacerbating or compounding effect. These include addressing the stresses that arise from tourism, fishing, coastal development, reduced beach sand supply and unsustainable aquaculture or agriculture.
2   *Protecting existing marine resources and assets.* Urgent attention should be given to identifying and protecting locations where organisms may be more robust or less exposed to climate change. This is in addition to restoring degraded but still existent sites. The latter may require *ex situ* conservation approaches.
3   *Applying integrated coastal zone management which recognises the changing resources.* Approaches to coastal development must integrate infrastructure and other land management practices with the changing ecosystems, e.g. accounting for shoreward shift or maintaining sediment supply to coastal areas to assist mangroves to keep pace with sea level rise.
4   *Balancing human and natural approaches.* It may prove more cost effective to pursue the maintenance, preservation and replacement of mangroves and tropical coral reefs as a viable complementary or preferable strategy for protecting coastal human communities. This is as opposed to other direct human interventions such as coastal hardening and the construction of seawalls and artificial reefs.
5   *Institutionalising fisheries management.* Fisheries management at local to regional levels will play the important roles of reducing stress on fish stocks and also helping communities and industries adapt to changing food-web structures and resources.
6   *Exploring alternative livelihoods.* In anticipation of the challenges to food and livelihoods of coastal communities, attempts will have to be made to

facilitate, where necessary, the diversification of livelihoods, the development of new sustainable industries and the reduction of dependency on threatened ecosystems.

7   *Introducing innovation.* Responding to the climate challenge will require new tools, technology, training, systems and procedures, legal and financial instruments, and methods of integrated planning that account not only for human communities and infrastructure, but also ecosystem responses and value. For example, improved safety-at sea training and associated equipment will be required, as well as early warning systems which are currently not prominent in small-scale fisheries across the Caribbean.

8   *Ensuring fairness and equity.* Adaptation options must ensure fair and equitable access to the economic opportunities associated with the marine resources.

A comprehensive mapping of the region's "blue carbon" resources will also be crucial to the region's response. Blue carbon refers to organic carbon captured and stored by oceans and coastal ecosystems, and in particular by vegetated coastal ecosystems such as seagrass meadows, tidal marshes and mangroves. The Caribbean has yet to quantify its blue carbon stocks, which limits its ability to leverage the public global good that their maintenance, conservation and preservation brings. Arguably the Caribbean should lead the efforts for equivalent compensation agreements as exists for the preservation and compensation of forestry (e.g. the REDD+ mechanism) given the size of the resources it may possess and the immense vulnerability of those resources to climate change.

Minimising the impact of climate change on the Blue Economy, while leveraging existing and future opportunities, will require an integrated, multi-sectoral and strategic framework that encompasses local, national, regional and even global scales. Such a framework is oftentimes difficult at sub-national scales, with even greater complexity and challenges introduced when coordinated multi-country action is required. The latter approach is, however, necessary given the interconnectedness of the marine environment, the shared nature of the ocean resource, the benefits to be had from economies of scale and collective action, and the far-reaching impacts of climate change. Political will, ownership and commitment will be key supporting pillars of the framework. The IPCC'S Special Report on Oceans and the Cryosphere (IPCC, 2019), Special Report on Global Warming of 1.5°C (IPCC, 2018), the World Bank's *Toward a Blue Economy: A Promise for Sustainable Growth in the Caribbean* (Patil et al., 2016) and the CDB's *Financing the Blue Economy* (CDB, 2018) are all key resources that can help guide the region toward the equitable and responsible development and management of the Blue Economy. Table 5.3 summarises some response measures needed at policy and programmatic levels as suggested by these documents.

58　*Michael A. Taylor et al.*

In the end, however, a resilient Blue Economy (across spatial and time scales) should form part of an overarching, cohesive sustainable development framework in the region even for physical, human, technical, financial and social systems indirectly associated with marine resources.

Table 5.3 Response measures for advancing the Blue Economy in the Caribbean

Recommendation/ response	*Examples of some key high-level actions to be implemented and areas to be addressed*
Enhance the policy, legal, institutional and regulatory framework to support holistic development of the Blue Economy, contingent on good sustainability practices and interwoven climate change consideration	Building on existing efforts at regional and national levels, a harmonised Caribbean-wide policy framework and implementation plan for management of the Caribbean Blue Economy should be effected. The framework should be supported by legislation and regulation and institutional arrangements at national and regional scales. It should also, among other things: • Mainstream climate change considerations; foster sustainable development, protection and conservation of marine resources; and ensure alignment with international policies, frameworks and standards • Define the Blue Economy in the Caribbean context and the conditions for long-term sustainability • Allocate government financing in order to achieve policy objectives, while pursuing other sources of funding (multilateral, private etc.) • Leverage opportunities and minimise impacts and risks, to the benefit of Caribbean peoples • Establish robust monitoring and evaluation frameworks that assess performance against targets, achievement of goals as well as documenting best practices and lessons learned and using these iteratively to guide future actions • Monitor and enforce to ensure compliance with standards, regulations and laws • Improve dialogue, coordination and collaboration among key stakeholders at sectoral, national and regional levels • Enhance the capacity of institutions to effectively undertake functions under the overarching framework
Establish/increase uptake of financing streams and mechanisms	Efforts must be made to take advantage of significant funds available under the global climate change financing architecture to support the Blue Economy in the Caribbean. Innovative financing mechanisms, such as blue bonds and debt-for-nature swaps, should be investigated for application within the Caribbean context. To foster sustainability, regional governments should also make budgetary allocation to ensure alignment with policy and strategic direction for the Blue Economy. Successful financial models should be replicated and upscaled

Implications of climate change 59

Recommendation/ response	Examples of some key high-level actions to be implemented and areas to be addressed
Establish a sustainability process for the effective implementation of adaptation and mitigation measures, leveraging co-benefits where possible	Within the region, adaptation and mitigation measures are sometimes not implemented as part of a broader, holistic approach, to the detriment of sustainability. As such, the development and implementation of adaptation and mitigation efforts should be supported by rigorous assessment, ranking and prioritisation, with significant consideration given to the effectiveness of the measures in a progressively warming world. Monitoring the measures over the long term to ensure expected benefits are being derived should be emphasised and any negative impacts are proactively addressed. Education, training and empowerment of local community groups in, or near to, the intervention areas will also be key
Prioritise research and development programmes aligned with Blue Economy agenda	The development of the Blue Economy in the region should be bolstered by an integrated research and development (R&D) agenda that: • Pulls from academia, government, private sector and multilateral resources (human and financial) to address current and future problems • Fosters evidenced-based decision-making • Promotes the development of new technologies, techniques, methods and tools • Focuses on maximising benefits, reducing threats, identifying new opportunities and where possible, converting threats into opportunities • Replicates and scales-up successful models The R&D efforts will need to be supported by dedicated funding as well as enhanced data collection, management and sharing systems. This should include mechanisms for capturing and making use of traditional knowledge and community-level data and information
Develop and conduct tailored capacity building, education, sensitisation and awareness programmes	To promote positive transformation in the knowledge, attitudes and practices of Blue Economy stakeholders, the following will be required: • Targeted education of stakeholders (directly and indirectly involved in the Blue Economy) on how to protect and conserve the marine environment • Development of a cadre of professionals that will lead implementation efforts • Enhanced capacity of governments and other stakeholders to effectively sensitise and educate users of marine resources as well as the general populace • Enhanced capacity to sustainably grow/manage local businesses that depend on, or impact, marine resources • Use of local creative capacity and expressive forms in education and awareness programmes • Capacity transfer at local, national and regional scales

References

Alvarez-Filip, Dulvy, L., Gill, N. K., *et al.* 2009. Flattening of Caribbean coral reefs: Region-wide declines in architectural complexity. *Proceedings of the Royal Society B: Biological Sciences*, 276: 3019–3025.

Asariotis R., Benamara, H. and Mohos-Naray, V. 2017. *Port Industry Survey on Climate Change Impacts and Adaptation*. UNCTAD/SER.RP/2017/18. Available at: https://unctad.org/en/PublicationsLibrary/ser-rp-2017d18_en.pdf.

Au, S. Y., Weinstein, C. M., van den Hurk, J. E. *et al.* 2017. Trophic transfer of microplastics in aquatic ecosystems: Identifying critical research needs. *Integrated Environmental Assessment and Management*, 13: 505–509.

Bates, N. R., Best, M. H. P., Neely, K. *et al.* 2012. Detecting anthropogenic carbon dioxide uptake and ocean acidification in the North Atlantic Ocean. *Biogeosciences*, 9: 2509–2522.

Burgess, C. P., Taylor, M. A., Spencer, N. *et al.* 2018. Estimating damages from climate-related natural disasters for the Caribbean at 1.5 °C and 2 °C global warming above preindustrial levels. *Regional Environmental Change*, 18: 2297–2312.

Burrowes, R., Wabnitz, C. and Eyzaguirre, J. 2019. *The Great Sargassum Disaster of 2018*. ESSA Technologies Ltd. Available at: https://essa.com/the-great-sargassum-disaster-of-2018/.

Cashman, A., 2014. Water security and services in the Caribbean. *Water*, 6: 1187–1203.

CDB. 2018. *Financing the Blue Economy: A Caribbean Development Opportunity*. Caribbean Development Bank. Available at: https://www.caribank.org/publications-and-resources/resource-library/thematic-papers/financing-blue-economy-caribbean-development-opportunity.

Coffel E. D., Thompson, T. R. and Horton. R.M. 2017. The impacts of rising temperatures on aircraft take off performance. *Climate Change*, 144: 381–388.

CRFM. 2019. *CRFM Research Paper Collection*, Volume 9. Caribbean Regional Fisheries Mechanism Secretariat.

CSGM (Climate Studies Group, Mona). 2020. *State of the Caribbean Climate*. Caribbean Development Bank (in press).

Franks, J. S., Johnson, D. R. and Ko, D. S. 2016. Pelagic sargassum in the tropical North Atlantic. *Gulf and Caribbean Research*, 27: SC6–SC11.

Friedrich, T., Timmermann, A., Abe-Ouchi, A., Bates, N. R. *et al.* 2012. Detecting regional anthropogenic trends in ocean acidification against natural variability. *Nature Climate Change*, 2: 167–171.

Green, S.O. and Webber, D. F. 2003. The effects of varying levels of eutrophication on phytoplankton and seagrass (*Thalassia testudinum*) populations of the southeast coast of Jamaica. *Bulletin of Marine Science*, 73: 443–455.

Guha-Sapir, D., Below, R. and Hoyois, P. 2015. *EM-DAT: International Disaster Database*. Brussels: Catholic University of Louvain.

Guinotte, J. M., Buddemeier, R. W. and Kleypas, J. A. 2003. Future coral reef habitat marginality: temporal and spatial effects of climate change in the Pacific basin. *Coral Reefs*, 22: 551–558.

Hallegatte, S., Green, C., Nicholls, R. J. *et al.* 2013. Future flood losses in major coastal cities, *Nature Climate Change*, 3: 802–806.

Hogarth, P. J. 2015. *The Biology of Mangroves and Seagrasses*. Oxford: Oxford University Press.

Implications of climate change 61

IPCC. 2013. *Climate Change 2013: The Physical Science Basis.* Working Group I Contribution to the Fifth Assessment Report of the Intergovernmental Panel on Climate Change (Stocker, T. F.*et al.*, Eds). Cambridge: Cambridge University Press. 1535 pp.

IPCC. 2014. *Climate Change 2014: Mitigation of Climate Change.* Working Group III Contribution to the Fifth Assessment Report of the Intergovernmental Panel on Climate Change (Edenhofer, O. *et al.*, Eds). Cambridge: Cambridge University Press.

IPCC. 2018. *Global Warming of 1.5°C: An IPCC Special Report on the Impacts of Global Warming of 1.5°C Above Pre-Industrial Levels and Related Global Greenhouse Gas Emission Pathways, in the Context of Strengthening the Global Response to the Threat of Climate Change, Sustainable Development, and Efforts to Eradicate Poverty* (Masson-Delmotte, V. *et al.*, Eds). Geneva: World Meteorological Organisation.

IPCC. 2019. Summary for policymakers. In: Pörtner, H.-O.*et al.* (Eds), *IPCC Special Report on the Ocean and Cryosphere in a Changing Climate* (in press).

Jackson J. B. C., Donovan, M. K. and Cramer, K. L. *et al.* (Eds). 2014. *Status and Trends of Caribbean Coral Reefs: 1970–2012.* Gland, Switzerland: Global Coral Reef Monitoring Network, IUCN. 304 pp.

Kroeker, K. J., Kordas, R. L., Crim, R. *et al.* 2013. Impacts of ocean acidification on marine organisms: quantifying sensitivities and interaction with warming. *Global Change Biology*, 19: 1884–1896.

Monnereau, I. and Oxenford, H. A. 2017. Impacts of climate change on fisheries in the coastal and marine environments of Caribbean Small Island Developing States (SIDS). Caribbean marine climate change report card: *Science Review* 2017: 124–154.

Monioudi, I. N., Asariotis, R, Becker, A. *et al.* 2018. Climate change impacts on critical international transportation assets of Caribbean Small Island Developing States (SIDS): the case of Jamaica and Saint Lucia. *Regional Environmental Change*, 18: 2211–2225.

Mycoo, M. A. 2018. Beyond 1.5 °C: vulnerabilities and adaptation strategies for Caribbean Small Island Developing States. *Regional Environmental Change*, 18: 2341–2353.

Nurse, L. 2011. The implications of global climate change for fisheries management in the Caribbean. *Climate and Development*, 3: 228–241.

Nurse, L., Cashman, A., and Mwansa, J. 2012. Confronting the challenges of sewerage management in the Caribbean: A case study from the island of Barbados. *Environment: Science and Policy for Sustainable Development*, 54: 30–43.

Oviatt, C. A., Huizenga, K., Rogers, C. S. *et al.* 2019. What nutrient sources support anomalous growth and the recent sargassum mass stranding on Caribbean beaches? A review. *Marine Pollution Bulletin*, 145: 517–525.

Patil, P. G., Virdin, J., Diez, S. M. *et al.* 2016. *Toward a Blue Economy: A Promise for Sustainable Growth in the Caribbean: An Overview.* Washington, DC: The World Bank.

Pulwarty, R. S., Nurse, L. A. and Trotz, U. O. 2010. Caribbean Islands in a changing climate. *Environment: Science and Policy for Sustainable Development*, 52: 16–27.

Reguero, B.G., Méndez, F. J. and Losada, I. J. 2013. Variability of multivariate wave climate in Latin America and the Caribbean. *Global and Planetary Change*, 100: 70–84.

62 Michael A. Taylor et al.

Rose, D. and Webber, M. 2019. Characterization of microplastics in the surface waters of Kingston Harbour. *Science of the Total Environment*, 664: 753–760.

Ross, P. M., Parker, L., O'Connor, W. A. *et al.* 2011. The impact of ocean acidification on reproduction, early development and settlement of marine organisms. *Water*, 3: 1005–1030.

Schell, J. M., Goodwin, D. S. and Siuda, A. N. 2015. Recent *Sargassum* inundation events in the Caribbean: Shipboard observations reveal dominance of a previously rare form. *Oceanography*, 28: 8–11.

Scott, D., and Verkoeyen, S. 2017. Assessing the climate change risk of a coastal-island destination. In: Jones, A. and Phillips, M. (Eds), *Global Climate Change and Coastal Tourism*. CAB International.

Simpson, M. C. *et al.* 2010. *Quantification and Magnitude of Losses and Damages Resulting from the Impacts of Climate Change: Modelling the Transformational Impacts and Costs of Sea Level Rise in the Caribbean*. UNDP.

Siung-Chang, A. 1997. A review of marine pollution issues in the Caribbean. *Environmental Geochemistry and Health*, 19: 45–55.

UNEP. 2018. *Sargassum white paper - Sargassum outbreak in the Caribbean: challenges, opportunities and regional situation*. UNEP(DEPI)/CAR WG.40/ INF8 30.

Wang, M., Hu, C., Barnes, B. B. *et al.* 2019. The great Atlantic Sargassum belt. *Science*, 365: 83–87.

WTTC. 2017. *Caribbean Resilience and Recovery: Minimising the Impact of the 2017 Hurricane Season on the Caribbean's Tourism Sector*. World Travel and Tourism Council. Available at: https://www.wttc.org/-/media/files/reports/2018/caribbean-recovery-report—full-report.pdf.

6 The role of coastal and marine planning in achieving Blue Economies

Lorna Inniss, Lucia Fanning, Robin Mahon and Margaux Remond

Introduction

Ensuring that Green and Blue Economies are integrated and that the relationship between land and ocean is fully considered is critical. Coastal and marine planning, or integrated coastal zone management (ICZM) is a well-established approach to addressing this relationship. In small countries that may be considered entirely coastal zones this warrants an "island systems" approach to coastal planning, extending seaward through marine spatial planning (Wong et al., 2005) Although Caribbean countries have been on this path for some time, the emergence of the Blue Economy as a driving force can catalyse action in the anticipated era of increasing climate change and variability. Blue Economy can also become a unifying element for policy, planning and practical coherence among the typically highly fragmented institutional arrangements for coastal and marine planning. With prospects of more coastal, nearshore and offshore development associated with fisheries, aquaculture, tourism, oil and gas, renewable energy and other economic arenas, this need is urgent. Planning at a whole-island or continental coast scale is becoming more accepted, as is the need to involve both place-based communities and communities of interest and practice in planning and management.

The coastal zone management planning (CZMP) process

Establishing the need for ICZM

Since its formal endorsement at the Rio Conference in 1992 (United Nations, 1992) and the demand for guidance for implementation (World Bank, 1993), ICZM has been used globally by countries to improve the quality of life of coastal residents and address emerging social, economic, and environmental issues affecting coastal areas (Cicin-Sain and Knecht, 1998; Greene, 2010; Hildebrand and Norrena, 1992; Sorensen, 2002). An essential first step of any coastal management programme is delineating the boundary to a clearly defined area over which the programme will apply (Fanning and Burbidge,

64 *Lorna Inniss et al.*

2010; Post and Lundin, 1996). As such, national and sub-national governments have been establishing or revising formal coastal policies and management programmes to include both the terrestrial and marine environment to maximise the benefits that can be gained from ICZM (e.g. see Albotoush and Shau-Hwai, 2019; Arkema et al., 2015; Goble et al., 2014; Lin et al., 2016). Failure to include important features and recognise key linkages among the components of the coastal system within and beyond a defined management area can seriously compromise success of a coastal policy. Therefore, clear articulation of goals and choice of boundaries are two critical steps in the coastal management process.

Structure of the ICZM process

Organisations, notably United Nations Environment (UNE) and the Intergovernmental Oceanographic Commission (IOC), have expended considerable effort over the past 25 years in providing detailed guidance on the ICZM process (UNEP, 2012; EC, n.d.). While the specific context (biophysical, socio-economic, political, legal and institutional) of a management area must be accounted for, the ICZM process engages stakeholders who can affect and/ or are affected by the state of the coastal and marine environment to maximise benefits while minimising detrimental consequences (UNEP, 2012). It provides a management framework for current and future multiple coastal zone uses and users, and is guided by principles aimed at building the resilience of the socio-ecological systems constituting the coastal zone to improve the quality of life in coastal areas and beyond (World Bank, 1993).

The ICZM process is iterative and follows a generic pattern encompassing four stages: (i) initiation; (ii) planning; (iii) implementation; and (iv) monitoring and evaluation, each with their respective tasks and tools. However, prior to initiating ICZM, a clear sense of the urgencies necessitating the onset of the process is needed. It may be driven by crises (such as conflicts among coastal sectors or increasing climate change impacts leading to coastal erosion and coastal disasters) or opportunities (such as tourism, renewable energy or other emerging Blue Economy activities) that arise from taking an integrated approach to managing the coastal zone.

Initiation

The realisation that ICZM is needed can also be stimulated by global or regional initiatives to promote ICZM. However, while increasing climate change impacts, industrialisation, commercial development and steadily growing population pressure in many places have resulted in an increase of erosion and flooding, loss of wetlands, pollution, disasters and over-exploitation of land and water resources in the coastal zone. Decision makers often fail to recognise the severity of the impacts until there is a crisis.

Planning

The planning stage develops a proposal calling for decision makers to establish continuous and integrated management of the coastal and marine area that addresses the issues identified during initiation. Necessitating the engagement and support of government and other stakeholders, key planning tasks include: clearly describing problems, goals and objectives; stating principles and policies to guide the programme; describing the area to be managed; describing required institutional arrangements, responsibilities and support; stating management actions to be taken; specifying funding and staffing requirements; outlining actions needed to adopt the plan and timetables for action; developing monitoring, reporting and evaluation schedules and responsibilities. An ICZM Planning Framework can provide guidance on a sequence of activities which ensures that information necessary to understand the anthropogenic and natural dynamics is gathered before the plan area is analysed; key issues and management options are not specified before a complete analysis of the dynamics of the plan area has been made; and emphasis on a single management option is not made before all possible management options have been identified (e.g. Le Tissier et al., 2004).

Implementation

Implementation requires resolving issues at the political level such as formal approval of the plan. Such endorsement holds that the changes in behaviours and ecosystems (proposed by the plan) can actually occur. It also requires addressing any policy gaps and legislative needs as well as putting in place the institutional arrangements necessary to facilitate integration. Operational implementation of the approved actions follows, oftentimes resulting in unanticipated conflicts among stakeholders as trade-offs become apparent. At this stage, enforcement and dispute resolution mechanisms identified during the planning phase can be implemented.

Monitoring and evaluation

Monitoring constantly gathers information which is evaluated and fed back into the other stages. This may lead to policy changes. Next, the data gathered is used to analyse and evaluate the extent to which the actions have addressed or solved the problems that were identified during planning. There are several practitioners for evaluating the success of ICZM initiatives that are currently outside the scope of this chapter to review in depth (e.g. Olsen, 2003; Billé, 2007). The evaluation should determine the goals and objectives of the next iteration of the ICZM process.

66 *Lorna Inniss et al.*

CZMP in the Wider Caribbean

Although it had been practised in many developed countries for decades, CZMP gained prominence during the Earth Summit (United Nations Conference on Environment and Development (UNCED)) process in 1992, in Chapter 17 of Agenda 21. ICZM was defined as "the comprehensive assessment, setting of objectives, planning and management of coastal systems and resources, taking into account traditional, cultural and historical perspectives and conflicting interests and uses" (Suman, 1998). Subsequently, many Caribbean countries have either initiated or upscaled their efforts at ICZM. Similar efforts have been ongoing globally. For example, in 2013 the European Union Commission adopted a new initiative on Maritime Spatial Planning and Integrated Coastal Management.[1] CZMP has been supported by major global programmes such as the UNEP Global Programme of Action (GPA), the FAO Code of Conduct for Responsible Fisheries (CCRF) and UNESCO's marine spatial planning initiative (Douvere, 2008).

Regional level policy support and initiatives

Although UNCLOS does not mention it explicitly, its provisions cover the practices that constitute ICZM. Similarly, neither the Cartagena Convention, nor any of its protocols mention ICZM per se, but their articles cover most relevant activities. The only regional seas conventions that have ICZM Protocols are the Barcelona for the Mediterranean and the Nairobi for the Western Indian Ocean, and these are quite recent. Nonetheless there have been regional initiatives for ICZM such as the Integrating Watershed and Coastal Area Management (IWCAM) Project covering 13 Caribbean SIDS, and IWEco covering 10 SIDS in aspects of ridge to reef management.

National level

Two country examples will be reviewed to illustrate the type of action needed at the national level.

Barbados

Barbados, successfully leveraging a combination of foresight, international support and local capacity to develop planning institutions, stands out as a Caribbean leader in ICZM. Fifty years after independence, Barbados demonstrates that "integrating sectors, levels of government and disciplines to address coastal zones both in the water and on dry land" (Scruggs and Bassett, 2013: 2) is important not only as an environmental programme, but also as a way to grow its economy. The island, by considering the synergic effects of coastal activities, successfully faces the challenge of contending with development patterns oriented toward the coast while managing the expanding threat of sea level rise. As any small island state, and although it has the advantage of being located east of the main arc of eastern Caribbean Islands, outside of the main Atlantic hurricane belt, Barbados will be disproportionately impacted by global climate change. The island is threatened by sea level rise, coupled with potential storm surge, in the event of a hurricane.

The coast of Barbados represents an "environment of tremendous intrinsic and extrinsic value in terms of its natural and human assets" (CZMU, 1998). The country's economy is highly dependent on its coast, especially for tourism – 80% of its US$4.4 billion GDP stems from tourism and the service industries. Following independence, sugar became economically less reliable as the UK and EU drew down preferential pricing and subsidies in a push for free trade. To mitigate this, the country heavily invested in tourism, resulting in strips of coastal development notably along the west coast and in the south, between the airport and Bridgetown.

The Coastal Zone Management Unit (CZMU) was created in 1996, with the mandate to "regulate, make recommendations and educate the Barbadian population about coastal management" (Scruggs and Bassett, 2013), to oversee the coral reefs around Barbados and all coastal engineering. The CZMU also serves as an adviser to the planning office for onshore coastal development. It implements coastal engineering projects to conserve the coastline and prevent beach erosion. It safeguards the coast with physical interventions such as breakwaters, seawalls and groynes (Figure 6.1). Natural conservation techniques include the restoration of sand dunes and mangroves, but such strategies are costly and less effective, and are primarily band-aid approaches. The CZMU operates along a strict policy of stakeholder consultation and can "leverage the political capital it earns from the private sector on such projects in order to make more demanding regulations become binding down the road" (Scruggs and Bassett, 2013). The CZMU undertook a comprehensive planning process based on extensive technical data (Table 6.1). It produced a series of Coastal Zone Management plans for Barbados and has been overseeing implementation of these plans.

Belize

Despite being a small developing coastal state in the western Caribbean, Belize has the distinction of being one of the first countries in the world to adopt an integrated approach to managing its coastal and marine resources.[2] Three years prior to the global endorsement of ICZM at the Rio Conference in 1992 (United Nations, 1992), government and other stakeholders met with the recognition that "an integrated, holistic approach to management of our coastal resources was necessary to ensure their use and protection in the long-term" (CZMAI, n.d.). This was sparked by both increasing opportunities for development in the coastal zone and the potential for threatening the very ecosystem services upon which those opportunities depended. These included

68 Lorna Inniss et al.

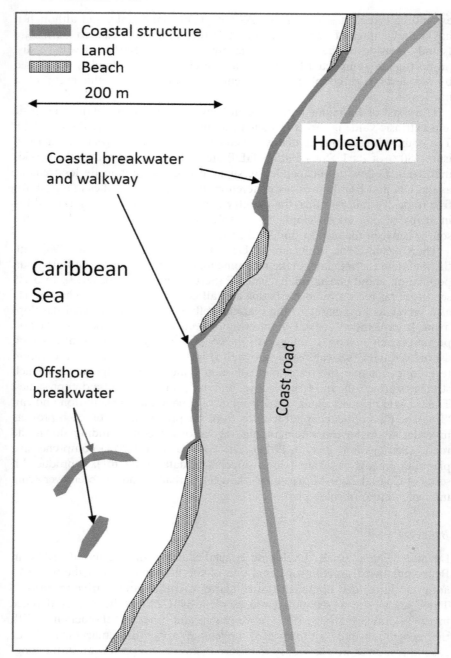

Figure 6.1 Sea defences at Holetown on the west coast of Barbados.

Coastal and marine planning 69

Table 6.1 Barbados ICZM planning: main tasks in technical feasibility study (Caribbean Environment Programme, 1996)

Coastal engineering	Terrestrial water	Marine water and EIA	Socio-economics	Pilot projects
1. Data acquisition: – wind, wave, current, tide, sediments, bathymetry 2. Shoreline mapping 3. Wave climate determination – deep and nearshore – west & south coasts 4. Tides & water levels 5. Coastal water circulation 6. Shoreline characterization: – sediment pathways, transport rates – shoreline predictions – sand nourishment sources 7. Beach/coast improvement techniques: – structural – non structural – drainage stabilization – pilot project design 8. Pilot project monitoring 9. Maintenance practices 10. Pre investment designs 11. CZM plan	1. Data acquisition: – sewage, fertilizers, pesticide, hydrogeology, lab capabilities, ranking pollution impacts 2. Measurement programme: – surface flow – rainfall – subsurface flow – water quality sampling 3. Analysis & modelling 4. Control options (evaluation): – agriculture management – sewage collection – stormwater management – education – legislation 5. CZM plan	1. Data acquisition: – sewage, fertilizers, pesticides, lab capabilities – reef & seagrass monitoring – vegetation identification 2. Marine ecosystem threshold 3. EIA pilot project 4. General environmental scoping 5. CZM plan	1. Develop CBA model 2. Tourism & recreation: – demand/supply – beach requirement 3. Land use issues: – regulations – zoning – open access – coastal structures & implications 4. Analysis of / land use control 5. Public participation programmes 6. CZM plan	1. Evaluation of engineering options relative to coastal problems 2. Select main option for further experimentation 3. Design pilot projects: – beach face dewatering – beach rock removal – submerged breakwaters – revetment – beach nourishment – reef rubble clearing 4. Modification of existing structures 5. CZM plan

"a rich diversity of habitats and attractions, including three offshore atolls, coastal plains and lagoons, mangrove forests, seagrass beds, coral reefs, and over 300 cayes" (CZMAI, n.d.). Additionally, the country's 280 km or more of barrier reef, part of the MesoAmerican Barrier Reef System representing the world's second longest unbroken reef system, with its associated mangroves, seagrass beds and lagoons (Cooper et al., 2009), provide significant provisioning (e.g. lobster and other fisheries), regulating (e.g. protection from storm surges), cultural (e.g. recreational activities) and supporting services (e.g. nutrient recycling). It has been estimated that almost US$500 million annually is generated through direct and indirect resource-based economic activity in the coastal zone (CZMAI, n.d.).

With the establishment of a coastal zone management unit and the subsequent approval of Belize's Coastal Zone Management Project by UNDP/GEF in 1993, Belize passed a Coastal Zone Management Act in 2000. The Act identifies Belize's coastal zone to include "the area bounded by the shoreline up to the mean high-water-mark on its landward side and by the outer limit of the territorial sea on its seaward side, including all coastal waters" (Belize, 2000, Part 1). The act also specified the management authority responsible for the provisions in the act and its role in advising the Minister on all matters relating to the development and utilisation of the resources of the coast zone (Clause 5), including the development and implementation of a coastal management plan (Clause 23). Part V of the act also calls for the revision of the plan every four years based on the monitoring and evaluation of the existing plan (Belize, 2000).

Initial funding for Belize's coastal management process and implementation was provided by the World Bank. The current iteration of the plan with its management zones (Figure 6.2) was approved in 2016 and has as its goal "To support the allocation, sustainable use and planned development of Belize's coastal resources through increased alliances, for the benefit of all Belizeans and the global community" (CZMAI, 2016). This version of the ICZM plan for Belize used a planning process (Figure 6.2) that built on current science-based tools informed by stakeholder knowledge regarding coastal and marine uses (CZMAI, 2016).

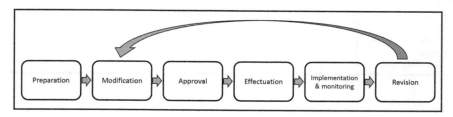

Figure 6.2 Planning process for ICZM in Belize.
Source: redrawn from CZMAI (2016)

Coastal and marine planning 71

In collaboration with the Natural Capital project (Arkema et al., 2015), a coastal and marine spatial plan was developed that "allows for the continuous delivery of environmental benefits to Belize by creating a zoning scheme to resolve conflicts in resource use and negotiate competing interests for management of the Belizean coastal zone" (CZMAI, 2016). Guiding the development of the plan was the desire among Belizeans to address the dilemma confronting most, if not all coastal states, namely, determine where can coastal development and associated uses of the coastal zone be expanded while minimising losses to ecosystem services. To answer this question, data collection focused on identifying the current level of human uses in Belize and on modelling the delivery of ecosystem services (in the form of lobster catch and value, visits and expenditures of tourists, and coastal protection) as provided by the country's coral reefs, mangroves and seagrass beds. In addition to the status quo use and provision of these services by the three habitat types, three additional possible futures with differing degrees of risk to the ecosystem and as such to the services they provide for the country were investigated, using a target year of 2025. These were identified as the development scenario (prioritising immediate development over sustainable use and future benefits from nature), the conservation scenario (prioritising ecosystem health through sustainable use and investment in conservation) and the informed management scenario which attempted to balance strong conservation goals with current and future needs of coastal development and marine uses (Arkema et al., 2015; CZMAI, 2016). The findings indicated that the informed management scenario best responded to the original question aimed at maximising benefits while minimising the risks posed to the sustainable provision of ecosystem services. By adopting a science-based approach to its ICZM plan that draws on input from all stakeholders and utilises current management tools to inform decision making, the Government of Belize has developed an action plan for the integrated management of its coastal resources that serves as a model for all countries in the Wider Caribbean Region and globally.

Approaching ICZM in the context of the Blue Economy

Marine spatial planning (MSP)

Coastal and marine management planning must ultimately be place based. Spatial planning for land use has been the norm worldwide for decades. More recently, integrated spatial planning has been extended to marine space (Frazão Santos et al., 2019). The uptake of marine spatial planning (MSP) has been rapid in most developed countries. In 2009 the USA released its Interim Framework on Coastal and Marine Spatial Planning (Stamoulis and Delevaux, 2015), and in 2014 the European Union adopted the Maritime Spatial Planning Directive "aimed at promoting the sustainable growth of maritime economies, the sustainable development of marine areas and the sustainable use of marine resources".[3] There are many resources to support

72 Lorna Inniss et al.

the development of coastal and marine spatial plans (e.g. Ehler and Douvere, 2009, Stamoulis and Delevaux, 2015).

Many Caribbean countries have adopted or are planning to adopt MSP.[4] The Organisation of Eastern Caribbean States (OECS) is pursuing MSP through its Caribbean Regional Oceanscape Project (CROP) (OECS/GEF/World Bank, 2019). Two notable examples of the successful application of MSP are the transboundary Grenadine Islands, St. Vincent and the Grenadines and Grenada, and in Belize as described below. In the Grenadines the full range of stakeholders needed for effective marine resource management was engaged in the development of participatory geographic information systems (PGIS), both in terms of the research process and the final product (geodatabase) developed to support MSP (Baldwin et al., 2013). This initiative demonstrated the value of incorporating local knowledge and ensuring stakeholder buy-in. The MSP that was produced was endorsed by both governments and will contribute to CROP.

Governance arrangements

National intersectoral bodies

ICZM is an intersectoral endeavour that requires collaboration among government agencies and engagement with civil society and the private sector. National Intersectoral Committees (NICs) are thought to be an appropriate way to achieve the desired collaboration and engagement. NICs are required by all GEF International Waters projects and have been pursued throughout the Caribbean Large Marine Ecosystem Initiative (CLME+) (McConney and Compton, Chapter 8).

Civil society

While national governments play a key role in ICZM by setting national policies, developing ICZM plans and legislation and enforcing regulations, engagement of stakeholders and the general public is critical for its successful implementation. This is particularly so in small developing countries where the resources needed for full implementation are seldom available. Rural areas may often be remote and central government operations there may be costly or impractical. In these circumstances, delegation of management to community-based organisations (CBOs) may be the most effective way to implement desired actions. This co-management approach must be provided for and measures for its promotion included in national level ICZM plans. Ideally, the coast of the country would be divided into management zones, and stakeholders in each zone invited to develop a CBO to lead development and implementation of a zone-specific ICZM plan in that zone. The CBO may be an existing NGO or developed anew. It may engage stakeholders directly or may be an umbrella NGO that engages through sectoral NGOs such as fisherfolk organisations, conservation groups and recreational user groups.

Although there are no known examples of a comprehensive national approach to delegation of ICZM to CBOs in the Caribbean, there are several examples where CBOs have played a leading role in some or all aspects of CZM. Most of these CBOs have arisen organically through community activity and pertain to a limited area in a given country. Some examples are summarised in Table 6.2. They range from having broad scope, as in the case of the Caribbean Coastal Area Management Foundation (C-CAM), Jamaica to being sector focused; for example, for fisheries and/or MPAs, as in the case of Bluefields, Jamaica, or tourism as is the case in Roatan, Honduras. The orientation depends on the primary activities and interests of the stakeholders in the particular area. Most are oriented towards MPAs. All, however, are oriented towards improving livelihoods of local coastal and marine resource users through sustainable use of coastal and marine ecosystems. A livelihoods orientation is essential if the benefits of blue growth are to be achieved at the local level by those who depend on blue resources.

An alternative to local co-management through a CBO is the establishment of an entity such as the Corporation for the Sustainable Development of the Archipelago of San Andrés, Providencia and Santa Catalina (CORALINA), Colombia. CORALINA is a public entity with administrative and financial autonomy and its own assets and legal status.[5] Its jurisdiction covers the entire Archipelago of San Andrés, Providencia and Santa Catalina, which is a UNESCO Man and Biosphere Program reserve, the Seaflower Biosphere Reserve since 2000. CORALINA is focused on equitable benefits and stewardship through ongoing education, outreach, and public involvement programmes (Taylor et al., 2013). Despite numerous challenges, primarily funding, it is considered to be an excellent example of an ecosystem based holistic approach to local level management of coastal and marine resources.

Although intuitively attractive, delegated co-management has had mixed success in the Wider Caribbean. Pomeroy et al. (2004) provide a set of conditions under which it is most likely to be successful:

- Membership is clearly defined as to who really has a stake in the issue.
- There is a shared recognition of a resource use problem that needs to be addressed.
- Clear objectives for management can be defined based on the problems and interests.
- Communication amongst the stakeholders is effective, and there is adequate networking.
- External agents provide support for management but do not encourage dependency.
- Management rules are enforceable by resource users and the management authority.

Pomeroy et al. (2004) also identified constraints to effective co-management. One of the key problems is inequity among stakeholders in capacity to

74   *Lorna Inniss et al.*

Table 6.2 Some examples of Caribbean CBOs that have taken on responsibility for aspects of ICZM

Organisation	Country/area	Role
Caribbean Coastal Area Management Foundation (C-CAM)	Jamaica, Portland Bight	Promote coastal conservation in the Portland Bight Protected Area. Strategies for reducing pollution, adapting to climate change, managing threats to forests, wetlands and fisheries (Baldwin and Mahon, 2015)
Soufriere/Scotts Head Marine Reserve Local Area Management Authority (SSMR LAMA)	Soufriere/Scotts Head Marine Reserve, Dominica	The SSMR LAMA began as an informal institution that was later formally institutionalised by law and administrative practice (McConney et al., 2010)
Southern Environmental Association (SEA)	Placencia, Belize	Co-management of Laughing Bird Caye National Park, Gladden Spit and Silk Cayes Marine Reserve, and Sapodilla Cayes Marine Reserve. Outreach activities and liaison with stakeholder organisations in the area (Peterson et al., 2014a)
Bluefields Bay Fishermen's Friendly Society (BBFFS)	Bluefields, Jamaica	Designation and co-management of the Bluefields Bay Fish Sanctuary. Sustainable fishing practices and alternative livelihoods that will enhance the quality of life and preserve the natural environment of the Bluefields ecosystem (Baldwin and Mahon, 2015)
Negril Coral Reef Preservation Society (NCRPS)	Negril, Jamaica	In 2002 the Jamaica Natural Resource Conservation Authority (NRCA) delegated management of the Negril Marine Park to the NCRPS (Blackman and McConney, 2008). The NRCPS included SCUBA operators, fishers, tourism and business operators
Roatan Marine Park	Roatan, Honduras	Co-management of Roatan Marine Park and liaison with local stakeholder NGOs representing different sectors (Peterson et al., 2014b)
Pearl Lagoon Inter Community Committee	Pearl Lagoon basin, Nicaragua	The committee was established to represent stakeholders and engage with the municipal government which ultimately endorsed the community based natural resource management plan (McConney and Pomeroy, 2006)
Stichting Nationale Parken Bonaire (STINAPA Bonaire)	Bonaire National Marine Park (BNMP) and the Washington Slagbaai National Park (WSNP)	STINAPA is a non-governmental, not-for-profit foundation commissioned by the island government to manage BNMP and WSNP. It has a mandate to self-finance by charging fees (STINAPA, 2015)

Coastal and marine planning 75

engage with the process. This may result in power imbalances, which can lead to failure. Co-management efforts therefore need to ensure that stakeholders are adequately empowered to participate on an equal basis.

Conclusion

The need for effective coastal and marine governance as a context for blue growth is a recurring theme of this book. As described in Chapter 9, governance is a multilevel endeavour with each level having an important role to play. Coastal and marine planning is the cornerstone of effective national level governance which communities, municipalities and parastatal bodies can play important roles in achieving. Especially in small countries where both coastal space and human resources are limited, coastal and marine spatial planning should be viewed as fundamental. Supported by clear policies, it provides a transparent and negotiated platform on which investors and other stakeholders can plan their activities. It is the foundation for the orderly development of sustainable Blue Economies.

Notes

1 https://ec.europa.eu/environment/iczm/index_en.htm.
2 Costa Rica is credited with being the first country in the Wider Caribbean Region to implement an ICZM approach in 1977.
3 Directive 2014/89/EU of the European Parliament and of the Council of 23 July 2014 establishing a framework for maritime spatial planning https://eur-lex.europa. eu/eli/dir/2014/89/oj.
4 http://msp.ioc-unesco.org/world-applications/overview/.
5 http://www.coralina.gov.co/nuevositio/en/.

References

Albotoush, R. and Shau-Hwai, A. T. 2019. Evaluating integrated coastal zone management efforts in Penang Malaysia. *Ocean & Coastal Management*, 104899.
Arkema, K. G., Verutes, S., Wood, C. *et al.* 2015. Embedding ecosystem services in coastal planning leads to better outcomes for people and nature. *PNAS*, 112 (24): 7390–7395.
Baldwin, K. and Mahon. R. 2015. *Rapid Fishery Sector Assessment of the Jamaican Seascape: Pedro Bank and the Southwest Coast of Jamaica.* For the Nature Conservancy, Caribbean Marine Biodiversity Program. Kingston, Jamaica. 105 pp.
Baldwin, K., Mahon, R. and McConney, P. 2013. Participatory GIS for strengthening transboundary marine governance in SIDS. *Natural Resources Forum*: Special Issue on Sustainable Development in Small Island Developing States, 37: 257–268.
Belize. 2000. *Coastal Zone Management Act Chapter 329 Revised Edition 2000.*
Billé, R. 2007. A dual-level framework for evaluating integrated coastal management beyond labels. *Ocean & Coastal Management*, 50 (10), 796–807.
Blackman, K. and McConney, P. 2008. *Information needed for the Negril Marine Park's Fisheries Management Plan.* CERMES Technical Report No. 21. 100 pp.

76 Lorna Inniss et al.

Caribbean Environment Programme. 1996. *Guidelines for Integrated Planning and Management of Coastal and Marine Areas in the Wider Caribbean Region.*

Cicin-Sain, B. and Knecht, R. W. 1998. *Integrated Coastal and Ocean Management: Concepts and Practices.* Washington, DC: Island Press.

Cooper, E., Burke, L. and Bood, N. 2009. *Coastal Capital Belize: The Economic Contribution of Belize's Coral Reefs and Mangroves.* WRI working paper. Washington, DC: World Resources Institute. 53 pp. Available at: http://pdf.wri.org/working_papers/coastal_capital_belize_wp.pdf.

CZMAI. 2016. *Belize's Integrated Coastal Management plan 2016: Promoting the Wise, Planned Use of Belize's Coastal Resources.* Available at: https://www.coastalzonebelize.org/wp-content/uploads/2015/08/BELIZE-Integrated-Coastal-Zone-Management-Plan.pdf.

CZMAI. n.d. Coastal Zone Management Authority and Institute. Available at: https://www.coastalzonebelize.org/about-czmai-2.

CZMU. 1998. *Integrated Coastal Management Plan for Barbados.* Volume 1 – *Integrated Coastal Management – the Barbados Policy Framework.*

Douvere, F. 2008. The importance of marine spatial planning in advancing ecosystem based sea use management. *Marine Policy*, 32 (5): 762–771. https://doi.org/10.1016/j.marpol.2008.03.021.

Ehler, C. N. and Douvere, F. 2009. Marine spatial planning: A step-by-step approach toward ecosystem-based management. *IOC Manuals Guide*, 53, 99. https://doi.org/10.5670/.

European Commission. n.d. Integrated maritime policy: Legislation to create a common framework for maritime spatial planning in Europe. Available at: https://ec.europa.eu/maritimeaffairs/policy/maritime_spatial_planning_en.

Fanning, L. and Burbidge, C. 2010. Towards a coastal area definition for Nova Scotia. *Ocean Yearbook*, 24: 239–267.

Frazão Santos, C., Ehler, C. N., Agardy, T. *et al.* 2019. Chapter 30 – Marine Spatial Planning, In: *World Seas: An Environmental Evaluation* (2nd Edition), Volume III: *Ecological Issues and Environmental Impacts.* New York: Academic Press 571–592.

Goble, B. J., Lewis, M., Hill, T. R. *et al.* 2014. Coastal management in South Africa: Historical perspectives and setting the stage of a new era. *Ocean & Coastal Management*, 91: 32–40.

Greene, D. R. 2010. *Coastal Zone Management.* London: Thomas Telford.

Hildebrand, L. P. and Norrena, E. J. 1992. Approaches and progress toward effective integrated coastal zone management. *Marine Pollution Bulletin*, 25: 94–97.

Le Tissier, M., Hills, J. M., McGregor, J. A. *et al.* 2004. A training framework for understanding conflict in the coastal zone. *Coastal Management*, 32: 77–88.

Lin, W-N., Wang, N., Song, N-Q. *et al.* 2016. Centralization and decentralization: Evaluation of marine and coastal management models and performance in the Northwest Pacific Region. *Ocean & Coastal Management*, 130: 30–42.

McConney, P. and Pomeroy, R. (Eds). 2006. *Reforming Governance: Coastal Resources Co-management in Central America and the Caribbean.* Final Report of the Coastal Resources Co-management Project (CORECOMP). CERMES Technical Report No. 5. 63 pp.

McConney, P., Pena, M., Haynes, C. *et al.* 2010. *An Institutional Perspective on the Local Area Management Authority of the Soufriere/Scotts Head Marine Reserve, Dominica.* Local Area Management Project. CERMES Technical Report No. 36. 84 pp.

Coastal and marine planning 77

OECS/GEF/World Bank. 2019. *Process Framework Report Coastal and Marine Spatial Plans and Training*. Castries, St. Lucia: Organisation of Eastern Caribbean States. 115 pp. Available at: https://www.oecs.org/en/ogu-resources/coastal-and-marine-spatial-plans-and-training.

Olsen, S. 2003. Frameworks and indicators for assessing progress in integrated coastal management initiatives. *Ocean & Coastal Management*, 46: 347–361.

Peterson, A., Turner, R., Gill, D. *et al.* 2014a. *Future of Reefs in a Changing Environment: An Ecosystem Approach to Managing Caribbean Coral Reefs in the Face of Climate change. Belize Country Profile*. CERMES Technical Report No. 71. 44 pp.

Peterson, A., Turner, R., Gill, D. *et al.* 2014b. *Future of Reefs in a Changing Environment: An Ecosystem Approach to Managing Caribbean Coral Reefs in the Face of Climate Change. Honduras Country Profile*. CERMES Technical Report No. 72. 47 pp.

Pomeroy, R., McConney, P. and Mahon, R. 2004. Comparative analysis of coastal resource co-management in the Caribbean. *Ocean and Coastal Management*, 47: 429–444.

Post, J. C. and Lundin, C. G. 1996. *Guidelines for Integrated Coastal Zone Management*. Environmentally Sustainable and Development Studies and Monographs Series Number 9. Washington, DC: The World Bank.

Scruggs G. R. and Bassett, T. E. 2013. Coastal zone management: The Barbados model. *Land Lines*, October: 1–7. Lincoln Institute of Land Policy.

Sorensen, J. 2002. *Baseline 2000 Background Report: The Status of Integrated Coastal Zone Management as an International Practice*. Boston: Harbour and Coastal Center, Urban Harbours Institute, University of Massachusetts.

Stamoulis, K. A. and Delevaux, J. M. S. 2015. Data requirements and tools to operationalize marine spatial planning in the United States. *Ocean & Coastal Management*, 116: 214–223.

STINAPA. 2015. *STINAPA Strategic Plan 2015–2020*. Bonaire: STINAPA. Available at: https://stinapabonaire.org/wp-content/uploads/2018/08/Strategisch-Plan-2015-2020-STINAPA.pdf.

Suman, D. 1998. Integrated coastal zone management in the Caribbean region. *University of Miami Inter-American Law Review*, 30: 31–52.

Taylor, E., Baine, M. Killmer, A. *et al.* 2013. Seaflower marine protected area: Governance for sustainable development. *Marine Policy*, 41: 57–64.

United Nations. 1992. *Report of the United Nations Conference on Environment and Development*, Rio de Janeiro, 3–14 June. A/CONF.151/26 (Vol. I), 12 August. New York: United Nations.

United Nations Environment Programme. 2012. *The ICZM Process: A Roadmap Towards Coastal Sustainability*. Split: UNEP/Mediterranean Action Plan/Priority Action Programme.

Wong, P. P., Marone, E., Lana, P. *et al.* 2005. Chapter 23 Island Systems. *In Millenium Ecosystems Assessment*. Island Press.

World Bank. 1993. *Noordwijk Guidelines for Integrated Coastal Zone Management*. Distributed at the World Coast Conference, 1–5 November, Noordwijk, The Netherlands.

7 Valuation of ecosystem services as a basis for investment in Blue Economies

Peter W. Schuhmann

Introduction

The foundation of the Blue Economy concept is managing coastal and marine resources in a way that maximises their economic value to society without jeopardising ecosystem health. Because many benefits from environmental goods and services are realised in the absence of formal transactions, market forces cannot be relied upon to provide the efficient provision of benefits from natural resources. Public and private sector investment, including investment in new policy interventions, will be required to transition from the traditional approach toward this sustainable paradigm.

Directing these interventions and investments toward their highest and best use is critical in the Caribbean. The region is endowed with a unique set of natural assets that, if properly managed, can make significant contributions to economic growth, employment and poverty reduction while enhancing resilience to climate change, natural disasters and economic shocks (Patil et al., 2016). Yet, implementing policies that maintain and/or improve the flow of benefits from nature to society will be difficult for many reasons, including complex interdependencies between ecosystems and the inherent conflicts between private and public uses of natural resources. Economic challenges in the Caribbean, including large public debt, high energy costs, limited access to credit, brain drain and the devastating impacts of natural disasters, create shortfalls related to technical capacity, data and budgetary resources (Alleyne et al., 2017) and compound the difficulties associated with sustainable management. These challenges also point to a critical need for sources of economic growth in the region that are ecologically sustainable.

The measurement and mapping of ecosystem service stocks, flows and economic values can assist policy makers in meeting these challenges and making the most of blue growth opportunities. The purpose of this chapter is to illustrate how the economic valuation of natural assets and ecosystem services can support the transition to a Blue Economy. Quantifying the costs and benefits associated with alternative uses of coastal and marine resources can form the foundation for investment planning, designing policies that

Valuation of ecosystem services 79

direct resources toward their highest and best use and communicating the importance of natural resources to the public.

Natural resource assets, human wellbeing and economic value

Natural resources such as coral reefs, beaches, seagrass beds, marine fisheries and offshore resources support Caribbean economies, functioning as the "natural capital" asset base and providing numerous contributions to economic activity and human wellbeing. These include the provision of food and water, the foundation for cultural activities and identity, attraction to tourists, risk reduction from storm damage and climate change, opportunities for recreation, energy creation, carbon storage and aesthetic appeal. Of course, human uses of coastal and marine resources also impair their ability to deliver benefits. Understanding the nature and scope of the economic benefits derived from ecosystem goods and services and the costs created by human activities is a core component of the Blue Economy concept.

Economists define the value of a good or service as what it is worth to people. Economic value can be measured in a variety of ways, including impacts on private and public sector revenues, employment, health care costs, damages to property and infrastructure and measures of willingness to pay (WTP) or willingness to accept (WTA). Importantly, economic value extends beyond transactions in the marketplace to "nonmarket" goods and services such as clean water, wide beaches and diverse ecosystems. Further, economic value can be derived in the absence of direct use or interaction with the natural environment. These "non-use values" include benefits derived from simply knowing that a species or ecosystem exists, and wellbeing associated with the knowledge that resources may be available in the future. Though intangible in many ways, these concepts are important components of economic value that should be measured and managed.

The Blue Economy requires government intervention

Moving toward the Blue Economy framework will require the correction of market inefficiencies. Basic economic theory suggests that free (unregulated) markets allow for the efficient allocation of goods and services, where "efficient" is synonymous with the maximisation of economic gains. This outcome is not planned, but rather is the result of individual decision makers seeking their own personal gains. As producers act to maximise profit and consumers act to benefit from consumption, the economy is guided toward the best outcome for society. The incentives created by self-interest guide markets to provide mutually beneficial outcomes. Indeed, free markets do many things very well. Markets allow individuals and businesses to specialise in producing certain goods and services while trading for others. This trade enhances productivity, allows access to goods and services from all over the world and gives people time to enjoy leisure.

80 Peter W. Schuhmann

However, human wellbeing is not limited to market-based metrics such as income, financial account balances and tangible assets such as real property. Economic value encompasses aspects of health, comfort and happiness that are enjoyed in the absence of markets and may not be directly associated with traditional measures of income or wealth. The natural resource assets of the Caribbean are a perfect example. While the benefits provided by natural systems such as habitat provision, scenic views, nutrient cycling, climate regulation and recreational opportunities create real economic value, we cannot expect market forces to reveal their true value or to deliver efficient quantities. Maximising the economic value of the natural resource assets that underpin Caribbean economies will require "non-market" valuation methodologies to measure value and interventions such as collective action or government provision to deliver these forms of wealth and wellbeing.

There are three basic reasons why markets will fail to provide the optimal amount of these valuable goods and services, all of which are relevant to the transition to the Blue Economy. The first pertains to situations where the benefits provided by the natural environment are shared and cannot be packaged and made available to buyers. Because people are generally unwilling to pay for things when the benefits are shared with others and because businesses cannot survive without profit, these characteristics eliminate the incentives that drive markets to mutually beneficial outcomes. The optimal amount of "public goods" like clean air, clean water and public beaches will not be provided by markets.

Related to public goods is the idea of common property, whereby the benefits from a natural resource accrue entirely to the user, but the costs are shared broadly. Freely accessible resources such as fisheries provide salient examples. The individual fisher realises the entire gain (i.e. revenue) from a day's catch but shares some of the costs (e.g. loss of ecosystem function or diminished fishery productivity) with others. In the absence of regulation, individuals have an economic incentive to continue using the resource, even if use leads to further degradation.

Finally, many market goods and services create costs that are not "paid" by the buyer or seller. Common examples fall under the general category of pollution which imposes real, but "hidden" costs on wellbeing and economic value. For example, the market price that consumers pay for energy produced with fossil fuels does not reflect the true cost of its production, which includes damages to human and environmental health. The price of coastal real estate developed to capture market benefits from housing, hospitality and tourism does not include the costs associated with coastal ecosystem degradation and heightened risk from flooding and storms.

Without some form of regulation or control by government, producers and consumers that impose costs on others will not consider these costs when determining the amount to supply or purchase. That is, costs associated with pollution and environmental degradation are logically ignored by businesses and individuals. As a result, the market prices of the goods that damage the environment are not an accurate reflection of the true cost of producing those goods. However, from society's perspective, the pollution or loss of ecosystem function are real costs associated with the market for this good. The resulting inefficient outcome is incompatible with the basic premise of the Blue Economy.

The Blue Economy involves trade-offs

The vision of the Blue Economy concept – managing human interactions with coastal and marine ecosystems in a way that generates a sustainable stream of benefits, promoting human wealth and wellbeing – is aspirational, intuitive and vague enough to garner widespread support. By focusing on both environmental sustainability and wealth generation the Blue Economy concept simultaneously appeals to conservation-minded individuals and those inclined to favour free markets and economic development – groups whose goals are often in conflict. While straightforward on the surface, translating this general vision into action will create an array of trade-offs that must be anticipated and managed.

It is important to recognise that the Blue Economy concept supports the need to use natural resources in ways that are not entirely compatible with conservation. Harnessing the economic power of blue zones while sustaining their ecological integrity does not mean that all damaging uses of coastal and marine resources are prohibited, but rather that impacts from such activities are mitigated in a way that promotes economic benefits while preserving, but not necessarily maximising, ecological function. Critical information for any country or territory seeking to advance human wellbeing through interactions with coastal and marine resources therefore includes understanding the desired mix of market and non-market contributions to wealth, analysing how these components of value are affected by ecological function and determining which interventions will best guide resource use toward desired outcomes.

Further, it is important to recognise that conserving and/or enhancing coastal and marine assets and the ecosystem services they deliver does not involve the management of natural systems, but rather the management of people and how they interact with nature (TEEB, 2012). Creating interventions that direct human actions toward sustainable outcomes, incentivising some behaviours and disincentivising others (Voyer et al., 2018), will naturally create winners and losers (Gill et al., 2019a). For example, as recently demonstrated in Jamaica, the establishment of marine protected areas (MPAs) to conserve or restore marine ecosystems may limit the short-term ability of those systems to provide sustainable livelihoods for nearshore fishers who lack alternative livelihood options (Chan et al., 2019). The same is likely to be true for recreation operators who may be dislocated by protected area restrictions. Similarly, directing capital toward the extraction of energy or mineral resources may promote short-term economic growth but may inhibit long-term economic gains from tourism and fisheries (Cisneros-Montemayor

82 *Peter W. Schuhmann*

et al., 2013) and may be incompatible with other national goals (e.g. carbon neutrality).

Recognising that moving toward a sustainable Blue Economy will involve trade-offs and synergies between market and non-market sources of value, economic sectors and stakeholders and short-term and long-term wellbeing, it seems logical that operationalising the Blue Economy in the Caribbean will not transpire through a one-size-fits-all approach or uniform set of guidelines. Each country or territory must define its own vision of the Blue Economy based on its priorities and environmental and socioeconomic conditions. A prerequisite for countries and territories seeking to transition away from status quo and toward a more sustainable approach is therefore the resolution of competing visions of the Blue Economy that will be held by different stakeholders (Silver et al., 2015; Voyer et al., 2018) and the identification of natural areas, markets and economic sectors that will be prioritised for investment and intervention. The establishment of these priorities will naturally rest on an a priori understanding of the costs, benefits and risks of alternative interventions and the distribution of these values across stakeholders and across time.

Valuation as a tool for operationalising the Blue Economy in the Wider Caribbean Region

To manage human activities in a way that enhances wellbeing it is necessary to understand the costs that people impose on natural systems and the benefits people derive from them. Measuring the contributions of ecosystem services to human wellbeing and the costs created by resource degradation is the domain of economic valuation. Economic valuation means estimating what something is worth to people, often in monetary terms, by observing what people are willing to give up (i.e., trade) to attain it. Valuation can serve many purposes, from informing policy to raising public awareness regarding the value of natural resources. Schuhmann and Mahon (2015) provide an overview of valuation methods and their use in the Caribbean. Below we present a blueprint for transitioning toward the Blue Economy framework, highlighting areas where valuation can serve to inform the inevitable trade-offs that will occur.

Establishing baseline economic values for natural capital stock

As the goal of a Blue Economy is to manage resources in a way that creates a sustainable stream of benefits, establishing baseline values against which to measure progress is an important first step. This is analogous to establishing a comprehensive understanding of one's physical and financial capital before endeavouring to manage and improve individual wealth. Establishing baseline economic values for natural assets will require a national inventory of those assets, the goods and services they deliver and appraisals of their

Valuation of ecosystem services 83

contributions to human wellbeing. Table 7.1 lists assets, services, stakeholders, benefits and measures of economic value associated with coastal and marine ecosystems in the Caribbean that could serve as a framework for national inventories of natural assets and their economic values. To further support comprehensive planning and management of natural assets, baseline values and threats to value should be spatially mapped and associated with human activities, allowing for identification of conflicts and synergies that may arise in the transition toward Blue Economy goals.

Measuring the costs and benefits of conservation and degradation

Akin to investing in the maintenance of physical capital such as roads and buildings, maintaining or enhancing the quality of natural resource assets through investment in conservation activities can create or enhance economic value. Likewise, human activities often damage or deplete natural capital, diminishing the ability of those assets to deliver economic benefits. In much the same way as financial or budgetary mismanagement constrains the economic returns from a portfolio of market assets, the degradation of natural capital via pollution, habitat modification or overuse limits the economic returns that those assets provide.

There is no shortage of evidence from the region to support these claims. Coral reefs provide economic benefits in the form of coastal defence (Burke et al., 2008; Cooper et al., 2009; van Zanten and van Beukering, 2012), recreation (Beharry-Borg and Scarpa, 2010; Schuhmann et al., 2013; Gill et al., 2015; Cazabon-Mannette et al., 2017) and support for fisheries (Failler et al., 2015; Gill et al., 2019b). Marine protected areas provide economic benefits by protecting coastal and marine ecosystem services from deterioration (e.g. Christie et al., 2015; Trujillo et al., 2016), and mangrove ecosystems provide economic value by protecting and stabilising coastlines, supporting fisheries and providing products that can be used for medicinal purposes (Kathiresan and Bingham, 2001).

Just as improvements to natural resource assets create economic benefits, losses create economic costs. For example, degraded mangroves and reefs provide less protection of coastal real estate and infrastructure than healthy ecosystems (Cesar et al., 2003). Eroded or littered beaches and polluted seawater are less attractive to tourists (Schuhmann et al., 2016; Schuhmann et al., 2019). Despite these well-publicised findings, resource damage and degradation continue as a matter of course. Coastal ecosystems are modified or destroyed to promote market-based returns from tourism; fisheries are depleted, yet continue to be subsidised to provide employment opportunities; and concessions are granted to the cruise industry to increase visitor spending despite the well-known environmental costs.

Calls to curtail such practices for the sake of ecosystem function are met with resistance. The benefits from conservation and the costs of degradation are commonly overlooked in favour of more tangible sources of wellbeing

Table 7.1 Coastal and marine ecosystems, assets, services, benefits and measures of economic value

Ecosystem	Natural assets	Ecosystem services	Stakeholders	Measures of benefits	Measures of economic value ($)
Coral reefs	Fish stocks Biodiversity Corals Clear seawater	Recreation Storm protection Food Carbon sequestration Cultural activities and identity	Fishers Tourists Divers / snorkellers Watersport operators Hoteliers Coastal communities	Annual catch Quality of recreational experiences Number of visitors Reduction in risk from loss Area (hectares) of habitat	Revenue & profit from catch Willingness to pay Revenue & profit from operations Avoided economic losses to coastal property Market value of carbon uptake
Intertidal zone	Beaches Biodiversity Seawater	Recreation Storm protection Cultural activities and identity	Tourists Bathers Watersport operators Hoteliers Coastal communities	Reduction in risk from loss from flooding and erosion Recreation quality Number of visitors Ease of access Beach width	Marginal contribution to real-estate prices by coastal amenity Avoided economic loss to coastal property Willingness to pay Revenue & profit from operations
Coastal lands	Coastal wetlands	Pollution / runoff assimilation Storm protection Cultural activities and identity	Tourists Divers / snorkellers Watersport operators Hoteliers Coastal communities	Reduction in risk from loss from flooding and erosion % Pollution assimilation Area (hectares) of habitat	Avoided water treatment costs Avoided losses of tourism and recreation due to beach closures Willingness to pay
Nearshore pelagic zone	Fish stocks Seawater	Food Recreation Cultural activities and identity	Fishers Watersport operators Coastal communities	Annual catch Quality of recreational experiences	Revenue & profit from catch Willingness to pay Revenue & profit from operations
Offshore / continental Shelf	Offshore minerals Offshore wind Fish stocks	Food Energy	Energy sector Fishers Tourism sector Coastal communities	Annual catch Kilowatt-hours of energy produced	Revenue & profit from catch Revenue & profit from operations Willingness to accept

Valuation of ecosystem services 85

such as income and employment. Conservation efforts are viewed as costly impediments to economic development, as they preclude market-based activities that generate more obvious or immediate financial rewards (Schuhmann et al., 2011). Much of the explanation for this resistance lies in the free-rider problem associated with the public nature of environmental benefits and the absence of monetary signals that allow comparison of non-market environmental values to returns from market activities.

Simply put, because market-based metrics such as jobs and revenues are easily understood, while measures of ecosystem health and function are not, economic actors respond in ways that prioritise market values. The result is a persistent inefficiency: environmental goods and services are under-valued and under-provided relative to the outcomes that would maximise societal welfare. Estimating and presenting the economic benefits from natural systems in monetary terms can help the transition toward sustainable outcomes by allowing "apples-to-apples" comparisons with market-based measures of value.

For example, valuation can be used to measure the expected change in human wellbeing associated with projects designed to restore or protect coastal and marine ecosystems (e.g. the creation of protected areas or restoration of damaged ecosystems), or projects designed to enhance the ability of the natural environment to deliver benefits (e.g. infrastructure near protected areas). These benefits can then be compared with the costs of conservation, facilitating cost–benefit analyses and estimates of the return on investment from specific projects and activities. Such analyses can serve to identify areas and/or ecosystems that display the highest economic value or highest vulnerability to loss, helping policy makers justify expenditures on conservation programmes and activities and providing evidence to target scarce budgetary resources toward actions that maximise societal benefits (Christie et al., 2015).

Correcting market failures by greening (bluing) fiscal policy

While it is easy to suggest that the economic benefits from the conservation of coastal and marine resources are "well known" based on a deep body of empirical research, we should not expect the general public to be familiar with valuation studies, or that the results of such studies alone will influence behaviour. Hence, while centralised policy options such as restrictions on development, establishing nature preserves or building coastal defence structures can be effective in protecting the economic value of natural resources from further deterioration, in the absence of public sector interventions or collective actions that incentivise sustainable behaviours, market-based incentives will continue to dominate the decision-making processes of households and businesses.

Mandates specifying allowable uses will not fully remedy the market inefficiencies associated with the under-provision of environmental goods and services. Incentive-based policies such as the establishment of clear property and access rights, subsidies for sustainable behaviours or corrective taxes and fees for damaging activities also serve important roles in transitioning toward the Blue Economy. Indeed, the "greening" of fiscal policy – shifting the burden of taxation toward activities, goods and services that impose environmental and social costs and away from than those that generate economic benefits such as employment – would appear to be a central tenet of the transition. By altering the tax structure so that the costs of environmental externalities are reflected in the market price of goods and services, fiscal policy can stimulate shifts in production, consumption and investment toward goods and services that are less environmentally damaging (Eni Enrico Mattei et al., 2015) improving overall market efficiency.

The economic foundation for incentive-based policies includes the "Beneficiary Pays Principle" (BPP) and the "Polluter Pays Principle" (PPP). BPP suggests that costs should be borne in proportion to benefits received. PPP suggests that individuals or groups that impose costs or risks on others through environmental damage should be held fiscally liable. Policy tools that are consistent with BPP include user fees, entry fees, property taxes, taxes on renewable natural capital and payments for ecosystem services (PES). Avenues that are consistent with PPP include pollution taxes, biodiversity offsets and some tourist fees and user fees. Valuation can inform the creation of such policies by measuring the economic returns resulting from changes in human behaviour. For example, WTP estimates can be compared to conservation costs to make a case for tax-based funding. Valuation played a critical role in adopting user fees at the Bonaire Marine Park, making it one of the few self-financed marine parks in the Caribbean (Waite et al., 2014).

In addition to understanding what people are willing to pay for access to natural resources, policy makers often must impose penalties or taxes for environmental damage or polluting behaviours (Lienhoop et al., 2015). Environmental taxes directly address the failure of markets to incorporate deleterious environmental impacts into the prices of goods and services by "pricing in" environmental costs associated with production or consumption (OECD, 2011). If the tax rate is set equal to the marginal damage imposed on others, the environmental cost that is otherwise "external" to the market is internalised into market prices and the associated decisions by buyers and sellers, improving overall market efficiency (Williams, 2016). A result where the market price of goods and services accurately reflects their true costs to society is the theoretical ideal for environmental taxes, and rests on estimating environmental costs in monetary terms.

Valuation can also be used to identify the most efficient uses of public sector revenues, a critical consideration for governments facing budget shortfalls. For example, valuation studies can be designed to understand the incentives required to encourage sustainable behaviours and expedite the transition toward cleaner energy and transportation by estimating the subsidy required to incentivise households to participate in waste recycling programmes, install solar technologies or purchase hybrid vehicles. Combining corrective pollution taxes on fossil fuels with such subsidies will pay multiple dividends related to the Blue Economy.

Incorporate the value of natural resources into national income accounts

The transition to the Blue Economy will require public support and targeted investments and will rest on widespread appreciation for the economic value of non-market goods and services. Hence, in addition to altering microeconomic signals (e.g. prices) to reflect the true value of environmental goods and services, it is critical to change the way macroeconomic wellbeing and economic progress are measured, tracked and reported.

The traditional framework for national income accounting calls for careful measurement of consumption, investment and government spending to track economic performance (Repetto et al., 1989). Apart from the value of market transactions (e.g. the sale of land or extracted resources or spending associated with recreation) this system fails to account for the productive role of natural resources (Repetto et al., 1989). Unlike the treatment of physical capital, changes in the value of natural capital are not recognised in aggregate measures of income. Yet, this is precisely the treatment that the Blue Economy concept promotes.

The greening of national accounts need not involve a wholesale dismissal of measures of aggregate economic activity such as Gross Domestic Product (GDP). Rather, GDP can serve as the foundation upon which to build a more comprehensive index that includes environmentally and socially oriented indicators of wellbeing (Giannetti et al., 2015). For example, the value of consumption or investment spending that degrades the natural resource asset base should be appropriately discounted, perhaps even reflecting net economic losses in cases of market activities that severely damage natural systems. Likewise, improvements in the value of the natural capital base or the production of ecosystem services should be included in aggregate measures of economic wellbeing.

Though difficult, incorporating the economic value of natural assets into national income accounts will allow for a more accurate appraisal of economic performance and national wealth (Dharmaratne and Strand, 1999) and will provide more appropriate signals for policy makers to follow when promoting the wellbeing of society. National accounting frameworks that capture environmental and social values include the System of Environmental-Economic Accounting (SEEA), Wealth Accounting and Valuation of Ecosystem Services (WAVES) and Inclusive Wealth Accounting (IWA). While the adoption of these frameworks as complements to the standard System of National Accounts is widespread and growing, their integration into public policy remains limited (Vardon et al., 2017).

Communication

Given that the transition to the Blue Economy will necessarily involve numerous trade-offs and policy changes that impact the general public, it is critical to communicate the nature, purpose and benefits of the new paradigm. Without such information, the public will naturally oppose new taxes, fees or restrictions on use, making the transition to the Blue Economy politically intractable.

Establishing baseline values against which to measure change, providing appropriate signals to guide policy toward sustainable outcomes, and measuring economic progress are essential roles that valuation can play in the transition toward the Blue Economy. Because monetary values are universally understood, value estimates can also serve an important role as a communication tool to: (i) assist in building awareness and sensitising public and private sector stakeholders to the relevance and economic value associated with ecosystem services; (ii) build support for projects and activities based on economic returns; (iii) provide value-based justification for budget allocations to environmental ministries (e.g. cost–benefit analyses, estimates of return on investment); and (iv) help to mainstream the economic value of natural resource management into public sector accounting.

Conclusion

The premise behind the Blue Economy concept is that the natural resource assets in the Caribbean have the potential to contribute to economic growth, poverty reduction and resilience to climate change, natural disasters and exogenous economic shocks (Patil et al., 2016). This vision will not be realised under the current market-based approach to capturing wealth and economic value. Purposeful management of natural resources as vital sources of wealth and wellbeing is required. This will rely upon the understanding, measurement and recognition of the "hidden" non-market benefits derived from natural assets, the economic losses induced by resource damage and the incorporation of those values into public spending, market prices and national income accounts.

Economic valuation provides a clear path toward these ends. Value estimates can serve to establish baseline measures of natural wealth against which to measure change, measure the costs and benefits of conservation and development projects, determine appropriate charges for ecosystem use or damage and target fiscal policy instruments that incentivise sustainable behaviours. Valuation can also serve to support a value-based paradigm for government budget allocations and communicate the value proposition associated with the transition to the Blue Economy to public and private sector stakeholders. When spatially mapped, value estimates can help facilitate the transition to a Blue Economy by improving our understanding of where different ecosystem services are delivered, where the benefits are enjoyed and by whom and what environmental and economic potential is unrealised. Spatial representation of value can also serve to identify areas at the greatest risk for loss of value and/or to target areas where programmes and interventions could yield the highest economic gains.

While much valuation research has been conducted in the Caribbean (Schuhmann and Mahon, 2015), valuation in the region has been piecemeal and ad-hoc, largely relying on academic rather than policy interest. While important for the purposes of communication and one-off policy design, the current state of knowledge regarding the economic values of natural resources in the region is insufficient to support the numerous changes that must occur if we are to be successful in realising the aspirational vision of the Blue Economy.

References

Alleyne, T. S. C., Ötker, İ., Ramakrishnan, U., Srinivasan, K. and Walutowy, M. F. (Eds). 2017. *Unleashing Growth and Strengthening Resilience in the Caribbean.* International Monetary Fund.

Beharry-Borg, N., Scarpa, R. 2010. Valuing quality changes in Caribbean coastal waters for heterogeneous beach visitors. *Ecological Economics*, 69: 1124–1139. doi:10.1016/j.ecolecon.2009.12.007.

Burke, L., Greenhalgh, S., Prager, D. and Cooper, E. 2008. *Coastal Capital: Economic Valuation of Coral Reefs in Tobago and St. Lucia.* June. World Resources Institute. Available at: https://wriorg.s3.amazonaws.com/s3fs-public/pdf/coastal_capital.pdf.

Cazabon-Mannette, M., Schuhmann, P. W., Hailey, A., Horrocks, J. 2017. Estimates of the non-market value of sea turtles in Tobago using stated preference techniques. *Journal of Environmental Management*, 192: 281–291. doi:10.1016/j. jenvman.2017.01.072.

Cesar, H., Burke, L. and Pet-Soede, L. 2003. *The Economics of Worldwide Coral Reef Degradation.* Cesar Environmental Economics Consulting (CEEC).

Chan, C., Armitage, D., Alexander, S. M. and Campbell, D. 2019. Examining linkages between ecosystem services and social wellbeing to improve governance for coastal conservation in Jamaica. *Ecosystem Services*, 39: 100997.

Christie, M., Remoundou, K., Siwicka, E. and Wainwright, W. 2015. Valuing marine and coastal ecosystem service benefits: Case study of St Vincent and the Grenadines' proposed marine protected areas. *Ecosystem services*, 11: 115–127.

Cisneros-Montemayor, A. M., Kirkwood, F. G., Harper, S., Zeller, D. and Sumaila, U. R. 2013. November. Economic use value of the Belize marine ecosystem: Potential risks and benefits from offshore oil exploration. *In Natural Resources Forum*, 37 (4): 221–230.

Cooper, E., Burke, L. and Bood, N. 2009. *Coastal Capital: Belize. The Economic Contribution of Belize's Coral Reefs and Mangroves.* WRI Working Paper. Washington, DC: World Resources Institute.

Dharmaratne, G. S. and Strand, I. 1999. *Approach and Methodology for Natural Resources and Environmental Valuation.* UWI Cave Hill, Barbados & University of Maryland, USA.

Eni Enrico Mattei, Fondazione, Pandey, S. and Stone, S. 2015. Why fiscal policy matters for a Green Economy transition. *Review of Environment, Energy and*

Economics (Re3). January. Available at: https://papers.ssrn.com/sol3/papers.cfm?abstract_id=2571317.

Failler, P., Pètre, É., Binet, T. and Maréchal, J. P. 2015. Valuation of marine and coastal ecosystem services as a tool for conservation: The case of Martinique in the Caribbean. *Ecosystem Services*, 11: 67–75.

Giannetti, B. F., Agostinho, F., Almeida, C. M. V. B. and Huisingh, D. 2015. A review of limitations of GDP and alternative indices to monitor human wellbeing and to manage eco-system functionality. *Journal of Cleaner Production*, 87: 11–25.

Gill, D. A., Cheng, S. H., Glew, L., Aigner, E., Bennett, N. J. and Mascia, M. B. 2019a. Social synergies, tradeoffs, and equity in marine conservation impacts. *Annual Review of Environment and Resources*, 44: 1–26.

Gill, D. A., Oxenford, H. A. and Schuhmann, P. W. 2019b. Values associated with reef-related fishing in the Caribbean: A comparative study of St. Kitts and Nevis, Honduras and Barbados. In Salas, S., Barragan-Paladines, M. J. and Chuenpagdee, R. (Eds), *Viability and Sustainability of Small-Scale Fisheries in Latin America and The Caribbean* (pp. 295–328). Cham: Springer.

Gill, D. A., Schuhmann, P. W. and Oxenford, H. A. 2015. Recreational diver preferences for reef fish attributes: economic implications of future change. *Ecological Economics*, 111: 48–57. doi:10.1016/j.ecolecon.2015.01.004

Kathiresan, K. and Bingham, B. L. 2001. Biology of mangroves and mangrove ecosystems. *Advances in Marine Biology*, 40: 81–251.

Lienhoop, N., Bartkowski, B. and Hansjürgens, B. 2015. Informing biodiversity policy: the role of economic valuation, deliberative institutions and deliberative monetary valuation. *Environmental Science & Policy*, 54: 522–532.

OECD. 2011. *Environmental Taxation: A Guide for Policy Makers*. Paris: Organisation for Economic Co-operation and Development.

Patil, P. G., Virdin, J., Diez, S. M., Roberts, J. and Singh, A. 2016. *Toward a Blue Economy: a Promise for Sustainable Growth in the Caribbean*. Washington, DC: World Bank.

Repetto, R. C., Magrath, W., Wells, M., Beer, C. and Rossini, F. 1989. *Wasting Assets: Natural Resources in the National Income Accounts* (No. INVES-ET P01 R425w). Washington, DC: World Resources Institute.

Schuhmann, P. W. 2012. *The Valuation of Marine Ecosystem Goods and Services in the Wider Caribbean Region*. CERMES Technical Report No. 63.

Schuhmann, P. W. and Mahon, R. 2015. The valuation of marine ecosystem goods and services in the Caribbean: A literature review and framework for future valuation efforts. *Ecosystem Services*, 11: 56–66.

Schuhmann, P. W., Casey, J. F., Horrocks, J. A. *et al.* 2013. Recreational SCUBA divers' willingness to pay for marine biodiversity in Barbados. *Journal of Environmental Management*, 121: 29–36.

Schuhmann, P. W., Bass, B. E., Casey, J. F. and Gill, D. A. 2016. Visitor preferences and willingness to pay for coastal attributes in Barbados. *Ocean & Coastal Management*, 134: 240–250.

Schuhmann, P. W., Skeete, R., Waite, R., Bangwayo-Skeete, P., Casey, J., Oxenford, H. A. and Gill, D. 2019. Coastal and marine quality and tourists' stated intention to return to Barbados. *Water* 11 (6), Article 1265.

Silver, J. J., Gray, N. J., Campbell, L. M., Fairbanks, L. W. and Gruby, R. L. 2015. Blue economy and competing discourses in international oceans governance. *The Journal of Environment & Development*, 24 (2): 135–160.

TEEB. 2012. *The Economics of Ecosystems and Biodiversity in Business and Enterprise* (Bishop, J., Ed.). London and New York: Earthscan.

Trujillo, C., Carrillo, B., Charris, C. A. and Velilla, R. A. 2016. Coral reefs under threat in a Caribbean marine protected area: Assessing divers' willingness to pay toward conservation. *Marine Policy*, 68: 146–154.

van Zanten, B. and van Beukering, P. 2012. *Coastal Protection Services of Coral Reefs in Bonaire*. 10 December.Amsterdam: IVM Institute for Environmental Studies. Available at: http://www.wolfscompany.com/wp-content/uploads/2014/07/Coastal-p rotection-value-Bonaire.pdf.

Vardon, M., Bass, S., Ahlroth, S. and Ruijs, A. 2017. *Forum on Natural Capital Accounting for Better Policy Decisions: Taking Stock and Moving Forward*. Washington, DC: WAVES, World Bank Group.

Voyer, M., Quirk, G., McIlgorm, A. and Azmi, K. 2018. Shades of blue: What do competing interpretations of the Blue Economy mean for oceans governance? *Journal of Environmental Policy & Planning*, 20 (5): 595–616.

Waite, R., Burke, L., Gray, E., van Beukering, P., Brander, L., Mackenzie, E., Pendleton, L., Schuhmann, P. and Tompkins, E. L. 2014. *Coastal Capital: Ecosystem Valuation for Decision Making in the Caribbean*. World Resources Institute.

Williams, R. 2016. *Environmental Taxation. Resources for the Future*. Discussion Paper 16–24. Washington, DC: Resources for the Future.

8 National ocean governance as a foundation for Blue Economic development

Patrick McConney and Sanya Compton

Introduction

Although the notion of a Blue Economy quickly became globally accepted after the Rio+20 (2012) UN Conference on Sustainable Development, given its promotion mainly by small island developing states (SIDS) and some international organisations, its national operationalisation has been limited. This is not surprising given the typical gap in practice, and lag in time, between socio-economic development concepts being articulated and implemented. However, successful implementation of Blue Economy will require national level ocean governance with sectoral integration across civil society, the public sector and the private sector. This is also the basis for national engagement with regional and global socio-economic development processes that rely on good and effective multi-level governance for advancing a Blue Economy (Bakshi, 2019).

Largely through a series of Caribbean Large Marine Ecosystem initiatives, the region has become increasingly familiar with visualising multi-level marine governance as occurring through polycentric vertical and horizontal networks, and linked policy cycles (Mahon and Fanning, 2019). For over a decade, regional and sub-regional projects have been geared towards operationalising these concepts. National inter-sectoral coordination mechanisms (NICs) are at the heart of good country-level governance arrangements, but currently more in theory than in practice (Compton et al., 2017; McConney et al., 2016a). A Blue Economy approach has the potential to be truly transformative in these circumstances, tipping the levels of interest and effort towards more comprehensive and sustainable national governance arrangements with performance better aligned to policy (World Bank and UNDESA, 2017).

Exactly how, in any country or territory, national governance arrangements intersect with Blue Economy initiatives will partly depend on the ocean orientation of the political directorate, which is often based on their assessment or perception of which sectors and strategies are likely to contribute towards socio-economic development (Keen et al., 2018). That argument also acknowledges that developing good and effective governance nationally is fundamental to Blue Economy progress. This is especially so, given the contiguous maritime jurisdictions in the Caribbean with high mobility of both living marine resources and human stakeholders (Fanning et al., 2011). There is guidance on how NICs can contribute to achieving good and effective national ocean governance, as well as help to provide a foundation for and means of nationally operationalising transboundary linkages (Compton et al., 2017). This chapter focuses on these aspects, paying most attention to the English-speaking SIDS for which examples are available. We outline ways in which establishing a Blue Economy in the Caribbean should and could be a national bottom-up process. Then we discuss the essential role of NICs in the Blue Economy. Finally, we link national governance to the regional level, with brief conclusions.

Becoming blue from the bottom up

No matter how one conceptualises Blue Economy (Keen et al., 2018; Voyer et al., 2018), in Caribbean countries, due to their small size and economies, a Blue Economy approach is likely to be everyone's business given the many interdependencies typical of SIDS (Bakshi, 2019). Regardless of the prior socio-economic and environmental paradigms in the country, the transition to a Blue Economy may require bottom-up change management from the individual through households, enterprises, communities and districts to the national level. As the transition to a Blue Economy moves beyond "business as usual" towards socio-economic development that aligns well with ocean and coastal environmental health in the Caribbean, there will be many stakeholders to take into account in making the required changes, and creating synergies, especially in small islands.

In SIDS, big issues occupy small physical spaces, and stakeholders may be numerous and/or diverse. Perhaps not all can be equally and simultaneously engaged due to limitations in their own capacities or other resources for transitioning to a Blue Economy. Citizens and firms may be less concerned about what Blue Economy means and how it is defined, than in how Blue Economy can benefit them and society, and by what means. Concerns and queries can mobilise stakeholders nationally based on their self-interest as well as altruism. Cohen et al. (2019) consider the transition to Blue Economy to be nationally transformative, but perhaps also deeply divisive based on power asymmetries and entrenched interests either dominating or coming under threat by such changes. Bearing in mind the paradox of participation in which greater numbers of participants may result in those with least voice becoming marginalised (de Vivero et al., 2008) it is necessary to carefully plan and prioritise stakeholder engagement within transformative participatory processes., This is especially relevant in cases where governance resources (e.g. time and money) are relatively scarce, as in many small states with large ocean spaces that are even more challenging to manage than their contested land areas (Bakshi, 2019).

The literature on resilience provides guidance for national transformation that fits well with current development theory (World Bank and UNDESA,

94 *Patrick McConney and Sanya Compton*

2017). First, there is a need to institutionalise exchange of information and mobilisation of knowledge widely, preferably at national and all lower levels, on Blue Economy. Communication features prominently in all subsequent stages. The next, very critical, step is to create a shared national vision for change and collective action. Third, the stakeholder groups sharing the vision need to direct their adaptive capacity towards implementing managed change (the transition or transformation) through formal and informal organisational and social networks. Some scholars suggest that there needs to be a window of opportunity (Olsson et al., 2004) to lower the threshold for achieving change, making it easier to overcome the inertia and resistance of "business as usual". In the case of the Caribbean the current global groundswell in favour of Blue Economy may provide the window of opportunity to transform, particularly if accompanied by external financial and technical assistance. Even so, the initial steps need to be nationally designed and driven, as discussed next.

The World Bank and UNDESA (2017) advise how each country can create a vision for its sustainable ocean (blue) economy with policies and plans that enable optimal use of ocean-related resources for the most benefit to human well-being and with the least harm to the environment. In Caribbean countries where maritime zones are huge compared to land masses, it can mean a merging of Green and Blue Economy approaches into one combined national direction to support the attainment of the agreed-upon vision. Responsibility for the Blue Economy is fragmented in many Caribbean countries, being tacked on to the main duties of a wide range of ministries and departments. In 2018, however, Barbados created a Ministry of Maritime Affairs and the Blue Economy, the first with such a clear titular mandate in the Caribbean Community (CARICOM). Yet, the ministry has had to seek assistance in determining its vision elements, areas of operation and functional mandate given the overlaps with several other government agencies and wide consultation is required to carve out a space in which to operate. A Blue Economy must envision how established marine activities transform/transition to becoming more environmentally responsible while still contributing substantially to socio-economic development. Often more important, the vision must set out how changes to attract new investment and industry under the banner of Blue Economy ensure that such responsibility is sustained by both local and foreign enterprises in all aspects of their value chains. It is in the context of visioning, that the national governance arrangements, information platforms and participatory processes are usually established, both formally and informally, rather than being created in a vacuum or on a blank page. As noted previously, some stakeholders will be watching closely to determine how national processes and outcomes are likely to affect them and their interests.

Globally, and thus in many Caribbean countries, clear and comprehensive policy and planning processes are often not well developed at the national level despite being essential for stakeholder engagement and co-creation of a common national vision for the Blue Economy (World Bank and UNDESA,

2017). Such engagement can be expected to consider, *inter alia*, resource efficiency in waste reduction, energy efficiency to reduce carbon footprint, decent employment for human well-being, innovative financing for improved technologies and capacity development to reduce reliance on external inputs of all types needed to provide sustainable environmental, social, and economic benefits.

Since significant policy interventions may be needed to achieve the envisioned Blue Economy benefits, stakeholders both inside and outside the policy domain may have concerns about consequent changes. For example, environmental NGOs may be concerned that associating Blue Economic development with the oceans will lead to further unsustainable ocean use, habitat degradation and social inequalities (Cohen et al., 2019; McConney et al., 2014). Firms (particularly small to medium enterprises) may be concerned that some competitors are allowed to continue unsustainable and inequitable actions to their disadvantage. However well-intentioned they may be, Blue Economy policies, plans and projects may inadvertently have significant adverse impacts on the environment and some segments of society even while benefiting other segments. Civil society organisations may be concerned that changes will trample upon the established rights and expected benefits of ordinary citizens, and especially groups perceived as disadvantaged, such as small-scale fishers (Cohen et al., 2019). "Ocean grabbing" has been a term applied to Blue Economy and other initiatives that ramp up tourism, coastal infrastructure, oil and gas extraction, marine renewable energy, transportation, mariculture, etc. in which some groups may lose control of, or access to, a marine space or resource that they previously enjoyed while "big business" benefits (Bennett et al., 2015). For example, in Trinidad and Tobago coastal seismic exploration for oil and gas has allegedly impacted small-scale fishers without adequate compensation (Gordon and Tupper, 2011). Fisherfolk, however, are using international agreements to influence regional policy in order to improve national level conditions for themselves within contested marine space (Compton et al., 2019). Oxenford and McConney (Chapter 10 this volume) further discuss fishing industry issues.

Environmentally sustainable increased economic growth and social development from coastal and marine resources will typically come with trade-offs among economic sectors and stakeholder groups. In inclusive, transparent and accountable participatory processes the decisions, outputs and outcomes should aim for equity, if equality is not feasible. The entire process of transition and transformation described above with its challenges, constraints, new prospects and opportunities calls for a robust and resilient national ocean governance arrangement to achieve trade-offs while maintaining engagement. The next section sets out NICs as such a type of governance arrangement.

National inter-sectoral coordination mechanisms

Multi-stakeholder multi-sector coordination is critical to achieving governance effectiveness (Mahon et al., 2010; McConney et al., 2016a; FAO, 2017).

It is primarily at the national level that implementation of management actions and policies occur. Therefore, meeting national ocean policy and plan goals and objectives, and by extension regional and international mandates, requires national-level coordination (Mahon et al., 2014). National inter-sectoral coordination mechanisms (NICs) are now being inserted into the heart of the design of some of Caribbean ocean governance arrangements such as the national Ocean Governance Committees of the Organisation of Eastern Caribbean States (OECS) that has also formed a sub-regional Ocean Governance Team for transboundary networking. However, arrangements such as these are still the exception. Many countries lack governance arrangements dedicated specifically to the ocean. Supporting the strengthening and establishment of NICs is a crucial early action needed to establish good and effective national and regional ocean and marine governance to support emerging Blue Economy initiatives.

Developing both good and effective governance at the national level is fundamental to progress. Arrangements such as NICs, in theory, can facilitate this because they provide that link between national and regional governance; for the improved management and sustainability of ocean and marine resources (Mahon et al., 2013). NICs can exist and evolve among various types of governance arrangements and modes of operation (structure and function as well as performance) based on specific aspects of the NIC. For example, these aspects relate to whether the NIC is formal or informal, has legislative or administrative mandate and authority, the timing of its formation or development, the composition of membership along several dimensions (e.g. sector, level, gender, state/non-state mix, etc.), the type and pathways of communication, how often the NIC is actually used for ocean governance outcomes, the process for documentation and or monitoring and evaluation, and so on (Mahon et al., 2010). For the purpose of Blue Economy advancement, relevant marine NICs may include Fisheries Advisory Committees (FACs) that use ecosystem approaches, ocean governance committees (OGCs), national sustainable development commissions, coastal management institutions, seascape-scale marine managed area authorities, comprehensive climate change committees or any other mechanism that facilitates marine inter-sectoral coordination nationally (Compton et al., 2017).

Since NICs can become an essential operational arm for the implementation of good and effective ocean governance, it is important to be clear on their design. Ideally, NICs operate as polycentric arrangements, that is, they function with a nested system of policy cycles creating multi-way linkages among national sectors, and between national and regional governance processes. NICs thus connect multi-level, multi-stakeholder systems with and among sectors at the national level laterally, while making transboundary connections vertically (Mahon et al., 2010; McConney et al., 2016a). These linkages extend into both the social and ecological parts of governance systems, arrangements and institutions. As an example, the Orange (creative) and Blue Economies may be combined in NICs when state and non-state stakeholders in cultural industries (song, dance, visual art, theatre, etc.) work along with coastal and fisheries authorities to reduce marine debris or land-based pollution, to promote marine renewable energy use, or to sensitise youth to coastal climate change adaptation issues and measures. NICs' design can facilitate the rapid diffusion of innovation across sectoral boundaries that must be achieved in developing a Blue Economy.

Conceptually, NICs are designed to provide the capacity needed for effective governance (nationally and regionally). It can be argued that for governance to be effective it must first be good (Mahon and Fanning, 2019). The extent to which governance arrangements and processes reflect internationally accepted norms, principles, and values is a direct reflection of good governance. A well-designed NIC should have all or most of the following features, among others:

- comprehensive inclusion of actors: state – government agencies, para-statal bodies; non-state – NGOs, CBOs and academia; and private sector – small, medium and large enterprises;
- supportive environment that creates opportunities for, and enables, sta-keholder participation, including encouraging individuals to become champions and leaders as change agents;
- non-partisan but politically endorsed both administratively and legally with a clear mandate;
- well-established reviewing processes for evaluating effectiveness that enhances capacity and self-organisation through monitoring, learning and adaptation;
- national multi-level integration of sufficient sectors with the stakeholders to make a difference;
- facilitation of linkages between national and regional level ocean governance processes;
- scope and mandate so that NICs can address or influence operationally critical functions and tasks.

Governance arrangement architecture and composition are among the most critical determinants of performance (Mahon et al., 2013). An almost infinite set of configurations is possible in NICs, and the available empirical evidence is insufficient to provide detailed guidance on which configurations best favour effective governance (Compton et al., 2017). Blue Economy initiatives offer an opportunity to test some of the good practices that seek to make NICs fit for purpose. Consider, for example, an island with a small number of high-capacity, corporate stakeholders compared to one with numerous, lower-capacity, small-scale enterprises in tourism, fisheries and shipping. While a simple, single-level NIC architecture may suit the former, a more complex, multi-level and representation-based NIC may be needed for the latter.

In addition, these two Blue Economy NIC scenarios may result in different good governance principles being valued for effective governance. In the first scenario the few corporate stakeholders may be more amenable to a formal legal structure oriented towards consensus-building and operational efficiency. An entirely different set of principles may be more effective in the second scenario with many small actors. In their case, inclusive and equitable participation with transparency and accountability may foster the trust and respect needed to counter possible disruptive power asymmetries. These are shown in Figure 8.1 as radar plots rating the preferences for the typical principles of good governance. Of course, these scenarios, stakeholder configurations and principles favouring effective governance are not static. As Blue Economic development proceeds any NIC will need to adapt over time in order to remain most effective. This is a new area for investigation in national ocean governance (Compton et al., 2017).

Currently, many Caribbean ocean governance initiatives are being undertaken through external projects. NICs have long been identified as a requirement for all Global Environment Facility (GEF) International Waters (IW) projects. There are at least a half-dozen currently being implemented that are relevant to Blue Economy advancement. Within recent years the Caribbean region has seen NICs integrated into many of its regional-based ocean and marine governance policies, programmes and initiatives. Having NICs operational in over 60% of its participating countries is a specific target under the GEF and UNDP funded CLME+ Project. Compton et al. (2017) investigated NIC institutional arrangements and their good practices for ecosystem approach to fisheries (EAF), marine spatial planning (MSP), integrated coastal management (ICM), marine managed and protected areas (MMAs and MPAs) and the like in order to produce guidelines for NICs that are also relevant to Blue Economy. As mentioned earlier, the OECS Commission's Ocean Governance and Fisheries (OGF) Unit is implementing the Caribbean Regional Oceanscape Project (CROP), the objectives of which are to strengthen ocean governance and improve the knowledge and capacity of citizens and institutions for ocean governance within the Eastern Caribbean. Embedded in these objectives is the development of policies, strategies and

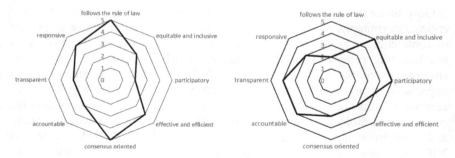

Figure 8.1 The relative importance and effectiveness of good governance principles will vary with the nature and complexity of the situation.

governance arrangements — Ocean Governance Committees (OGC) — for improved ocean governance. Yet it must be remembered a call for establishing NICs in SIDS is not new and it precedes the concept of Blue Economy. For example, the SIDS Programme of Action (POA) called for coordinating mechanisms to guide and provide oversight of national and regional SIDS POA implementing processes for oceans (Roberts and Ali, 2016).

Regional frameworks such as the Large Marine Ecosystem (LME) Governance Framework (developed for the Caribbean LME) have been proposed to support improved governance of marine resources. So there must be national capacity to facilitate effective participation in regional and international processes (Mahon et al., 2014). The Sustainable Development Goals (SDGs) connect the socio-economic and ecological aspects of the global ocean environment. SDG 14 on life below water specifically refers to ocean conservation and sustainable use of marine resources. The value of goods and services provided by coastal and ocean ecosystems and their contribution to poverty eradication; livelihoods; and economies led to the concept of the Blue Economy. With NICs in place and functioning well, countries should be better positioned for achieving this and other international sustainability goals. Utilising NICs as platforms for successfully integrating sectoral approaches to oceans within the Blue Economy will have to take into consideration at least the following: (1) if adaptation is to be dynamic and demand-driven, and (2) achieving sustainability of national ocean governance in a Blue Economy also requires attention to operationalising concepts such as the ecosystem approach to fisheries (EAF), ecosystem-based management (EBM), climate change adaptation (CCA) and disaster risk management (DRM) that must be embedded into NICs and the Blue Economy.

- Gender (i.e. SDG 5) in supporting participatory governance arrangements (i.e. NICs), the power dynamics of gender equality and equity, particularly as it relates to the involvement of men and women in leadership and decision-making, is critical.
- NICs are based on the principles of good governance, which is essential for enabling conditions favouring the success of Blue Economy activities, but understanding which good governance principles would be most effective is critical for optimising NIC performance.
- A key feature of any NIC is the comprehensive inclusion of stakeholders, preferably as sector representatives so that in an ideal situation, NICs can facilitate stakeholder engagement and buy-in to Blue Economy concepts and initiatives, which is especially important if there is low trust of leadership or suspicion of elite capture (e.g. big businesses or tourism being treated preferentially as a sector).
- Further to implementing the Blue Economy approach using NICs is the significant role for civil society, and small and medium-sized enterprises in making the transformation or transition, but low civil society capacity may be a constraint typical of Caribbean SIDS.

- One of the challenges to a successful outcome, both for NICs and in implementing Blue Economy approaches, is the cost associated with sustaining engagement among stakeholders with diverse interests and trade-off expectations. As such, change-management must be factored into participatory monitoring and evaluation if adaptation is to be dynamic and demand-driven.
- Achieving sustainability of national ocean governance in a Blue Economy also requires attention to operationalising concepts such as the EAF, EBM, CCA and DRM that must be embedded into NICs and the Blue Economy.

NICs should be ideal governance arrangements for successfully achieving national to international goals in ocean governance. Therefore, a Blue Economy approach serves to benefit from incorporating NICs. However, establishing and sustaining NICs is challenging. Processes in NICs throughout the Wider Caribbean Region are poorly documented and understood at the level of detail required to take remedial action or to optimise effectiveness under different, dynamic conditions (Compton et al., 2017). Much support is still needed for NICs if they are to play their perceived important role in implementing a Blue Economy.

National need for transboundary linkages

National ocean governance arrangements through NICs are necessary, but not sufficient, for a successful Blue Economy. Transboundary linkages are vital in the Caribbean due to the many complex interactions and interdependencies described previously here and in other chapters of this volume. However, the vertical ties between national and (sub-) regional levels of governance require some attention as understanding and managing them is crucial and often not simple. Mahon et al. (2010) examined the process of connecting national to regional marine science to policy across science-policy interfaces in Caribbean countries. It is clear that, even without a Blue Economy thrust, national science and policy processes need to interface better, and this is also true at the regional level (McConney et al., 2016b). NICs and the various working groups, or similar, of regional intergovernmental organisations and regional NGOs can play a major role in such reformation through both their design and performance. Regarding NICs, not only must there be flows of information from the regional level to inform their advice or decision-making, but their outputs must in turn be effectively channelled towards the relevant regional organisations and policy cycles (Mahon et al., 2014). Both processes are far more national than regional in character and locus of action, since nation-states set regional agendas. Ideally, they will demand information to assist NICs, and exercise influence at the (sub-) regional level to advance their collective national agendas.

A passive national arrangement will not result in the information flows and decision-making required for a successful national Blue Economy. Furthermore, both the national demand and supply should serve to make regional level governance better, such as more transparent, accountable, inclusive and especially responsive to participation. Various initiatives such as those under the CLME+ SAP and Project (Debels et al., 2017) are promoting multi-level approaches to regional ocean governance with such transboundary network interactions (Mahon and Fanning, 2019). Initiatives such as these are addressed in more detail in Fanning and Mahon, Chapter 9 on regional ocean governance.

Conclusion

Caribbean countries have historically not sought to strategically optimise the benefits from marine ecosystem services as their outlooks, from colonial times, have mainly been landward and were only recently couched in terms of Green Economy and now Blue Economy. With independence came more attention to coastal tourism and fisheries in most locations, and seabed hydrocarbons in some. Although the concept of Blue Economy is new to Caribbean development paradigms, the conventional economic activities are well established. Most existing coastal and marine activities are now billed as components of Blue Economy initiatives. A good and effective national approach to Blue Economy has the potential to be truly transformative in the Caribbean, tipping the levels of interest and the entrepreneurial effort towards more sustainable intersectoral governance structures with functions that are well aligned with their enabling sectoral parent policies and plans. However, in many Caribbean countries, the national vision, enabling policies and planning frameworks, with good and effective governance arrangements for a comprehensive and coherent transition to a Blue Economy may be deficient. Yet, these countries are making the transition and there is guidance on how to do so at the national level (Compton et al., 2017). In conclusion, some of the elements required for the national transition to a Blue Economy include:

- appreciation of the value of marine resources and their corresponding ecosystem services;
- acceptance of the need for a people-centred framework for ecosystem-based management;
- stakeholder analysis and engagement to ensure that appropriate groups are fully involved;
- establishment and institutionalisation of information exchange and knowledge mobilisation;
- effective and creative co-production of a vision with a set of enabling policies and plans;
- translation of the vision into action through broad and resilient partnerships and networks;

102　*Patrick McConney and Sanya Compton*

- governance to grow a Blue Economy through national inter-sectoral coordination mechanisms;
- implementation of complete policy cycle with adequate stakeholder participation at all stages;
- use of a fully functional NIC to sway decision-makers to evidence-based decision making;
- indicators to measure and track progress for evaluation, review, learning and adaptation.

Successful Blue Economy requires national ocean governance arrangements in place, linked to regional level processes as discussed in the next chapter.

References

Bakshi, A. 2019. Oceans and small island states: Prospects for the blue economy. *International Research Journal of Human Resources and Social Sciences*, 6: 43–60.

Bennett, N. J., Govan, H. and Satterfield, T., 2015. Ocean grabbing. *Marine Policy*, 57: 61–68.

Cohen, P., Allison, E. H., Andrew, N. L., Cinner, J. E. *et al.* 2019. Securing a just space for small-scale fisheries in the blue economy. *Frontiers in Marine Science*, 6. Available at: https://www.frontiersin.org/articles/10.3389/fmars.2019.00171/full.

Compton, S., McConney, P., Monnereau, I., Simmons B. and Mahon, R. 2017. *Good Practice Guidelines for Successful National Intersectoral Coordination Mechanisms (NICs)*. Report for the UNDP/GEF CLME+ Project (2015–2020). CERMES Technical Report No. 88. Centre for Resource Management and Environmental Studies, The University of the West Indies, Cave Hill Campus, Barbados. 14 pp.

Compton, S., McConney, P., Murray, P., Nembhard, N. and Phillips, T. 2019. Influencing regional Caribbean small-scale fisheries policy through protocol. In Westlund, L. and Zelasney, J. (Eds), *Securing Sustainable Small-Scale Fisheries: Sharing Good Practices from Around the World*, pp.109–131. FAO Fisheries and Aquaculture Technical Paper No. 644. Rome. 184 pp.

de Vivero, J. L. S., Mateos, J. C. R. and del Corral, D. F. 2008. The paradox of public participation in fisheries governance. The rising number of actors and the devolution process. *Marine Policy*, 32: 319–325.

Debels, P., Fanning, L., Mahon, R., McConney, P., Walker, L., Bahri, T. and Toro, C. 2017. The CLME+ Strategic Action Programme: An ecosystems approach for assessing and managing the Caribbean Sea and North Brazil Shelf large marine ecosystems. *Environmental Development*, 22: 191–205.

Fanning, L., Mahon, R. and McConney, P. 2011. *Towards Marine Ecosystem-based Management in the Wider Caribbean*, Amsterdam: Amsterdam University Press.

FAO. 2017. *Implementing 2030 Agenda for Food and Agriculture: Accelerating Impact through Cross-Sectoral Coordination at the Country Level*. Rome: FAO.

Gordon, A. and Tupper, M., 2011. *Small-scale fisheries and oil and gas operations in Trinidad and Tobago. A scoping study*. WorldFish Center, Malaysia.

Keen, M. R., Schwarz, A. M. and Wini-Simeon, L. 2018. Towards defining the blue economy: Practical lessons from Pacific Ocean governance. *Marine Policy*, 88: 333–341.

Mahon, R and Fanning, L. 2019. Regional ocean governance: Integrating and coordinating mechanisms for polycentric systems. *Marine Policy*, 107. https://doi.org/10.1016/j.marpol.2019.103589.

Mahon, R., McConney, P., Parsram, K., Simmons, B. *et al.* 2010. *Ocean governance in the Wider Caribbean Region: Communication and coordination mechanisms by which states interact with regional organisations and projects.* CERMES Technical Report No. 40. Centre for Resource Management and Environmental Studies, The University of the West Indies, Cave Hill Campus, Barbados. 84 pp.

Mahon, R., Cooke, A., Fanning, L. and McConney, P. 2013. *Governance Arrangements for Marine Ecosystems of the Wider Caribbean Region.* CERMES Technical Report No. 60. Centre for Resource Management and Environmental Studies, The University of the West Indies, Cave Hill Campus, Barbados. 99 pp.

Mahon, R., Fanning, L. and McConney, P. 2014. Assessing and facilitating emerging regional ocean governance arrangements in the Wider Caribbean Region. *Ocean Yearbook*, 28: 631–671.

McConney, P., Pomeroy, R. and Khan, Z. 2014. ENGOs and SIDS: environmental interventions in small island developing states, In Garcia, S. M., Rice, J. and Charles, A. (Eds), *Governance of Marine Fisheries and Biodiversity Conservation: Interaction and Co-evolution*, pp. 360–373. Chichester: Wiley-Blackwell.

McConney, P., Monnereau, I., Simmons, B. and Mahon, R. 2016a. *Report on the Survey of National Intersectoral Coordination Mechanisms.* CERMES Technical Report No. 84. Centre for Resource Management and Environmental Studies, The University of the West Indies, Cave Hill Campus, Barbados. 75 pp.

McConney, P., Fanning, L., Mahon, R. and Simmons, B. 2016b. A first look at the science-policy interface for ocean governance in the wider Caribbean region. *Frontiers in Marine Science*, 2: 119.

Olsson, P., Folke, C. and Hahn, T. 2004. Social-ecological transformation for ecosystem management: the development of adaptive co-management of a wetland landscape in southern Sweden. *Ecology and Society*, 9 (4): 2. Available at: http://www.ecologyandsociety.org/vol9/iss4/art2.

Roberts, J. P. and Ali, A. 2016. *The Blue Economy and Small States.* Commonwealth Blue Economy Series, No. 1. London: Commonwealth Secretariat. Available at: http://www.cpahq.org/cpahq/Cpadocs/The%20Blue%20Economy%20and%20Small%20States.pdf.

Voyer, M., Quirk, G., McIlgorm, A., and Azmi, K. 2018. Shades of blue: What do competing interpretations of the blue economy mean for oceans governance? *Journal of Environmental Policy & Planning*, 20: 595–616.

World Bank and United Nations Department of Economic and Social Affairs. 2017. *The Potential of the Blue Economy: Increasing Long-term Benefits of the Sustainable Use of Marine Resources for Small Island Developing States and Coastal Least Developed Countries.* Washington, DC: World Bank.

9 Regional ocean governance

An imperative for addressing Blue Economy challenges and opportunities in the Wider Caribbean

Lucia Fanning and Robin Mahon

Introduction

For Blue Economic growth to take place sustainably and equitably, good governance must be in place. Ocean governance is inevitably multilevel, from local to global. However, due to their transboundary nature most ocean issues require a regional approach to governance. Such approaches are in various stages of development in most ocean regions globally (Mahon and Fanning, 2019a; 2019b). In the case of the Wider Caribbean Region (WCR), while considerable activity has been oriented towards ocean governance at the regional level, it has been fragmented. This and other weaknesses have long been known and were articulated by the Transboundary Diagnostic Analysis (TDA) for the Caribbean Large Marine Ecosystem (CLME) Initiative which took place in two phases between 2006 and 2013 and is concluding its third phase (2015–2020).[1] The topic of regional ocean governance also increased in prominence with the advent of the Sustainable Development Goals (SDGs), especially the Ocean SDG14 and the pursuit of blue economic growth within the region (CDB, 2018; Fanning and Mahon, 2017).

This chapter focuses on the imperative of a regional approach to governing the challenges and opportunities associated with the transboundary nature of the Caribbean Sea which provides the basis for the Blue Economy being sought by countries in the WCR. It builds on the understanding of a Blue Economy as articulated by Clegg et al. (Chapter 2 this volume). It provides an overview of the key transboundary issues confronting the region and an exploration of the regional approaches that have been emerging over the past several decades, building on the analysis of Mahon et al. (2014). We suggest that these approaches will need to be expanded and strengthened if the requirements of Blue Economies within the WCR are to be met. We conclude that the negative consequences of not pursuing regional approaches may be considerable.

Transboundary issues affecting the WCR

The WCR is arguably the world's most geopolitically complex region, with 29 countries and 18 territories that are departments of France, or dependencies of the United Kingdom, United States and the Netherlands. Most states are developing countries and 16 are Small Island Developing States (SIDS). The exclusive economic zones (EEZs) of these states cover all marine space in the region out to 200 nautical miles east of the Lesser Antilles, resulting in extensive sharing of living marine resources and a diversity of associated transboundary resource management issues. The geopolitical complexity of the WCR has considerable implications for ocean governance. It includes some of the largest (e.g. Brazil, USA) and smallest countries (e.g. Barbados, St Kitts and Nevis) as well as the most developed (e.g. USA, France) and the least developed (e.g. Haiti, Guyana) countries, resulting in an extremely wide range in their capacities for governance. There is also a diversity of language, culture and administrative arrangements as part of their colonial heritage.

The TDA for the CLME Initiative explored the weakness in transboundary governance and noted that all three major categories of impacts on marine ecosystems in the WCR – overexploitation, pollution and coastal habitat destruction – have transboundary aspects that require collaboration among countries. Effluents of large continental rivers such as the Amazon, Essequibo and Orinoco carry pollutants that disperse throughout the region. Living marine resources may be shared by all WCR states as in the case of migratory large pelagic species or just a subset of states as in the case of Central American lobster. The countries recognise that to address these risks, international collaboration is essential to build collective capacity and take transboundary action necessary for achieving the 2030 SDGs, particularly Goal 14, and associated Blue Economies.

The TDA noted the inadequacy or absence of institutional arrangements for dealing with shared living marine resource issues. This is despite there being around 25 regional organisations with mandates for various aspects of sustainable use of marine ecosystems. The countries and organisations sharing the WCR marine space have recognised that effective ocean governance is essential if the critical goods and services that support coastal economies are to be sustained (Debels et al., 2017).

The United Nations Convention on the Law of the Sea, of which most WCR states are parties, obligates countries to collaborate to ensure the sustainability of transboundary resources. The complexity of ocean management and the need for integration also demand regional collaboration as the WCR moves towards ecosystem-based management (Fanning et al., 2011). WCR countries have also committed to collaboration in ocean governance through United Nations Convention on the Law of the Sea (UNCLOS), Agenda 21, Convention on Biological Diversity, SIDS Barbados Program of Action and other multilateral agreements (Singh and Mee, 2008). The Cartagena

106 *Lucia Fanning and Robin Mahon*

Convention and its Protocols are of special significance in this regard, as they are region specific (UNEP, 1983).

Many Caribbean countries, and all SIDS, are predominantly coastal. Climate change impacts will also be prominent in ocean and coastal areas globally. Expected climate change impacts in the region include coastal erosion and inundation, increased intensity of tropical cyclones, degradation of reefs due to coral bleaching and ocean acidification and changes in the distribution of fish stocks (Oxenford and Monnereau, 2018; Taylor et al., Chapter 5 this volume). In the WCR, healthy coastal and marine systems will be important for climate change adaptation (Oxenford and Mahon, Chapter 4 this volume). All these factors contribute to the importance of a regional approach to ocean governance.

Efforts to promote regional ocean governance

In an effort to address the significant transboundary challenges in the WCR, institutional arrangements for regional ocean governance have been emerging through the ongoing efforts of some 25 sub-regional, regional and international organisations with mandates for various aspects of living marine resource governance in the WCR (Mahon et al., 2014) (Figure 9.1). They include political integration organisations,[2] sector-specific sub-bodies of these organisations, regional bodies of UN agencies, NGOs and a small number of private sector organisations. Geographically, these operate at several overlapping, nested or linked levels. This diverse array of regional and sub-regional organisations has emerged to address both the challenges and opportunities of ocean governance. To some extent, they have paralleled the global sequence of ocean related multilateral environmental agreements and their regional subsidiaries.

Three regional initiatives that focus on integrated regional ocean governance within the WCR are:

- the Association of Caribbean States (ACS), Caribbean Sea Initiative, 1999 – ongoing;
- the Organisation of Eastern Caribbean States (OECS), Eastern Caribbean Regional Ocean Policy (ECROP), 2010 – ongoing;
- the UNDP Caribbean Large Marine Ecosystem (CLME) Initiative funded by the Global Environment Facility (GEF), 1999 – ongoing.

Their progress and relevance to the development of Blue Economies are reviewed below. While the Central American Integration System (SICA) and CARICOM have ocean-related activities through their agencies and associated civil society organisations they have not yet explicitly taken up the mantle of integrated ocean governance.

The ACS Caribbean Sea Initiative

The Caribbean Sea Initiative is led by the ACS for which "The preservation and conservation of the Caribbean Sea" is a focal area. The ACS was established in 1994 by 29 Caribbean states. In 1999, ACS Member States submitted a proposal for a resolution at the United Nations General Assembly (UNGA) calling for designation of the Caribbean Sea as a "special area", under UNCLOS (Berry, 2014, p. 342). The UNGA did not endorse the proposal. Instead it adopted a variation as Resolution A/RES/54/225, "Promoting an integrated management approach to the Caribbean Sea within the context of sustainable development", which emphasised the need for an

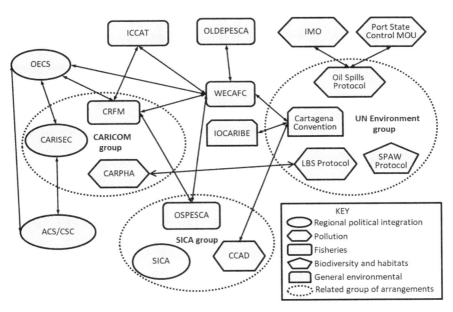

Figure 9.1 The Wider Caribbean Regional ocean governance cluster.
Notes: ACS/CSC, Association of Caribbean States/Caribbean Sea Commission; CARICOM, Caribbean Community; CARISEC, Caribbean Resilience & Security Conference; CARPHA, Caribbean Regional Public Health Agency; Cartagena Convention, Convention for the Protection and Development of the Marine Environment of the WCR; CCAD, Central American Commission for Environment and Development: CRFM, Caribbean Regional Fisheries Mechanism; ICCAT, International Commission for the Conservation of Atlantic Tunas; IMO, International Maritime Organisation; IOCARIBE, Regional Sub commission of the Intergovernmental Oceanographic Commission; LBS, Land Based Sources of Pollution; OECS, Organisation of Eastern Caribbean States; OLDEPESCA, Latin American Organisation for Fisheries Development; OSPESCA, Central America Fisheries and Aquaculture Organisation; Port State Control MOU, MOU for Port State Control in the Caribbean Region; SICA, Central American Integration System; SPAW, Specially Protected Areas and Wildlife; WECAFC, Western Central Atlantic Fisheries Commission.

108 *Lucia Fanning and Robin Mahon*

integrated approach to ocean governance in the WCR (Parris, 2016). This resolution has been revised and renewed every two years, most recently in 2018 as Resolution A/RES/73/229 (UNGA, 2019).

Numerous regional intergovernmental arrangements have a mandate for aspects of ocean governance in the WCR. The arrows in Figure 9.1 indicate known formal interactions.

In 2006, urged by the UNGA to demonstrate capacity and willingness to manage the Caribbean Sea, the ACS established the Caribbean Sea Commission (CSC) to promote and oversee the sustainable use of the Caribbean Sea as per the UNGA Resolution. The objective of the CSC is "to carry out the strategic planning and technical follow-up work for the advancement of the Caribbean Sea Initiative and to formulate a practical and action-oriented work programme for the further development and implementation of the Initiative".[3] In 2010, the CSC was identified as the most appropriate regional organisation to coordinate regional level policy, and this role was endorsed by the majority of regional organisations that it would coordinate (ACS/CERMES-UWI, 2010). This proposal was incorporated in the draft CLME Strategic Action Programme (SAP), but was vetoed by the USA at the CLME Project Steering Committee meeting in 2013 because the USA is not entitled to be a member of the ACS (Mahon et al., 2014). Instead, the USA demanded that the appropriate coordinating mechanism be identified in the 2015–2020 phase of the CLME Project (now ongoing). The CSC continues to pursue the concept of making the Caribbean Sea a "special area" by updating and resubmitting the UNGA Resolution every two years. However, since 2015, due to a change of focus for the CSC towards project implementation, it has shown little interest in pursuing the coordination role for which it was deemed best suited.

The OECS Ocean Governance Initiative

The revised Treaty of Basseterre, 2010, mandates the OECS Commission to pursue a common policy for "matters relating to the sea and its resources".[4] In 2013, OECS countries adopted the Eastern Caribbean Regional Ocean Policy (ECROP) promoting a common approach to ocean governance in all member states and requiring that each member develop a national ocean policy to support the regional policy. Most ECROP priorities and goals are synergistic with the SDGs. In 2014, implementation of ECROP commenced and has: (i) developed a structure for research to strengthen the science-policy interface (including a marine research strategy, a code of conduct for responsible marine research, a data platform to support greater access to information and a guideline of marine standards); (ii) established an OECS Ocean Governance Team (OGT) comprising one nominated representative of each member State who supports the connectivity and articulates the needs on behalf of the state; and (iii) developed five National Ocean Policies (Patil et al., 2016). While this is commendable progress towards the establishment of institutional arrangements, it is too early to comment on their performance. For the remaining (non-OECS) CARICOM countries, the CARICOM Secretariat has not pursued ocean policy as intensively as the OECS. Nor has this been the case for SICA and its associated organisations, likely due to lack of resources and capacity, and greater focus on trade and economic integration.

The CLME Initiative

Initiatives towards sustainable fisheries have been the main drivers towards marine ecosystem-based management (EBM) and associated governance of transboundary living marine resources in the WCR. These have been consolidated by the GEF-supported CLME Initiative, which included two development phases (1998–1999, 2006–2008) and two full phases (2009–2013, 2015–2020). The first full phase adopted the United Nations Food and Agriculture Organisation (FAO) Ecosystem Approach to Fisheries (EAF) (CLME, 2011). It identified the three major marine ecosystems of the WCR as the context for its work: the open-sea/pelagic ecosystem, the coral reef ecosystem and the continental shelf ecosystem (CLME, 2011). This shift to EAF/EBM was a conscious effort to broaden the scope of the CLME Initiative beyond fisheries to include the full range of uses of living marine resources and the users. Recognising that EBM or any other kind of management cannot be pursued effectively unless governance institutions are in place and operational, the CLME Projects placed considerable emphasis on facilitating ocean governance in the WCR (Mahon et al., 2014).

This governance focus began by examining the emerging situation and considering the options available. Conventional approaches to regional ocean governance have usually been oriented towards establishing a single organisation or commission, created by a binding treaty, with responsibility and authority to pursue transboundary ocean governance (Duda, 2016). It was recognised early on that this was probably not feasible for a complex region such as the WCR in which a great deal had already been invested in many multilateral organisations. Consequently, the approach to governance arrangements in the WCR was based on emerging ideas that take a broader view of possibilities for functional governance systems than has conventionally been applied to transboundary situations. The emerging approach in the Caribbean follows more of an adaptive governance model in which control is decentralised and flexibility of response is emphasised. Although just two years old, the Interim Coordination Mechanism (ICM) formed under the CLME+ Project as a precursor to a permanent mechanism has played an important role in advancing regional cooperation for ocean governance. Analysis of regional ocean governance globally has since demonstrated that many regions have encountered similar circumstances to those found in the WCR and are following a similar path (Mahon and Fanning, 2019b).

110 *Lucia Fanning and Robin Mahon*

Operationalising regional ocean governance in the Caribbean

In seeking to operationalise the decentralised or networked regional ocean governance approach mentioned above, it was noted that the key component of governance policy coordination and harmonisation was absent. The system had been emerging on its own in a somewhat haphazard way. It was therefore thought that an appropriate direction for the CLME Project would be to rationalise and guide the emerging ocean governance regime by:

1 developing a conceptual framework at the LME level for regional ocean governance in the WCR, based on current governance research and theory;
2 using the framework to assess the governance arrangements in the WCR;
3 formulating the next phase of the project to guide efforts to improve regional ocean governance in the WCR.

The conceptual framework

The LME Governance Framework was developed for the WCR to capture the key features of transboundary governance that could be assessed and strengthened (Fanning et al., 2007). The framework emphasises governance architecture as the context for governance processes and interactions. It is based on linked policy cycles operating geographically at multiple levels (local, national, regional and global) (Figure 9.2). The framework emphasises the importance of having complete and functional policy cycles that address specific issues and are linked vertically and laterally. The suite of governance arrangements needed to address specific issues in the WCR, and their interactions, make up the ocean governance regime. This regime and the performance of the arrangements that comprise it were assessed with a view to developing interventions to improve its structure and effectiveness. The long-term goal is a suite of functional arrangements with appropriate policy cycles and interactions within and between arrangements (Fanning et al., 2007). While the LME Governance Framework is a simplification of a complex situation, it aims to depict and communicate the core ideas of scale, process and interaction in a way that stakeholders can use to understand the relationship between individual governance arrangements and the overall governance regime and ultimately get involved in assessing and improving them.

The first full phase of the CLME Project was based on the LME Governance Framework. It (a) assessed the extent to which the network of governance arrangements that had emerged could be considered complete and comprehensive, and (b) explored applicability of the framework in the WCR through "learning by doing" pilot projects and case studies (UNDP, 2008). The assessment provided a considerably improved understanding of the functioning of ocean governance in the WCR. The LME Governance Framework was tailored to the requirements of the WCR as determined by the

Regional ocean governance 111

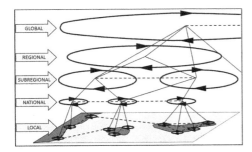

Figure 9.2 Graphical representation of the Large Marine Ecosystem Governance Framework showing (left) the need for process at multiple levels, lateral and vertical linkages among them, and (right) the stages of the policy process that are required for effective governance.
Source: Mahon et al. (2014)

assessment and the experience of the pilots. These were combined to produce a Regional Governance Framework (RGF) for the WCR (Mahon et al., 2014). The geopolitical complexity of the region and the nested, multi-scale and multi-level nature of the living marine resources and the ecosystems that support them, led to a set of nested arrangements at both operational and policy levels (Figure 9.3).

A 10-year Strategic Action Programme (SAP) was developed to address the identified governance deficiencies. Strengthening the framework involved by engaging the key organisations to determine if they were willing to: (a) continue these roles; (b) expand their mandates and activities to take up appropriate functions within the framework; and (c) develop the interactions and linkages that would be essential if the framework was to function effectively. Particular attention was paid to the need for overarching architecture that would integrate the issue-specific arrangements within the WCR. The SAP took a "learning by doing' approach to strengthening governance (CLME, 2013; Debels et al., 2017). Strategies focused on:

- developing a mechanism for overall coordination of ocean affairs in the WCR;
- a regional mechanism for environmental issues; namely pollution and biodiversity;
- a regional mechanism for fisheries;
- specific activities to strengthen transboundary governance of selected resources and sub regions;
- a monitoring programme for SAP implementation based on the Governance Effectiveness Assessment Framework (GEAF) (Mahon et al., 2017).

The SAP was signed by ministers in 25 countries in 2014, which led to the provision of US$12.5 million in funding from the GEF to catalyse its implementation over five years. The resulting CLME+ Project began in 2015 and ends in 2020. Implementation is primarily through the key regional and sub-regional partners, with the Project Coordinating Unit (PCU) and the ICM, comprising the key IGOs, in a coordinating role, pending the identification and operationalisation of the permanent mechanism. Implementation of the SAP has helped elevate the discourse on regional ocean governance among countries.

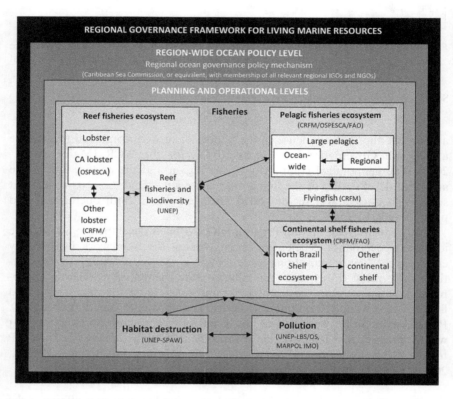

Figure 9.3 Diagram of the nested, multi-scale level nature of the proposed operational Regional Governance Framework for living marine resources in the WCR.
Notes: (a) Likely lead organisations for arrangements are shown in parentheses. (b) Nesting implies that there are vertical linkages with the overarching entity. (c) Nesting

Interactions among the initiatives

Since the RGF focuses on the overall coordination of activities oriented towards sustainable use of oceans in order to minimise inefficiency of resource use, close collaboration among these initiatives is highly desirable. This has been the case between the OECS initiative and the current CLME+ Project.

The OECS Commission, represented by its Ocean Governance & Fisheries Coordinator, is a partner in CLME+ SAP implementation and a member of the ICM. There is significant effort underway to align the two programmes. In contrast to the OECS, the degree of interaction between the ACS/CSC and the CLME Projects has been limited. During the first full phase of the CLME Projects the Secretary General represented the ACS on the Steering Committee, with a strong commitment to having the CSC play a central role in regional ocean governance (ACS/CERMES-UWI, 2010). Following the veto of this role at the end of the first full phase by the US, the CSC has been less engaged as previously mentioned. Another source of disconnect between the CSC and the CLME Initiative is national representation. The CSC is primarily addressed through ministries of foreign affairs, whereas the CLME Initiative is through ministries of fisheries and environment. There is often limited interaction among these ministries at the national level, and this impacts directly on the level of collaboration on these initiatives.

The situation described above reflects the generally limited arrangements in place at the national level for integration across ocean sectors (McConney et al., 2016), which also results in a weak interface between national and regional level initiatives. If not improved, this will limit the effectiveness of the regional initiatives described above. In this regard, the OECS's focus on the establishment of National Ocean Committees is a welcome and leading development in the region. The CLME+ Project has a focus on strengthening national level integration mechanisms and has been making slow but steady progress. This focus is expected to continue into subsequent initiatives in the region.

Lessons learned with establishing regional ocean governance

Key lessons derived from pursuing an adaptive approach to regional ocean governance in the Caribbean relate to country capacity, tensions between regional mandates and national sovereignty.

Supporting aspects

Several factors have contributed to the acceptance of the RGF and SAP by the countries and regional organisations in the WCR. Foremost is the prominent role of regional ocean governance organisations in the CLME Initiative from the outset. They were included by conceiving regional ocean governance in the WCR as a network of arrangements addressing the diversity of issues. In this context, the key regional and sub-regional organisations in the WCR with responsibility for sustainable use of the ocean were engaged so that the mandates and activities of these organisations, and their inter-relationships, were understood and accommodated in operationalising the RGF. Another key factor was the development of a conceptual framework that stakeholders could understand and work with, but that still accommodated critical governance concepts. The framework allowed the complex

114   *Lucia Fanning and Robin Mahon*

situation to be broken down into components for assessment and development of remedial interventions. It allowed organisational actors to see the system as a whole and their role within it; including what needed to be done to enhance their capacity to play that role. A third supporting feature was that from the outset, the process emphasised that the long-term success of regional ocean governance was the collective responsibility of the regional organisational partners. It sought to put them in the lead and to facilitate their cooperation, rather than taking on the persona of a pseudo-regional organisation as large projects often do.

Challenges

The process was not without challenges. In the context of the CLME Initiative, the governance focus brought unfamiliar vocabulary and ideas into the arena. Countries were inclined to send technical representatives with backgrounds in fisheries and environmental sciences. Therefore, governance concepts such as architecture, nesting, subsidiarity, institutional arrangements, etc., were unfamiliar to many. The other major concern of countries has been to avoid establishing another regional institution that will require financial support. Therefore, sustainable financing that does not depend on country contributions has been a priority in designing the coordination mechanism. Regional organisations were also at times uncomfortable with these concepts or with an RGF that might constrain their flexibility. Some were concerned that buying in to the framework might place demands upon them that they did not have the capacity to support. Consequently, at times, organisations tried to fit the CLME activities into their ongoing programmes, rather than to adjust the programmes to accommodate what they had agreed to in the context of the CLME Initiative. The concept of an overarching policy coordination mechanism for the WCR also caused some initial concern among regional organisations. This lingered until it was clear that the objective was not to create a new organisation that would direct and dictate to the existing regional organisations, but rather to create a mechanism for policy coordination that included all existing organisations. At the national level, although countries are currently engaged, the long time-frame for fully implementing a regional approach to governance in the WCR may mean that implementation is given low priority as countries are forced to deal with more pressing issues. Another major challenge is the prevalence of territories and overseas departments that share marine space and resources but whose engagement is not supported by their metropolitan countries. Lastly, while this chapter does not seek to expand on the political tensions between the USA and Venezuela or Cuba, this has exacerbated efforts aimed at a fully integrated regionalised approach as the latter two countries have had limited engagement in the CLME+ Project. Challenges such as those described above can be expected to re-emerge as implementation of the SAP proceeds and personnel change. They will require on-going management.

Conclusion – the way ahead with the RGF and SAP

The assessment of regional ocean governance arrangements and the development of an RGF and SAP to facilitate effective regional ocean governance for the WCR are first steps only. This is a long-term initiative with a decadal timeframe. Much remains to be done conceptually and practically with implementation of the framework. There is also the need to ensure adaptability and resilience in the ocean governance initiatives for the WCR. The threat of climate change continues to evolve and requires flexibility to address emerging issues. Taking the framework as the way forward with ocean governance in the WCR, it is important to view it as a whole and to focus on building and strengthening the entire system. To achieve this, the reliance on project funding, as has been the case so far, will need to transition to more sustainable sources of financing.

Despite the apparent political acceptance of the LME Governance Framework and the RGF through endorsement of the CLME+ SAP, there is still a great deal of awareness building needed, both nationally and among regional organisations, to mainstream it into the activities of the key players. The current emphasis on living marine resources means that only ministries of fisheries and/or environment have been integrally involved in the work of the CLME Projects. Foreign affairs, tourism, energy (oil and gas) and marine transportation are other key ministries whose awareness and engagement will be critical. In the long term, all ocean-use activities must be brought into the RGF if it is to be comprehensive and complete. The planned development of a CLME Partnership as well as two complementary SAPs for civil society and the private sector have the potential to contribute significantly to this engagement.

The WCR experience indicates that conventional approaches to ocean governance in the form of commissions based on binding agreements may not be appropriate in complex regions where countries are diverse in terms of size, wealth and power. For the WCR and possibly for other regions as well, it is important to recognise that capacities and interests among countries and regional organisations may differ sufficiently to preclude a binding arrangement that covers the entire range of ocean issues. Nonetheless, as shown here, this does not preclude efforts to develop and implement more effective regional ocean governance.

Notes

1 See www.clmeproject.org
2 At the overarching level in the WCR, there are four regional political integration organisations: (1) the Caribbean Community (CARICOM) formed in 1973 by 12 former British colonies and Montserrat (a UK overseas territory), and subsequently joined by Suriname and Haiti; (2) the Organisation of Eastern Caribbean States (OECS) formed in by ten island nations in the Eastern Caribbean, all CARICOM Member States; (3) the Central American Integration System (SICA) formed by

116 Lucia Fanning and Robin Mahon

seven countries in Central America and the Dominican Republic; (4) the Association of Caribbean States (ACS), comprising all countries in the region with the exception of the United States of America.
3 http://www.acs-aec.org/index.php?q=csc.
4 Revised Treaty of Basseterre Establishing the OECS Economic Union. http://www.oecs.org/lsu-resources?task=document.viewdoc&id=679.

References

ACS/CERMES-UWI. 2010. *Report of the Expert Consultation on the Operationalisation of the Caribbean Sea Commission: Building a Science-Policy Interface for Ocean Governance in the Wider Caribbean.* CERMES Technical Report No. 33. University of the West Indies, Cave Hill Campus, Barbados, 7–9 July. 90 pp.

Berry, D. S. 2014. *Caribbean Integration Law.* Oxford: Oxford University Press.

Caribbean Development Bank (CDB). 2018. *Financing the Blue Economy: A Caribbean Development Opportunity.* Barbados: Caribbean Development Bank.

CLME Project. 2013. *The Strategic Action Programme for the Sustainable Management of the Shared Living Marine Resources of the Caribbean and North Brazil Shelf Large Marine Ecosystems (CLME+SAP).* Cartagena, Colombia: The UNDP/GEF Caribbean Large Marine Ecosystem and Adjacent Areas (CLME) Project, 123 pp.

CLME. 2011. *Caribbean Large Marine Ecosystem Regional Transboundary Diagnostic Analysis.* Cartagena, Colombia: The Caribbean Large Marine Ecosystem and Adjacent Areas (CLME) Project, 153 pp.

Debels, P., Fanning, L., Mahon, R., *et al.* 2017. The CLME+ Strategic Action Programme: An ecosystems approach for assessing and managing the Caribbean Sea and North Brazil Shelf large marine ecosystems. *Environmental Development*, 22: 191–205.

Duda, A. M. 2016. Strengthening global governance of large marine ecosystems by incorporating coastal management and marine protected areas. *Environmental Development*, 17: 249–263.

Fanning, L. and Mahon, R. 2017. *Implementing the Ocean SDG in the Wider Caribbean: State of Play and Possible Ways Forward.* IASS, IDDRI, & TMG. Available at https://www.gstss.org/2018_Ocean_SDGs/documents/Fanning-Mahon%202017%20Ocean%20SDG%20in%20the%20Wider%20Caribbean.pdf.

Fanning, L., Mahon, R., McConney, P. *et al.* 2007. A large marine ecosystem governance framework. *Marine Policy*, 31: 434–443.

Fanning, L., Mahon, R. and McConney, P. 2011. *Towards Marine Ecosystem-based Management in the Wider Caribbean.* Amsterdam: Amsterdam University Press.

Mahon, R. and Fanning, L. 2019a. Regional ocean governance: Polycentric arrangements and their role in global ocean governance. *Marine Policy*, 107, https://doi.org/10.1016/j.marpol.2019.103590.

Mahon, R. and Fanning, L. 2019b. Regional ocean governance: Integrating and coordinating mechanisms for polycentric systems. *Marine Policy*, 107, https://doi.org/10.1016/j.marpol.2019.103589.

Mahon, R., Fanning, L. and McConney, P. 2014. Assessing and facilitating emerging regional ocean governance arrangements in the Wider Caribbean Region. *Ocean Yearbook*, Leiden, Brill, 28: 631–671.

Mahon, R., Fanning, L. and McConney, P. 2017. Assessing governance performance in transboundary water systems. *Environmental Development*, 24: 146–155.

McConney, P., Monnereau I., Simmons, B. and Mahon, R. 2016. *Report on the Survey of National Intersectoral Coordination Mechanisms.* Report prepared for the CLME + Project by the Centre for Resource Management and Environmental Studies, University of the West Indies, Cave Hill Campus, Barbados. 74 pp.

Oxenford, H. A. and Monnereau, I. 2018. Chapter 9: Climate change impacts, vulnerabilities and adaptations: Western Central Atlantic marine fisheries. In: Barange, M., Bahri, T., Beveridge, et al. (Eds), *Impacts of Climate Change on Fisheries and Aquaculture: Synthesis of Current Knowledge, Adaptation and Mitigation Options*, pp. 147–168. FAO Fisheries Technical Paper 627.

Parris, N. 2016. The Caribbean Sea Commission (CSC): defining the 'Special Area'. *Social and Economic Studies*, 65: 145–151.

Patil, P. G., Virdin, J., Diez, S. M., Roberts, J. and Singh, A. 2016. *Toward a Blue Economy: A Promise for Sustainable Growth in the Caribbean: An Overview.* Washington, DC: The World Bank.

Singh, A. and Mee, L. 2008. Examination of policies and MEAs commitment by SIDS for sustainable management of the Caribbean Sea. *Marine Policy*, 32: 274–282.

UNDP. 2008. *Sustainable Management of the Shared Living Marine Resources of the Caribbean Large Marine Ecosystem (CLME) and Adjacent Regions.* UNDP/UNOPS/GEF Project Document. New York: United Nations, 106 pp.

UNEP. 1983. *Cartagena Convention.* Available at http://cep.unep.org/cartagena-convention/text-of-the-cartagena-convention.

UNGA. 2019. *Towards the Sustainable Development of the Caribbean Sea for Present and Future Generations.* UN General Assembly Resolution A/RES/73/229. New York. Available at https://digitallibrary.un.org/record/1660785.

10 Fisheries as a key component of Blue Economies in the Wider Caribbean

Hazel A. Oxenford and Patrick McConney

Introduction

The Wider Caribbean is characterised by multi-species, multi-gear, small-scale fisheries (SSF) supporting coastal community food security and livelihoods, and in the case of some high-value species (e.g. tunas, conch, lobster, shrimps), also larger-scale fisheries with significant national export earnings. Fisheries employ hundreds of thousands of directly dependent fisherfolk and indirectly dependent fishery workers in the harvest sector, post-harvest sector and fisheries-linked industries across the region (Oxenford and Monnereau, 2018). Fisheries are particularly critical to low income and pro-poor labour force mobility. They often serve as a social safety net in the 29 small island developing states (SIDS) within the Caribbean, where productive agricultural land and alternative employment opportunities may be extremely limited or seasonal, and national economies are particularly vulnerable to external shocks (global economic conditions, international fuel prices, natural hazards *inter alia*) including climate variability and change (Monnereau et al., 2017).

Further and more sustainable development of the fisheries sector is an essential component of any Blue Economy (Cohen et al., 2019). However, fisheries are poorly recognised and rewarded for their substantial contribution to social and economic growth in this region. This contribution is both direct, and through intersectoral linkages such as with the tourism and hospitality industries that are the fragile mainstay of many small Caribbean economies (Clegg et al., Chapter 11 this volume). Valuing, managing and integrating sustainable fisheries into the Blue Economy will require: (1) addressing the reasons for the general perception of low value attributed to the sector; (2) tackling the current issues threatening the sustainability of fisheries; and (3) investing in the support of responsible fisheries with value-added fishery products having intersectoral linkages to deliver more societal benefits.

The first point requires attention to collection of fishery data, full analysis of these data, greener national accounting and better information sharing at all levels within and among countries. The second point requires that countries address critical issues such as the common practice of allowing open access, which inevitably leads to severe resource depletion, habitat damage

Fisheries   119

from land-based activities (particularly in the case of shallow-shelf, coral-associated resources), and low management capacity. The third point indicates the most promising direction for further development of the fishing industry in this region; a complete sustainable fisheries value chain approach with active intersectoral linkages. Although there are already efforts to address these issues, a strong fishery sector in the Blue Economy will require more and better attention to ensure that all three complex points are adequately tackled.

Fisheries overview

Importance of fisheries

The fishing industry, with its long and productive history, is a well-established sector within the economies of the Wider Caribbean. It has a critical role to play in the emerging Blue Economies of this ocean-dominated region.

Diverse fisheries fleets and resources

The fishing industry of the Wider Caribbean is dominated by SSF operating with privately owned vessels close to home, targeting multiple species with a variety of non-specific, artisanal gear. Most fishers are considered to be commercial, although some are entirely subsistence fishers. There is also an unknown, but likely substantial, number of recreational fishers that are poorly documented throughout the region (Southwick et al., 2016), except perhaps in the USA, where licensing is mandatory. There are also some semi-industrial and a few large-scale industrial fleets, mostly operating within the exclusive economic zones (EEZs) of the Wider Caribbean, from South and Central America and especially in the Gulf of Mexico (Oxenford and Monnereau, 2018).

The Wider Caribbean is one of the most bio-diverse areas of the world's oceans (Linardich et al., 2017), supporting an enormous diversity of finfish and shellfish, many of which are commercially important. They can be categorised into five multi-species groups that are targeted by different fisheries: (1) coastal benthic and coral reef-associated species which include over 100 finfish species and high-value invertebrates such as queen conch, spiny lobster, blue crab, American cupped oyster and octopuses; (2) coastal schooling pelagic finfishes including sardines, pilchards, scads and jacks; (3) continental shelf shrimps and groundfishes including penaeid shrimps and weakfishes; (4) deep-slope benthic finfishes including deep-water grouper and snapper species; and (5) open ocean, highly migratory, pelagic finfishes including surface species (e.g. dolphinfish, wahoo, flyingfish) and subsurface species (e.g. large tunas, sharks, billfishes).

The Wider Caribbean encompasses distinctly different biogeographic regions; notably four Large Marine Ecosystems (Caribbean Sea, North Brazil

120   Hazel A. Oxenford and Patrick McConney

Shelf, Gulf of Mexico and Southeast USA Shelf), and the open ocean of the Western Central Atlantic with very different marine environments and fishery production potential. It is also one of the most geopolitically complex regions of the world, comprising 28 nation states and 16 territories belonging to the UK, USA, Netherlands and France with a complex mosaic of adjoining EEZs where states have exclusive rights over fishery resources. Consequently, most commercially important fishery resources are shared among two or more (often multiple) states, when boundaries dissect the stock's natural ranges, or when adults or early life history stages migrate or are dispersed across boundaries by water currents.

Appreciating fisheries assets

Annual fishery production in the Wider Caribbean (Caribbean Sea, Gulf of Mexico and North Brazil/Guianas shelf) is currently around 1.9 million tonnes, with 80% from marine capture fisheries (WECAFC, 2019a). However, the real value may be considerably higher, as significant under-reporting is likely given the high proportion of unmonitored SSF across the region (WECAFC, 2019a). The current yield is lower than recorded landings in the early 1980s, and this is largely explained by a significant reduction in foreign fleets fishing in the region following the establishment of EEZs under the United Nations Convention on the Law of the Sea (UNCLOS). Catches from this region have always represented a relatively small contribution to global fish yield, reflecting the typically low biological productivity of tropical and sub-tropical ocean waters (Die and Rodriguez Casariego, 2016). However, the fisheries sector remains vitally important, contributing significantly to nutrition and food security, supporting livelihoods in coastal communities, and in the case of some high-value species such as conch, lobster and shrimp, providing significant export earnings in countries like Guyana, Jamaica and The Bahamas. The sector is also important for tourism, a major economic sector in the Caribbean, providing recreational fishing opportunities and local seafood (CRFM, 2016). The fisheries sector employs hundreds of thousands of fisherfolk in harvesting, post-harvest activities and associated industries regionwide (Oxenford and Monnereau, 2018; WECAFC, 2019a). Whilst harvesting is male dominated, women are central in post-harvest activities (GIFT, 2017). Indigenous fisherfolk play a significant role on the Caribbean coast of Central America (WECAFC, 2019a). Data for 37 states suggest that there are more than 754,000 marine fishers in the region, and the SSF sector is crucial for livelihoods. In some rural areas at least 15% of the work force is engaged in the harvest and post-harvest activities (WECAFC, 2019a). Ancillary activities provide an additional three million jobs, and the annual gross revenue from fisheries and aquaculture in the Wider Caribbean was estimated at US$6.9 billion in 2012 (Patil et al., 2016).

Many fisheries-dependent communities live a precarious and vulnerable existence because of poverty, and inadequate public services and essential infrastructure (McConney et al., 2016). For them, fisheries are an essential social safety net, especially after natural disasters or significant external shocks to other key employment sectors such as tourism and agriculture, when they help avert poverty and food insecurity. Fisheries are particularly critical to the livelihoods, diets and wellbeing in the 29 Caribbean SIDS, which are particularly vulnerable to external shocks including climate variability and change (Monnereau et al., 2017). Furthermore, fishing is important to the culture of SIDS populations. For example, in Barbados, flyingfish is part of the island's identity (featured on the currency, in national passports, in the national dish, and tourism and business logos). Elsewhere, conch or lobster may be iconic, such that fishing holds deep cultural value which has potential to add to the tourism product.

Threats and challenges

It is vital to fully appreciate that many of the serious threats and challenges that face fisheries worldwide are also evident in the Wider Caribbean. These must be addressed for fisheries to become sustainable. Many threats and challenges are situation specific, but some issues are crosscutting.

Status of fishery resources

Insufficient and unreliable data on fish landings and fishing effort is typical of SSF, since they do not require centralised facilities, are often widely dispersed and are difficult and expensive to monitor. Data-poor fisheries are difficult to assess, which contributes to management challenges faced in the region (WECAFC, 2019a). Although formal assessment of the status of commercial fishery stocks is very limited in this region (Singh-Renton and McIvor, 2015), the majority of stocks are considered fully or over-exploited, whilst a few are under stock-rebuilding programmes (NOAA, 2019; WECAFC, 2019a). It is also considered that marine habitats essential for commercially important fishery species have suffered significant degradation from localised, mostly land-based, anthropogenic stressors (e.g. increased sediment, nutrient and pollutant loading of coastal waters) over the last three decades (Burke et al., 2011; Jackson et al., 2014), thus lowering their capacity to support and sustain fish biomass (Oxenford and Mahon, Chapter 4 this volume). Climate variability and change is also negatively impacting critical fishery habitats, particularly coral reefs, but also the open ocean. This compromises production potential of commercially important species through loss of habitat, and through biophysical changes to the species that affect their life cycles (Oxenford and Monnereau, 2017; Taylor et al., Chapter 5 this volume). Most commercially important fishery species are expected to be under high conservation risk, regardless of the carbon emission pathway followed over the next few decades, as their habitats will become increasingly unsuitable (Cheung et al., 2019). Consequently, the outlook for fishery production in this region is one of expected decline, with the coastal benthic and coral reef-associated species, that support the majority of Caribbean fisheries livelihoods, being most severely affected in the short term (Oxenford and Monnereau, 2018; Cheung et al., 2019).

Management scale mismatches

Fisheries governance is weak in most Caribbean countries especially for SSF. Shared resources require collaborative management, yet there is no overall Regional Fishery Management Organisation (RFMO) serving this region, although the efforts of the Western Central Atlantic Fishery Commission (WECAFC) and two sub-regional organisations in fisheries management are well recognised. These include the Caribbean Regional Fishery Mechanism (CFRM) with 17 members and the Fisheries and Aquaculture Organisation for Central America (OSPESCA) with 8 Central American members plus the Dominican Republic. Recently, they have adopted harmonised regulations and/or regional or sub-regional management plans for several key fishery species (flyingfish 2014, conch 2015, lobster 2015 and billfishes 2018. However, there are few fully operational institutional arrangements for shared management. Even highly migratory species that are shared Atlantic-wide (e.g. large tuna and billfish species) and under the management authority of the International Commission for the Conservation of Atlantic Tunas (ICCAT) are over-exploited and under stock-rebuilding plans (WECAFC, 2019a).

Access, tenure and enforcement

Most fisheries in the region are open access, which has typically resulted in over-exploitation (WECAFC, 2019a). Where fishery regulations do exist, there is often little enforcement capacity (largely through inadequate budgets) and/or insufficient political or public sector will to enforce. This causes a low level of fisheries management performance nationally and regionally for most of the region's commercially important fisheries (Singh-Renton and McIvor, 2015). Most species do not even have national or sub-regional fishery management plans. There are some notable exceptions such as conch in Jamaica (Aiken et al., 2006).

Low enforcement capacity, low penalties and in many cases the close proximity of adjacent EEZs, contributes to illegal, unreported, unregulated (IUU) fishing. IUU fishing is commonplace, particularly within and among Wider Caribbean states (domestic vessels in their own national waters; vessels from other regional countries in national waters) and also international high seas fleets (CRFM, 2014). IUU landings in this region are thought to be 20–30% of reported landings with an annual value of US$700–930 million (FAO, 2018). As elsewhere in the world, IUU fishing has contributed significantly to fishery depletion and undermines national and regional efforts to manage fisheries sustainably and to conserve marine biodiversity. IUU fishing, often for the most lucrative species, puts legitimate fishers and entire fisheries value chains at an unfair disadvantage, robbing coastal communities of livelihoods, market share, well-being and threatening food security. Furthermore, some instances of IUU fishing in the Caribbean have been associated with transnational organised crime and violations of labour laws and human rights (CRFM, 2014).

Fractured value chains

The concept of a fisheries value chain is often incorrectly taken as a linear production line. In a Blue Economy it more resembles chainmail, or a rather more intricately networked conceptual framework of how fisheries fit into ecosystem-based, intersectoral development. In order to advance, we must first identify fractures in the network.

Intersectoral integration

Fisheries sector development, especially in Caribbean SIDS, is hampered by the lack of the integrated legal, policy and planning framework needed to address fisheries value chains alone and together with interconnected economic sectors. This is not only about governance (McConney and Compton, Chapter 8 and Fanning and Mahon, Chapter 9 this volume); it concerns technical and economic ties such as between fisheries and aquaculture which are seldom integrated and may even compete. Given the stagnation of capture fisheries worldwide, aquaculture has become the major growth sector in aquatic food production globally. Consequently, there is increasing interest in financing aquaculture investment in the Caribbean, especially for high-priced, export-oriented species (CDB, 2018). One of the challenges for the Blue Economy will be to ensure that aquaculture expansion is sustainable, taking advantage of ecosystem-based management and ecosystem approaches to aquaculture. Development opportunities in SIDS aquaculture are challenged *inter alia* by limited land, coastal and marine space; environmental concerns; and maintaining economic viability in global trade. All these are exacerbated by the limited understanding of the aquaculture sector's potential and its contributions to socio-economic development as a complement to marine fisheries.

Links to tourism have been mentioned several times. However, we see persistent socio-cultural barriers to integration with fisheries in locations where the cultural significance of fisheries value chains is not appreciated. This extends from the tourist-attracting artisan craftsmanship of wooden boat-building to the culinary experiences of Caribbean cooking at the other end of the value chain. Although fisheries have recently become better embedded in tourism food service, the emphasis is still on harvest rather than developing the entire value chain with linkages. Similar can be said for services such as

124 *Hazel A. Oxenford and Patrick McConney*

water-taxi and yacht provisioning services offered part-time by fishers. The significant roles played by women and indigenous communities in fisheries is also currently overlooked in labour force planning across sectors.

Undervaluing the value chain

The Wider Caribbean is a net importer of fishery products, with net imports rising sharply in the decade 2003–2013 to around 250,000 tonnes (WECAFC, 2019a). The economic deficit between fish imports and exports is, however, relatively small due to the high value of the regions' export species (shrimp, lobster, conch), but still reached an estimated US$42 million in 2017 (WECAFC, 2019a). Thus, in considering value chains there is need to carefully consider policies on fish export/import. Fish consumption per capita is very high in some Caribbean SIDS (e.g. Guyana, Montserrat, Turks and Caicos) although below global average across the whole region (WECAFC, 2019a). Seafood production, consumption and trade statistics do not, however, measure all facets of fisheries value chains.

Linking back to the first of the three main points in this chapter, the undervaluation of SSF in particular with regard to actual landings, social safety net, etc. results in the entire value chain having low political priority and receiving inadequate development support. Many countries do not have a fisheries policy and so cannot use it to integrate fisheries into the Blue Economy. National accounts communicate that fisheries' overall contribution to GDP in the region is low, on average around 1%, but measuring the real contribution requires better accounting to capture the entire value chain. According to the CRFM (2014):

> The fisheries sector in CRFM member countries provides a range of benefits to the region, including employment, poverty alleviation, food security and foreign exchange earnings. Some of these benefits are not sufficiently understood and valued. Additionally, fisheries issues are usually managed under the general portfolio of agriculture, but are often marginalised, and as a consequence, attract low investment. This low investment has stifled the advancement of statistics, research, and development for supporting resource management, technological developments and marketing and trade. At present, land and marine space use and planning do not reflect holistic consideration of the various sectoral needs, with low priority given to fisheries and aquaculture.

A way forward: securing fisheries in a Blue Economy

As a way forward, fisheries sector development in the Wider Caribbean Blue Economy will need to focus on: (1) acknowledging the true value of fisheries to social and economic development in order to attract the necessary support;

(2) institutionalising sustainable ecosystem-based management that considers climate change and other uncertainties; and (3) unlocking the potential for adding socio-economic value to fisheries by supporting responsible innovation and closer intersectoral linkages.

Valuing fisheries differently

Improving and acknowledging the value of fisheries requires comprehensive sex-disaggregated data to quantify the value of the industry (participants, dependants, costs and earnings along the value chain, investment performance, economic multipliers, etc.), allowing evidence-based analysis to guide policy (e.g. whether to support development of no-take recreational fishery, sell catch on the local market or export, develop a particular fleet type, etc.).

Adopting data-poor management approaches that include better use of "traditional" (mainly fisherfolk) knowledge is essential for the best information. As countries invest in new technologies (e.g. smartphone apps) and open data to improve data collection and analysis, it is likely that such improvements can be cost-effective and not burdensome.

Subsidies that promote fisheries' over-capitalisation at any point along the value chain should be eliminated, discouraged or linked to promotion of responsible fishing practices, development of value-added fishery products and other necessary short-term incentives to support longer-term adaptation and changes in practices. Enhanced national accounting can ensure that the value of fisheries is not masked by subsidies that cause problems in regional and international trade and other arenas.

Fisherfolk organisations can be key in enhancing the value of fisheries, which is important for their self-image and policy influence. Recent initiatives include regional and local fisherfolk organising for collective action and influence, as well as demonstrating leadership in the implementation of instruments such as the Voluntary Guidelines for Securing Sustainable Small-Scale Fisheries in the Context of Food Security and Poverty Eradication (SSF Guidelines, FAO, 2015) (McConney et al., 2017). Costa Rica is a leading example of using the SSF Guidelines to actively implement fisheries policy, and the CRFM countries have similar intentions.

Sustaining fisheries improvement

The means of implementing and sustaining fisheries improvement vary with location, situation, period and actors involved. Here we focus on a few of the critical aspects that are closely linked to the Blue Economy concept. The CLME + Strategic Action Programme (SAP) is an ecosystem-based approach for assessing and managing the Caribbean Sea and North Brazil Shelf Large Marine Ecosystems with a major focus on fisheries, that is highly compatible with enabling Blue Economy initiatives (Debels et al., 2017). Many recommendations fit within the SAP (Mahon et al., 2014). Foremost is support for the formation of

126 *Hazel A. Oxenford and Patrick McConney*

a regional fisheries management organisation (RFMO) to coordinate the management of shared and straddling stocks not covered by other RFMOs.

An RFMO could facilitate implementation of the 2019 Regional Plan of Action to Prevent, Deter, and Eliminate IUU Fishing (RPOA-IUU) (WECAFC, 2019b) and adopt EBM/EAF for better integration of management across sectors to mitigate habitat degradation (largely from land-based sources) (Fanning et al., 2011). Binding decisions could implement measures to prevent unsustainable harvesting (or in some cases recovery of overfished resources) with catch, effort and access controls harmonised to scale-up sustainability (Selig et al., 2017). The RFMO could also provide a forum for information exchange and collective action among Wider Caribbean countries on a wide range of ecological, socio-economic and governance matters that do not require binding decisions. For example, countries may be encouraged to try new approaches to tenure and access that have shown promise, e.g. the Managed Access of Belize, quotas in the Jamaica industrial conch fishery, market-based incentives such as Marine Stewardship Council certification of Suriname and Guyana seabob fisheries.

Since climate change, extreme events and coastal pollution are all negatively impacting the fisheries sector (Monnereau and Oxenford, 2017; WECAFC, 2019a), countries have agreed that fisheries plans must have climate strategies and intersectoral approaches (McConney et al., 2015) that include mitigation and disaster risk management, such as through insurance (CCRIF SPC, 2019). Marine spatial planning (MSP) that incorporates coastal and fisheries management out to the limits of the EEZ, as being pursued through the Caribbean Regional Oceanscape Project (CROP), is also compatible with a Blue Economy. MSP can rationalise fisheries in conjunction with integrated coastal management, provide replenishment (e.g. via Marine Protected Areas) and establish fishing priority areas for tenure and equity, whilst reducing coastal conflicts (Inniss et al., Chapter 6 this volume). It is a major Blue Economy challenge to ensure that these initiatives involve fisheries stakeholders and satisfy the needs of fishers, in order to be truly successful over the long term (McConney et al., 2019). This reinforces the need for people-centred approaches that increase stakeholder involvement and responsibility in decision-making, to improve accountability, transparency, trust and compliance (Jentoft et al., 2018; Kalikoski et al., 2019).

Unlocking intersectoral investment

Blue Economy fisheries value chains must be highly adaptive to challenges such as climate-induced changes in species composition in multi-species fisheries, increased variability in catches and landings, loss of species due to migration and increased abundance of new species that will require flexibility in marketing, distribution and trade (Johnson et al., 2019). Given the mosaic of EEZs in the Wider Caribbean there should be both national and transboundary movement of people and capital between fisheries value chains and across marine industries in a regional fisheries Blue Economy. Value chain investment opportunities are improving in some areas such as the eastern Caribbean due to integration of fisheries into ocean governance with transboundary and intersectoral dimensions (Compton et al., 2017). OSPESCA countries also have far-reaching integration.

CRFM and OSPESCA countries have discussed strategies to harness Blue Economy benefits (CRFM, 2019). Global and regional instruments can help make fisheries sector investment more coherent when led by the industry participants. We see this as fisherfolk urge their countries to adopt and mainstream the SSF Guidelines, and in so doing develop a sense of dignity and worth (CRFM, 2014). Since the SSF Guidelines cover governance and tenure, value chains, decent work, post-harvest, trade, gender equality, disaster risk reduction, climate change, institutional collaboration, capacity development, monitoring, research and communication, they provide a comprehensive frame for moving forward. SSF Guidelines implementation will also deter marginalisation of fisherfolk groups and reduce management costs through fisherfolk organisation collaboration (McConney et al., 2017).

CRFM (2014) reminds that the value chain concept is used as a way to add value, improve food security, employment and socio-economic stability and domestic growth in countries, highlighting points at which to reduce high levels of imported food, increase production and strengthen competitiveness by providing a larger portion of the market share to fisherfolk. CRFM (2014) states that while enhancing fisherfolk input into intersectoral Blue Economy policy development and implementation, there should be parallel efforts to educate and engage the public about the potential of fisheries and aquaculture. This will make it easier for the fisheries sector to gain their support for successful policy implementation and attract new sectoral and intersectoral investment along the entire fisheries value chain.

Such investment includes value-added processing (filleting, loining, smoking, salting, fish burgers and sausages, etc.) as well as utilising current waste (fish offal for meal and silage, conch shells for craft, fish skins for leather, jewellery from lionfish "feathers" etc.). Reducing waste supports a circular Blue Economy. Marine recreational fisheries are underdeveloped throughout the region despite their significant contribution to the economy of some countries, e.g. USA, Bahamas. In the latter, recreational fisheries contribute more than US$500 million to the economy annually and employ 18,000 Bahamians (WECAFC, 2019a). Valuation of billfish recreational fisheries versus commercial fisheries reinforces the high value of the former that is often linked to niche tourism (Gentner and Whitehead, 2018. Countries should thus consider investing in recreational/charter boat fisheries through appropriate private sector incentives. Innovation in the sector could be supported to develop new or more energy efficient boat designs and equipment, potentially fuelling an increase in blue jobs. Newly commercial species being harvested as a result of sargassum and climate change may be prime candidates for value-added domestic or export markets following appropriate investment.

Conclusion

The Blue Economy thrust should be to harvest more responsibly and add value to the product. A frequent concern with the Blue Economy is that there will be too much emphasis on market-use values and large enterprises but too little on non-market values and small enterprises. This concern extends to a fear that Blue Economy may become synonymous with ocean grabbing and further marginalisation, especially of SSF (Cohen et al., 2019). This is not likely to be the case in the Wider Caribbean, which favours SSF (e.g. artisanal, subsistence and recreational) and agrees with Pauly (2018) that SSF are more consistent with Blue Economy than larger-scale fisheries. The prospects for fisheries becoming a key component in the Blue Economy are good, but only if SSF are properly valued, sustainably managed and attract new value chain investments.

References

Aiken, K., Kong, A., Smikle, S. *et al.* 2006. Managing Jamaica's queen conch resources. *Ocean and Coastal Management*, 49: 332–341.

Burke, L., Reytar, K., Spalding, M. and Perry, A. 2011. *Reefs at Risk Revisited.* Washington, DC: World Resources Institute. 130 pp.

CCRIF SPC. 2019. Caribbean countries to benefit from access to insurance for the fisheries sector. Available at: https://go.nature.com/2WLw5yD.

CDB. 2018. *Financing the Blue Economy: A Caribbean Development Opportunity.* Barbados: Caribbean Development Bank.

Cheung, W., Reygondeau, L., Wabnitz, G. *et al.* 2019. Climate change effects on Caribbean marine ecosystems and fisheries: Regional projections. *CRFM Research Paper Collection*, 9: 10–97.

Cohen, P., Allison, E. H., Andrew, N. L. *et al.* 2019. Securing a just space for small-scale fisheries in the blue economy. *Frontiers in Marine Science*, 6: 171. Available at: https://www.frontiersin.org/articles/10.3389/fmars.2019.00171/full.

Compton, S., McConney, P., Monnereau, I. *et al.* 2017. *Good Practice Guidelines for Successful National Intersectoral Coordination Mechanisms (NICs).* Report for the UNDP/ GEF CLME+ Project (2015–2020). CERMES Technical Report No. 88. 14 pp.

CRFM. 2014. *Report of the CRFM / CNFO / CTA Regional Fisheries Workshop: Investing in Blue Growth, St. George's, Grenada on 20–21 November 2014.* CRFM Technical & Advisory Document, No. 2014/5. 113 pp.

CRFM. 2016. *Promoting Regional Trade and Agribusiness Development in the Caribbean: Case Studies on Linking Fisheries to Tourism-Related Markets.* CRFM Technical & Advisory Document, No. 2016/3. Belize City. 101 pp.

CRFM. 2019. *Report and Proceedings of the Second High-Level CRFM & OSPESCA Ministerial Meeting, Belize City, Belize, 2 October.* Volume 2. CRFM Management Report PY 2019/20. 16 pp.

Debels, P., Fanning, L., Mahon, R. *et al.* 2017. The CLME+ Strategic Action Programme: An ecosystems approach for assessing and managing the Caribbean Sea and North Brazil Shelf large marine ecosystems. *Environmental Development*, 22: 191–205.

Die, D. and Rodriguez Casariego, J. 2016. *Review of the state of fisheries in the WECAFC region.* 16th Session of the Western Central Atlantic Fishery

Commission, Guadeloupe. WECAFC/XVI/2016/2. Available at: ftp://ftp.fao.org/FI/DOCUMENT/wecafc/16thsess/2e.pdf.

Fanning, L., Mahon, R. and McConney, P. 2011. *Towards Marine Ecosystem-Based Management in the Wider Caribbean*, Amsterdam: Amsterdam University Press.

FAO. 2015. *Voluntary Guidelines for Securing Sustainable Small-Scale Fisheries in the Context of Food Security and Poverty Eradication*. Rome: Food and Agriculture Organisation, 18 pp.

FAO Western Central Atlantic Fishery Commission. 2018. *Report of the First Meeting of the Regional Working Group on Illegal, Unreported and Unregulated (IUU) Fishing, Barbados, 1–2 March 2017*. FAO Fisheries and Aquaculture Report No. 1190. Bridgetown, Barbados.

Gentner, B. and Whitehead, J. 2018. *Expenditure and Willingness-to-Pay Survey of Caribbean Billfish Anglers: Summary Report*. FAO Fisheries and Aquaculture Circular No. 1168. Rome. 54 pp.

GIFT. 2017. *Gender Scoping Preliminary Report: Caribbean Fisheries in the Context of the Small-Scale Fisheries Guidelines*. Gender in Fisheries Team (GIFT), CERMES Technical Report No. 86. 64 pp.

Jackson, J. B. C., Donovan, M. K., Cramer, K. L. and Lam, V. V. (Eds). 2014. *Status and Trends of Caribbean Coral Reefs: 1970-2012*. Global Coral Reef Monitoring Network, Gland, Switzerland: IUCN. 304 pp.

Jentoft, S., Bavinck, M. and Alonso-Población, E. *et al.* 2018. Working together in small-scale fisheries: Harnessing collective action for poverty eradication. *Maritime Studies*, 17: 1–12. https://doi.org/10.1007/s40152-018-0094-8.

Johnson, J., Monnereau, I., and McConney, P. *et al.* 2019. Climate change adaptation: Vulnerability and challenges facing small-scale fisheries on small islands. In Johnson, J., De Young, C., Bahri, T. *et al.* (Eds) *Proceedings of FishAdapt: The Global Conference on Climate Change Adaptation for Fisheries and Aquaculture, Bangkok, 8–10 August, 2016*. FAO Fisheries and Aquaculture Proceedings No. 61. Rome: FAO. 240 pp.

Kalikoski, D. C., Jentoft, S., and McConney, P. *et al.* 2019. Empowering small-scale fishers to eradicate rural poverty. *Maritime Studies*, 18: 121–125. https://doi.org/10.1007/s40152-018-0112-x.

Linardich, C., Ralph, G., Carpenter, K. *et al.* 2017. *The conservation status of marine bony shorefishes of the Greater Caribbean*. Gland, Switzerland: IUCN. 75 pp.

Mahon, R., Fanning, L. and McConney, P. 2014. Assessing and facilitating emerging regional ocean governance arrangements in the Wider Caribbean Region. *Ocean Yearbook*, 28: 631–671.

McConney, P., Charlery, J., Pena, M. *et al.* 2015. *Disaster risk management and climate change adaptation in the CARICOM and wider Caribbean region – Formulating a strategy, action plan and programme for fisheries and aquaculture*. Regional Workshop,10–12 December 2012, Kingston, Jamaica. FAO Fisheries and Aquaculture Proceedings, No. 35. Rome. 123 pp.

McConney, P, Phillips, T., Lay, M. *et al.* 2016. Organizing for good fisheries governance. *Social and Economic Studies*, 65: 57–86.

McConney, P., Phillips, T., Nembhard, N. *et al.* 2017. Caribbean fisherfolk engage the small-scale fisheries guidelines, pp. 451–472 in Jentoft, S., Chuenpagdee, R., Barragán-Paladines, M.*et al.* (Eds), *The Small-Scale Fisheries Guidelines: Global implementation*. MARE Publication Series, Vol. 14. Cham: Springer.

McConney, P., Pereira Medeiros, R., Pascual-Fernández, J. L. *et al.* 2019. Stewardship and sustainable practices in small-scale fisheries. In Chuenpagdee, R. and Jentoft, S. (Eds), *Transdisciplinarity for Small-Scale Fisheries Governance*, pp. 181–201. MARE Publication Series, Vol. 21. Cham: Springer.

Monnereau, I., Mahon, R., McConney, P. *et al.* 2017. The impact of methodological choices on the outcome of national-level climate change vulnerability assessments: An example from the global fisheries sector. *Fish and Fisheries*, 18: 717–731.

Monnereau, I. and Oxenford, H. A. 2017. Impacts of climate change on fisheries in the coastal and marine environments of Caribbean Small Island Developing States (SIDS). Commonwealth Marine Economies Programme. *Caribbean Marine Climate Change Report Card: Science Review*, 2017: 124–154.

NOAA. 2019. *Status of stocks 2018: Annual Report to Congress on the Status of US Fisheries*. National Oceanographic and Atmospheric Administration, National Marine Fisheries Service, USA, 11 pp.

Oxenford, H. A. and Monnereau, I. 2017. Impacts of climate change on fish and shellfish in the coastal and marine environments of Caribbean small island developing states (SIDS) Commonwealth Marine Economies Programme. *Caribbean Marine Climate Change Report Card: Science Review*, 2017: 83–114.

Oxenford, H. A. and I. Monnereau. 2018. Chapter 9: Climate change impacts, vulnerabilities and adaptations: Western Central Atlantic marine fisheries. In: Barange, M., Bahri, T., Beveridge, M. *et al.* (Eds), *Impacts of Climate Change on Fisheries and Aquaculture: Synthesis of Current Knowledge, Adaptation and Mitigation Options*, pp. 147–168. FAO Fisheries Technical Paper 627.

Patil, P. G., Virdin, J., Diez, S. M. *et al.* 2016. *Toward a Blue Economy: A Promise for Sustainable Growth in the Caribbean*. Washington, DC: The World Bank, 91 pp.

Pauly, D. 2018. A vision for marine fisheries in a global blue economy. *Marine Policy*, 87: 371–374.

Selig, E. R., Kleisner, K. M., Ahoobim, O. *et al.* 2017. A typology of fisheries management tools: using experience to catalyse greater success. *Fish and Fisheries*, 18: 543–570.

Singh-Renton, S. and McIvor, I. 2015. *Review of Current Fisheries Management Performance and Conservation Measures in the WECAFC Area*. FAO Fisheries and Aquaculture Technical Paper No. 587, Bridgetown, Barbados. 293 pp.

Southwick, R., Maycock, D'S. and Bouaziz, M. 2016. *Recreational Fisheries Economic Impact Assessment Manual and its Application in Two Study Cases in the Caribbean: Martinique and The Bahamas*. FAO Fisheries and Aquaculture Circular 1128, SLC/FIAP/C1128. 107 pp.

WECAFC. 2019a. *State of fisheries and aquaculture in the WECAFC Area*. 17th Session of the Western Central Atlantic Fisheries Commission, Miami, Florida, USA, 15–18 July 2019, WECAFC/XVII/2019/02.

WECAFC. 2019b. *The Regional Plan of Action to Prevent, Deter and Eliminate Illegal, Unreported and Unregulated (IUU) Fishing in WECAFC Member Countries (2019–2029)*. 17th Session of the Western Central Atlantic Fisheries Commission, Miami, Florida, USA, 15–18 July 2019, WECAFC/XVII/2019/14.

11 Tourism in the Caribbean and the Blue Economy
Can the two be aligned?

*Peter Clegg, Janice Cumberbatch and
Karima Degia*

Introduction

The tourism industry is absolutely central to the economies of the Caribbean, and is thus extremely important within the Blue Economy agenda. Tourism is influenced heavily by domestic and external factors, including climate change, and thus must adjust to overcome, or at the very least mitigate, the challenges that are posed. Tourism also contributes to some of the negative issues related to environmental and social sustainability, and so changes must be made within those contexts too. This chapter provides an overview of why and how tourism developed in the Caribbean; its advantages and disadvantages to the region's economy today; the threats aligned against it; and how within the frame of the Blue Economy, the tourism industry can adjust to ensure its long-term sustainability. The chapter shows that despite numerous examples of creativity and initiative, much more needs to be done to safeguard and realign the industry in the Wider Caribbean.

Origins and development of the tourism industry

Tourism is now synonymous with the Caribbean, but that was not always the case. It is really over the last five decades that the industry has established itself, developed and transformed into what we see today. Up until the 1960s, tourism was a niche industry for the region; other sectors predominated, particularly agriculture and mineral extraction. With the exception of Haiti and the Dominican Republic, the links with the colonial powers remained strong, and much of the production and export that took place was directed towards Europe, and to a lesser extent the United States. Key agricultural exports, such as sugar, bananas and rum were well established, and under preferential arrangements saw decent rates of return and employed significant numbers of workers. In other countries such as Jamaica (bauxite) and Trinidad and Tobago (oil and natural gas) non-agricultural sectors were equally, if not more important, and these too were seen as key drivers towards development. It was at this time, of course, that many countries in the region were either gaining independence or at the very least more autonomy, and

132 *Peter Clegg et al.*

profound political and economic debates were taking place about how the Caribbean could break away from its perceived dependency on traditional exports and markets.

The work of Lloyd Best, a Trinidadian economist, and Sir Arthur Lewis, an economist from St Lucia, were highly influential at this time. They spoke of "Industrialisation by Invitation" – an attempt to reduce the reliance on agriculture in particular and to increase the range of employment opportunities. It was hoped that by establishing an attractive environment for foreign investment, foreign companies would move into the region and in time this would lead to self-sustaining growth in manufacturing. There were some successes, but clear limitations too. A little later, there were more radical ideas from the New World Group, linked to the University of the West Indies but whose influence extended beyond the English-speaking Caribbean, about how concerns over economic dependency could be more profoundly challenged. This group of academics, which included amongst them Lloyd Best, argued that small size should not be a constraint on development, rather strong and effective policy could alter fundamentally the way in which Caribbean economies operated. The work of the Group was prominent in the 1960s and 1970s, and certainly helped to guide the reformist programmes instituted in Jamaica and Grenada. However, by the early 1980s these ideas had been discredited (at least in the eyes of many) and also superseded by the strengthening wave of neoliberal thought, which was also undermining the concept of preference. So under these circumstances, many countries put greater emphasis on tourism, an industry that had already become an important feature of many economies in the region.

Indeed, from the 1960s with the growth of international air travel and the greater control over domestic economic planning, tourism's role in the Caribbean grew quickly. This was assisted by Cuba's withdrawal from the industry after the Revolution in 1959. The government in Havana felt that tourism embodied many of the failings in the economy and society that they wanted to overcome. But most other countries in the region subscribed to the argument of Peters (1969): "that income from international travel can bring the foreign exchange essential for major investment" (quoted in Mullings, 2004, p. 98). As a consequence, significant infrastructure was developed, particularly in the form of hotels to accommodate mass tourism, and enhanced links with air transport companies and tour operators. By 1970, almost four million tourists were visiting the region (Spencer, 2018). However, it was clear even at this time that tourism was not going to be the panacea for development suggested by some, including powerful international organisations such as the World Bank. For example, Patullo (2005) noted that tourism in this period was seen as a demeaning industry with its close parallels to the region's recent colonial past of slavery, exploitation and dependency. This unease was exacerbated by the sizeable role of foreign ownership. A majority of hotels were foreign-owned, with some of the smaller islands barely having any local ownership (Mullings, 2004). Further, the hope that tourism would create significant links to other parts of the economy, such as manufacturing and agriculture, was not realised. Rather than linkages there were significant leakages, where a majority of the profits went abroad. This trend was worsened by countries' reliance on international carriers bringing in tourists. Attempts were made to establish local airlines, such as British West Indian Airways (BWIA), Air Jamaica, and the Leeward Islands Air Transport Company (LIAT), but all struggled financially. The creation of the all-inclusive model of tourism in the late 1970s and the growth of cruise ship tourism in the 1990s significantly expanded the industry within the Caribbean, but they did not reverse the view that tourism in the region was dominated by foreign interests (Patullo, 2005; Spencer, 2018).

The industry today

According to the World Travel and Tourism Council (WTTC, 2019a), travel and tourism accounted for 15.5% of the Caribbean economy in 2018, equating to US$62.1 billion. This was 2.1% up on the year before. Travel and tourism contributed 2.4 million jobs, or 13.4% of total employment. Most visitors arrived from the United States (43%), followed by Canada (13%), France (6%) and the United Kingdom (4%). The WTTC suggests that the Caribbean ranks first with regard to the contribution of travel and tourism to GDP and employment; in second place is South East Asia. There are, of course, some differences in terms of the contribution of travel and tourism to particular countries in the region. In the Bahamas, over 40% of the economy is supported by travel and tourism and close to 50% of total employment (WTTC, 2019b). There is a similar level of dependency in Antigua and Barbuda, with a contribution of 44% to both GDP and employment (WTTC, 2019c). In contrast, the contribution of travel and tourism to the economy of Trinidad and Tobago is somewhat less: 7.6% to GDP and 9.5% to employment (WTTC, 2019d). In Puerto Rico also, the role is less important: 6.7% to GDP and 5.8% to employment (WTTC, 2019e). Finally, what about Cuba, that for so long did not engage with the industry? Tourist numbers have increased markedly since the early 1990s and in 2018 its contribution to GDP and employment was close to 10% (WTTC, 2019f). So it is clear that despite some variations tourism is a key industry for the region. Let us now consider some of the issues that shape it today.

The most significant change in tourism has been the large increase in cruise ship visitations. Indeed, the Caribbean has now the largest share of cruise visitors; accounting for 50% of global market share by vessel calls and passenger count (Commonwealth Secretariat, 2016). The top Caribbean cruise ship destinations are the Bahamas (where cruise arrivals contributed over 70% of all arrivals in 2013), Cayman Islands, US Virgin Islands and Puerto Rico (Spencer, 2018). Other islands, although less popular destinations, still depend heavily on cruise ship visitors. In Dominica and St Kitts and Nevis, cruises represent around 80% of total arrivals (IDDRI, 2019). Many reports

134 *Peter Clegg et al.*

suggest that there are real economic benefits to the region from cruise ship tourism. The Association of Caribbean States (ACS) in a recent report noted that "cruise ships ... generate a significant amount of economic revenue and employment for the Region" (2016, p. 2). A report by the Business Research and Economic Advisors in 2015 concurred, calculating that cruise ship passengers spent almost US$2.5 billion when visiting onshore, creating 45,000 direct onshore jobs (Honey, 2019). Similarly, Spencer (2018, pp. 51–52) argued:

> Undoubtedly, cruise tourism facilitates employment of locals, both directly and indirectly. Direct employment opportunities include tour operators, store clerks, taxi drivers, craft vendors, port pilots, port security, and port restaurant staff ... This in turn facilitates buoyancy in the economy ...

However, as the Commonwealth Secretariat (2016, p. 3) stated: "cruise tourism in the region has been characterised by high volumes and low value". For example, "cruise passengers typically stay for one day in each destination, and on average spend 94% less in the country than stay-over (or long-stay) visitors" (Caribbean Development Bank, 2018). Revenues from taxation are also much lower for cruise tourists. As Spencer (2018, p. 66) argued: "[land-based tourists] pay significant departure taxes while [cruise passengers] pay only a token port charge, if anything". Further, the negative environmental impacts are significant. As Honey (2019, p. 146) argued, "seventy percent of cruises take place in sensitive biodiversity 'hotspots', including those in the Caribbean, and environmental monitoring is notoriously difficult". "Ballast water, grey and black water, chemical pollution, solid waste, and oil are some of the pollutants created and expelled by cruise ships" (Spencer, 2018, p. 53). Also, the impacts of dredging reef areas and construction of port facilities to accommodate the ever-increasing size of cruise ships is of considerable concern. It should be mentioned, however, that with the designation of the Wider Caribbean Region as a Special Area under the International Convention for the Prevention of Pollution from Ships (MARPOL) Annex V, the restrictions on the discharge of garbage into the sea from ships has placed additional strain on receiving ports waste collection infrastructure (Association of Caribbean States, n.d.).

Greenhouse gas emissions are also significant. The effects of these can be found at sea and in port and coastal areas. Past efforts have been made to construct a unified Caribbean response to mitigate some of these concerns, but they have been largely unsuccessful. For example, plans for a Caribbean Community (CARICOM)-wide standard tax on cruise ship passengers collapsed after the cruise lines threatened to remove destinations from their itineraries (Patullo, 2005; Honey, 2019).

For most destinations in the Caribbean, traditional mass tourism remains of central importance, both in terms of its direct and indirect contribution. In

2018, the most popular destinations were the Dominican Republic with 6.57 million stop-over visitors and Jamaica with 2.47 million. Tourism products rely on coastal pursuits such as sunbathing, swimming, snorkelling and surfing, as well as maritime activities, such as boating and yachting (CDB, 2018). A recent study in Barbados found that visitors place significant economic value on the quality of coastal and marine resources such as wide beaches, sea-water quality and thriving coral reefs (Schuhmann et al., 2017). Notwithstanding, the long-standing concerns related to mass tourism remain, including the damage to vulnerable marine and land-based ecosystems from poorly planned coastal development. For example, it is estimated that 85% of waste water releases from tourist facilitates are untreated (IDDRI, 2019); there is a limited role for local stakeholders; and there remains a significant level of leakages from the domestic economy. Thus, efforts have been made to diversify the tourism product.

Ecotourism that focuses on nature experiences while aiming for environmental sustainability is one example; others include community-based and heritage tourism. In recent years, countries in the region have become more successful in marketing particular products and using information and communication technology (ICT) to do so. The Toucan Trail in Belize is a case in point (Spencer, 2018, p. 63). More niche, higher-end, tourism products with greater rates of return have also been developed, such as medical and sports tourism, as well as weddings and honeymoons. St Lucia has been particularly successful in relation to the latter. So there is undoubtedly a recognition that although mass tourism remains the bread-and-butter product for the region, new products and new approaches are required to maintain an acceptable balance between the economic benefits of tourism and environmental and social sustainability. As Neil Waters, acting Secretary-General of the Caribbean Tourism Organisation, argued: "the industry [must] shift away from excessive standardisation and embrace the unique culture of the destinations in the Caribbean" (Caribbean News Now, 2019). However, with growing environmental threats, more needs to be done to address the challenges that are already presenting themselves.

External environmental threats and implications

In addition to the negative environmental effects caused by tourism in the locale, there are significant changes to the global environment, which are clearly having impacts on the Caribbean. The World Tourism Organisation (2009, p. 2) called the travel and tourism sector "highly climate sensitive" as climate "defines the length and quality of tourism seasons, affects tourism operations, and influences environmental conditions that both attract and deter visitors". The most significant risks for the region from climate change are coastal flooding and inundation, loss or reduction of beaches, and loss of coastal ecosystems such as coral reefs, and salt marshes and mangroves that provide valuable ecosystem services such as buffer zones that protect the coast

136 *Peter Clegg et al.*

from storm surges (Thomas & Benjamin, 2015). Climate change could also contribute to increased incidences of vector-borne diseases such as dengue fever, chikungunya and zika virus, which could negatively impact on tourist arrivals to the region and affect its image as a destination. In Jamaica, for example, a one-metre rise in sea level will likely inundate 100% of port lands, 20% of airport lands and 2% of road networks (Trotz, 2014). Similarly, Thomas and Benjamin (2015) estimated that in the Bahamas, sea level rise will lead to displacement of coastal communities, coastal erosion and loss of land, salination in aquifers and damage or loss of coastal infrastructure amounting to billions of dollars. Further, if sea level increases 0.5 metres, tourism income is expected to fall by 62% in Barbados and 34% in Bonaire (Pulwarty et al., 2010, in IDDRI, 2019).

A further related outcome of climate change is more frequent and stronger hurricanes. This was illustrated very clearly in September 2017 with the passage of Hurricanes Irma and Maria through the Caribbean. Both were Category 5 hurricanes and caused severe damage to several countries, including Antigua and Barbuda (15% of GDP), the British Virgin Islands (350% of GDP), Dominica (224% of GDP), and the Turks and Caicos Islands (51% of GDP) (Caribbean Development Bank, 2018). The hurricanes destroyed or damaged much of the infrastructure, which had a knock-on impact on the tourism industry. In the British Virgin Islands, for example, more than 80% of the 4,000-strong charter sailing fleet was destroyed or damaged. Although the recovery was swift the initial effects were significant. An associated issue is to what extent prospective tourists consider the risks of hurricanes when they plan their trip. Forster et al. (2012) suggested that it is an important issue. They concluded that 40% of visitors to Anguilla considered hurricane season when making a booking, and respondents were less likely to choose a destination if the frequency and intensity of hurricanes increased. Further, as Honey and Bray (2019, p. 41) argued, "Increasingly cruise ships are ... forced to delay or cancel departures or divert course and alter itineraries to avoid extreme weather events".

Can the Blue Economy offer a viable way forward?

In relation to tourism, "the concept of the Blue Economy is expected to ensure the sustainability of resource availability, ecosystem balance and environmental health, and encourage the effective utilization and management of resources" (Tegar & Gurning, 2018, p. 128). In its report entitled *The Potential of the Blue Economy,* the UN and World Bank detailed a number of initiatives that should help to move tourism in the right direction. These included: improving local stakeholder engagement; reducing leakages by enhancing local productive capacity; ensuring the effective handling and disposal of waste; strengthening coastal and biodiversity conservation; implementing adequate disaster risk reduction policies and practices; diversifying the tourism product; and improving planning and development control policies (World Bank Group / United Nations, 2017, p. 17). So in short, as the Caribbean Development Bank noted, "The blue economy calls for the intelligent management of coastal resources to drive economic growth while protecting ocean and coastal ecosystems" (2018, p. 26). Indeed, the study by Schuhmann et al. (2017) found that visitors were highly sensitive to environmental degradation as a major consideration in whether or not they would make a return visit. Making the necessary changes and safeguarding the natural environment are of course easier said than done, given the significant challenges posed by mass and cruise ship tourism in particular. In addition, there is the ongoing threat of climate change, which is way beyond the Caribbean's control. Nevertheless, tourism in the region must take advantage of and advance the benefits within the Blue Economy.

The region has a well-developed governance framework to support tourism and the Blue Economy. There are various inter-governmental associations and organisations assembled for regional integration at the political level, including in particular the ACS and CARICOM. For coordination with regard to governance of the Caribbean Sea, there is the UN's Caribbean Environment Programme (one of its Regional Seas Programmes) and the Caribbean Sea Commission of the ACS. Under the auspices of CARICOM, there are also inter-governmental bodies mandated with coordinating the region's efforts in response to climate change (Caribbean Community Climate Change Centre) as well as tourism development (Caribbean Tourism Organisation, CTO). Regional private sector associations such as the Caribbean Hotel and Tourism Association, and non-government organisations, such as the Caribbean Natural Resource Institute (CANARI), also play an important role.

There is a slow but positive move by the tourism industry to begin contributing to efforts to sustain the natural environment on which their business depends Some large-scale tourism actors have established foundations or associations which support various environmental conservation projects. Marketing is helping to promote more sustainable tourism products, and ICT is being used "as a means of anticipatory warning and post-impact crisis management and in controlling their harmful effects on tourism" (Spencer, 2018, p. 99). For example, the Caribbean Institute of Meteorology and Hydrology has partnered with the CTO to develop a tourism-climate spatio-temporal modelling framework that predicts the influence of intra- and extra-regional climate on tourist arrivals to the Caribbean.

The following case studies highlight some of the challenges and the responses which represent real progress in meeting the Blue Economy agenda in regard to tourism. The case studies have been selected to showcase examples of good governance and beneficial interventions that address underlying issues such as coastal erosion and land based sources of pollution, as well as to highlight the value of individual and collective action by local small-scale actors to secure local livelihoods, the future of the industry and stewardship of key resources.

138   *Peter Clegg et al.*

The Barbados model for coastal zone management

Already presented in Chapter 6, the Barbados-based Coastal Zone Management Unit is a best practice in managing the coastline. The Unit has installed protective infrastructure that serves the primary purpose of providing shoreline protection, while at the same time enhancing the tourism product by offering continuous lateral access along stretches of beach that were once impassable in many sections due to erosion. In addition, the seating and landscaping provide amenity and recreational value in a densely developed urban setting that lacks outdoor public spaces. In short, the more visible and popular function is the use of the timber-deck walkway by visitors and locals alike for a range or recreational pursuits, including walking, fishing and photography.

In a contingent valuation study, results revealed that such investments had a positive impact on enhancing cultural and aesthetic ecosystem services, for both tourists and residents alike. Between 23% and 30% of tourists were drawn to the beaches because of the improved beach conditions. Visitors showed even stronger preferences for the improved conditions with over 60% stating that they were less likely to visit if the beach returned to its pre-improved condition. Moreover, tourists were found to value the improvements at Holetown and Rockley beach at BBD$51 per visitor and BBD$43 per visitor, respectively (Banerjee et al., 2018).

Individual and collective action by small-scale actors

Watersports and diving are key attractions for many tourists visiting the Caribbean, and represent economic opportunities for locals to make their livelihoods through the provision of these services to tourists. However, the capacity to leverage such economic opportunities is dependent on having the requisite knowledge and in-water competencies, and despite living on islands surrounded by the sea, many Caribbean people are unable to swim or are uncomfortable in the marine environment. They are therefore unable to take advantage of these opportunities. Fortunately, several watersports and/or dive operators across the region have taken the initiative to build capacity in Caribbean young people by offering swim and dive classes as well as marine awareness and education programmes. For example, Serenity Dive in St Vincent and the Grenadines has launched a school awareness programme, while in Jamaica, Yardie Divers and Environmental Conservationists was founded by two local marine biologists with the motto "Discover, Educate, Conserve". The business offers a diversity of services, including SCUBA diving, environmental consultancy and conservation tours. Also, "Dive Fest" in Barbados represents an example of collective action among dive operators to promote dive tourism, while incorporating activities to raise awareness of environmental issues and provide capacity building for local children.

Other opportunities for local small-scale actors may be found in the link between tourism and fisheries in the Caribbean. In some destinations, the tourism industry creates demand for fish and seafood; it is common and often expected that there is a "catch of the day" on restaurant menus. Sport fishing is also an attraction for some visitors, and may provide a niche-market for local operators. Many small-scale businesses are engaged in a variety of activities across sectors, for example, many divers also fish, and some local fishers also offer fishing charters to tourists. In the Dominican Republic, local NGO Reef Check DR has launched AquaCheck, a Marine Environmental Gastronomic Certification Program targeting businesses that use food from the sea, with the purpose of helping to educate and involve these businesses in the incorporation of sustainable options for responsible use of fish and seafood (Reef Check DR, 2018).

Tourism and the (Green and) Blue Economy – ridge to reef management

Tourism in the Caribbean is primarily located in low-lying coastal areas. Properties are therefore at risk from flooding because of poorly designed and maintained public drainage systems. In addition, reefs and other coastal and marine resources which underpin the industry are subject to pollution and sedimentation from land-based sources inland. These issues are exacerbated by climate change, which is predicted to cause increased intensity of extreme rainfall events which would increase the risk of flooding and associated damage. In response, several Caribbean countries are implementing Ridge to Reef projects, and although they are not explicitly Blue Economy projects, they provide critical support to the coastal tourism product and the Blue Economy by alleviating flooding and protecting coastal and marine resources. One such project was implemented in Barbados by the then Ministry of Environment and Drainage in 2014, entitled "Adaptation Measures to Counteract the Effects of Climate Change with a focus on Water Resources Management and Flood Alleviation" (AMCECC).[1] This project was implemented in the Holetown and Trents area, where several major tourism properties are located. It included a management plan for the Holetown Lagoon, the largest remnant wetland on the west coast, which lies between two beachfront hotels. In addition, a capital works programme was developed to design and implement interventions for flood alleviation for the area.

Such interventions by government to address national issues are made for the collective public good, and it is sometimes difficult to relate the specific benefits to individuals. In this case, we can offer an example with clear links to the Blue Economy. Michael Marshall is a resident of Trents, on the eastern side of the west coast road, across from a large hotel and the land-based park facility of the Folkestone Marine Reserve. He makes his livelihood as a small-scale actor in the Blue Economy – he is a watersports operator promoting snorkelling tours and other activities. Michael will benefit as a reduction in land-based sources of pollution will lessen stress on the natural resources that he relies upon for his livelihood. Recognising this, Michael has engaged with executing agency of the works, reaching out to inform on issues that arise,

140   *Peter Clegg et al.*

acting as a point-of contact in the community and assisting with setting up meetings. Such an integrated approach (of government action and local stakeholder engagement) to environmental management and the protection of tourism services is one that can and should be embraced further across the region.

Conclusion

The examples in the previous section indicate that action can be, and is being, taken by governments, international governmental organisations, businesses, NGOs and private individuals to align tourism with the Blue Economy agenda and vice versa. It is clear that key stakeholders across the Caribbean are aware of the challenges and opportunities that are present. Some of the work already being seen in countries such as Barbados, Belize, the Dominican Republic and Jamaica is important and effective. Further, there is a growing regional infrastructure that is being put in place to help the tourism industry align with the Blue Economy agenda. But there is clearly much more to do. Regional actors must be better coordinated and pro-active; national governments need to more effectively challenge long-held accepted norms, particularly around mass overnight and cruise ship tourism, and local communities should play a more central role. Perhaps the ideas of the New World Group are important here, in that strong and effective policies are fundamental in bringing about change. However, as this chapter has also highlighted, the challenges facing the region in terms of climate change and environmental degradation, dependency on mass tourism and the foreign companies that (largely) run the industry, and the small-island capacity and character of the countries in question mean that the significant step-change that is required remains out of reach. Perhaps as policy, action and threat increase that step-change will come, but for the moment at least, tourism and the Blue Economy agenda remain largely separate bedfellows.

Note

1 Information on the AMCECC Programme was provided courtesy of the Project Management Coordination Unit (PMCU) of the Ministry of Environment and National Beautification.

References

Association of Caribbean States. 2016. *Research Paper: Cruise Tourism in Greater Caribbean Region*. ACS Directorate of Sustainable Tourism, July. Available at: http://www.acs-aec.org/sites/default/files/cruise_tourism_in_the_greater_caribbean.pdf.

Association of Caribbean States. n.d. Marine pollution and Caribbean maritime transport industry. Available at: http://www.acs-aec.org/index.php?q=fr/node/5972.

Banerjee, O., Boyle, K., Rogers, C., Cumberbatch, J., Kanninen, B., Lemay, M. & Schling, M. 2018. Estimating benefits of investing in resilience of coastal infrastructure in small island developing states: An application to Barbados. *Marine Policy*, 90, April: 78–87.

Caribbean News Now. 2019. Caribbean urged to look within to grow tourism, 25 July. Available at: https://www.caribbeannewsnow.com/2019/07/26/caribbean-urged-to-look-within-to-grow-tourism/.

Caribbean Development Bank (CDB). 2018. *Financing the Blue Economy: A Caribbean Development Opportunity*. Bridgetown, Barbados: The Caribbean Development Bank (CDB). Available at: https://issuu.com/caribank/docs/financing_the_blue_economy-_a_carib.

Commonwealth Secretariat. 2016. *The Blue Economy and Small States*. Commonwealth Blue Economy Series No. 1. London, Commonwealth Secretariat. Available at: http://www.cpahq.org/cpahq/Cpadocs/The%20Blue%20Economy%20and%20Small%20States.pdf.

Forster, J., Schuhmann, P. W., Lake, I. R., Watkinson, A. R. & Gill, J. A. 2012. The influence of hurricane risk on tourist destination choice in the Caribbean. *Climate Change*, 114(3/4): 745–768.

Honey, M. 2019. Conclusions: lessons learned and recommendations. In Honey, M. (ed.), *Cruise Tourism in the Caribbean: Selling Sunshine*. Abingdon, Oxford, pp. 144–156.

Honey, M. & Bray, S. 2019. Environmental "footprint" of the cruise industry. In Honey, M. (ed.), *Cruise Tourism in the Caribbean: Selling Sunshine*. Abingdon, Oxford, pp. 32–51.

Institute for Sustainable Development and International Relations (IDDRI). 2019. *Sustainable Blue Tourism: Blue Tourism Study*. June. Available at: https://www.iddri.org/sites/default/files/PDF/Publications/Hors%20catalogue%20Iddri/20190620_BLUE%20TOURISM%20STUDY_EN.pdf.

Mullings, B. 2004. Caribbean tourism: trouble in paradise? In Skelton, T. (ed.), *Introduction to the Pan-Caribbean*. London, Arnold, pp. 97–117.

Patullo, P. 2005. *Last Resorts: The Cost of Tourism in the Caribbean*. London, Latin America Bureau.

Reef Check DR. 2018. AquaCheck. Available at: http://www.reefcheckdr.org/programas-aquacheck.html.

Schuhmann, P., Skeete, R., & Waite, R. 2017. *The Economic Importance of Coastal and Marine Resources to Tourism in Barbados*. Bridgetown, Barbados. Available at: https://www.onecaribbean.org/wp-content/uploads/Economic-Importance-of-Coastal-and-Marine-Resources-to-Tourism-in-Barbados.pdf.

Spencer, A. 2018. *Travel and tourism in the Caribbean: challenges and opportunities for small island developing states*. Cham, Switzerland: Palgrave Macmillan.

Tegar, R. D. & Gurning, R. O. S. 2018. Development of marine and coastal tourism based on blue economy. *International Journal of Marine Engineering, Innovation and Research*, 2(2), March: 128–132.

Thomas, A. & Benjamin, L. 2015. Climate loss and damage and the Bahamas. *The Nassau Guardian*. Available at: https://thenassauguardian.com/2015/09/16/climate-loss-and-damage-andthe-bahamas/.

Trotz, U. 2014. *Climate change and environmental challenges*. Paper presented at the Tourism as a Key Sector for Development in Islands States conference, Nassau, 19–20 February.

World Bank Group / United Nations. 2017. *The Potential of the Blue Economy: Increasing Long-term Benefits of the Sustainable Use of Marine Resources for Small*

142 *Peter Clegg et al.*

Island Developing States and Coastal Least Developed Countries. Washington, DC. Available at: https://openknowledge.worldbank.org/bitstream/handle/10986/26843/115545.pdf?sequence=1&isAllowed=y.

World Tourism Organisation. 2009. *From Davos to Copenhagen and beyond: advancing tourism's response to climate change.* UNWTO Background Paper. Available at: http://sdt.unwto.org/sites/all/files/docpdf/fromdavostocopenhagenbeyondunwtopaper electronicversion.pdf.

World Travel and Tourism Council (WTTC). 2019a. *Caribbean: 2019 Annual Research: Key Highlights.* Available at: https://www.wttc.org/economic-impact/coun try-analysis/region-data/.

World Travel and Tourism Council (WTTC). 2019b. *Bahamas: 2019 Annual Research: Key Highlights.* Available at: https://www.wttc.org/economic-impact/country-ana lysis/country-data/.

World Travel and Tourism Council (WTTC). 2019c. *Antigua and Barbuda: 2019 Annual Research: Key Highlights.* Available at: https://www.wttc.org/economic-impa ct/country-analysis/country-data/.

World Travel and Tourism Council (WTTC). 2019d. *Trinidad and Tobago: 2019 Annual Research: Key Highlights.* Available at: https://www.wttc.org/economic-impa ct/country-analysis/country-data/.

World Travel and Tourism Council (WTTC). 2019e. *Puerto Rico: 2019 Annual Research: Key Highlights.* Available at: https://www.wttc.org/economic-impact/coun try-analysis/country-data/.

World Travel and Tourism Council (WTTC). 2019f. *Cuba: 2019 Annual Research: Key Highlights.* Available at: https://www.wttc.org/economic-impact/country-analysis/country-data/.

12 The role of shipping and marine transport in developing Blue Economies

David Jean-Marie

The Caribbean Blue Economy

While it has been attracting significant attention in recent times, the Caribbean Development Bank (CDB) report, 'Financing the Blue Economy: A Caribbean Development Opportunity', notes that for the Caribbean region, the concept of the Blue Economy is not new (CDB, 2018). Indeed, traditional fishing and shipping activities have dominated regional ocean activity for centuries (Table 12.1). Perhaps the most significant development in marine-based activity in the region has been the growth of the cruise industry. The Caribbean's cruise industry accounts for 33.7% of the global cruise market share of vessel calls and passengers (FCCA, 2018).

The CDB defines the Blue Economy as one that comprises economic activities that directly take place in the ocean and seas, or use outputs from the sea for consumption or as a source of income and recites multiple Blue Economy initiatives which can be highlighted in the Caribbean (CDB, 2018). However, the report suggests that the scope and scale of these activities in the region have failed to reach their full potential because the Blue Economy has not been formally recognised as an important economic driver.

Some Caribbean countries have been making significant strides towards the development of Blue Economy activities (Clegg et al. Chapter 2). Barbados has taken the lead with the 2018 creation of a ministry of government dedicated to the Blue Economy. The Organisation of Eastern Caribbean States (OECS) is developing a Green-Blue Economy Strategy and Action Plan, the first of its kind in the region, under a Memorandum of Understanding (MOU) signed in June 2019 between the Caribbean Natural Resources Institute (CANARI) and the OECS Commission. Meanwhile, the first Caribbean Blue Economy major event was held in October 2019, co-hosted by the CDB and New Energy Events. The event was successful in bringing together multilateral agencies, funding agencies, industry stakeholders and solutions providers. It also served as a forum for heads of government to discuss policy and next steps.

Leveraging a Blue Economy strategy will allow Caribbean countries to more effectively drive the triple bottom line of sustainable development: growing the economy, protecting the environment and advancing social well-being. At the same time, it can usher in a new Caribbean economic development paradigm that is more diversified and less vulnerable to external shocks

144 *David Jean-Marie*

Table 12.1 Caribbean Blue Economy activities, industries and growth drivers

Activity	Related industry	Drivers of growth
Commercial shipping	Marine transport, manufacturing, retail	Import & export trade
Marine services	Marine transport	Import & export trade Tourism
Boat maintenance	Seafaring	Demand for maritime transport
Cruising	Tourism, leisure & entertainment	Increasing leisure travel Demand for leisure activity
Waste disposal	Cruise tourism	Environmental conservation
Coastal protection	Environmental protection	Habitat protection Coastal restoration
Coastal development	Tourism, construction	New business investment Demand for housing
Fresh water generation	Desalination	Demand for potable water
Seafood harvesting	Fisheries, trade of seafood products, aquaculture, manufacturing	Demand for food & nutrition Hotel and restaurant cuisine Demand for cosmetic and pharmaceutical products
Recreation, e.g. big game fishing, regattas, diving	Leisure & entertainment, watersports	Demand for on the water & underwater activity
Entrepreneurial development	Trade in services, retail Tourism	Self-employment
Mineral extraction	Oil and gas	Demand for energy
Offshore wind and wave energy	Renewable energy	Demand for renewable energy sources

(CDB, 2018). To support the Blue Economy approach and investment however, the CDB insists that appropriate policies, legislation, incentives and infrastructure must be accommodative to facilitate the transition. In other words, the policy mix, legislation and regulation, processes and other governance structures should align with the strategy, in order to maximise economic potential and value added. This chapter examines the role of shipping and marine transport in the transition to Blue Economies.

Quantifying shipping and transport activities

The annual economic value of the ocean economy in the Caribbean in 2012 was estimated at US$407 billion (Patil et al., 2016). This assessment consisted almost entirely of market-based activities, since the non-market values of

Shipping and marine transport 145

many ecosystem services are not easily valued monetarily (Schuhmann, Chapter 7). The value of the ocean economy is therefore dominated by the estimated value of the volume of cargo shipped through the Caribbean Sea, together with tourism, oil and gas (Patil et al., 2016). Gross revenues for the same period were estimated at US$53 billion, an estimate which the World Bank said is likely conservative and even low (given that estimates of shipping activity and values are not available) (Patil et al.., 2016).

Where shipping activity is concerned, data provided by the UN Economic Commission for Latin America and the Caribbean (ECLAC) suggest that container throughput in ports of Latin America and the Caribbean increased by 7.7% in 2018 compared to 2017. ECLAC annually updates its report of container port throughput, which shows the cargo volume in containers in the ports of the region, based on data obtained directly from port authorities and terminal operators. This analysis is based on the performance of a sampling of 31 countries and 118 ports and port areas in the region (ECLAC, 2019).

The 2018 activity was drawn from 118 ports analysed, with a total volume of approximately 53.2 million Twenty-foot Equivalent Units (TEUs). Of the total sample, 66 ports and port areas saw their figures improve versus 2017. The total volume of activity in 2018 represents 7.1% of global throughput, marking a slight increase in the rate versus the previous year when it amounted to 6.6% of global throughput. The ten countries contributing the most to the total volume of cargo handled represented 84.1% of regional movement. These are, from highest to lowest based on the quantity of TEUs mobilised: Brazil, Mexico, Panama, Colombia, Chile, Peru, Argentina, Ecuador, the Dominican Republic and Jamaica. The Caribbean showed 12% growth in total throughput, while Central America (excluding Mexico) had more subtle growth of 7% only on the West Coast, since the East Coast essentially maintained the same activity levels as in 2017 (ECLAC, 2019).

In keeping with industry trends, regional gateway container demand is expected to increase further, supported by the expansion of the Panama Canal. With the opening of the new locks, many Caribbean ports and cruise terminals have been expanding their facilities to accommodate larger ships and increased maritime traffic. The pace of ships' growth has indeed been spectacular. Some 25 years ago, a regular container carrier had a capacity of 1,000 to 2,000 TEUs. Today some of the larger vessels boast a capacity of 18,000 TEUs, necessitating substantial changes in ports and port operations.

Cruise tourism numbers have similarly been showing dramatic growth, proving the fastest growing segment of the travel industry for the past 20 years, with an annual growth rate of 7.4%. According to Florida Caribbean Cruise Association (FCCA) and Cruise Line International Association (CLIA) statistics, cruise passenger arrivals in the Caribbean region increased from 3 million in 1980 to an estimated that 27.2 million passengers in 2018 – a 10% increase over 2016 (FCCA, 2019). The economic contribution of cruise tourism in the Caribbean is tracked by the Business Research and Economic Advisors (BREA). The study is engaged by the FCCA in partnership with

146   *David Jean-Marie*

destinations every three years as one of many ways to foster the understanding of cruise tourism, its benefits and how to best actualise its potential. According to the latest 2018 study released by BREA, cruise tourism directly generated US$3.36 billion in total cruise tourism expenditures – more than 6% higher than the record set by the previous study in 2015, along with nearly 79,000 jobs paying more than US$900 million in wage income in the 36 participating destinations (BREA, 2018).

The US$3.36 billion in expenditures in cruise tourism is up 6.3% compared to the last study in 2015. Some 78,954 jobs attributable to the industry, were up 5.2% compared to the last study, paying a total employee wage income of US$902.7 million. According to the study, Caribbean destinations welcomed 25.2 million onshore visits from cruise passengers, with an average spend of US$101.52, generating a total of US$2.56 billion and 4.4 million onshore visits from crew, with an average spend of US$60.44, generating a total of US $265.7 million. The 29.6 million passenger and crew visits represent a 5.2% increase compared to the previous study, and the 32 common destinations in the 2015 and 2018 studies experienced a 6.5% increase in passenger visits. Cruise lines spent US$534 million, an average of US$14.8 million per destination (BREA, 2018). These numbers confirm the increasing importance of marine transport and shipping within the Caribbean and the increasing relevance of the region in the maritime arena. Across the region today, there are 351 ports and over 15 different types of ships transiting (Trillo, 2018).

Environmental sustainability

The Caribbean Shipping Association (CSA), established in 1971 to facilitate development of an efficient, viable Caribbean shipping industry, is the collective of the regional shipping industry. Its membership comprises 12 national shipping associations and over 100 individual member entities, including port authorities, terminal operators, shipping agents, shipping lines, tug and salvage companies, consultants, freight forwarders, leasing companies and others.

Given the fact that ports are critical infrastructure assets to economic development, and that maritime transportation is essential for most Blue Economy activities, an efficient, modern and environmentally friendly shipping industry is essential to Blue Economy growth. The need to prioritise sustainability has therefore never been more urgent than it is today, particularly as it relates to the environmental issues of our time. Shipping companies globally are under greater scrutiny in this area, and there is an increasing demand for accountability and transparency from key stakeholders including customers, partners, investors and government agencies.

The shipping industry in the Caribbean is conscious of its responsibility to promote environmental sustainability. No longer is this viewed as a side-line or fringe activity. Sustainability has in fact become central to our core business, given the emergence of the Blue Economy. As such, the CSA is committed to supporting sustainable marine economic activities that meet the needs of current and future generations. This is by no means an easy task for us in the Caribbean. Blue growth will require investments in infrastructure, conservation, research and development, institutional and human capacity development, as well as greater technological penetration, information-sharing and knowledge-building.

Within the shipping and transport sector, much has been done in the field of environmental protection in recent years, largely driven by the International Maritime Organisation (IMO), a United Nations (UN) agency with responsibility for shipping, and the United Nations agency itself. The International Convention for the Prevention of Pollution from Ships (MARPOL) is the main international convention covering prevention of pollution of the marine environment by ships from operational or accidental causes (IMO, 2020a). MARPOL has been updated by amendments through the years, buoying the responsible and eco-friendly disposal of maritime waste to the top of the agenda for ports everywhere. It is a matter of particular concern for Caribbean countries, which have been struggling to comply with the requirements of the MARPOL convention. While 86% of Caribbean countries have ratified MARPOL, only 25% have implemented the minimum legislation requirements to enforce MARPOL in the region (Trillo, 2018). Caribbean countries are therefore vulnerable to maritime accidents and shipping companies are challenged to comply with environmental regulations and standards.

This vulnerability increases the reliance on Port State Control (PSC) regimes, which carry out inspections on ships to monitor and enforce compliance with international regulations. The IMO's report of a growing number of PSC regimes implementing targeted inspections mechanisms and incentive schemes, is therefore comforting. According to that report, ships found in compliance with international standards are subject to fewer inspections, while substandard ships are targeted more often (IMO, 2017). At a 2017 workshop of PSC MOU member countries, PSC regimes pledged to strengthen collaboration, harmonisation and information sharing, further goods news in the efforts to reduce maritime accidents and enforce environmental standards and regulations (IMO, 2017).

The pledge to preserve the Caribbean Sea is further bolstered by the Convention for the Protection and Development of the Marine Environment in the Wider Caribbean Region (WCR), also known as the Cartagena Convention. It is a regional legal agreement which was adopted in Cartagena, Colombia on 24 March 1983 and entered into force on 11 October 1986. The Convention is supported by three technical agreements or Protocols on Oil Spills, Specially Protected Areas and Wildlife (SPAW) and Land Based Sources of Marine Pollution (LBS). As at January 2019, 11 of the 25 United Nations Member States in the WCR had ratified all three protocols. Nine had ratified two and the remaining five, just one (UNEP, 2019).

Beyond the prevention of marine pollution by ships, waste disposal and management is a major concern to regional environmental sustainability.

148 *David Jean-Marie*

Since the first attempt in 1991 to designate the WCR as a Special Area – one defined under MARPOL as an area for which stringent requirements apply to the discharge of garbage from ships, there has been little progress in expanding reception facilities at ports in the region (IMO, 2020b). A resolution established 1 May 2011 as the date of entry into force of garbage discharge requirements for the WCR. Vessels operating within the WCR are now prohibited from discharging any garbage into the sea, except food waste which may be discharged if the vessel is at least 12 nautical miles from the nearest land, or further if practicable. Ground food wastes that are capable of passing through a screen with openings no greater than 25 mm may be discharged if the vessel is at least three nautical miles from the nearest land, or further if possible (IMO, 2010).

While most of the States bordering the WCR Special Area have given notice to the IMO that they now have adequate reception facilities in the relevant ports, the reality is that only a few countries accept oily waste, fewer accept sewage and most accept garbage with significant restrictions on organic materials, biomedical and hazmat (Trillo, 2018). Operational and legislative differences between countries generate a large disparity in the management of cargo residues and waste and there remains a need to better address marine port inefficiencies in environmental sustainability. It was suggested by the Inter American Committee on Ports of the Organisation of American States that a regional plan is needed to enforce MARPOL in order to make its implementation more feasible (IACC, 2018).

When it comes to air pollution, environmental studies suggest that carbon dioxide is the primary source of global warming. About 30% of it comes from the transport sector and of this 30%, sea shipping is responsible for a relatively small portion – about 1.8% to 3.5%. Though ships have the lowest energy demand of all transport modes per one tonne of goods, the shipping industry continues to be criticised as a source of pollution and for not working hard enough to minimise exhaust emissions from vessels.

The IMO has agreed to reduce total greenhouse gas emissions from shipping by at least 50% by 2050, and has pledged to pursue efforts towards phasing them out entirely (IMO, 2018b). Shipping via the sea and inland waterways, though considered one of the most environmentally friendly modes of transport, impacts many aspects of the environment. Human health is affected the substances found in the emissions, such as particulate matter (PM), volatile organic compounds (VOCs) and nitrogen oxides (NOXs). Exposure to such substances can lead to severe public health issues. Local flora is also damaged by ship emissions, while ecosystems and freshwater quality are affected by acid rain which comes from emissions of sulphur and nitrogen oxides.

The IMO's strategy to tackle emissions notes that technological innovation and the global introduction of alternative fuels and/or energy sources for international shipping will be integral to achieve the overall goal. The race is now on to identify technologies capable of decarbonising the 50,000-plus

Shipping and marine transport 149

tankers, freighters, container vessels and ferries that comprise the world's shipping fleet. Wind power is one of the options being discussed and there are ongoing debates on how to build more environmentally friendly ships.

Support for implementation of the IMO's energy-efficiency measures comes through two major global projects executed by the IMO: The Global Maritime Energy Efficiency Partnerships Project (GloMEEP Project) is aimed at supporting the uptake and implementation of energy efficiency measures for shipping, thereby reducing greenhouse gas emissions from shipping. The GloMEEP project was launched in 2015 in collaboration with the Global Environment Facility and the United Nations Development Programme. A 'Global Industry Alliance to Support Low Carbon Shipping' (or GIA), launched in 2017 under the auspices of the GloMEEP Project, is identifying and developing solutions that can support overcoming barriers to the uptake of energy efficiency technologies and operational measures in the shipping sector (IMO, 2018a, 2018b).

The Global Maritime Technology Network (GMN) project, funded by the European Union, has established a network of five Maritime Technology Cooperation Centres (MTCCs) in Africa, Asia, the Caribbean, Latin America and the Pacific. Through collaboration and outreach activities at a regional level, the MTCCs will focus their efforts on helping countries develop national maritime energy-efficiency policies and measures, promote the uptake of low-carbon technologies and operations in maritime transport and establish voluntary pilot data-collection and reporting systems (IMO, 2018c).

The stricter environmental emissions regulations raise questions on whether these are too much for the industry and whether the industry is able to cope with the legislative burden. In addition to the IMO emissions reduction efforts, among the more significant of environmental protection initiatives is the ballast water management convention which entered into force in 2017. The International Convention for the Control and Management of Ships' Ballast Water and Sediments BWM Convention was adopted in 2004 to introduce global regulations to control the transfer of potentially invasive species. With the treaty now in force, ships need to manage their ballast water (IMO, 2019). Ballast water may be taken on-board by ships for stability and can contain thousands of aquatic or marine microbes, plants and animals, which are then carried across the globe. Untreated ballast water released at the ship's destination could potentially introduce new invasive marine species. Hundreds of such invasions have already taken place, sometimes with devastating consequences for the local ecosystem.

Under the Convention, all ships in international traffic are required to manage their ballast water and sediments to a certain standard, according to a ship-specific ballast water management plan. All ships have to carry a ballast water record book and an international ballast water management certificate. The ballast water management standards are being phased in over a period of time. New ships must meet the ballast water treatment standard. Existing ships should exchange ballast water mid-ocean but they will be

150 *David Jean-Marie*

required to meet the ballast water treatment standard by the date of a specified renewal survey. Eventually, most ships will be required to install an on-board ballast water treatment system.

Official communication has been sent to the IMO from the Regional Activity Centre/Regional Marine Pollution Emergency, Information and Training Centre, Wider Caribbean Region which includes: Antigua and Barbuda, Belize, Colombia, Costa Rica, Cuba, Dominican Republic, El Salvador, Guyana, Honduras, Jamaica, Mexico, Nicaragua, Panama, Saint Kitts and Nevis, Saint Lucia, Saint Vincent and the Grenadines, Suriname and Trinidad and Tobago (IMO, 2018d). The communication contained guidelines as part of a regional strategy on ships' ballast water management and invasive species, developed within the Wider Caribbean Region Strategic Action Programme (SAP) (IMO, 2018e). These Guidelines do not replace the requirements of the Ballast Water Management Convention, but provide an interim Ballast Water Regional Management Plan for the Wider Caribbean Region until all member states have ratified, and all applicable ships implemented, the BWM Convention.

Further still, the United Nations General Assembly has adopted the 2030 agenda for sustainable development listing a bold set of 17 global goals related to: no poverty; zero hunger; good health and well-being; quality education; gender equality; clean water and sanitation; affordable clean energy, decent work and economic growth; industry, innovation and infrastructure; reduced inequalities; sustainable cities and communities; responsible production and consumption; climate action; life below water; life on land; peace, justice and strong institutions and partnerships for the achievement of the goals. These all have implications for the maritime sector.

Critical role of ports

It is clear that the regulatory and legislative changes facing the shipping and transport industry are challenging, wide-ranging and far-reaching: from decarbonisation to the need to plan a future that is both environmentally and economically sustainable. Globally, we are at the threshold of a new wave of industrialisation and exploitation of the ocean, which holds the promise of more innovation, economic growth and jobs. Efforts therefore must be made to ensure that maritime industries and the use of ocean space, resources and ecosystems are ecologically sustainable, and that economic activities are in balance with the long-term carrying capacity of the ocean ecosystems (Visbeck et al., 2014; Silver et al., 2015). Working towards a cleaner environment, however, will not go far without the smooth incorporation of ports in this process. Particular consideration has to be given to port capacity.

The FCCA and CLIA member cruise lines have 50 vessels on order between 2018–2025, representing 220,000 lower berths and an investment value of more than US$51 billion. Most of these vessels are large in both features and capacity, with the average new build on order tipping the scales

Shipping and marine transport 151

at more than 155,000 Gross Registered Tonnage (GRT), with more than 4,000 lower berths (FCCA, 2018). Caribbean port capacity will have to increase proportionally with projected increased vessel size.

Infrastructural work has already started in this regard with terminals being built and expanded to ensure there is enough room. Royal Caribbean invested US$250 million to launch Terminal A at Port Miami, often referred to as the cruise capital of the world (Mody, 2018). Norwegian Cruises in conjunction with Port Miami is also constructing a terminal which is expected to be fully operational by February 2020. Miami-Dade County is spending US$100 million on the new terminal, while the cruise line is allocating up to US$65 million to cover costs among other items (Mody, 2018).

However, for Caribbean ports, investment in port infrastructure has to go far beyond investing simply for increasing capacity. As evidenced by the 2017 impact of hurricanes, the capacity and resources of Caribbean countries to plan, invest and react effectively is insufficient. Resilience is a key factor to successfully rebounding from a hurricane or other disaster. The immediate priority therefore has to be infrastructure-building capacity that will reduce or prevent damage/destruction in the event of a disaster (Swoboda, 2018).

Ports provide security, reliability, safety, efficiency and predictability for the transport of supplies during any disaster event and can serve as platforms to facilitate mass evacuations. Ports can guarantee the sustainability of the population, provide reliable connectivity and facilitate the efficient planning and distribution of supplies. They are critical infrastructures in the global transportation system facilitating resource mobilisation, but often disconnected from disaster management frameworks (Dennie, 2019).

As part of the resiliency-building effort within the region, there is a need for research-informed engineering and construction of facilities that will sustain little or no damage during natural disasters. Careful attention must be given to the quality of infrastructure and capabilities that exist at seaports. Emphasis also has to be on designing, implementing and sustaining a vibrant disaster management plan, fully capable of mitigating against man-made events, responsive to natural disasters and incorporating a prominent role for ports in the logistics architecture. Priority also has to be given to human capacity-building to ensure that the persons employed in the maritime industry have the training that will enable them to prepare for natural disasters, and the know how to operate during and after an event.

It is clear in all this that the role of ports has evolved. Ports are now repositioned as multi-activity facilitators of the emerging maritime trends and gateways to a Blue Economy. Ports have come to be considered the nerve centres for numerous Blue Economy activities and services in shipping and ancillary sectors. In keeping with this expectation, some regional ports have been modernising infrastructure in preparation for new maritime-related activities. Efforts are also underway to implement technology, safety, health and environmental programmes/controls to support the adoption of relevant conventions, codes and standards for safety and the environment.

152 David Jean-Marie

Trends to note

As the capacity-building investments continue, there has been some concern expressed in the Caribbean about the cruise companies' growing interest in private islands and enclaves of the kind that now exist in the Bahamas, Haiti and the Dominican Republic. There is also concern about the growing emphasis on ever-larger cruise ships marketed as destinations in their own right, and the absence of any commitment on the part of the companies to long-term on-shore economic sustainability. Some too, have begun to look nervously at the growing civic protests in European cities like Venice and Barcelona, which are overwhelmed with cruise tourism and simmering anti-cruise controversies in iconic US destinations, such as Charleston, Maine and Key West. It is considered that what is now happening in Venice and Barcelona, namely the disruption of communities, endangering of cherished buildings, environmental damage, congested streets, packed beaches and ruined experiences of travellers and visitors alike, should be viewed as "the canaries in the coal mine" for what poorly controlled cruise tourism could mean for ports in the Caribbean.[1]

The World Tourism Organisation (UNWTO), in examining the European scenario has defended the cruise sector, calling on local authorities to do more to manage growth in a sustainable manner. The UNWTO is of the view that ensuring that tourism is an enriching experience for visitors and hosts alike, demands strong, sustainable tourism policies, practices and the engagement of national as well as local governments and administrations, private sector companies, local communities and tourists themselves (Rifai, 2017). This is sound advice that Caribbean countries should heed, given their small land mass and the close proximity of seaports to already densely populated urban areas.

Looking to the future, while ports will have to comply with stricter guidelines and adjust to a greener profile, supporting activities which are not now considered as essential, should also factor into development plans. Consider for a moment Liquefied Natural Gas (LNG) becoming the ship's fuel of the future and the build out of new ships with dual-fuel engines. To accommodate these LNG vessels, we must be able to provide the infrastructure and specialised services. There is likely to be a huge shift when it comes to fuelling the ships, with demands for the production of energy within the ports, aiming at a zero-emission strategy.

Conclusion

Having examined the Caribbean shipping and transportation sector in the context of building a Caribbean Blue Economy, it is clear that the region faces significant national and regional challenges and constraints. It is equally clear, however, that the prospects for developing a Blue Economy and transforming the nascent conceptual framework are real and can be achieved. The

Shipping and marine transport 153

Caribbean's quest for sustainability of shipping and ports over the years has revolved around expansion of infrastructure, equipment upgrade and tackling of environmental concerns. In spite of its reputation of being conservative and slow to change, the shipping industry is eager and moving to address a number of significant gaps and barriers. What is needed, however, is significant progression in innovation and new paradigm thinking in science, technology, R&D, manufacturing, infrastructural design, consultation and decision-making processes. The long-term potential for growth and job creation must in addition be backed by efforts to improve integrated ocean management, including ecosystem preservation at the local, regional and international level.

In the same vein, the role of the port must also be expanded well beyond the conventional expectation. Seaport support to Blue Economy opportunities will, however, require funding, technical capacity-building, as well as a more supportive policy environment. Small island states are failing to attract investments and financing for several blue growth sectors, thus underlining the need for new, innovative financing mechanisms to tackle budget constraints. Private–public partnerships should therefore be encouraged as there is tremendous scope for the development of partner initiatives, to help the region transform concepts into implementation. To enhance technical capabilities, issues surrounding the ease of labour mobility between industries and technological impairment will have to be tackled. In the Caribbean context, serious consideration has to be given to fostering technical knowledge of marine ecosystems; highly skilled and knowledgeable human capital; effective project management and evaluation.

A more supportive policy environment should extend to institutional, regulatory and legislative requirements to support regional enforcement of international maritime conventions such as those established by MARPOL and the IMO. Enhanced governance in the form of more effective inter-ministerial communication; speedier government approval of projects would further support a more enabling framework for the Blue Economy. With a cohesive vision, strategic thinking and coordinated effort, we will achieve significant progress towards realising the development of the Blue Economy in the region.

Note

1 www.caribbean-council.org, 2018.

References

BREA. 2018. *Economic Contribution of Cruise Tourism to the Destination Economies, a Survey-Based Analysis of the Impacts of Passenger, Crew and Cruise Line Spending*: Volume II, *Destination Reports*. Business Research and Economic Advisors, October. Available at: https://www.f-cca.com/downloads/Caribbean-Cruise-Analysis-2018-Vol-II.pdf.

154 *David Jean-Marie*

CDB. 2018. *Financing the Blue Economy, A Caribbean Development Opportunity.* Caribbean Development Bank, Bridgetown, Barbados, 114 pp.

Dennie, C. 2019. The crucial role of port in humanitarian logistics. *Portside Caribbean*, 3 (13): 36–37. Available at: https://ufdc.ufl.edu/AA00062974/00013.

ECLAC. 2019. *Port Activity in 2018: The Top 20 Ports in Latin America and the Caribbean for 2018.* Economic Commission for Latin America and the Caribbean, Santiago, Chile. Available at: https://www.cepal.org/en/infographics/ports-activity-2018-top-20-ports-latin-america-and-caribbean accessed 6 April, 2019.

FCCA. 2018. *2018 Cruise Industry Overview.* Florida Caribbean Cruise Association, Pembroke Pines, Florida. Available at: https://www.f-cca.com/downloads/2018-Cruise-Industry-Overview-and-Statistics.pdf accessed 7 April, 2019.

IACC. 2018. Green logistics and port reception facilities: A key to competitiveness. *Caribbean Maritime*, 33: 18.

IMO. 2010. Establishment of the date on which regulation 5(1)(h) of MARPOL Annex V in respect of the Wider Caribbean Region Special Area shall take effect. Resolution MEPC.191(60). Available at: http://www.imo.org/en/KnowledgeCentre/IndexofIMOResolutions/Marine-Environment-Protection-Committee-(MEPC)/Documents/MEPC.191(60).pdf.

IMO. 2017. Port State control regimes move to boost collaboration, harmonization and information sharing. Available at: http://www.imo.org/en/MediaCentre/PressBriefings/Pages/30-PSC-workshop.aspx (accessed11 February 2020).

IMO. 2018a. Global maritime energy efficient partnerships. Available at: http://glomeep.imo.org/.

IMO. 2018b. *UN Body Adopts Climate Change Strategy for Shipping.* International Maritime Organization (IMO), London, Briefing 06, 13/04/2018. Available at: http://www.imo.org/en/MediaCentre/PressBriefings/Pages/06GHGinitialstrategy.aspx.

IMO. 2018c. Global network for energy-efficient shipping. Available at: http://gmn.imo.org/.

IMO. 2018d. Communication received from the Regional Activity Centre/Regional Marine Pollution Emergency, Information and Training Centre – Wider Caribbean Region (RAC/REMPEITC-Caribe). Available at: http://www.ics.org.ir/Downloads/CLD/News/BWM.3-Circ.2%20-%20Communication%20received%20from%20the%20Regional%20Activity%20CentreRegional%20Marine%20PollutionEmergency...%20(Secretariat).pdf.

IMO. 2018e. *Guidelines for Ballast Water Management in Wider Caribbean Region Areas.* Choice Ballast Solutions, Cleveland, Ohio. Available at: https://choiceballast.com/guidelines-for-ballast-water-management-in-wider-caribbean-region-areas/.

IMO. 2019. *International Convention for the Control and Management of Ships' Ballast Water and Sediments (BWM).* International Maritime Organization, London. Available at: http://www.imo.org/About/Conventions/ListOfConventions/Pages/International-Convention-for-the-Control-and-Management-of-Ships%27-Ballast-Water-and-Sediments-(BWM).aspx.

IMO. 2020a. *Marpol Convention.* International Maritime Organization, London. Available at: http://www.imo.org/en/About/Conventions/ListOfConventions/Pages/International-Convention-for-the-Prevention-of-Pollution-from-Ships-(MARPOL).aspx.

IMO. 2020b. *Special Areas under MARPOL.* International Maritime Organization, London. Available at: http://www.imo.org/en/OurWork/Environment/SpecialAreasUnderMARPOL/Pages/Default.aspx.

Mody, S. 2018. Cruise lines build up capacity despite global headwinds, hoping for better days ahead. Available at: https://www.cnbc.com/2018/11/04/cruise-lines-build-up-capacity-despite-global-headwinds.html.

Patil, P.G., Virdin, J., Diez, S. M., *et al.* 2016. *Toward a Blue Economy: A Promise for Sustainable Growth in the Caribbean; an Overview.* The World Bank, Washington DC.

Rifai, T. 2017. *Tourism: Growth is not the Enemy; it's How we Manage it that Counts.* PR No.: Opinion article 1, United Nations World Tourism Organization. Available at: https://www.unwto.org/taxonomy/term/32?page=21.

Silver, J. J., Gray, N. J., Campbell, L. M., *et al.* 2015. Blue economy and competing discourses in international oceans governance. *The Journal of Environment and Development*, 24 (2): 135–160. https://doi.org/10.1177/1070496515580797.

Swoboda, M. 2018. *Disaster management and emergency response initiative.* Port Management Association of the Caribbean 21st annual general meeting, The Jewel Dunn's River Resort, June. Available at: http://www.pmac-ports.com/news/109-pmac-agm-2018-disaster-management-and-emergency-response-initiative.

Trillo, A. 2018. Implementation of MARPOL in the Caribbean. *Caribbean Maritime*, 33: 17.

UNEP. 2019. *The Convention for the Protection and Development of the Marine Environment in the Wider Caribbean Region (WCR).* United Nations Environment Programme, Caribbean Environment Programme, Kingston, Jamaica. Available at: http://cep.unep.org/cartagena-convention.

Visbeck, M., Kronfeld-Goharani, U., Neumann, B., *et al.* 2014. Securing blue wealth: The need for a special sustainable development goal for the ocean and coasts. *Marine Policy*, 48: 184–191.

13 Renewable energy
An emerging Blue Economy sector

Indra Haraksingh

Introduction

The energy sector in the Caribbean is still very much fossil-fuel centred. Apart from Trinidad and Tobago, the Caribbean Community (CARICOM) member states are largely net importers of energy in the form of petroleum and petroleum products. This places our countries in a very vulnerable position due to fluctuating world oil prices. Additionally, the Caribbean region continues to suffer from ever increasing and more intensified natural hazards, and climate vulnerability. While there have been concerted efforts to diversify energy generation capabilities by injecting renewable energy technologies into our generation mix, there has not been enough focus on energy diversification through our marine space. This chapter explores the scope of the Blue Economy for the Caribbean region and investigates ways of enhancing our energy security and economic competitiveness through this medium. It explores the range of marine renewable energy technology solutions in an effort to decarbonise the fragile economies of our Small Island Developing States (SIDS). One immediate challenge is lack of adequate expert capacity in the region. This must be addressed in the short term in order for the region to be equipped to embrace the benefits of renewable energy technologies and the Blue Economy. Some of the efforts already existing will be highlighted, and recommendations will be proposed for charting the way forward.

Electricity tariffs in many Caribbean countries are among the highest in the world. Energy security remains a major concern for the region. Energy is critical to most sectors of the economy, and inadequate energy capacity directly undermines economic competitiveness in Caribbean states. There have been different financial schemes which have served to support Caribbean countries. One of these, the PetroCaribe arrangement with Venezuela, which provided for discounted oil, was an important source of assistance, particularly when prices were high. However, with the collapse of the Venezuelan economy and the retrenchment of PetroCaribe, this facility is unreliable or even non-existent. It is therefore imperative that the region moves swiftly to adopt clean renewable energy technologies as a matter of urgency. And this must be extended to the marine opportunities encompassing the Blue Economy.

Most Caribbean countries have already established national targets for the uptake of renewables, and regional targets were established at the Council for Trade and Economic Development (COTED) meeting in March 2013 in Trinidad. This in itself is a breakthrough in terms of sensitisation and the realisation that countries must adhere to established international protocols. What needs to be investigated is the vast potential for renewable "blue energy" production from wind, wave, tidal, thermal and biomass sources, and the extent to which these can be adopted.

Caribbean countries depend to a large extent on tourism. There is the perception that marine energy development would negatively impact the tourism industry, including water-sporting activities. However, we must look beyond this narrow viewpoint and establish activities that would attract tourists and create financial gain to further enhance the economy. A simple example would be tourist visits to marine renewable energy sites, such as an off-shore wind farm. Many tourists would welcome such a visit. The ocean is also a source of livelihood for many in the region through fishing. There is concern among many about the impact the development of blue energy would have on the fishing industry. Investigations must be undertaken on a continuous basis to ensure that the fishing industry is not compromised.

Policy

Significant work has already been done on policy development for renewable energy in the Caribbean region (CARICOM, 2013). However, this should be streamlined to incorporate the Blue Economy needs for the region. A concerted effort must be made to increase investment in climate and environmental information services and modelling capability for prediction of future climatic events. This will help to strengthen our early warning systems capability and better prepare the region for the onslaught of some of the severe disasters which have been so seriously affecting the region. Some countries have already established governance frameworks that includes marine spatial planning, such as the draft national marine policy for the Bahamas and regional oceans policy adopted by the Organisation of Eastern Caribbean States (OECS) (UNCTAD, 2014).

While many of the countries in the region have national policies and targets for renewable energy implementation, there is also a regional target set by members of CARICOM. Regional energy Ministers approved an initial target of 47% renewable energy contribution to total electricity generation in the region by 2027 at the COTED Energy meeting in 2013 (Worldwatch, 2013). Interim targets of 20% and 28% renewable energy for 2017 and 2022 were also set at this meeting. It is hoped that this would be achieved through developments in solar, wind, hydro, geothermal and bio-energy. Some of this can be achieved through development of marine renewable energy (MRE). Following this is the Caribbean Sustainable Energy Roadmap and Strategy (S-SERMS), which aims to steer CARICOM Member states with a coherent

158 *Indra Haraksingh*

strategy for the transition to a sustainable energy future (Worldwatch, 2013). More recently, through the 11th European Development Fund, the Technical Assistance Programme for Sustainable Energy in the Caribbean (TAPSEC) was established to help drive the development of renewables as well as build capacity and expertise the region.

Building of national and regional capacity in renewable energy, especially with a focus on marine renewables, is necessary and critical to development of the Blue Economy. To this end, international partnerships and collaborations must be established to help the region achieve its targets. Sensitisation programmes to raise awareness of the population at large and specific stakeholders are essential. Strengthening of legislation and policy development are also necessary for promotion of blue energy. Data acquisition and management are critical for informed policy decision-making.

Technology solutions

The Caribbean region has made strides in deploying land-based renewable energy technologies. Some countries are more advanced than others, but few have embraced off-shore solutions for sustainable energy development. Most of these are in the infancy stage of development, with many hurdles to overcome in the initial stages. One issue that is common to most of the technologies is the fact that extensive resource assessment must be done in order to establish feasibility of a particular technology. This could be quite challenging for SIDS. Adoption of marine renewables is slow due to many reasons. The barriers include:

- inadequate policy;
- financial capital;
- difficulty in working in the marine environment;
- lack of awareness of the general public;
- transportation within the marine environment;
- lack of clarity with respect to border restrictions;
- technological solutions which are not easily adaptable for SIDS.

Some of the technologies to be considered for the Caribbean situation are:

- off-shore wind energy;
- ocean thermal energy conversion (OTEC);
- wave energy;
- tidal energy;
- sea water air conditioning (SWAC);
- salt gradient;
- bio-energy.

Renewable energy   159

However, even before starting the projects there is much initial investigatory work to be done, such as:

- general marine spatial planning;
- assessment of the possibilities and local opportunities;'
- investigation of bathymetry and geology of the areas under consideration;
- local sea-bed conditions, proximity to oil rigs, underground pipes and high-tension cables;
- resource assessments to in order to assess feasibility of projects;
- assessment of vulnerability to natural disasters such as hurricanes;
- understanding of sensitive areas such as coral reefs, sea turtles' nesting sites.

Off-shore wind energy

Of all the marine renewable energy technologies, the most developed and accessible currently is off-shore wind. Some land availability issues and visual impacts can be addressed by the use of this technology. The fact that the wind regimes are more consistent off-shore than on land means that the problem of intermittency is significantly reduced. What is key here is that the most appropriate size and design of wind turbines for SIDS are adopted. Similarly, the best choice of foundation designs and cost must be made. Wind turbines can be classified as:

- fixed-speed;
- variable-slip;
- doubly fed induction generator;
- full-converter.

Increasingly, the full-converter seems to be the preferred choice for wind turbines. Worldwide, Europe led grid-connected off-shore wind power in 2019 with Great Britain highest (1,760 MW), followed by Germany (1,111 MW) and Denmark (374 MW) (WindEurope, 2020).

Special attention needs to be paid to the foundations for off-shore wind turbines. The type of fixed foundation depends on the water depth, hence the importance of bathymetry studies, sea-bed conditions and costs. The main foundation types (Aqua-RET, 2012; Miceli, 2012) are:

- monopile;
- jacket frame;
- tripod;
- gravity;
- floating.

160 *Indra Haraksingh*

Of these, the monopile seems to be the most adopted foundation type up to approximately 30 metres water depth. In water too deep for fixed-foundation turbines, floating structures are more feasible as this allows the turbine to be located at any depth. Clearly, water depth, among other factors mentioned, plays an important role in the selection of the foundation type to be employed for Caribbean territories.

> For most onshore wind power generation sites, the yearly CF [Capacity Factor] varies between 20% and 40%. Full load hours vary between 1800 and 3500 per year. Offshore locations, and some extreme case sites onshore, may achieve up to between 4,000 and 5,000 full load hours per year. ... Simulations of offshore wind power production for countries bordering the North Sea, based on six years of reanalysis data, generated a CF of between 0.39 and 0.43 [39% and 43%].
>
> (Graabak and Korpås, 2016)

The big disadvantage is the enormous capital investment. Marine conditions can be very abrasive. Consequently, all the infrastructures and equipment are more expensive than on-land installations. Additionally, access is more difficult than on land. In general, overall cost of an off-shore wind farm is roughly two to three times that on land. But the big advantage is that the power output can be double. Usually off-shore wind farms tend to utilise large turbines (approx. 5 MW) and up to 80 turbines. However, for SIDS, the better choice is probably smaller and fewer wind turbines (approx. 3 MW) placed closer to land. The smaller capacity wind turbines with traditional foundation designs are cheaper to install and to maintain (Greenhill et al., 2016).

Before the Caribbean can embark on off-shore wind energy development, a comprehensive wind resource assessment is needed. Theoretically, while global wind maps exist, they use re-analysis data. Re-analysis data depends on global atmospheric models, using different processing systems, yielding different wind speeds. Hence all data need to be verified with actual measurements. It is therefore recommended that actual measurements are taken at different hub heights, 80 m and higher. Orkney Islands off Scotland had more than 120% of their energy demand met by renewables in 2017 (Aquatera, 2014). The Orkney Islands experience can provide a unique example for the Caribbean.

Ocean energy

Ocean thermal energy is derived from the heat of the sun and mechanical energy from the tides and the waves. The ocean is often considered the world's largest solar collector and is inherently a huge source of energy. Because oceans occupy 70% of the Earth's surface this resource is almost limitless.

Ocean thermal energy conversion (OTEC)

The surface of the ocean is warmer than the deep ocean. The significant temperature difference between the surface and bottom of the ocean leads to the possibility of OTEC, which has the advantage that it is a fairly constant source. A very small portion of this energy could be used to power the world; the big problem is harnessing this energy. There are technologies which are already developed. Adaptation to SIDS requires expertise, experience and financial capital, which SIDS seldom have. However, the Caribbean region, lying in the tropics, has the distinct advantage of having reasonably large temperature differences between surface and deep water, approximately 20°C to 25°C, deeming them suitable for OTEC as the heat engines will be able to run with greater efficiency.

There are numerous applications for ocean thermal energy, the main one being electricity generation through:

- Closed-cycle systems using a working fluid such as ammonia, with a low boiling point, which is cooled at depth then warmed by the ocean's surface heat and allowed to vaporise. The vapour expands and turns a turbine which activates a generator producing electricity.
- Open-cycle systems that boil sea water by operating at low pressures. The steam produced passes through a turbine generator system creating electricity.
- Hybrid systems that incorporate both closed-cycle and open-cycle systems.

Some countries in the Caribbean are already embarking on OTEC projects.

The Bahamas

The Bahamas has favourable operating conditions for OTEC applications. OTEC International is investigating the possibility of small Floating Power Platforms (FFPs) close to the shore, providing up to 5 MW of base-load power to serve the island communities. Larger commercial plants would need to be installed further off-shore because they need the cold deep sea water to achieve the required temperature difference for effective operations.

The smaller, barge-based FPP is recommended for The Bahamas, as it can withstand most hurricanes. The plant can be configured so that the barge can be detached from the mooring lines and piping, and towed into safe harbour. After the hurricane the FPP can be reinstalled. Using FPPs, the Bahamas can realise significant benefits, such as lower power costs, scalable solutions, employment and training opportunities. It is expected that OTEC will provide economical, environmentally sound energy, and increased energy security for the Bahamas.

162 *Indra Haraksingh*

Cayman Islands

OTEC International hopes to deliver up to 25 MW of renewable electricity to the Public Electric Power Utility Company in Grand Cayman (CUC) utilising FPPs on the north side of Grand Cayman Island. CUC generates an average of 70 MW of power each year, with peak demand of 100 MW from diesel generation. The first phase of the Cayman project would be the generation of 6.25 MW renewable electricity from an FPP that would be permanently moored less than a mile off-shore. The visual impact will therefore be minimal. The power generated from the FPP would be transmitted via cable to a substation onshore where it will be connected to the CUC grid.

Barbados

Barbados has been making strides in its clean energy development, which includes marine renewable energy. The work is part of the island's EU-IDB funded Public Sector Smart Energy Programme, which aims to promote renewable energy and energy efficiency in Barbados (Renews Ltd, 2018). Barbados has carried out an ocean energy scoping study to determine potential for OTEC and off-shore wind. Following this, all nearshore activities were mapped in a GIS. Suitable areas for OTEC, off-shore wind and wave energy were also mapped. The next stage is to conduct feasibility studies for ocean power in Barbados with a focus on off-shore wind and OTEC. These studies will include policy and regulatory frameworks; tourism impacts; and economic, financial, technical and environmental assessments.

Tidal and wave energy

Ocean mechanical energy deals with tidal and wave energy. Tidal energy is derived primarily by the gravitational pull of the moon. It is based on the vertical height difference between successive high and low tides. Wave energy is influenced primarily by the winds. Like many renewable energy sources, tidal and wave energy are intermittent. In areas where the wave and tidal resources are high, it is feasible to develop these resources. There are some such areas in the Caribbean, but it is necessary to conduct assessments before embarking on any such project.

Key areas of investigation are the timing and magnitude of tides which depend on:

- the alignment of the sun and the moon;
- the shape of the coast;
- water depth and bathymetry;
- location of the amphidromic points (points of zero tidal amplitude).

Tidal energy is harnessed using a barrage or dam to force the water through turbines, activating a generator. Tidal stream devices capitalise on the constant flow of water to drive the turbines. Speeds of approximately 4–5 m/s are ideal. Closeness to the shore is an asset since the length of power lines can be greatly reduced. Commercial-scale tidal energy projects are currently emerging for small island nations.

Sea currents are developed by tidal currents, density differences due to salt and temperature, and wind run-up. Sea current turbines can operate under certain conditions, such as when there are strong currents and shallow waters. There may be potential in the Caribbean but this will have to be determined by measuring the speed of the currents. It can be economically viable if the velocity is greater than 1.0 m/s. Currently, large projects for SIDS are still costly, but scalability is possible. In areas where the resource is available, tidal energy is a good option.

Wave energy technologies are still in developmental stage and not yet commercially available. Wave energy conversion uses three basic systems:

- channel systems which direct the waves into reservoirs;
- float systems which drive hydraulic pumps;
- oscillating water column systems that use the waves to compress air within a container, creating mechanical power which activates a generator.

Progress has been made in Europe and the United Kingdom, supported by policy and investment. The European Marine Energy Centre has its testing facility in Orkney, Scotland. Many studies in ocean energy have been carried out there. One of the main technological challenges that has been identified is the harsh ocean environment and its effect on machinery. The Ocean Energy Forum (OEF) hosted by the European Commission, together with industry and other stakeholders, has been working on a strategic roadmap for development of ocean energy to the year 2020. It is hoped that this document will serve as a guide for countries involved in ocean energy, including SIDS (Ocean Energy Forum, 2016).

Sea water air conditioning (SWAC)

Energy generation, cooling and desalination can be derived from deep sea water resources, with added benefits of aquaculture and agriculture by-products. This is a valuable natural resource in the Caribbean. The most economically viable use of this resource is to provide air-conditioning in buildings through SWAC systems. A SWAC system consists of a cold intake sea water supply pipe, a pumping unit and heat exchanger located close to the shoreline, and a closed loop with fresh water distribution to supply cooling needs of each building, connected through a secondary heat exchanger (Water and Sewage Corporation, 2018).

SWAC can provide up to 90% savings over conventional air conditioners. Many large facilities, such as hotels, large commercial and industrial complexes, universities, hospitals, airports, etc., can gain significant benefits from SWAC. Chillers used in conventional air conditioning can be quite costly as these systems account for approximately 40% of the total energy consumption in such large buildings.

There are numerous benefits to be derived from SWAC. This is an environmentally benign technology and is not easily affected by price volatility. Other benefits include reduction in energy and cooling power, and consequently costs. This technology can help to realise growth and economic development. This can help to attract other industrial activities and reduce electricity peaks for the utility. The Caribbean region is a favourable location for this technology (Bardot Ocean, 2020).

Since 2014, CAF, the Development Bank of Latin America, invested US $200,000 in a preliminary assessment of the technical and economic implications of the introduction of SWAC in four islands, Jamaica, Dominican Republic, Guadeloupe and Martinique, with co-financing from the French Development Agency (AFD). This assessment showed that SWAC was both technically and economically feasible in these locations. The Caribbean Development Bank (CDB) is also investing in the development of ocean resources as the blue energy is high on their agenda. Other international institutions, such as the World Bank and IRENA, are also promoting the Blue Economy in the Caribbean by investing funds to develop the ocean energy in the Caribbean.

There are a few SWAC projects in their early stages in the Caribbean. A SWAC project under development for the airport in Curacao is due to become operational in 2020. This project, being developed between Curacao Airport Holding and International Ecopower, is expected to bring opportunities for new economic activities in the vicinity of the airport. Other projects are being planned for Grenada, Jamaica, Cayman Islands and other Caribbean islands. SWAC can significantly benefit the tourism sector in the Caribbean, on which many of the islands depend for their survival.

Research work done

Research has been conducted on wave energy potential in the region. One such study is "Wave energy potential assessment in the Caribbean Low Level Jet using wave hindcast information". The wave energy potential in the Caribbean Sea was studied using a 30-year wave hindcast. There is an easterly zonal wind up to 13 m/s known as the Caribbean Low-Level Jet (CCLJ) that determines what the wave climatology in the Caribbean Sea will be. Information from altimetry (Globwave) and buoy (DIMAR) data from the Colombian Caribbean Sea is used to validate the wave hindcast information. Findings from this study show good correlation at two locations, but an under-prediction of extreme events at another location. Results indicate that

Renewable energy 165

there is high potential for wave energy in the CLLJ region (Appendini et al., 2015).

Case study

Another study (White, 2016) investigated the feasibility of developing a co-located off-shore wind and wave generation system for Trinidad with installed capacity of 15 MW and 5 MW, respectively. The test area was Guayaguayare Bay on the southeast coast of Trinidad. Data for the project was obtained from existing data sets, research and field visits. A constraints analysis was done using ESRI ArcMap. The Annual Energy Production for the wind system was estimated using WindPRO and Weibull distribution.

The constraints analysis consisted of three parts. The first step was to identify all constraints for Trinidad. These included routine checks, such as Bathymetry, geology, etc. and took into consideration oil and gas activities. The data was fed into ArcMap which yielded several possibilities with high potential for off-shore wind and wave energy around Trinidad. The second part involved utilising the wind resource map for Trinidad for selection of the optimum off-shore wind and wave site. The south-east coast of Trinidad showed the area with high wind resource potential. The third part dealt with legal considerations. A 5 km distance from the coast emerged as a reasonable distance as it would fall within the archipelagic baseline as well as the exclusive economic zone (EEZ) and out of major shipping routes.

The analysis indicated that the wind and wave parks must be at least 5 km off-shore and would occupy an area of 2 km^2. The proposed devices were oriented to capture the north-easterly trade winds: five Vestas 112–3.0 MW wind turbines that can each produce 7,122.8 MWh and three WaveSurfers that can each produce 59.84 MWh. The levelised cost of energy (LCOE) for the wind park was calculated to be 1.4589 TTD/kWh and Wave Park was 0.7484 TTD/kWh.

Environmental impact analysis showed that the proposed project would have a substantial impact on CO_2 emissions reduction – 52.5 Mt. Social analysis indicated that the residents in the area are highly interested in renewable energy and this project. In summary, while the co-located wind and wave energy generation system showed environmental, social and financial feasibility, the technical feasibility was questionable since there was significant disparity in power generation of the two independent systems. The independent wind energy system was deemed to be technically feasible, while the wave energy system was not. This was largely because there was not adequate data to support the study.

This project can be further developed by considering the lessons learnt from the study. Different project layout configurations can be simulated in order to obtain feasibility of other pilot projects, such as creating an off-shore wind and wave hybrid system utilising existing oil platforms which may be converted into multi-use off-shore platforms.

166   *Indra Haraksingh*

Ongoing activities in support of marine renewable energy

CARIMET Forum

The CARICOM Secretariat, serving as the coordinating body for renewable energy development in the region, has taken many initiatives to catalyse the movement towards achieving its target. In November 2019, CARICOM, the Government of Grenada, Caribbean Centre for Renewable Energy and Energy Efficiency (CCREEE), the German Technical Corporation GmbH (GIZ) and SIDS Sustainable Energy and Climate Resilience Initiative (SIDS DOCK) hosted the Caribbean Marine Energy Technology (CariMET) Forum, to kick off the CARICOM Energy Month. The deliberations centred on the development and deployment of marine renewable energy: ocean thermal energy, including SWAC, and kinetic marine energy, including offshore wind, tidal and wave. Financial aspects and cost-reduction strategies for cutting-edge marine renewable energy technologies within the region were explored.

The main objectives of the Forum were knowledge sharing on marine renewable energy and investigation of opportunities for off-shore grid and off-grid energy service generation. The meeting sought to develop a strategic research agenda on marine renewable energy projects for SIDS in the CARICOM region, and to create a framework for businesses, and prospective developers and investors to actively engage governments on exploration opportunities and the way forward.

On-going training

There are numerous capacity-building efforts across the Caribbean region in renewable and sustainable energy. These include Masters, MPhil and PhD degrees and training programmes at The University of the West Indies and other academic institutions in the region. One which specifically targets the technology aspects is the MSc in Renewable Energy Technology at The UWI in Trinidad.

Conclusion and recommendations

Caribbean countries lying in and adjacent to huge marine areas have an advantage in developing Blue Economies (Roberts and Ali, 2016). Despite the many barriers to its development, there have been concerted efforts to seek international cooperation and to explore funding possibilities through international financial institutions. The region has made significant strides in its development of terrestrial-based renewables but is currently taking concrete initiatives to advance or to promote the growth of marine renewables. The recent activities indicate that some of the islands are already engaged in marine renewable projects and have had substantial initial success it its development, with the expectation that some projects will become operational in 2020. As the MRE sector is not yet mature in the region, and recognising that the operations are expensive, especially working in the marine environment, investments can be risky. The small size of SIDS also presents challenges regarding economies of scale and market development. Technology developers are therefore focusing on innovative designs and smaller, site-specific projects with the expectation of achieving phased expansion. It is imperative, however, that this is supported by integrated and strategic action to ensure a coherent and supportive policy framework.

Renewable energy generation policy must work in tandem with measures to address efficiency and demand (World Bank and United Nations Department of Economic and Social Affairs. 2017). While there are many similarities among the SIDS, such as available on- and off-shore resources, local institutional capacity, etc., strategies to develop MRE must be well planned and coordinated. Strategic marine spatial planning must entail resource assessment and national priorities in order to ensure the selection of the most appropriate locations for MRE development, taking into consideration ecological sensitivity, visual impacts, etc. Engaging civil society early is critical for gaining acceptance and fostering long-term success and ownership and sensitisation programmes are needed for all stakeholders. SIDS should continue to work together sharing experiences among themselves as well cooperating with regional mechanisms to establish best practices for development of MRE projects. This can also serve to attract donor funding, as well as investment by technology developers.

The way forward for Caribbean countries SIDS must include the following:

- policy development through a strategic roadmap for MRE as a core aspect of the blue economy ensuring high-level support for comprehensive planning and regulatory framework development;
- relevant data and scientific approaches must be applied to inform policy and decision making;
- research to ensure the best options are developed or selected for the unique situation of individual nations;
- capacity strengthening for knowledge and self-sufficiency of the local community;
- collaboration with international partners and financial institutions to secure support;
- engaging local coastal communities to enable the assessment of possible impacts and to establish acceptance of projects;
- financing must be realigned to support blue economy activities;
- a specific CARICOM renewable energy target needs to be defined for MRE.

Developing Blue Economies through MRE is a novel and important means of ensuring energy security and addressing the United Nations SDGs for the benefit of the Caribbean countries.

168 *Indra Haraksingh*

References

Appendini, C., Urbano-Latorre, C., Figueroa, B., Dagua-Paz, C. *et al.* 2015. Wave energy potential assessment in the Caribbean Low Level Jet using wave hindcast information. *Applied Energy*, 137 (1), 375–384.

Aqua-RET. 2012. Aqua-RET. Available at: http://www.aquaret.com.

Aquatera. 2014. *A Review of the Potential Impacts of Wave and Tidal Energy Development on Scotland's Marine Environment*. Aquatera Ltd. for Marine Scotland.

Bardot Ocean. 2020. Sea water air conditioning. Available at: https://www.bardotocean.com/pages/swac-sea-water-air-conditioning-by-bardot-group. Accessed January 2020.

CARICOM. 2013. *CARICOM Energy Policy*. Georgetown: CARICOM Secretariat.

Graabak, I. and Korpås, M. 2016. Variability characteristics of European wind and solar power resources – a review. *Energies*, 9 (6), 449.

Greenhill, L, Day, J. G., Hughes, A. and Stanley, M. S. 2016. *Marine Renewable Energy*. Commonwealth Blue Economy Series, No. 4. London: Commonwealth Secretariat.

Miceli, F. 2012. Offshore wind turbines foundation types. 4 December. Available at: http://www.windfarmbop.com/offshore-wind-turbines-foundation-types/.

Ocean Energy Forum. 2016. *Ocean Energy Strategic Roadmap, Building Ocean Energy for Europe.*

Renews Ltd. 2018. reNEWS.BIZ. July. Available at: https://renews.biz/46158/barbados-mulls-offshore-options/.

Roberts, J. P., and Ali, A. 2016. *The Blue Economy and Small States*. Commonwealth Blue Economy Series, No. 1. London: Commonwealth Secretariat.

Sustainable Blue Economy. 2018. *The Nairobi Statement of Intent on Advancing the Global Structure*. Sustainable Blue Economy Conference, Nairobi, Kenya. 1–14.

United Nations Conference on Trade and Development (UNCTAD) and Commonwealth Secretariat. 2014. *The Oceans Economy: Opportunities and Challenges for Small Island Developing States (SIDS)*. New York and Geneva: United Nations Publication.

Water and Sewage Corporation (The Bahamas). 2018. *Water Supply, Sanitation, & Resources Management in The Bahamas; Benchmarking of the Caribbean Water Utilities along with WSC (Bahamas)*. The Bahamas Water & Sewage Resources Management Unit.

White, T. 2016. *Feasibility Study for Development of a Co-located Off-shore Wind and Wave Energy Generation System for Trinidad*. MSc. Thesis, The University of the West Indies, St. Augustine.

WindEurope. 2020. *Offshore Wind in Europe: Key Trends and Statistics 2019*. Brussels: WindEurope.

World Bank and United Nations Department of Economic and Social Affairs. 2017. *The Potential of the Blue Economy: Increasing Long-term Benefits of the Sustainable Use of Marine Resources for Small Island Developing States Coastal Least Developed Countries*. Washington, DC: World Bank.

Worldwatch. 2013. *Caribbean Sustainable Energy Roadmap (C-SERMS): Phase I Summary and Recommendations for Policymakers*. CARICOM.

14 Is there a future for the oil and gas sector within the Caribbean's Blue Economy?

Anthony T. Bryan

Introduction

The ocean is the new economic frontier. It promises immense resource wealth, great potential for boosting economic growth, employment and innovation. But crucially, within the context of this chapter, can oil and natural gas production and consumption in the Caribbean be incorporated within, and responsive to the needs of, the Blue Economy? Answers to that question require first a detailed look at the contribution past, present and future of offshore oil and gas in the Caribbean, and second a discussion of maritime zones and delimitations of cross-border acreage, which can form the basis of an integrated and better-managed sector that can complement the Blue Economy agenda. But before we explore these issues it is important to note some inconvenient truths about oil and gas, which mean their contribution to the Caribbean (and global) economy will continue for some time to come.

According to the report of an expert conference at Wilton Park, Sussex, UK in 2011, despite the aspirations to reduce the use of hydrocarbons and increase renewables with a view to minimising carbon dioxide emissions, hydrocarbons will dominate the energy mix at least until 2035. Unconventional fossil fuels such as oil from sands and shale, shale gas and gas from coal (through underground coal gasification) have challenged the concept of "peak oil". The geographical distribution of unconventional sources is wide and technological developments, particularly drilling techniques, are enabling extraction at an economic price. These have the potential to alter significantly the current understanding of energy security and the medium-term contribution of oil and gas.

The need to reduce carbon emissions poses considerable challenges to the development of unconventional fossil fuels. All fossil fuel use can be linked to carbon capture and storage to whatever degree is rewarded by the market. The need to protect the environment, reduce greenhouse gas emissions and protect the public is a *sine qua non* for the successful future development of the sector. To that end, innovative technology and energy education are necessary in order to allow governments, regulators and the industry to cooperate effectively (Wilton Park, 2011).

170 Anthony T. Bryan

According to Bailey (2020), a noted expert on global energy, while transportation might be the main use, petroleum and its derivatives are in almost everything. It may be safe to assume that oil demand will persist even with net zero carbon, although the size and shape of future demand is up for debate. From an industry perspective, oil wells decline naturally, so new development and investment is needed to maintain supply. Oil companies and service companies will still be needed, though many will be challenged by growing uncertainty and fluctuations in prices and geo-political volatility. So in short, any discussion of the Blue Economy in the Caribbean must include the hydrocarbons sector.

Oil and gas in the Caribbean: The current state of play and a future outlook

A retrospective look

Historically, only Trinidad and Tobago, Cuba and Suriname were the oil producers of the Caribbean. In addition to these three, other countries such as Curaçao, Aruba and St Croix (part of the US Virgin Islands) operated oil refineries. Trinidad rapidly emerged as the Caribbean's major oil producer. Its first well (61 metres deep) was drilled onshore in 1857 in the vicinity of the Pitch Lake at La Brea in the southwest of the island. By 1908, commercial oil production began in the same locale. Its first export cargo of crude oil was shipped by tanker in 1910. Its first refinery was built in 1912. By 1930, oil production had increased to 10 million barrels per year. That same year, Venezuelan oil was imported to be refined locally. By 1940, the country's refining capacity was at 285,000 barrels per day (bpd). In 1954, offshore drilling for oil began off the southeast coast of the island. In 1971, when drilling began off the north coast of Trinidad, natural gas was discovered. In 1999, Atlantic built what would be the first of 4 LNG (Liquefied Natural Gas) trains that would put the country ahead of most of the world in the monetisation of natural gas (Gov.tt, 2020). Soon after Trinidad became a natural gas economy, replacing oil as its main energy staple for economic growth. Utilising the advantage of cheap natural gas, the government entered into a joint venture with local businesses to establish the Point Lisas Industrial Estate. Today, the estate is home to approximately 103 companies involved in a range of industrial activities (PLIPDECO, 2020).

The petrochemical sector is dominant, however, with many multi-national production plants operating on the estate. Ease of access to vast resources of natural gas has been a strong incentive for some of the world's leading manufacturers of ammonia, urea, methanol, other petrochemicals and steel. It is the site of two power stations and a large desalination plant. Most of the industry located at Point Lisas is dependent on cheap natural gas which is produced off the east coast of Trinidad and transported by pipeline across the island. Trinidad's energy success story was not replicated by either Cuba or

Suriname. Both countries remained producers of heavy grade onshore oil. There is little doubt that much of Trinidad's fortune is due to its geology and proximity to Venezuela which has one of the world's largest deposits of oil.

The search for the frontier provinces

Beginning in 2015 there was a rush to develop the "frontier provinces" of oil and gas in the Caribbean. Encouraged by the discoveries in Guyana that year, a number of international oil companies (IOCs) and state companies (NOCs) moved in to tie up acreage in bid rounds in the expectation that their investments would eventually pay off. The development of technology to facilitate the exploration and accessing of hydrocarbon resources in deep water accelerated the interest shown in the countries of the Caribbean. The geological surveys demonstrate that the region consists of a series of structural elements, the most prominent being the Venezuelan and Colombian deep sea suboceanic depressions, the Nicaraguan Rise and the Greater and Lesser Antilles bordering the Caribbean Sea in the North and East.

In a 2012 report, the United States Geological Survey (USGS) of 31 priority geological provinces in South America and the Caribbean assessed the undiscovered conventional hydrocarbon potential at 126 billion barrels of crude oil and 679 trillion cubic feet (tcf) of natural gas. In the Guyana–Suriname Basin (GSB), the crude oil potential was assessed at 13.6 billion barrels and natural gas at 21 tcf. Thirty-one geologic provinces were assessed in the study which represented at the time, a complete reassessment of the South America/Caribbean region (USGS, 2012). Since that time, a series of world-class discoveries made by US oil major ExxonMobil off the coast of Guyana has been forcing the USGS to reassess its estimated petroleum reserves in the GSB which could see its previous estimates increase. The whole area appears to be characterised by excellent quality reservoirs in deep and also shallow waters.

The current big picture of Caribbean oil and gas

Since 2014 there have been some dramatic changes in the global picture of oil and gas. Oil prices fell dramatically in that year. The consequences of the fall in oil prices produced mixed results for the Caribbean. Oil importing countries saw their bills drop by half, while low prices created additional opportunities for upstream projects. Oil and natural gas exporting countries such as Trinidad faced declining revenues from the sector, resulting in serious budgetary constraints and economic adjustments. In a low oil price environment, when contracts have to be renegotiated, the IOCs put a great deal of pressure on oil exporting countries to adjust (i.e. lower) their tax codes to compensate for IOC development costs over previous years (Bryan, 2018).

172 *Anthony T. Bryan*

Even after the fall, the oil markets only rebounded slightly and starting in 2020 went from bad to worse. The global environment faces dual challenges of an oil price crash and the Covid-19 pandemic, with competitive pressures and disruptions to supply chains. The volatile nature of the oil and gas market is now in stark exposure. Until recently, the so-called OPEC+ arrangement (an alliance of crude-oil producers, who have been undertaking corrections in supply in the oil markets since 2017) had successfully managed supply to keep the oil price up in the face of a global slow-down in demand, but within a matter of months all that has changed.

In mid-March 2020, Norway-based Rystad Energy's forecast for global oil demand projected a decrease of 0.6%, or 600,000 bpd, year-on-year. Total oil demand in 2019 was approximately 99.8 million bpd, which is now projected to decline to 99.2 million bpd in 2020. This severe downgrade, compared to previous estimates, takes into account the quarantine lockdowns in Europe, a disastrous Covid-19 pandemic in the United States, massive cancellations of flights by airlines, the travel ban between Europe and the US, and the reduced global demand for road traffic fuel. Consequently, the impact on global oil demand so far has been staggering.

The Caribbean regional energy picture is now complicated further by the global shift in exploration from mature fields and basins to new and emerging plays; the drop (3 million bpd or 20% of total consumption) in Chinese oil demand since the onset of Covid-19 forcing a decline in crude-oil prices; the challenge for exploration companies now faced with a global glut of oil; and the global movement to a lower-carbon and renewable energy future. These trends are all interconnected and will continue to have an impact on the regional oil and gas picture.

Before the current crisis, there was a positive outlook for the energy sector in the Caribbean with new discoveries in deep water and the increasing penetration of renewable energy in other island territories. Fortunately, exploration and production have not come to an end. In the big picture, Guyana has joined Trinidad and Suriname as oil producers and exporters in the 15-member Caribbean Community (CARICOM) bloc of nations. Suriname has discovered two large offshore wells to go along with the 16,000 barrels of heavy crude that it has continued to produce from onshore land wells for several decades. These are Suriname's first offshore wells, just a few miles away from two of the largest of the 17 that Exxon and its partners, and UK-based Tullow Oil have found so far off Guyana. Barbados also produces about 1,600 barrels of oil daily from a small collection of onshore wells. The Guyana discovery has sparked deeper interest in the region with The Bahamas, Jamaica, Barbados and Grenada all moving to step up exploration. While Guyana is in the most dynamic and productive region so far, several other countries in the circum-Caribbean region continue to open their territorial waters to deep-water exploration for oil and gas. The results have been mixed.

A closer look and current snapshot of some individual countries

French Guiana

French Guiana is the country that inspired the Caribbean's momentum in deep-water exploration. It began following the discovery of the Zaedyus well by Tullow Oil in late 2011. The Zaedyus well substantiated the theory of Tullow geologists that the geological features of offshore Ghana (where the huge Jubilee field had been discovered in 2007) are replicated on the opposite side of the Atlantic, in the now-named Guyana–Suriname Basin. In 2011, French Guiana was actually the hottest of the deep-water "frontier provinces" – the P10 (10% probability) reserve estimate of the Zaedyus was 840 million barrels of oil equivalent (Bryan, 2013). However, in French Guiana, expectations of a boom have given way to disappointment. After the Zaedyus find in 2011, four other appraisal wells were unsuccessful. A partnership of Shell, Tullow, Northpet and Wessek Exploration failed to discover commercial hydrocarbons in French Guiana's exploration acreage. It is difficult to predict the results of future activities, but to date initial expectations have not been realised.

Guyana

There has been significant success in the discovery of more than eight billion barrels of recoverable hydrocarbons in Guyana's deep water. ExxonMobil made its first lift of Guyana crude in January 2020 and the first lift for Guyana during February. By 2025 production could be 750,000 bpd and by the end of the decade, more than one million bpd of oil equivalent. Under the current Production Sharing Agreement the IOCs have a 75% cost recovery with the remaining 25% profit equally split between the licensees and Guyana. The current royalty rate is 2%. The impact on the Guyanese economy could be convulsive. In 2020 it was forecast to grow by 86%, and the per capita income could more than double to US$$10,000. This is now in doubt because of the effects of, and responses to, Covid-19, but Rystad Energy estimates that national revenue will amount to more than US$117 billion over the lifetime of the projects. With the windfall, and a population of less than 800,000, Guyana could become one of the world's richest nations per capita. Obviously it will not happen overnight. The IOCs have to recover their investment and projected peak production is still some years away. But a national sense of euphoria is high and caution may be in short supply. This is concerning because Guyana faces some harsh realities. It must provide the necessary legislation, institutional structures and management for the industry. Further, it is vulnerable to the many "above ground" pitfalls that could accompany the boom. For example, the explosion of money might be difficult to absorb and to manage; traditional economic sectors might lose out if Guyana becomes overly dependent on exports of a single commodity, the so-called "Dutch disease"; and corruption and poor governance are significant

174　*Anthony T. Bryan*

risks, in a country that has real problems in these areas. So Guyana has a great opportunity to improve its economic and social position, but the jury is still out as to whether the resource wealth and the expectations of its people can be managed effectively.

Suriname

The Republic of Suriname could become the Caribbean and South America's newest energy power. In November 2019, the American company Apache and the French company Total announced the discovery of significant oil deposits offshore. The maritime geology is similar to that of neighbouring Guyana. The expected energy windfall could be substantial. It could be a game changer for a nation of a little under 600,000 people. The country is seen to be well prepared to handle the largesse, because of the regulatory system for oil and gas, the resident skills and the negotiating capacity to deal with the IOCs built up over the years by the state oil company Staatsolie. However, corruption is an issue, the politics is uncertain and the macroeconomic environment may be seen as risk factors for other investments.

Trinidad and Tobago

As noted previously, the country is the region's oldest oil and gas economy, but its place as the primary hydrocarbons economy is being superseded by Guyana, and quite possibly by Suriname too. But given its 110-year status as a mature oil province, Trinidad's oil and gas service companies and investors now have a major presence in the Guyanese energy landscape. Domestically, crude-oil production remains low and there has not been a major oil discovery in more than a decade. Indeed, oil production fell by 27% during the period 2015–2019. Offshore drilling activity reveals more gas-prone than oil-rich plays. The only bright spot is the potential *onshore* discovery by Touchstone in the Ortoire block in November 2019. With respect to natural gas, currently, BHP Billiton has found significant gas offshore and remains optimistic about the possibility of further discoveries. Unfortunately, Trinidad's energy sector remains temporarily becalmed because of natural gas curtailment, with plants at the massive Point Lisas industrial estate having shut down and others engaging in difficult price negotiations with the National Gas Company. Further, the outlook for crude refining remains uncertain. In September 2019, Patriotic Energies was the successful bidder for the former (now mothballed) Petrotrin refinery. But a reopening date for the refinery has not been announced.

The Caribbean's future in oil and gas

On the positive side, the Southern Caribbean (from Barbados down to Trinidad, Venezuela and to the "Three GUIANAS") is oil and gas rich. In fact, it is a new axis of oil and gas development in the region. Trinidad (despite the challenges to its traditional leadership in the regional energy space), Guyana and Suriname are the game changers for a new era in oil and geopolitics for the Caribbean.

It is time for an accelerated regional energy policy. Several countries in the Caribbean have launched their own national energy policies. The only regional policy plan is the CARICOM Energy Policy (CEP) that has the goal of assuring access to affordable, adequate, safe and clean energy products necessary for the development of the member states of the Community. In order to fulfil the goal, the Community is expected to develop a programme of regional actions related to the respective objectives of the CEP, including: timely access to adequate, reliable and affordable supplies of energy; least-cost hydrocarbon resources for each member state and the appropriate standards for petroleum and related products; diversification of energy resources through the increased use of renewable energy; promotion of fuel switching to cleaner energy sources and greater efficiency use in the transport sector; fair pricing and access to hydrocarbon resources by member states; and development of strategies for taking advantage of opportunities for trade in energy services regionally and internationally (CARICOM.org, 2013). Transformation of energy markets in the Community requires every member state to mobilise large amounts of capital. Progress is slow and incremental, but is sustained via the special meetings of the Council for Trade and Economic Development (COTED) on Energy.

On the negative side, it is hard to avoid the conclusion that given the oil collapse induced by Saudi Arabia, the impact of Covid-19 on tourism and a world that seems to be moving toward recession and diminished global confidence, the Caribbean will not be immune from an economic shock that will require significant economic and social adjustments. Indeed, for all oil and gas producers in the Caribbean and elsewhere, the loss of revenue is likely to be substantial. Lower oil prices are expected to put severe fiscal strain on a number of the most important producers. While Caribbean nations that import oil and gas are likely to benefit from lower prices, this is not likely to compensate for the fall in visitor arrivals and attendant taxes for the tourism dependent countries. For the Caribbean energy exporters, in the current circumstances, oil and gas are no longer the panaceas for economic distress. Economic diversity is the new mantra.

As discussed, the oil and gas sectors are important elements of the Caribbean's regional economies. It is also clear that the global energy landscape is changing dramatically characterised by high levels of uncertainty inherent in the system, as well as the enormous impact energy has on development, security, the environment, the economy and geopolitics. The global energy system is undergoing a transition away from a nearly complete dependence on fossil fuels toward a greater reliance on clean and renewable energy sources. Because this low-carbon energy transition will fundamentally alter the relationship between energy producers and consumers, its geopolitical ramifications are now a key concern of global energy leaders.

176 *Anthony T. Bryan*

Among the foreign policy tools that can be leveraged to support a country in managing the geopolitical consequences of an energy transition, diplomacy is one of the most important. The results demonstrate the strategic importance of fostering bilateral energy diplomacy with countries that can provide security of domestic energy supply, markets for the long-term monetisation of hydrocarbon resources and support for economic diversification. These strategic relations have energy at the core but should extend to joint investment and science and technology collaboration in order to have maximum value (Griffiths, 2018).

The notion of an "energy transition" remains an inchoate concept. Classically understood to encompass shifts in the national supply of energy or the discovery of new energy resources, energy transitions are now also conceptualised to include transformations in the markets that deliver energy, in addition to conversions in end-use devices. In its recent formulation, the transition refers to a confluence of issues from rapid cost declines in renewable energy systems like wind and solar, to the US shale "revolution", to IT advances in smart grids, to innovative business and contract models. The Caribbean has to get on board in the energy transition that will depend heavily on the Blue Economy.

Offshore oil and gas resources in the emerging Blue Economy of the Caribbean

The preceding discussion has emphasised that offshore oil and gas production should be regarded as one of the major components of the Blue Economy in the Caribbean and is projected to increase significantly in the future. The ongoing strategic shift in oil and gas developments from onshore to offshore, means that the offshore, "blue", component of the oil and gas sectors is likely to be of increasing significance to the region's economic and developmental future. But can these resources be shared throughout the region? In this context some discussion of maritime zones, maritime boundaries and cross-border negotiations is important for gauging the regional Blue Economy potential.

Subsea petroleum development has played a huge role in the industry, and the control of oil and gas fields beneath the sea surface remains vital for both domestic and international interests of almost every nation. Every nation and oil and gas company desires efficient, safe, environmentally mindful and profitable oil and gas production. Despite the international community's best efforts, maritime border disputes still exist in certain areas around the world, sometimes impeding the development of oil and gas. The role maritime law plays in relation to the access and control of subsea oil and gas in disputed territorial claims around the world indicates that there may have to be multiple approaches to find resolutions to certain maritime border disputes (Charney and Alexander, 1993; 1998).

The rights of coastal states to exploit and regulate areas of the ocean under their jurisdiction are key foundations of the Law of the Sea Convention

Oil and gas sector 177

(LOSC). These rights need to be balanced with the freedom of the seas, and the navigation and access to resources outside of state control. To demarcate the proverbial rules of the road, the LOSC permits coastal states to establish several different maritime zones, and these zones give coastal states different jurisdictional rights. In general, a state has more rights in zones near to its coastline than it does further into the ocean. The main challenges associated with these zones are how variations in geography affect where zones end and where new zones begin.

The LOSC employs what it terms "baselines" to draw maritime zones. Rather than having moving maritime boundaries, the baseline is fixed to begin at the low-water line along the coast. The low-water line is derived from the coastal state's own charts. These zones are measured using nautical miles, a measurement based on the circumference of the Earth. One nautical mile is equal to approximately 1.15 miles on land.

The LOSC divides the ocean into six different zones:

1 Internal Waters;
2 Territorial Sea;
3 Contiguous Zone;
4 Exclusive Economic Zone (EEZ);
5 Continental Shelf;
6 High Seas & Deep Ocean Floor.

While the LOSC specifically defines the various maritime zones and their features, there are continuing controversies worldwide over the definition of the features and the zones they produce. One challenge centres on the *definition of islands*. So there is an incentive for states to obtain island status for their deep-ocean exploits. Islands project a full territorial sea with over-flight (national airspace) control and a full EEZ. Even small islands such as the Isla de Aves (Bird Island), a dependency of Venezuela, is the subject of numerous territorial disputes with Dominica and the Netherlands. Isla de Aves is 375 metres (1,230 ft) in length and never more than 50 metres (160 ft) in width, and rises 4 metres (13 ft) above the sea on a calm day. Under a particular interpretation of the United Nations Convention on the Law of the Sea (UNCLOS) it could be classified as a rock, which would give Venezuela only a 12-nautical-mile EEZ. But Venezuela claims it is an island, which grants it a 200-mile (320 km) EEZ.

Local issues and geopolitical realities

Offshore oil and gas projects face numerous technical and legal risks not typically encountered in onshore exploration and production activities. Among these risks is the possibility that the relevant licence/concession area in which an oil and gas company is entitled to explore and/or produce falls within or near an area subject to an international maritime border dispute. In

178 Anthony T. Bryan

this context, different sources of law applicable to offshore oil and gas projects amid maritime border disputes, include: (a) the provisions of the UNCLOS; (b) the law applicable to the exploration and exploitation of offshore oil and gas resources under joint development agreements negotiated amid maritime territorial disputes; and (c) the law applicable to the exploration of offshore oil and gas resources amid unresolved maritime territorial disputes pursuant to relevant international case law.

Sometimes both hindrances and opportunities for the development of oil and natural gas have regional or local origins, while other times wider geopolitical and economic interests are hurdles to finding a workable solution. For example, disputes over the sovereignty of maritime hydrocarbon resources are ongoing in the South China Sea, the Eastern Mediterranean Sea and in the Persian/Arabian Gulf. In other areas, delimitations of the EEZ have had to be settled before the expansion of offshore production could commence. Some might say that there is no EEZ solution for some disputes. However, in practice, most countries rely on international law to establish rules and legal mechanisms for dealing with trans-boundary hydrocarbon deposits. Coastal states worldwide have made such arrangements to overcome potential political or technical obstacles to the development of their hydrocarbon resources in maritime areas, either jointly or on the basis of an agreed upon sharing.

Current international law that applies to the cooperative development of petroleum resources imposes few procedural requirements on states. In the event of a failure to agree they may choose to make further efforts at developing cooperative agreements or go ahead alone and develop the resource. But with respect to the economic development of disputed maritime areas, UNCLOS advances the argument that in the absence of an agreed boundary or a provisional co-operative agreement, none of the states concerned operates legitimately by unilaterally undertaking petroleum operations in the disputed area, including seismic surveys, if the conduct of such operations proves to aggravate the dispute.

In sum, coastal states are under a procedural duty to negotiate in good faith with a view to reaching some form of cooperative joint agreement pending the final settlement of their boundaries. Ultimately, in the absence of an agreed boundary, only provisional interstate cooperation, such as joint exploration and development, can enable disputing parties to facilitate investments and realise the economic potential of disputed areas. In this context, the Guyana–Venezuela border dispute (which is now before the International Court of Justice, ICJ) does pose a calculated risk for the large offshore IOCs which would normally avoid venturing into those areas. The matter is further complicated by the current internal politics of Venezuela.

At present there are at least 16 maritime disputes in the circum-Caribbean region. Most relate only to territorial waters. But some emanate from land boundary disputes such as between Guatemala and Belize, and Guyana and Venezuela. Territorial tensions in the Caribbean Sea, involving Nicaragua, Colombia and Costa Rica, have flared up during recent years, with

Nicaragua and Colombia granting oil exploration licences in areas claimed by others, followed by both sides making regular claims to the ICJ to determine their maritime boundary. And there will be more to come as countries pursue their options of energy and resource extraction in the region. There are two recent developments of note.

First, as a result of major oil finds offshore Guyana, authorities in Trinidad have moved to apply to the relevant world bodies to extend its country's continental shelf as far as possible southeast toward the outer edge of its continental margin that is proximate to the Guyana–Suriname Basin. The initiative is intended to come as legally close as possible to the fields of the GSB. Similarly, exploration companies in Suriname to the east want to readjust their search areas as the latest Exxon wells off Guyana are close to their common maritime border.

Second, another development is Venezuela's plan to remap its offshore oil territory in order to be specific about its Caribbean oil and gas prospects. The seismic survey will include an eastern area of Venezuela that borders Guyana. Venezuela has mapped its offshore territory for oil deposits in the past, but some areas remain uncharted. The new survey will also include areas bordering Caribbean islands such as Grenada and St Vincent and the Grenadines. Several surveys are pending to identify viable commercial options for natural gas. In the past, the state oil company Petroleos de Venezuela SA (PDVSA) was always focused on oil. But now it has become more interested in its oil and gas projects in the east near Trinidad and Guyana. The remapping initiative may further aggravate the dispute with Guyana and collide with the Exxon Mobil venture in the GSB. In fact, following an encounter in December 2018 with the Venezuelan navy, one of the two ships hired by Exxon to conduct seismic surveys in Guyanese waters has stayed away from the border.

As maritime disputes increase, some recent bilateral agreements in the Caribbean seek to go beyond the cooperation established under bilateral delimitation treaties. They suggest a preference to design innovative legal frameworks in which different, sometimes diverging interests may be managed. One of the important regional initiatives to resolve differences about subsea petroleum rights outside of an appeal to the Law of the Sea concerns the Loran-Manatee natural gas field that crosses the maritime boundary between Venezuela and Trinidad. For the interests to be properly divided, the two nations negotiated for more than a decade to establish ownership.

The field contains an estimated 10 tcf of natural gas sandstone reservoirs that span the area around the two nations' borders. Venezuela and Trinidad allowed for various international gas companies to research and explore the gas contained within the field and more particularly, which nations controlled the right to produce or sell the rights to production. The Loran–Manatee agreement recognises two particularly important issues with the development of subsea petroleum rights. First, the extensive research done demonstrates the importance of definitively establishing ownership interests prior to

180   *Anthony T. Bryan*

development for each field discovery to prevent future disputes. Second, it demonstrates the role that corporate entities can play in the development of subsea petroleum, establishing and gathering all the information about the different petroleum rights. So oil and gas companies can play an important role in resolution schemes in future disputed territories.

Development of subsea petroleum involves significant investment in terms of money and time. As exemplified in the decade-and-a-half-long negotiation between Venezuela and Trinidad, the research and development of these significant resources can often be too great for individual nations to take on. For this reason, countries may choose to exchange the rights to develop the petroleum in exchange for the oil and gas companies to put in the upfront costs of establishing and gathering all the information concerning the different petroleum rights. Thus, oil and gas companies can play a very important role in resolution schemes in future disputed territories. As one analyst suggests, when mediations led by state actors or international governing bodies have not led to successful settlements of certain maritime disputes, rather than doubling down on the efforts for state actors to resolve these disputes or force the parties into international court or arbitration, perhaps a new route could be attempted. Despite the global sceptical perception of corporate involvement in international legal affairs, private involvement could help the process (Brooking, 2017). In short, there are legal and administrative roadmaps for cooperative approaches that could allow the entire region to benefit from the oil and gas resources in its Blue Economy.

Conclusion

This chapter has addressed the potential for oil and gas in the Caribbean's Blue Economy. Future regional energy demands and foreign exchange earnings depend a great deal on this sector. There will be demands for continuing investment in further exploration, shortening the transition from exploration to production, negotiating maritime boundaries and ensuring a stable political and regulatory environment for regional energy cooperation. While it is acknowledged that at present and for the future, the region's overall development as an offshore/Blue Economy will depend on hydrocarbons, there also will have to be options developed to minimise the risks associated with the offshore hydrocarbons industry and provide the opportunity for more sustainable Blue Economy activities to grow. Such options might include the application of marine protected areas, marine spatial planning, the use of ecosystem-based management, and integrated coastal management. The literature on the Blue Economy is replete with such recommendations. There are many options to be discussed in the larger Blue Economy framework, bearing in mind the importance of offshore oil and gas in the equation. The most important takeaway is that the oil-producing Caribbean countries should be included in the formulation of economic policies that will be anchored in the Blue Economy. Such inclusion and the promotion of oil and gas into the regional energy mix will facilitate an increase in regional access to energy and help to further industrial development in the blue/green Caribbean.

References

Bailey, J. 2020. Climate change and the oil sector. Available at: https://www.iamericas.org/documents/energy/webinars/presentations/bailey_webinar_climate_change_oil_sector.pdf.

Brooking, D. R. 2017. The curse of black gold: How maritime oil reserves can sink international negotiations. *Oil and Gas, Natural Resources, and Energy Journal*, 2 (6) March, pp. 651–684. Available at: https://digitalcommons.law.ou.edu/cgi/viewcontent.cgi?article=1080&context=onej.

Bryan, A. T. 2013. Oil and gas in the Caribbean: What's at the finish line? *PetroleumWorld*, 11 April. Available at: http://www.petroleumworld.com/lagniappe13041101.htm.

Bryan, A. T. 2018. Caribbean energy outlook. In: B. Bagley*et al.* (Eds), *After the Fall: Energy Security, Sustainable Development, and the Environment*, London, Lexington Books.

CARICOM.org. 2013. The CARICOM Energy Policy in Bullets. Available at: https://caricom.org/the-caricom-energy-policy-in-bullets-2/.

Charney, J. I. and Alexander, L. M. (Eds). 1993. *International Maritime Boundaries*, Volumes I and II, Dordrecht, Martinus Nijhoff.

Charney, J. I. and Alexander, L. M. (Eds). 1998. *International Maritime Boundaries*, Volume III, Dordrecht, Martinus Nijhoff.

Gov.tt. 2020. Historical facts on the petroleum industry of Trinidad and Tobago. Available at: http://www.energy.gov.tt/historical-facts-petroleum/.

Griffiths, S. 2018. Bilateral energy diplomacy in a time of energy transition. *EDA Insight*, December. Available at: https://eda.ac.ae/docs/default-source/Publications/eda-insight_fret-ii_bilateral-diplomacy_en.pdf?sfvrsn=2.

PLIPDECO. 2020. Overview – Point Lisas Industrial Estate. Available at: http://www.plipdeco.com/main/index.php?page=estate-management-overview.

United States Geological Survey (USGS). 2012. *Assessment of Undiscovered Conventional Oil and Gas Resources of South America and the Caribbean*, May. Available at: https://pubs.usgs.gov/fs/2012/3046/fs2012-3046.pdf.

Wilton Park. 2011. Conference Report, New Energy Frontiers: What role for hydrocarbons in global energy security? June, Wilton Park, WP 1111. Available at: https://www.wiltonpark.org.uk/wp-content/uploads/wp1111-report.pdf.

15 The future of deep-seabed minerals and marine genetic resources in Blue Economies

Laleta Davis-Mattis

Introduction

Deep-seabed minerals are one of the many categories of economic goods that can be derived from the ocean and are potentially a significant part of Blue Economic growth for some countries. Demand for basic and rare-earth minerals is expected to increase substantially around the globe in the coming decades. Some estimates predict that global mineral demand will be 60 percent higher in 2050 than it is today. For more traditional minerals such as copper and nickel, demand could triple in that time (Madiraju, 2019).

The high seas constitute about half of Earth's surface and 95 percent of the volume of the world ocean (Payne, 2019). The Clarion–Clipperton Zone (CCZ) is an area of seabed of about six million km^2, with depths of 4,000–6,000 m, located in the Eastern Central Pacific Ocean and bounded to the North and South by the Clarion and Clipperton Fracture Zones. It is comparable in area to Europe and is a prime location for commercially viable deposits of polymetallic nodules which have been the subject of scientific investigation, mineral prospecting and exploration since the 1960s (Lodge et al., 2014). One estimate is that the CCZ contains 6,000 times more titanium than all land reserves combined. Other areas were calculated to have several times more cobalt and yttrium, and significant amounts of copper, lithium and manganese. A 2012 European Commission Report estimated that by 2030 as much as 10 percent of the world's mineral requirements could come from deep-seabed mining (DSM) (Madiraju, 2019).

Genetic resources also constitute a significant potential contribution to the Blue Economy. At the 2012 UN Conference on Sustainable Development (Rio+20), states committed themselves

> to address, on an urgent basis ... the issue of the conservation and sustainable use of marine biological diversity in areas beyond national jurisdiction, including by taking a decision on the development of an international instrument under the United Nations Convention on the Law of the Sea [UNCLOS].

The Draft Agreement calls for states to cooperate towards the conservation and sustainable use of marine biological diversity in areas beyond national jurisdiction (ABNJ), and to cooperate towards the promotion of marine scientific research (United Nations, 2019).

The deep-seabed, often referred to as the final frontier, remains largely unexplored. However, existing knowledge reveals a variety of habitats with a rich and unique biodiversity, as well as ecosystems discovered only some 40 years ago. Deep-seabed resources are thought to be the future of the planet as mankind pursues an anthropogenic trajectory towards development considered essential to high-tech applications and switches to a Blue Economy (Cuyvers et al., 2018). This chapter explores the challenges faced by Caribbean countries in obtaining the benefits from these resources, as well as the opportunities for capacity building and other ocean-governance-related benefits to be had from engaging with these processes.

Deep-seabed minerals

Opportunities

Deep-seabed minerals and genetic resources present a special case for the development of Blue Economies for Caribbean countries. While Caribbean countries are not known to have significant deep-seabed mineral resources within their Exclusive Economic Zones (EEZs), there may be benefits to be derived from participating in the mining of such minerals in the Area (deep-seabed beyond national jurisdiction) in an effort to capitalise on the new "gold rush". The matter of sharing the benefits from these common property resources based on the Common Heritage of Mankind (CHM) principle is currently being developed by the International Seabed Authority (ISA) and experts from around the globe. Caribbean states should position themselves to take advantage of these opportunities as they seek to resolve and catch up from the vestiges of colonisation.

The debate on the economic implications for the commercial exploitation of polymetallic nodules commenced early in the discussions on commercial exploitation of the resources of the Area. The discussion did not anticipate the rapid growth in technology and investor interest in deep-seabed resources so that the notion in 1994, based on technological and related factors prevailing in 1989, that it was unlikely that commercial mining of polymetallic nodules would begin in the decade 2001–2010, has been self-defeated (United Nations, 1994).

Indeed, it was posited during the UNCLOS III deliberations, for some developing countries, that the rules concerning the control and management of deep-seabed resources constituted a significant test case for the implementation of the New International Economic Order (NIEO) (Kirton and Vasciannie, 2002). Developing countries argued that these resources should be considered the common heritage of mankind, meaning that they should be

184   *Laleta Davis-Mattis*

treated as the property of all mankind and not be exploited solely for the benefit of countries and companies with advanced technology. The NIEO position indicates that revenues obtained from mining the nodules should be distributed to reduce economic disparities between developing and developed countries. The common-heritage concept, as applied to seabed mining, is a fundamental and integral part of efforts to establish an NIEO (Payne and Nassa, 1982). However, it has been argued that the concerns of developing countries have been superseded by The 1994 Implementation Agreement, that has created a final regime and the establishment of the International Seabed Authority (ISA, The Authority) which, though sensitive to developing country concerns on some points, concedes substantial influence and authority to states which have the financial resources and technological expertise in the area of DSM (Kirton and Vasciannie, 2002).

The significance of the part to be played by developing countries was self-evident before the adoption of the International Convention on the Law of the Sea Convention (UNCLOS). Indeed, with respect to the organisation of the ISA, two issues assumed prominence from the outset. First, as noted in the Declaration of Principles (United Nations, 1970; see especially Articles 1 and 7), there was early agreement on the idea that the resources of the deep-seabed and ocean floor constituted the common heritage of mankind, and therefore, the Area and its resources should be explored and exploited in the interests of mankind as a whole, with particular consideration being given to the needs of developing countries. Secondly, it was acknowledged that the technological and financial resources needed to exploit the Area and its resources, and to make full use of the data and new materials derived from deep-seabed activities were in the possession of only a few, industrialised countries. Such technical and financial resources were also very often in the hands of private enterprises, rather than State entities, in the industrialised countries (Kirton & Vasciannie, 2002). Other areas of concern and discontent during the UNCLOS III negotiations pertained to technology transfer and production policies. However, although the UNCLOS made some effort to reflect developing country perspectives, the Implementation Agreement has shifted the balance significantly away from that result (Kirton and Vasciannie, 2002).

Developing states are disadvantaged, for several reasons including lack of economic and technical competence to participate in the "big boys' club". Article 148 of the Convention exhorts states parties to promote the effective participation of developing states in activities in the Area having due regard to their special interests and needs, and in particular to the special need of the land-locked and geographically disadvantaged among them. However, this acknowledgement presents little comfort to developing states. Article 144, among other things, exhorts the Authority to "promote and encourage" the transfer of deep-seabed technology to developing countries, and mandates the Authority and states so to do. However, it is argued that Section 5(2) of the Annex to the Implementation Agreement has nullified Annex IE, Article 5 of

Deep-seabed minerals 185

the Convention; or, in other words, the Implementation Agreement has removed all provisions that could justify the mandatory transfer of technology from developed country operators to the Enterprise or to developing countries for seabed mining purposes. The Enterprise is the organ through which the Authority carries out the functions referred to in the Convention; pursuant to article 153, paragraph 2(a), as well as the transporting, processing and marketing of minerals recovered from the Area. In place of this mandatory transfer regime, the Implementation Agreement contemplates a scheme in which the Enterprise and developing countries shall seek the requisite technology "on fair and reasonable commercial terms and conditions in the open market, or through joint-venture arrangements" (Kirton and Vasciannie, 2002).

The argument by Kirton and Vasciannie is further advanced through the proposition that the Implementation Agreement indicates that where the Enterprise or developing countries are unable to obtain DSM technology (presumably on the open market), the Authority "may request" contractors and sponsoring states to cooperate with it in facilitating technology acquisition by the Enterprise or developing countries "on fair and reasonable commercial terms and conditions, consistent with the effective protection of intellectual property rights" (Kirton and Vasciannie, 2002)

With specific reference to Caribbean economies, it is unlikely that any one or even a consortium of countries could invest in such technology. Deep-sea exploration, not to mention mining, is an expensive exercise that no Caribbean country is likely to be able to afford to invest in, even though investments can be attracted from far afield. The long-term return on investments could also pose a deterrent to private sector enterprises within the Caribbean. An overview of the DSM value chain, the technologies and the estimated costs reveals that exploration will cost more than US$100,000 a day. Most exploration trips need a budget of US$50–200 million. For exploitation, the costs run in hundreds of millions of US dollars, depending on the deposit and location (EPRS, 2015). The largest costs are the costs of the vessel, drilling and crew. In terms of economic benefits, much is decided by the previously mentioned exogenous factors, mainly depending on what the market price for the specific resource at the time of sale and the cost savings DSM can generate vis-à-vis terrestrial mining (EPRS, 2015).

The Commonwealth Blue Charter, an agreement by all 53 Commonwealth countries to actively co-operate to solve ocean-related problems and meet commitments for sustainable ocean development, reaffirms the commitment to recognising the primacy of UNCLOS as the legal framework within which all activities in the oceans must be carried out, supported by other applicable treaties to which Commonwealth member countries are parties and affirming the rights of landlocked member countries as stipulated in UNCLOS (Commonwealth Secretariat, 2018). The Charter notes that the seabed and its resources beyond the limits of national jurisdiction are the common heritage of humankind, as governed by the regime in Part XI of UNCLOS.

186 *Laleta Davis-Mattis*

Despite this, many Caribbean countries are yet to fully capitalise on the ocean's capacity to deliver equitable and sustainable economic growth particularly from new blue growth sectors (marine biotechnology, DSM and ocean renewable energy) (Ram, 2018). It is notable that the report, though proposing that Caribbean economies can benefit from exploiting deep-seabed resources to their own benefit and in accordance with their own developmental principles (the right to development), fails to progress the topic of DSM any further. It appears, that though all Caribbean states are parties to UNCLOS and have sat at the negotiating table, there have been no strategic efforts at the CARICOM sub-regional level to acknowledge any potential benefits from a regional approach to DSM.

Jamaica's courtship with DSM

On the eve of the celebration of the 25th year of the ratification of the UNCLOS, Jamaica indicated its intention to join the band of a select group of countries and a mix of private entities sponsored by national governments, including China, France, Germany, India, Japan, the Republic of Korea, the Russian Federation and the Interoceanmetal Joint Organisation (a consortium of Bulgaria, Cuba, the Czech Republic, Poland, the Russian Federation and Slovakia), as well as small island states such as the Cook Islands, Kiribati, Nauru, Singapore and Tonga. This move represents the first of its kind in the English-speaking Caribbean. The occasion was the meeting of Cabinet Ministers on 4 March 2019 which heralded Jamaica into a new era of oceans management, this time in ABNJ.

The 29 exploration contracts granted to date by the ISA pursuant to the mining code represent a set of legislative instruments, procedures and guidelines for managing the exhaustive deep-seabed minerals for present and future generations. This will be done through a comprehensive system of contracts which grant rights and obligations to sponsoring states, their contractors and the ISA itself, presenting a complex evolving regime destined to end in a sharing of benefits from these minerals for the common heritage of mankind and for generations yet unborn. The ISA through its Enterprise will be held accountable for its management of these resources which in a sense are held on trust for this common heritage, yet to be fully articulated and defined (Aldred, 2019).

Applications have been made to the ISA for an Exploration License for Polymetallic Nodules in "the Area" (Aldred, 2019). Jamaica has signed a contract with Blue Minerals Jamaica, a company registered in Jamaica. In the language of the UNCLOS, Jamaica would be a sponsoring state and Blue Minerals Jamaica the contractor. Blue Minerals Jamaica's activities will be focused on the exploration and eventual exploitation of polymetallic nodules containing high concentrations of nickel, copper, cobalt and manganese.

Role of sponsoring states – implications for Caribbean countries

The Prime Minister of Jamaica, in engaging in contractual relations with Blue Minerals Jamaica, assured concerned persons that the government of Jamaica is committed to embodying a robust legislative framework to ensure Jamaica's obligations under the convention and that its accountability framework is consistent with the mining code.[1] The principal provisions governing the roles of sponsoring states in the Area are captured in Article 139, paragraph 1; Article 153, paragraph 4; Annex III, and Article 4, paragraph 4, of the Convention.

Article 139, paragraph 1 provides that:

> States Parties shall ensure that activities in the Area, whether carried out by States Parties, or state enterprises or natural or juridical persons which possess the nationality of States Parties or are effectively controlled by them or their nationals, shall be carried out in conformity with this Part. The same responsibility applies to international organisations for their activities in the Area.

Article 153, paragraph 4 stipulates that:

> The Authority shall exercise such control over activities in the Area as necessary for securing compliance with the relevant provisions of this Part and the Annexes relating thereto, and the rules, regulations and procedures of the Authority, and the plans of work approved in accordance with paragraph 3. States Parties shall assist the Authority by taking all measures necessary to ensure such compliance in accordance with article 139.

Annex III, article 4, paragraph 4 requires that:

> The sponsoring State or States, pursuant to article 139, have the responsibility to ensure, within their legal systems, that a contractor so sponsored shall carry out activities in the Area in conformity with the terms of its contract and its obligations under this Convention. A sponsoring state shall not, however, be liable for damage caused by any failure of a contractor sponsored by it to comply with its obligations if that state Party has adopted laws and regulations and taken administrative measures which are, within the framework of its legal system, reasonably appropriate for securing compliance by persons under its jurisdiction.

This provision requires the enactment of robust legislative regimes within each sponsoring state to ensure compliance.

From the text above, sponsoring states are provided with a due diligence defence if they have taken legislative and administrative measures which are,

188   Laleta Davis-Mattis

within the framework of its legal system, reasonably appropriate for securing compliance by persons under its jurisdiction. The International Seabed Disputes Chamber in an Advisory Opinion (Seabed Disputes Chamber, 2011) sought to clarify the role of sponsoring states in DSM. Specifically, the questions posed to the Chamber were:

1. What are the legal responsibilities and obligations of States Parties to the Convention with respect to the sponsorship of activities in the Area in accordance with the Convention, in particular Part XI, and the 1994 Agreement relating to the Implementation of Part XI of the United Nations Convention on the Law of the Sea of 10 December 1982?
2. What is the extent of liability of a State Party for any failure to comply with the provisions of the Convention, in particular Part XI, and the 1994 Agreement, by an entity whom it has sponsored under Article 153, paragraph 2 (b), of the Convention?
3. What are the necessary and appropriate measures that a sponsoring State must take in order to fulfil its responsibility under the Convention, in particular, Article 139 and Annex III, and the 1994 Agreement?

The Chamber refrained from elaborating on the precise nature of the level of due diligence required, other than to indicate that the standard of due diligence is more severe for activities involving higher environmental risks (Poisel, 2012). The Chamber opined that a requisite step toward achieving this protection from liability is for a sponsoring state to put in place necessary measures, including legislation, to ensure contractor compliance with Part XI of the UNCLOS, the ISA contract and the ISA rules; and that this obligation applies equally to developed and developing states (Lily, 2018).

The Chamber made the distinction between direct and indirect responsibilities. Article 145 of The Convention articulates the role of the Authority in the protection of the marine environment and provides that the Authority should adopt rules for the prevention, reduction and control of pollution and other hazards to the marine environment, including the coastline, and of interference with the ecological balance of the marine environment, particular attention being paid to the need for protection from harmful effects of such activities as drilling, dredging, excavation, disposal of waste, construction and operation or maintenance of installations, pipelines and other devices related to such activities; (b) the protection and conservation of the natural resources of the Area and the prevention of damage to the flora and fauna of the marine environment.

The Chamber also amplified the obligations of sponsoring states and stipulated that the obligations of sponsoring states are not limited to the due diligence "obligation to ensure". Under the Convention and related instruments, sponsoring states also have obligations with which they must comply independently of their obligation to ensure a certain behaviour by the sponsored contractor. These obligations may be characterised as "direct obligations". Paragraph 122 of the Opinion provides that among the most important of these direct obligations incumbent on sponsoring states are:

1. the obligation to assist the Authority in the exercise of control over activities in the Area,
2. the obligation to apply a precautionary approach,
3. the obligation to apply best environmental practices,
4. the obligation to take measures to ensure the provision of guarantees in the event of an emergency order by the Authority for protection of the marine environment,
5. the obligation to ensure the availability of recourse for compensation in respect of damage caused by pollution; and the obligation to conduct environmental impact assessments.

Further, The Chamber pronounced that the notions "of due diligence" and "of conduct" are connected and impose an obligation on the sponsoring state to "adopt regulatory or administrative measures and to enforce them" in order to prevent, as far as possible, damage resulting from the contractor's activities. Sponsoring states are expected to act with caution and prudence to ensure that conservation measures are taken (Seabed Disputes Chamber, 2011).

The Opinion, whilst clarifying the roles of sponsoring states, highlights the challenges faced by Caribbean states seeking to engage in activities far from their shores and with persons from other jurisdictions whose avenue for control is perhaps primarily through local legislation to be enforced against a company formed solely for the purpose of satisfying the standing issue to engage in DSM. Caribbean countries need to negotiate contractual terms that will ensure benefit to their economies while the exploration activities are underway. Negotiation may include capacity building and technological transfers.

Investments in deep-seabed minerals: Caribbean perspectives

Mineral prices are volatile, generating long-term cyclical swings in revenue. Mining requires lengthy periods of exploration and development during which no revenue is generated. DSM equipment is highly specialised, and much of the technology remains under development, further lengthening the time prior to mining and increasing risk. Sources of risk include exploration, mineral prices, cost uncertainty, technology development, environmental damage and policy-regulatory uncertainty. The capital required during the development and construction phase is relatively larger than in most other industries (Van Nijen et al., 2019). These facts underlie the reluctance of Caribbean governments to enter the race, bearing in mind their vulnerable economies.

190   *Laleta Davis-Mattis*

Contractors and investors bear the principal risks and face a long investment period prior to production. There is a preference for full cost-recovery before paying royalties (Van Nijen et al., 2019). Investors ask the following questions when considering whether to invest in a project: how much is needed; what is the risk; what is the return; and when can the project be exited? Investors use tools such as the weighted average cost of capital (WACC), internal rate of return (IRR), and net present value (NPV), and consider other risk factors (e.g., technology and market maturity) around financing DSM activities. Financing differs between the pre-feasibility, feasibility and construction phases of development. Investors require much higher rates of return on the earlier phases, when risk is higher. For example, an investor might want 20–40 times their investment in the pre-feasibility phases versus 10–20 times their investment in the feasibility phase. The financing costs for the pre-feasibility, feasibility and construction phases should be considered in financial modelling (Van Nijen et al., 2019). However, in the case of Caribbean states, investors may be reluctant or unable to invest in such long-term investments. The resources of the deep-seabed are vested in humankind, as common property to ensure to the benefit of humankind, an undefined group of persons within the context of sustainability. The benefits from the spoils of mining are to be shared equitably based on economic models being developed. The concept of the common heritage of mankind is not a widely applied concept, confined at best to global international arrangements the implementation of which is primarily dependent on the definition of the concept by the ISA (Cuyvers et al., 2018).

The common heritage of mankind

The "common heritage of mankind", sometimes also called the common heritage of humankind or humanity, represents the notion that certain global commons or elements regarded as beneficial to humanity as a whole should not be unilaterally exploited by individual states or their nationals, nor by corporations or other entities. Instead, the preferred and only equitable option is for earth's resources especially those beyond areas of national jurisdiction to be exploited under some sort of international arrangement or regime for the benefit of mankind. The concept though having some previous incarnation, gained prominence from the speech of Arvid Pardo, the Maltese Ambassador to the United Nations, delivered at the United Nations General Assembly in November 1967, calling for the deep-seabed beyond national jurisdiction and the resources contained therein to be declared the common heritage of mankind (Taylor, 2011).

The application of the CHM is perhaps one of the more controversial and challenging concepts to articulate with any level of precision within the context of DSM, and the benefits to be derived by developing countries, which by virtue of their economies are challenged in participating in this race against time. The CHM principle is not confined to DSM, but perhaps will provide a practical platform from which to articulate and implement the principle not only for developing states but for present and future generations. The lack of proximity in terms of knowledge and geography in of itself poses a problem for Caribbean states. The development agenda and investment climates are not necessarily commensurate with the uncertainties of risks, benefits to sponsoring states, contractors and investors who in relation to the latter class are not willing to invest large sums in a market that can only reap rewards in an uncertain future.

The ISA's 168 members must agree on how the fragile and unique ecosystems of the Area will be protected, how the potentially multibillion-dollar industry will be regulated, how any profits will be shared equitably and how it can demonstrate accountability and transparency.

Biodiversity Beyond Areas of National Jurisdiction

The development of the international agreement on Biodiversity Beyond Areas of National Jurisdiction (BBNJ) is now at an advanced stage. Here the benefits relating to BBNJ are to be derived from bioprospecting for genetic resources for medical purposes. In this case, application of the CHM principle is being debated. UNCLOS, the ozone, climate change, and biodiversity agreements introduced treaty elements intended to address the disparate situation of states that had been colonised and that therefore lagged in economic development. These included recognition of some resources as the CHM, finance for capacity building and technology transfer. The BBNJ agreement will likely follow suit (Payne, 2019), while the ISA struggles to implement the CHM principle, recognising the challenges being experienced by small island developing states in having their fair share of the resources of the deep-seabed.

The Caribbean has been identified as one of the world's top biodiversity hotspots (CARICOM, 2018). Caribbean countries continue to grapple with the challenges of balancing poverty alleviation, economic growth, the right to development and biodiversity conservation. BBNJ presents enormous opportunities for Caribbean states, whilst recognising that there has been substantive underperformance in the area of managing and sustainably exploiting our terrestrial and marine biodiversity. The current engagements recognise gaps in capacity both in terms of human resources and finances. The deep-seabed exhibits an extensive array of geological features, from immense abyssal plains to towering mountain chains and deep trenches. Life here faces harsh conditions: no sunlight (and hence no photosynthesis), immense pressures, low but generally consistent temperatures and varying oxygen levels. Food is often scarce and, with few exceptions, limited to organic material that slowly trickles down from more productive regions near the surface or to other deep-sea organisms (Cuyvers et al., 2018).

In spite of these challenging conditions, the deep-sea supports a rich and often unique biodiversity with which the Caribbean can interface. Capacity development for BBNJ is critical to participation in these emerging

192 *Laleta Davis-Mattis*

economies of scale. Capacity building must aim to achieve the effective implementation of the new International Agreement on BBNJ by all countries by strengthening their ability to fulfil their rights and obligations as stated in the Agreement. Ultimately, capacity development will support the conservation and sustainable use of marine biodiversity in ABNJ, as well as the ability of all countries to participate in a sustainable ocean economy. (Cicin-Sain et al., 2018). Capacity building should include, area-based management, including marine protected areas (MPAs); Environmental Impact Assessments (EIAs) and Strategic Environmental Assessments (SEAs); marine genetic resources; marine scientific research and monitoring; and climate change (Cicin-Sain et al., 2018).

Conclusion

Caribbean states ought to make DSM an agenda item to remain at the successive meetings of the heads of governments. There ought to be a special committee established to examine the costs of benefits of DSM, and the potential for benefits to be derived therefrom. The establishment of a consortium of interested states may very well suit the region. A CBS News[2] report advances the notion that America is being left out of one of the most high-stakes races in history with colossal riches waiting for the winners, and editorialises that around the world, thousands of engineers and scientists are in fierce competition to build the first undersea robot that can mine the ocean floor. The reporter laments the absence of the USA from the race, since the latter is not a party to UNCLOS. The Caribbean Community (CARICOM), a grouping of 20 countries (15 Member States and 5 Associate Members) and home to approximately 16 million citizens could perhaps take the baton from Jamaica and continue the race, whilst including non-CARICOM Caribbean states in the race.

BBNJ should be added to the list of potential benefits from the Blue Economy. Caribbean countries have not yet begun to capitalise on their own biodiversity within national borders. They must stay current and active at the respective negotiating tables, bearing in mind that the competing global interests, the disparate distribution of wealth and opportunities must only serve to encourage regional engagement at unprecedented levels. The race is not for the slow, nor is it only for the mighty. The race is for the strong through perseverance, representation and investment.

Notes

1 "Legislation Being Advanced to Ensure Compliance with Rules of Seabed Exploration'; Jamaica Information Service; https://jis.gov.jm/legislation-being-adva nced-to-ensure-compliance-with-rules-of-seabed-exploration/.
2 "United States sitting out race to mine ocean floor for metals essential to electronics". https://www.cbsnews.com/news/united-states-sitting-out-race-to-mine-ocea n-floor-for-rare-earth-elements-metals-electronics-60-minutes-2019-11-13/.

References

Aldred, J. 2019. The future of deep-seabed mining. *The Maritime Executive*, 1 March. Available at: https://www.maritime-executive.com/editorials/the-future-of-deep-sea bed-mining.

CARICOM. 2018. *The State of Biodiversity in the Caribbean Community: A Review of Progress Towards the Aichi Biodiversity Targets*. CARICOM Secretariat, Georgetown, Guyana. Available at: https://caricom.org/documents/16630-un_environment_-_the_state_of_biodiversity_in_the_caribbean_community_b5....pdf.

Cicin-Sain, B., Vierros, M., Balgos, M. *et al.* 2018. *Policy Brief on Capacity Development as a Key Aspect of a New International Agreement on Marine Biodiversity Beyond National Jurisdiction (BBNJ)*. Global Ocean Forum. University of Delaware, Newark, 84 pp. Available at: http://www.fao.org/fileadmin/user_upload/comm on_oceans/docs/policy-brief-on-bbnj-capacity-development-aug-2018.pdf.

Commonwealth Secretariat. 2018. *Commonwealth Blue Charter. Shared Values, Shared Ocean: A Commonwealth Commitment to Work Together to Protect and Manage Our Ocean*. Commonwealth Secretariat, London. Available at: https://blue charter.thecommonwealth.org/wp-content/uploads/2019/08/Commonwealth_Blue_ Charter.pdf.

Cuyvers, L., Berry, W., Gjerde, K. *et al.* 2018. *Deep-seabed mining: A rising Environmental Challenge*. IUCN and Gallifrey Foundation, Gland, Switzerland, 74 pp. Available at: https://portals.iucn.org/library/sites/library/files/documents/2018-029-En.pdf.

EPRS. 2015. *Deep-Seabed Exploitation study: Tackling Economic, Environmental and Societal Challenges*. European Parliamentary Research Service, Brussels. Study IP/ G/STOA/FWC/2013–2001/Lot3/C4, 82 pp. Available at: https://www.europarl. europa.eu/RegData/etudes/STUD/2015/547401/EPRS_STU(2015)547401_EN.pdf.

Kirton, A. G. and Vasciannie, S. C. 2002. Deep-seabed mining under the law of the sea convention and the implementation agreement: developing country perspectives. *Social and Economic Studies*, 51 (2): 63–115.

Lily, H. 2018. *Sponsoring State Approaches to Liability Regimes for Environmental Damage Caused by Seabed Mining*. Liability Issues for Deep-Seabed Mining Series, Paper No. 3. Centre for International Governance Innovation (CIGI), Waterloo, Canada, 14 pp. Available at: https://thecommonwealth.org/sites/default/files/inline/ Seabed%20Minerals%20State%20Liability%20paper%20Hannah%20Lily%20Dec% 202018%20%28003%29.pdf.

Lodge, M., Johnson, D., Le Gurun, G. J. *et al.* 2014. Seabed mining: International Seabed Authority environmental management plan for the Clarion–Clipperton Zone: a partnership approach. *Marine Policy*, 49: 66–72.

Madiraju, K. S. 2019. Contemplating a domestic regulatory and enforcement framework for deep-seabed mining. *Natural Resources and Environment*, 34 (2): 17–21.

Payne, C. R. 2019. New law for the high seas. *Ecology Law Quarterly*, 46: 191–214.

Payne, R. J. and Nassa, J. R. 1982. The new international economic order at sea. *Journal of Developing Areas*, 17 (1): 31–50. doi:10.15779/Z38RX93D7B.

Poisel, T. 2012. Deep-seabed mining: Implications of Seabed Disputes Chamber's advisory opinion. *Australian International Law Journal*, 19: 213–233.

Ram, J. 2018. *Financing the Blue Economy: A Caribbean Development Opportunity*. Caribbean Development Bank, Barbados. ISBN: ISBN: 978-976-96037-96038-3, 28 pp.

Seabed Disputes Chamber. 2011. *Responsibilities and Obligations of States Sponsoring Persons, and Entities with Respect to Activities in the Area*. Seabed Disputes

194 *Laleta Davis-Mattis*

Chamber of the International Tribunal for the Law of the Sea Year. Advisory Opinion, 76 pp. Available at: https://www.itlos.org/fileadmin/itlos/documents/cases/case_no_17/adv_op_010211.pdf.

Taylor, P. 2011. Common heritage of mankind principle. In K. Bosselmann, D. Fogel and J. B. Ruhl (Eds), *The Encyclopedia of Sustainability*, Vol. 3: *The Law and Politics of Sustainability*, pp. 64–69. Berkshire Publishing, Great Barrington, MA.

United Nations. 1970. *Declaration of Principles Governing the Seabed and the Ocean Floor, and the Subsoil Thereof, beyond the Limits of National Jurisdiction.* Official records United Nations General Assembly, 25th Session. Available at: https://undocs.org/en/A/PV.1933.

United Nations. 1994. *United Nations Preparatory Commission for the International Seabed Authority and for the International Tribunal for the Law of the Sea, Twelfth Session: Report of the Croup of Technical Experts to the General Committee of the Preparatory Commission for the International Seabed Authority and for the International Tribunal for the Law of the Sea*, UN Doc. LOS/PCN/BUR/ R.32, 1 February, 14 pp.

United Nations. 2019. International legally binding instrument under the United Nations Convention on the Law of the Sea on the conservation and sustainable use of marine biological diversity of areas beyond national jurisdiction. IUCN Comments. 15 August. Available at: https://www.iucn.org/sites/dev/files/iucn_comments_on_bbnj_draft_text_-_august_2019.pdf.

Van Nijen, K., Van Passel, S., Brown, C. G. *et al.* 2019. The development of a payment regime for deep sea mining activities in the Area through stakeholder participation. *International Journal of Marine and Coastal Law*, 34: 571–601.

16 The role of waste management in underpinning the Blue Economy

Christopher Corbin

Introduction

Coastal and marine ecosystems and water quality in the Wider Caribbean Region (WCR) are negatively impacted by increasing volumes of solid and liquid wastes. These can be in the forms of untreated wastewater, nutrients from agricultural run-off, or marine litter, including plastics. The quantity of pollution entering the Caribbean Sea has been directly correlated with coastal population densities and extent of activities in watersheds draining into the oceans (World Bank, 2019). Global population growth predictions of 9.6 billion by mid-century raise concerns about the increased demand on our oceans and seas for food, energy, medicines and other products and services while continuing to receive increased discharges of solid and liquid wastes (World Bank, 2016). For Caribbean people, whose lives and livelihoods are heavily dependent on the Caribbean Sea, any efforts to develop new and innovative Blue Economy approaches must ensure long-term sustainability while reducing the negative impacts of pollution from land and marine-based sources and activities.

It has been estimated that by 2050 the ocean's content will consist more of plastic than of fish if no drastic actions are taken (World Economic Forum et al., 2016). At a global level, less than a fifth of the 300 million tonnes of plastic produced each year is recycled (Geyer et al., 2017). Waste that is not recycled gets dumped on land or in the sea, resulting in up to 12 million tons of plastic in our seas and oceans (Jambeck et al., 2015). In the Caribbean in particular, anywhere from 0.16 to 0.42 million tons of plastic has entered the sea yearly since 2010 and this number was projected to double by 2025. The region is estimated to have high levels of plastic concentration compared to other marine ecosystems (World Bank, 2016). Plastics have detrimental effects on ocean and marine ecosystems, causing injury and death to marine life. Like many coastal and marine areas, the Caribbean Sea receives excess nutrients from the discharges of untreated or partially treated domestic wastewater and surface run-off from poor agricultural practices. Nutrient pollution impacts coastal and marine ecosystems and processes and their ability to provide critical inputs to other ocean-based economic sectors.

Human activities that continue to contribute to the pollution of the Caribbean Sea must be addressed effectively to ensure that the full potential for new Blue Economy approaches are realised and allow sustainable contributions to economic growth while maintaining environmental integrity (Report on the Sustainable Blue Economy, 2018). The direct and indirect impacts from pollution on important economic sectors in the WCR will hinder efforts to transition to more sustainable uses of coastal and marine resources. The transition to a Blue Economy presents an opportunity for regional governments to take a more proactive approach to integrated solid and liquid waste management and enhance national and regional efforts to control, reduce and prevent marine pollution. Converting waste into a resource through, for example, repurposing marine litter, energy from waste, or nutrient recovery from wastewater are all under-explored opportunities. Other considerations such as management of transboundary wastes need to be at the core of any new ocean governance and Blue Economy frameworks.

For the WCR, the most important regional legal framework for the control, reduction and prevention of marine pollution is the Cartagena Convention for the Protection and Development of the Marine Environment and its Protocol concerning pollution from Land-based Sources and Activities (LBS Protocol). The Protocol includes regional effluent limitations for domestic wastewater (sewage) and requires the development of plans to address agricultural non-point sources of pollution. The LBS Protocol provides general obligations and a legal framework for regional co-operation. It also describes the work that each Contracting Party must do and gives guidance for the development of regional actions.

Pursuing Blue Economy strategies should be a pathway to achieving sustainable development for countries of the WCR and can directly assist with the issue of pollution and waste management. The World Bank (2017, p. 6) defines the Blue Economy as "the sustainable use of ocean resources for economic growth, improved livelihoods and jobs, while preserving the health of marine and coastal ecosystems". Linked closely to this is a focus on the "Green Economy", which the United Nations Environment Programme (UNEP, 2012, p. 3) describes as a vision of "improved wellbeing and social equity, while significantly reducing environmental risks and ecological scarcities". An important factor is the realisation that the sustainable management of ocean resources requires collaboration across nation-states and across the public–private sectors, and on a scale that has not been achieved previously. This realisation underscores the challenge facing countries in the WCR as they turn to better managing their Blue Economies.

The ocean influences the livelihoods of about 40% of the world's population living at or near the coast, and its contribution to current and future economic growth is significant. For small islands and coastal developing states such as in the Caribbean, the ocean's role as an important generator of subsistence and income is magnified. In the Caribbean, leveraging the ocean as a natural resource could lead to faster economic growth, improve social inclusion and protect coastal environments and marine life. So, a healthy ocean is fundamental to a prosperous and sustainable Blue Economy. However, plastics, including microplastics, have polluted the ocean environment and marine food chain as well as impacting aquatic food sources and national economies.

Addressing issues related to pollution and waste management are vital to enable the transition to a Blue Economy for countries in the region. In promoting Blue Economy approaches, management of solid and liquid wastes, including plastic and microplastic management, are key activities for reducing pollution of the coastal and marine environment. Waste management, including transboundary waste management, as well as reducing, recycling and reusing waste has huge social, environmental and economic benefits. This will promote decoupling of the relationship between economic growth and degradation of the Caribbean ocean, and will contribute to sustainable management of marine ecosystems while building resilience. In addition, through transfer of appropriate technologies and capital investments, the industry could be replicated where it is not in use.

This chapter on the Blue Economy and waste management will elaborate on: (i) the main sources of marine pollution; (ii) challenges for reducing pollution from solid and liquid wastes in the WCR; (iii) impacts and threats for current and future efforts to develop Blue Economies; (iv) opportunities for integrated approaches to a Blue Economy while improving waste management and reducing pollution; and (v) conclusions and recommendations.

Land-based pollution sources and impacts

Environmental impacts and related socio-economic costs of land-based pollution are attributed, to a great extent, to inadequate waste management practices and inadequate local, national and regional governance frameworks in the WCR which are reflected in the following:

- high percentage of untreated wastewater;
- inadequate discharge of black and grey water, particularly among low-income households;
- inadequate or non-existent systems for collection, recycling and disposal of urban and industrial waste;
- lack of/inadequate policies, legislation and regulations as well as limited monitoring of agricultural and industrial production and disposal of wastes, in particular from the pharmaceutical and mining industries.

Urban wastewater

Approximately 85% of the domestic wastewater that is discharged into the Caribbean Sea is partially treated or untreated. Increases in coastal population, expansion of the tourism sector, and coastal development continue to place heavy demands on wastewater treatment infrastructure (UNEP-CEP,

198 Christopher Corbin

2019). Urban wastewater is defined by the European Union (EU) as domestic wastewater or the mixture of domestic wastewater with industrial wastewater and/or run-off rainwater. It is estimated that in 2015, 12 billion m^3 of domestic wastewater was generated in the WCR; however, only 40% reached treatment plants, while the remaining 60% of untreated wastewater was disposed of in coastal waters (CReW+, n.d.).

Poor wastewater treatment infrastructure along with expanding urban populations are the main causes of untreated or poorly treated domestic wastewater discharges into fresh-water bodies or directly into the Caribbean Sea. Even in places where treatment occurs, the generated effluent may often not meet national sewage effluent standards. While domestic sewage is bio-degradable, the large quantities of sewage discharged in many locations throughout the WCR exceed natural decomposition and dispersal capacity levels of the recipient water bodies, resulting in water quality degradation (SOCAR, 2019). According to the 2019 State of Convention Area Report (SOCAR) on marine pollution in the WCR, many areas suffer from elevated levels of nutrients, i.e. dissolved inorganic nitrogen (DIN) and dissolved inorganic phosphorus (DIP), from sources including human faecal pollution (UNEP-CEP, 2019).

Untreated domestic wastewater is considered to be the most serious problem because of its direct threat to public health. It represents a multiple stressor to the coastal and marine environment with negative impacts associated with high levels of nutrients, organic matter, pathogenic microorganisms, chemicals, suspended solids and contaminants of emerging concern such as endocrine disruptors and hormones, among others (SOCAR, 2019).

Apart from indirect and direct impacts on human health, economic sectors such as tourism and fisheries are negatively impacted due to the degradation of coastal and marine ecosystems with coastal waters being made unsuitable for recreational use and fisheries. Exposure of bathers to contaminated recreational waters and consumption of contaminated seafood may lead to gastrointestinal illness, and ear, eye and skin infections are other possible human health impacts. Pollution from domestic wastewater directly impacts national economies and sectors that are dependent on the Caribbean Sea for livelihoods, tourism and fisheries (SOCAR, 2019).

Agricultural nutrients

Coastal and marine ecosystems are vulnerable to the impacts of excess nutrients that result not only from domestic wastewater but from agrochemical groundwater leaching and surface run-off associated with poor agricultural practices and excessive use of artificial fertilisers. It is estimated that nutrient loads that are transported from land to sea have increased threefold from pre-industrial levels (UNEP, 2013). The Caribbean Sea is highly vulnerable to heavy sediment loading from some of the world's major rivers, including the Amazon, Mississippi, Magdalena and Orinoco River. These rivers drain vast watersheds and are located in areas with large urban centres, with heavy concentrations of agricultural and industrial activities. As they drain into the Caribbean Sea, heavy metals such as mercury and lead, nitrates and phosphates and sediments impact coastal and marine ecosystems. Additional threats are posed to public health from the increased microbiological content of run-off with a high nutrient content (SOCAR, 2019).

Continuous flow of high loads of organic matter reaching the coasts can lead to eutrophication and eventually hypoxia (oxygen deficiency in a biotic environment). Dead zones have been identified in the Gulf of Mexico due to oxygen levels being so low that it became impossible to sustain marine life (CReW+, n.d.). Corals are highly susceptible to deoxygenation – in combination with increasing water temperatures and higher acidity levels – causing coral bleaching and eventually leading to coral death (Altieri, 2017). At the same time, the excessive nutrients stimulate the growth of algae that may compete with the coral. An additional threat to the health of humans and aquatic organisms are endocrine-disrupting compounds (chemicals that can interfere with hormone systems) that pose serious risks to human health (World Bank, 2018).

Urban solid waste

Solid waste, marine litter and plastics have emerged as a major threat for the development of a Blue Economy and for the sustainability of sectors such as fisheries and tourism. Persistent litter along coastal and marine areas has become a common sight in many countries. The resident population of the WCR generated about 79 million tonnes of solid waste in 2015, projected to have increased to 84 million tonnes by 2020 (SOCAR, 2019). According to the 2017 International Coastal Clean-up organised by the Ocean Conservancy, the Caribbean region contained more litter than the global average. The average litter concentration for the Caribbean was 2,014 items/km, whilst the global average was 573 items/km (Ocean Conservancy, 2017).

Plastics products are now among the top items collected during Annual International Coastal Clean-up exercises including plastic beverage bottles, plastic bottle caps, plastic grocery bags and plastic lids (Ocean Conservancy, 2017). While plastics represent on average between 20 and 30% of the solid waste generated in the WCR, its persistence requires targeted priority action as part of any pollution control measures (World Bank, 2019). The influence of plastics and other marine litter on marine life can be devastating. The different ways in which aquatic life can be hindered include injury, ingestion, suffocation, infection and entanglement – all of which could lead to death. Studies have found that large marine mammals are especially vulnerable to ingestion of plastic bags. These are often found in whales' stomachs, causing death due to critical obstruction in digestive systems.

Microplastics is the term used to refer to small plastic particles, increasingly found in cosmetics and cleansers (World Bank, 2019). It also refers to

200 *Christopher Corbin*

microscopic pieces of plastic resulting from the structural breakdown of larger plastics due to wave action and sunlight. These tiny particles, of 5 millimetres or less, have been shown to reduce fertility and contribute to declines in the populations of some marine animals. Marine filter feeders such as baleen whales, whale sharks and manta rays that feed on plankton or other tiny organisms are particularly susceptible to microplastics. The manner in which these marine animals feed by filtering thousands of cubic metres of seawater – most likely containing microplastics – puts them at high risk of toxin exposure (Germanov et al., 2018). Other marine animals such as fish and shellfish are also highly susceptible to microplastics. This is especially worrying since microplastics have been demonstrated to adsorb chemicals from industrial and manufacturing activities. There is increasing concern about the long-term human health implications from consuming seafood containing microplastics (Smith et al., 2018).

Ocean-based pollution sources

Coastal resources are not only impacted from land-based sources of pollution resulting from poor solid and liquid waste management, but also by pollution from marine-based sources and activities. Sectors such as maritime transportation and offshore mining are significant contributors to ocean-based pollution impacting coastal and marine environments. While considered to be a potential opportunity for expanding Blue Economies, measures to minimise polluting impacts should be implemented.

Maritime transportation

While most of the marine litter originates from land, substantial quantities are also generated by maritime activities like shipping, cruising, fishing and military activities. These can be in the form of plastics, wood, metal, rubber, etc. that eventually wash onto the shores of several of the islands in the Caribbean, contaminating beaches and affecting aesthetics (Čulin and Bielić, 2016). Caribbean countries – especially Small Island Developing States (SIDS) – are highly vulnerable to the waste generated by the international shipping sector (World Bank, 2019). Furthermore, ships discharge wastewater into coastal waters, which may, especially in the case of static discharge from small vessels near the shoreline, contribute significantly to the levels of nitrogen and phosphate being released locally, with subsequent impact on biota and the marine environment (Mearns et al., 2003).

Offshore mining

Dredging and shallow-water mining for sand, gold, tin and diamonds has direct ecological consequences and can negatively impact marine flora and fauna living on/in the sea floor (Desprez, 2000). The recent increased interest

Oil and gas extraction are other potentially highly polluting activities. According to the US Geological Survey (2020), the Caribbean region holds up to more than 120 billion barrels of offshore oil and significant natural gas reserves. Several countries in the region, including Guyana and Suriname, have contracted exploration licences in the past decade. Significant mining activities that take place in offshore waters have increased risk for oil spills that can cause major harm to ecosystems: changes in seawater quality, mortality of marine life and seabirds, and damage to coral reefs, seagrass beds and mangroves. Furthermore, all stages of oil and gas production can result in undesirable discharges of liquid, solid and gaseous wastes. This is in addition to the environmental impacts and pollution caused by construction, operation and decommissioning of the platforms required for oil and gas extraction.

Marine pollution: Impacts and threats to a Blue Economy

Countries of the WCR are dependent on a few major economic sectors i.e., tourism and recreation, fisheries (including aquaculture), maritime transportation and offshore mining, which rely on coastal and marine assets. These sectors are directly or indirectly negatively impacted by inadequate management and disposal of land and marine-based solid and liquid waste. Pollution from wastes affects coastal and marine ecosystems and will hinder future efforts to enhance these marine-based sectors as part of efforts to develop Blue Economies in the region.

Tourism and recreation

The tourism sector continues to be a key pillar for the economies of many Caribbean countries. It is estimated that the sector generates approximately US$47 billion in annual revenue in the region and "healthy beaches" are a key factor that draw tourists to the region (see Clegg et al., Chapter 11 this volume). The industry is characterised by land-based activities, cruise tourism and beach-related activities such as sailing and diving (SOCAR, 2019). However, the impact of solid and liquid waste on coastal and marine ecosystems and the provision of ecosystem goods and services has had detrimental effects on coral reefs, beaches and water quality – the basis for a sustainable tourism industry.

The long-term sustainability and potential for further expansion of the tourism sector as part of a Blue Economy is heavily dependent on coral

202 Christopher Corbin

reefs – so called reef-adjacent tourism. Indirect services provided by coral reefs include aesthetic value, calm waters, coastal protection, beach generation and high-quality seafood (SOCAR, 2019). Poor aesthetics are a major threat to both land and marine-based tourism activities especially when associated with visible land or marine pollution. Marine pollution leads to degradation of natural assets such as beaches, sand dunes, coral reefs and mangroves. With the growing dependence of Caribbean governments on tourism, any declines will have significant impacts on businesses associated with the tourism supply such as manufacturing and agriculture (World Bank, 2019). According to a recent study carried out in Barbados, visitors have a high preference for clear water, healthy coral reefs and high-quality beaches, and reported not being interested in returning if the quality of these were to worsen in the future (Schuhmann et al., 2017).

Hotels, guest houses and the tourism accommodation sector have a major role to play in the control, reduction and prevention of marine pollution from solid and liquid wastes. Many existing municipal wastewater facilities do not meet national environmental standards as far as the quality of effluent discharged into coastal and marine areas. Large hotels in many countries are required to establish their own on-site wastewater treatment plants and the proper maintenance and operations of these systems are critical to protect human health, meet recreational water quality standards levels and ensure aesthetic attractiveness (CReW+, n.d.).

Fisheries

Despite not having extensive large commercial fisheries operations, the fisheries sector in the WCR is an important socio-economic activity for the region (see Oxenford & McConney, Chapter 10 in this volume). Some countries are highly dependent on fish as the main protein source contributing directly to food security, and for many coastal populations is a major source of livelihoods having great economic significance for millions (SOCAR, 2019). Pollution from solid and liquid wastes may reduce the numbers of commercial species by degrading coastal and marine habitats and nursery areas. Consumption of seafood from polluted waters poses an additional human health risk. Coastal waters contaminated with chemicals, toxic heavy metals and disease-causing microorganisms can have direct or indirect human health impacts. Once seafood is contaminated by these pollutants, their commercial value is impacted, threatening livelihoods. Pollution from domestic wastewater has been reported to reduce the productivity of nursery areas, including marine habitats such as coral reefs, mangroves and sea grass beds (World Bank, 2019).

A growing sector with great potential for Blue growth opportunities is aquaculture (including mariculture). Aquaculture is considered by many to be a sustainable way of supplying seafood to meet the demands of growing populations (Lu et al., 2019). Future production levels in the WCR are projected to be about 40 million tons of seafood per annum while occupying less than 1.5% of the countries' Exclusive Economic Zones (EEZ) (SOCAR, 2019). However, poorly managed aquaculture and mariculture activities could lead to increased nutrient run-off into the Caribbean Sea and occurrences of Harmful Algal Blooms (HAB). In other regions, such as Europe, HABs have disrupted maritime-based activities and led to billions of dollars in annual losses (Lu et al., 2019). Increased discharges of nutrients associated with unplanned aquaculture and mariculture expansion may further exacerbate the impacts of Sargassum in the Caribbean Sea. Sargassum could pose a direct threat to the sustainability of aquaculture or mariculture operations when thick mats of seaweed disturb the near coast, as well as offshore farming. The seaweed can, furthermore, cause alterations in water quality and death of marine life when it starts decomposing, leading to hypoxia and the release of poisonous hydrogen sulphide (Pfaff, 2015).

Waste management challenges

Countries of the WCR are facing several challenges in controlling, preventing and reducing the impacts of pollution from solid and liquid wastes. Table 16.1 presents a summary of some of these challenges, as well as capacity building needs to allow governments to improve solid and liquid waste management (GEF CreW, 2013).

Catalysing Blue Economy approaches through improved waste management

As the previous sections have described, the countries in the WCR are dependent on a few economic sectors for which healthy oceans are crucial. It is, therefore, important to strengthen the already established sectors, and address the threats that pollution can further impose in the future. Nonetheless, it is crucial to create alternatives in addition to strengthening the already established Blue Economy sectors. Hence, more and more countries are fostering and exploring ways the ocean can support new types of industries. What is key in these innovations is to help create new markets by stimulating demand for alternative forms of goods, services and energy. Some options are noted here to help establish a fulling functioning circular economy.

Repurposing plastic

A circular economy approach involves maximising recovery, reuse and/or recycling of wastes to reduce wastage and pollution. Solid wastes and specifically plastics offer tremendous opportunities for repurposing the use of plastics given its persistence and reuse potential. According to the EU, one million tonnes of recycled plastic is equivalent to taking one million cars off

204 *Christopher Corbin*

Table 16.1 Waste management challenges and needs

Challenges	Needs
Lack of financing	Funding for the development of laboratory capacity in support of monitoring programmes
Inadequate (and sometimes uncoordinated) policy, legislative and institutional frameworks	Formulation and implementation of relevant policies
Lack of human, financial and technical resources	Enhancing institutional capacity through training and the provision of technical and other assistance
Old infrastructure leading to increased pollution of the environment	Review of national legislative and regulatory frameworks, including drafting of legislation to address the weaknesses and gaps identified
Lack of adequate maintenance and poor operational wastewater systems	Design and implementation of public awareness and environmental educational programmes
A need for sustained water quality monitoring programmes and more comprehensive information management systems	Accessing and adopting more appropriate and cost-effective technologies
A need for more focused public awareness and environmental education programmes	Establishing data management systems both for national analytical purposes and for facilitating the exchange of information at national and regional levels
	Valuation of the economic impacts of pollution resulting from nutrients and wastewater
	The provision of "easy" financial arrangements to assist industries in upgrading their treatment
	Guidance on the development of wastewater permitting systems

the road in terms of carbon emissions (WTO, 2018). To foster more circular economy approaches for plastics management, plastics need to be designed to allow greater durability, reuse and recycling in a cost-effective manner. Increased investments in recycling capacity are needed given that recycled plastics have the potential to become a valuable feedstock for industries locally and abroad, as well as generating new employment opportunities (European Commission, 2018).

Repurposing marine litter

Marine litter and coastal debris found along beaches and coastal areas can be collected, and in a process of "up-cycling", be transformed into useful products and/or art. There are many new initiatives that are transforming what is considered to be waste into fashion items. Amongst the most common materials that are recycled are: discarded fishing nets (estimated to be 650,000 tons lying at the ocean bottom), PET plastic bottles, tyres, post-consumer coffee, post-industrial cotton and post-industrial wool. The movement referred to as "Upcycling the Oceans programme" is being applied in Korea, Spain and Thailand and has great potential for being part of the Blue Economy for countries of the WCR.

Energy generation: waste-to-energy

Biogas is a renewable energy source that is produced by the breakdown of organic matter. The production of biogas is a convenient solution for the disposal of organic wastes such as agricultural waste, animal manure, plant material, wastewater sludge/biosolids, or food waste. When organic matter decomposes in an environment absent of oxygen (anaerobic environment) it releases a mixture of gases, primarily methane and carbon dioxide. The high content of methane makes biogas flammable, and therefore, useful as a renewable energy source. This process, also called anaerobic digestion, helps address two major environmental problems: the waste problem in the Caribbean that emits daily dangerous levels of methane gas into the environment, and dependency on fossil fuel energy to meet increasing energy demand. The biogas generated can be used as gas, electricity, heat and transportation fuels.

Nutrient recovery from wastewater

Domestic wastewater contains valuable nutrients such as phosphorus, nitrogen and potassium. These minerals are important components of artificial fertilisers used in the agricultural industry and important for food security. Estimates of the reserves of phosphate rock on Earth have increased four-fold since 2010, on grounds still widely debated (Edixhoven et al., 2014): the most optimistic evaluations estimate continental reserves as high as 260 times the current yearly phosphorus production (USGS, 2020), but it should be noted that the use of phosphorus in agriculture has been projected to increase by up to 80% as early as 2050 (Mogollon et al., 2018). Recycling nutrients is therefore a topic of growing interest. Recovering valuable nutrients from domestic wastewater will help reduce the polluting impacts on coastal and marine environments while providing significant cost-savings and contributing to more sustainable food production. It is estimated that a quarter of the worldwide artificial phosphorus demand for fertiliser use can be supplied

206 Christopher Corbin

through the recovery of black water (toilet water) and food wastes (Wageningen University, n.d.).

Shift to biodegradable materials

Biodegradable materials, also called bio-waste, include human and animal waste, plant products, wood, paper, food waste, leaves, grass clippings and remains of dead animals and plants, which can be decomposed by bacteria, fungi and small insects following exposure to water, light and oxygen. Non-biodegradable items include glass, metals, plastics, electronic devices and some medical waste. While these items do not decompose, they can be reused to make other products. Global efforts to reduce single-use plastic packaging offer opportunities for more sustainable and biodegradable alternatives which result in reduced pollution. Bio-waste bags and cups, plates and cutlery and film can be used to store short shelf-life food products. However, further commercialisation and research to improve quality while maintaining food standards are required.

Conclusion

The future growth and opportunities of the ocean economy in the Caribbean Sea would be increased by transitioning to the Blue Economy with investments in natural and produced capital. For example, the waste disposal sector of the region's ocean economy, where the Caribbean Sea provides implicit or explicit services of disposal of wastes and particularly excess nutrients, provides a flow of outputs in the form of pollution to the ecosystems and ecosystem processes. One specific example of the circular interaction between different sectors of the ocean economy and the natural capital of the Caribbean Sea is the above depiction of the waste disposal function of the ocean and its impact on ecosystems and ecosystem processes such as coral reefs, beaches and water quality, all of which are inputs and factors of production for the tourism sector. While the value of the waste disposal segment has not been quantified, the tourism sector in the waters of the islands alone generates tens of billions of dollars each year, accounting for 14% of the region's GDP, and depends heavily on ocean ecosystems and ecosystem processes as an input. The Caribbean Development Bank has highlighted that the economic cost of doing nothing is also significant. Estimates reveal that the Caribbean region could lose up to 5% of its GDP over the next decade if governments fail to step up their resilience efforts and adapt to climate change. This may be underestimated and some of those losses will be permanent and irreversible (loss accumulation) and the rate of loss will increase with time, eventually reaching a tipping point, where the entire economy collapses. These losses will be as a result of a range of impacts including from ocean acidification, more intense storms, floods, droughts, rising sea levels and higher temperatures.

This will negatively impact marine and coastal ecosystems, consequently affecting Caribbean livelihoods.

Putting the Blue Economy conceptual framework into action would measure both the ocean economy and the natural capital that underpins it, combined as the Blue Economy. Activities such as repurposing plastic debris collected from the marine and coastal environment into up-scaling products and art, as well as other innovative activities, such as using biodegradable materials, would directly support this framework. The Blue Economy offers countries of the WCR the opportunity to diversify from a narrow production base, invest in and develop growth and employment opportunities in a wide range of both existing and new sectors and industries, and move away from predominantly land-based industries toward those that integrate and sustainably develop a broader range of land-based, coastal and ocean-based sectors. In the context of the circular economy, the issues and industries dealing with solid and liquid waste management, including marine plastics, can be a leading part of the Blue Economy in the region.

In order to qualify as components of a Blue Economy activities need to: (1) provide social and economic benefits for current and future generations; (2) restore, protect and maintain the diversity, productivity, resilience, core functions and intrinsic value of marine ecosystems; and (3) be based on clean technologies, renewable energy and circular material flows that will reduce waste and promote recycling of materials. Integrating waste management and pollution prevention efforts with Blue Economy approaches offers countries in the WCR the opportunity to:

1   enhance efficiency in the use of resources and natural capital and reducing waste;
2   spur innovation of new technologies to simultaneously increase economic growth as measured by GDP, enhance natural capital, with a focus on the energy system and prevent/reduce pollution from waste;
3   create new markets by stimulating demand for green technologies, goods and services;
4   measure natural capital as part of the economy, thereby incorporating considerations of the environment and coastal and marine resources into broader economic decision-making;
5   boost investor confidence through greater predictability and continuity in addressing environmental issues, while better understanding the scale of risks.

References

Altieri, A. H. 2017. Tropical dead zones and mass mortalities on coral reefs. *Proceedings of the National Academy of Sciences*, 114 (14): 3660–3665.

208 *Christopher Corbin*

CReW+. n.d. An integrated approach to water and waste water management using innovative solutions and promoting financing mechanisms in the Wider Caribbean Region, Global Environment Facility. Available at: https://www.thegef.org/project/crew-integrated-approach-water-and-wastewater-management-using-innovative-solutions-and.

Čulin, J., & Bielić, T. 2016. Plastic pollution from ships. *Pomorski zbornik*, 51 (1): 57–66.

Desprez, M. 2000. Physical and biological impact of marine aggregate extraction along the French coast of the Eastern English Channel: Short-and long-term post-dredging restoration, *ICES Journal of Marine Science*, 57: 1428–1438.

Edixhoven, J. D., Gupta, J., & Savenije, H. H. G. 2014. Recent revisions of phosphate rock reserves and resources: a critique. *Earth System Dynamics*, 5: 491–507.

European Commission. 2018. A European strategy for plastics in a circular economy. Available at: https://eur-lex.europa.eu/legal-content/EN/TXT/?qid=1516265440535&uri=COM:2018:28:FIN.

GEF CreW. 2013. *Assessment Report for Select Countries in Respect of the Protocol concerning Pollution from Land-based Sources and Activities*. January. Available at: https://www.gefcrew.org/images/reports/project_final_reports/CReW_C2_Regional_FINALLBSProtocolAssessmentReportselectedcountries_Final_Jan2013.pdf.

Germanov, E. S., Marshall, A. D., Bejder, L., Fossi, M. C., & Loneragan, N. R. 2018. Microplastics: No small problem for filter feeding megafauna. *Trends in Ecology & Evolution*, 33 (4): 227–232.

Geyer, R., Jambeck, J. R., & Lavender Law, K. 2017. Production, use, and fate of all plastics ever made. *Sciences Advances*, 3 (7).

Jambeck, J. R., Geyer, R., Wilcox, C., Siegler, T. R., Perryman, M. Andrady, A., Narayan, R., & Law, K. 2015. Plastic waste inputs from land into the ocean. *Science*, 347(6223): 768–771.

Lu, W., Cusack, C., Baker, M., *et al.* 2019. Successful blue economy examples with an emphasis on international perspectives. *Frontiers in Marine Science*, 6: 1–14.

Mearns, A., Stekoll, M., Hall, K., Krause, C. J. B., Watson, M., & Atkinson, M. 2003. Biological and ecological effects of wastewater discharges from cruise ships in Alaska. In: *Proceedings, Oceans 2003 Conference*, Marine Technology Society, Columbia, Maryland. 737–747.

Mogollon, J. M., Beusen, A. H. W., Grinsven, H. J. M. van, Westhoek, H., Bouwman, A. F. 2018. Future agricultural phosphorus demand according to the shared socio-economic pathways. *Global Environmental Change*, 50: 149–163.

Ocean Conservancy. 2017. *Together for Our Ocean: International Coastal Clean-up 2017 Report*. Available at: https://oceanconservancy.org/wp-content/uploads/2017/04/2017-ICC_Report_RM.pdf.

Pfaff, M. 2015. Key scientific questions addressing environmental drivers and effects of periodic mass deposits of a brown seaweed (golden tides) along the Sierra Leone coast. Draft report for Oceans and Coastal Research, Directorate: Biodiversity and Coastal Research.

Report on the Sustainable Blue Economy. 2018. Sustainable Blue Economy Conference, Nairobi, Kenya, 26–28 November. Prepared by SBEC technical documentation review committee at a retreat held at Lake Naivasha Simba Lodge, Kenya, 5–9 December. Available at: http://www.blueeconomyconference.go.ke/wp-content/uploads/2018/12/SBEC-FINAL-REPORT-8-DECEMBER-2018-rev-2-1-2-PDF2-3-compressed.pdf.

Schuhmann, P., Skeete, R., & Waite, R. 2017. *The Economic Importance of Coastal and Marine Resources to Tourism in Barbados*. Bridgetown, Barbados. Available at: https://www.onecaribbean.org/wp-content/uploads/Economic-Importance-of-Coastal-and-Marine-Resources-to-Tourism-in-Barbados.pdf.

Smith, M., Love, D. C., Rochman, C. M., & Neff, R. A. 2018. Microplastics in seafood and the implications for human health. *Current Environmental Health Reports*, 5 (3): 375–386.

SOCAR. 2019. *An Assessment of Marine Pollution from Land-based Sources and Activities in the Wider Caribbean Region*. May.

UNEP. 2012. *What do We Mean by Green Economy? – Briefing*, May. UNEP, Nairobi, Kenya. Available at: https://wedocs.unep.org/bitstream/handle/20.500.11822/8659/-%20Green%20economy_%20what%20do%20we%20mean%20by%20green%20economy_%20-2012Main%20briefing%202012–Final.pdf?sequence=2&isAllowed=y.

UNEP. 2013. *Green Economy in a Blue World: Full Report*. Available at: https://wedocs.unep.org/bitstream/handle/20.500.11822/12715/GreenEconomyinaBlueWorld%20FullReport.pdf?sequence=1&isAllowed=y.

UNEP-CEP. 2019. *State of the Convention Area Report. Water Quality*. Available at: http://cep.unep.org/content/about-cep/amep/environmental-monitoring-assessment.

US Geological Survey. 2020. Phosphate rock. In: *Mineral Commodity Summaries*. Available at: https://pubs.usgs.gov/periodicals/mcs2020/mcs2020.pdf.

Wageningen University. n.d. Recovering nutrients from wastewater. Available at: https://www.wur.nl/en/show/Recovering-nutrients-from-waste-water.htm.

World Bank. 2016. *Toward a Blue Economy: A Promise for Sustainable Growth in the Caribbean*, September. Available at: https://openknowledge.worldbank.org/bitstream/handle/10986/25061/Demystifying0t0the0Caribbean0Region.pdf?sequence=4.

World Bank. 2017. *The Potential of the Blue Economy: Increasing Long-Term Benefits of the Sustainable Use of Marine Resources for Small Island Developing States and Coastal Least Developed Countries*, World Bank, Washington, DC.

World Bank. 2018. *Successful Models to Reduce Wastewater, Agricultural Runoff, and Marine Litter*. September. Available at: http://documents.worldbank.org/curated/en/651521537901259717/Solving-Marine-Pollution-Successful-Models-to-Reduce-Wastewater-Agricultural-Runoff-and-Marine-Litter.

World Bank. 2019. *Marine Pollution in the Caribbean: Not a Minute to Waste*. March. Available at: http://documents.worldbank.org/curated/en/482391554225185720/Marine-Pollution-in-the-Caribbean-Not-a-Minute-to-Waste.

World Economic Forum, Ellen McArthur Foundation, McKinsey & Company. 2016. *The New Plastics Economy: Rethinking the Future of Plastics*.

World Trade Organization. 2018. Plastic waste, 'Blue Economy' among issues taken up at trade and environment committee. 30 November. Available at: https://www.wto.org/english/news_e/news18_e/envir_30nov18_e.htm.

17 Financing the Blue Economy in the Wider Caribbean

Justin Ram and Donna Kaidou-Jeffrey

Introduction

Burdened by the cost of building resilience to climate change, reconstruction costs after disasters and other fiscal contingent liabilities, high fiscal deficits, debt overhang and declining Official Development Assistance, the Caribbean requires new and innovative financing initiatives to advance the Blue Economy. Ten years after the global economic crisis, Caribbean economies are still facing structural social, environmental and economic challenges that limit the ability of governments to finance new and emerging investment opportunities such as the Blue Economy. There are, however, other resources and emerging sources of finance, particularly within the climate change agenda, blended finance and impact investments and other private sector resources including digital resources and Fintech solutions, which could be leveraged for Blue Economy projects. In addition, innovative financing instruments, particularly those which have been tested for the Green Economy, may be extended to the Blue Economy. This chapter gives a brief overview of the fiscal and debt challenges which compromise the ability of many Caribbean countries to invest in the Blue Economy. Options such as blended finance, blue bonds, debt swaps, development impact bonds, insurance, international climate finance and Fintech solutions are examined. It also focuses on where the Caribbean needs to improve its own practices in relation to leveraging available resources more efficiently; aligning resources more strategically to Blue Economy priorities; and enhancing its capacity to develop and implement viable projects. This includes a recognition of the role of the development community, private sector and civil society.

Challenges to financing the Blue Economy in the Caribbean

The negative relationship between public debt and growth poses significant risks to sustainable development and poverty reduction, particularly the ability of governments to invest in growth inducing initiatives such as that of the Blue Economy (CDB, 2018). Even fiscal consolidation and debt restructuring programmes which several Caribbean countries have undertaken, sometimes more than once, carry heavy social and economic costs which are borne by the population. Development of the Blue Economy agenda requires mobilising resources to finance long-term investments and policy reforms. However, several challenges and risk factors may hamper the ability of Caribbean countries to participate in and derive the full potential of the Blue Economy. These include the following.

Marginal scope for debt finance

Decades of low growth, compounded by high and increasing expenditures have contributed to relatively high and persistent fiscal deficits in most Caribbean countries. Consequently, debt build-up, particularly in many small Caribbean states, has also created a drag on growth, and a resultant debt overhang cycle. A 1% increase in the debt to gross domestic product (GDP) ratio can be attributed to an estimated 0.015% decline in real GDP growth for the countries in the Caribbean (McLean & Charles 2018). With a general increase in public debt since 1997, debt trajectories in the Caribbean have generally worsened since the 2008 crisis (Kathuria et al., 2005; Wright et al., 2017). At the end of 2018, public debt in the Caribbean was in excess of US $57 billion with the majority of countries having debt to GDP ratios in excess of the generally accepted prudential benchmark for fiscal sustainability of 60% (see Figure 17.1) (CDB, 2018).

Exogenous economic shocks and natural disasters, when combined with limited scope and capacity for adequate policy responses, have contributed to

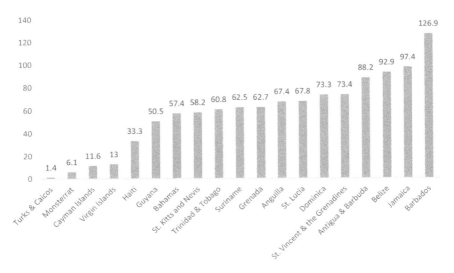

Figure 17.1 Selected Caribbean countries' debt to GDP Ratios (2018).
Source: Caribbean Development Bank

212 *Justin Ram and Donna Kaidou-Jeffrey*

the increasing debt ratios in some Caribbean countries (Acevedo et al., 2013; Alleyne et al., 2018). These impacts are expected to continue as the frequency and intensity of climate-change-related hazards are expected to increase. The cost of rehabilitation and reconstruction following major natural disasters impose significant financing constraints on small island states, adding to the national debt. High economic, social and environmental vulnerability, according to the multidimensional vulnerability index recently computed by Ram et al. (2019), also exacerbates the debt burden in the region. The economic cost of disasters to the Caribbean exceeded $22 billion (in constant 2009 dollars) between 1950 and 2016, which excludes the Category 5 Hurricanes of 2017 (Otker & Srinivasan, 2018). These costs are related to the immediate aftermath and recovery needs as well as long-term infrastructural and development needs.

Other factors which have contributed to the general increase in debt include other contingent liabilities such as debt contracted by state-owned enterprises (SOEs), a reduction in aid, limited access to concessional financing and in some instances institutional weaknesses, which have led to inadequate planning and fiscal mismanagement.

Declining development aid and finance

Official Development Assistance (ODA) flows to the Caribbean have declined significantly from 0.72% of global ODA in 2000 to 0.52% in 2016 (CDB, 2018). The decline in development aid and concessional financing to the Caribbean has been impacted mainly by the criteria for allocation and access. Many Caribbean countries have graduated from upper-middle-income to high-income status based on per capita income and rankings on the UN's human development index. ODA flows to the Caribbean in 2016 represented 1.1% of the region's gross national income, lower than the registered 3.1% average in the 2000s and the 4.4% average for the 1980–2016 period (ECLAC, 2018).

In addition to a significant reduction in the amount of ODA allocated to the Caribbean, the objectives of development funding have shifted from broad poverty reduction, health and education to environmental and climate-change-related targets. The share of ODA allocated for environmental protection has increased from an average of 4.1% between 2003 and 2007 to an average of 8.2% between 2012 and 2016, reflecting the shift in focus towards the environment and climate change (ECLAC, 2018).

Despite close alignment of environmental and climate change objectives to the Blue Economy, the Caribbean's ability to access funding remains challenging. Weak capacity for project identification, development of proposals and implementation are most prevalent factors affecting the ability of many Caribbean countries to access finance and complete projects (CDB, 2017). Therefore, accessing ODA for development of the Blue Economy will require a combination of concessional finance and technical support. In addition to

Financing the Blue Economy   213

capacity building in project identification, preparation and implementation, technical support will be required to help develop and test new financing models.

Investing in the Caribbean Blue Economy

Innovative financial instruments and mechanisms for the Blue Economy

The acknowledgement that Caribbean states having as much as 80 times more ocean space than land mass, coupled with the advent of the Blue Economy paradigm, has given Caribbean Small Island Developing States (SIDS) and indeed all SIDS the ability to change the narrative of their development towards Big Ocean Developing States (BODS). However, traditional and current financing models are widely inadequate for the level of investments needed to meaningfully develop the Blue Economy and transform the Caribbean. Different levels of interventions and investments tailored to country specific circumstances will be required to meet infrastructure, conservation, governance, planning, research and development, institutional-strengthening and capacity-building needs.

Development finance should incorporate innovative instruments and mechanisms which complement international resource flows. Financing for development has matured with the emergence of several new sources of finance related to the Sustainable Development Goals (SDGs), climate change and environmental protection. As such, opportunities for the Caribbean to leverage financing for the Blue Economy are more readily available. Innovative finance tools include but are not limited to the identification of new revenue streams, debt-based instruments related to the environment such as debt for nature swaps and blue or green bonds. More recently, calls for building financial resilience to climate change have proposed building fiscal buffers, contingency reserves and natural disaster funds.

Challenges to development of the Blue Economy, particularly investments in infrastructure, are expected to be hindered by a multitude of factors, especially around the upfront costs. Low appetite for risk by the private sector has left many development projects to be financed by the public sector through multilateral development institutions (CDB, 2018). In addition, a "pipeline" of feasible projects around the Blue Economy remains undeveloped. Many Caribbean countries are only beginning to apply an investment lens to traditional sectors such as fisheries, ecosystem restoration and marine conservation to name a few.

But, there are a number of avenues through which financial innovation could support the Blue Economy even within the wider sustainable development agenda. However, different approaches will be needed to cater for country specific circumstances, although some general concepts and principles will be applicable across the board. This section explores a few innovative finance models and their application to the Blue Economy in the Caribbean.

214 *Justin Ram and Donna Kaidou-Jeffrey*

Mobilising capital market finance for the Blue Economy

Blended finance

Blended finance is broadly described as the use of development finance and philanthropic funds to incentivise or mobilise private capital flows such that investor risks can be mitigated and returns managed more efficiently in the market. Through the collaboration between development finance and philanthropic funds, capital is risk adjusted for impact investments particularly related to development. Blended finance has been used increasingly by multilateral and bilateral development agencies to more effectively mobilise private resources to address investment needs related to achieving the SDGs and close the estimated annual US$2.5 trillion investment gap between funding needs and available public and private investment (Andersen, et al. 2019). In just over four years, the Organisation for Economic Co-operation and Development (OECD) estimates that over US$81 billion has been generated in blended finance specifically for the SDGs (OECD, 2018). Meanwhile, Convergence[1] estimates that blended finance has reached over US$100 billion, reflecting over 300 blended finance transactions globally. Concessional debt or equity and grant funding are the most common form of public and philanthropic funder participation in blended finance transactions, used to attract commercial investment (OECD, 2018). Latin America and the Caribbean accounts for approximately 20% of blended finance, with an average deal size of US$186 million (OECD, 2018).

Blended finance is strongly aligned to the SDGs, particularly the goals on Partnerships (Goal 17), No Poverty (Goal 1), Industry, Innovation and Infrastructure (Goal 9) and Decent Work and Economic Growth (SDG 8). As the market for blended finance continues to mature and concerns for the environment, particularly the state of the world's oceans, become increasingly more prominent, new niche themes such as Life Below Water (Goal 14) are also attracting blended finance. Althelia's Sustainable Ocean Fund is one such example of a blended finance fund which is built around a specific theme. Within the Blue Economy context, blended finance can be utilised for development of sustainable fisheries industries, including marine aquaculture, ocean renewable energy or marine renewable energy and conservation and marine protected areas, amongst others.

Blended finance transactions facilitate a number of benefits across agencies such as the sharing of best practices, skills enhancement and the creation of markets by testing new and emerging sectors and markets. This is especially important in the Blue Economy context where upfront costs and risks are also high. The concessional finance element in blended finance packages can also help to drive the Blue Economy objectives in a number of ways. For example, the technical assistance component can be used for project scoping and preparation or to underwrite the risks to the investors. The objective of development financial institutions and the inclusion of concessional funding is to reduce the financing costs and make investments viable for the private sector. In the context of the Caribbean, sound policies and institutional capacity around financial innovation, investment and innovation around Blue Economy entrepreneurship, project proposal development and monitoring and evaluation is necessary to help build stable Blue Economy project pipelines. In some instances, pilot projects may help build confidence and a track record for consideration of larger blended finance transactions. This would help overcome some of the constraints related to technical capacity for designing, managing and executing blended finance instruments. Building awareness and consideration for the social and environmental impacts are also important in the Caribbean context given the current vulnerabilities. Less-concessional finance, however, must be reviewed carefully given the high debt burdens in the Caribbean and issues surrounding fiscal space, the cost of disasters and country specific development challenges.

Blended finance principles have been developed and adopted by the OECD and the Development Finance Institutions (DFI) working group led by the International Finance Corporation. The OECD Principles include a five-point checklist to ensure blended finance meets certain standards and achieves impact, but also meets the objectives of blended finance with respect to concessionality,[2] additionality[3] and transparency.[4] The DFI Working Group's Enhanced Principles for Blended Concessional Finance for Private Sector Projects seek to strengthen the effective and efficient use of concessional resources in private sector projects so that market distortions or crowding out of private capital is reduced. As such, the principles promote commercially sustainable vehicles using the minimum amount of concessionality, but stress the importance of high social, environmental and governance standards. A talent pool across the Caribbean with expertise in innovative finance, project scoping, development and implementation would help to accelerate the awareness and appetite in blended finance for the Blue Economy. Blended finance transactions in the Caribbean remain low, as reflected in the low track record for using innovative financing instruments. Thus there is a requirement to develop capacities around new financial instruments to capitalise on private finance for development needs in relation to climate change and the Blue Economy. Furthermore, the Caribbean could consider setting up a Blue Economy finance credit rating agency, similar to the resilience credit rating agency proposed by Ram et al. (2019). This agency, using ex-ante valuation and scoping studies would score Blue Economy projects on criteria such as overall risks, credit worthiness of the project or its sponsor, economic and social impacts as well as overall Blue Economy impacts, thereby giving investors information that would allow them to compare the viability and efficacy of Blue Economy projects across countries and regions.

Blue bonds

Bonds are fixed income instruments or investments, where bond investors are paid a fixed interest rate (coupon) on a fixed schedule and will be returned their initial investment (principal) upon maturity of the bond (Roth et al., 2019). Bonds are issued by public and private entities for differing financing objectives. In the case of development bonds issued by development financial institutions, the objective is related to longer-term development and sustainability priorities in the areas of climate change, SDGs, conservation and now oceans. Blue bonds, designed on the concept of "green Bonds" represent but one of the more innovative ocean financing instruments developed more recently. Funds raised from the issue of blue bonds are earmarked exclusively for ocean-related projects, unlike green bonds which focus on wider land-based environmental projects. Blue bonds leverage private sector capital to support the ocean-related activities, and by extension the Blue Economy. While the green bond market is relatively more mature, blue bonds are newer, with the first issuance in 2018 by the Republic of Seychelles. This was the world's first sovereign blue bond, developed with support from the World Bank, and targeted towards Blue Economy activities, such as supporting conservation of marine resources and expanding seafood value chains. The instrument was a demonstration of the potential impact of capital markets financing for development projects related to the environment.

Development of blue bonds has seen increased collaboration between a wide cross-section of institutions, including multilateral and development banks, capital markets and non-profit groups. Following the success of Seychelles blue bonds, in 2019, the Nordic Investment Bank issued the Nordic-Baltic Blue Bond to the amount of €194 million[5] for water- and sewage-related projects and water-related climate change adaptation. Also, Morgan Stanley in collaboration with the World Bank raised US$10 million in blue bonds for plastic pollution in the oceans.

Blue bonds could potentially alter the financing landscape in the Caribbean. The Nature Conservancy (TNC) is working with governments across the Caribbean and beyond to leverage blue bonds which, similar to the case of Seychelles, will seek to reduce debt, but also promote marine conservation and the expansion of seafood value chains. To realise this potential however, a number of areas with respect to capacity building related specifically to project identification, negotiations, implementation and monitoring must be addressed. This will require the collaboration of different agencies across multilateral and private finance institutions, government authorities and non-profit organisations. Similar to blended financing, there may be a need for the development of principles or industry standards to ensure that all parties abide in good faith and be guided by industry best practice.

TNC recently launched a blue bonds initiative to raise US$40.5 million in philanthropic finance which could be used to catalyse an estimated US$1.6 billion specifically for ocean conservation. This project is targeting 20 island

Financing the Blue Economy 217

and coastal countries across the Caribbean, the Pacific Islands and the East Indian Ocean which will seek to enhance the management of marine areas and create new marine protected areas over the next five years. The Caribbean stands to gain from the objectives of this initiative which envisions a multiplier of up to 40 times based on the expected ripple effects from financial savings that national governments could re-invest in natural resource conservation, creating livelihoods in local communities and preserving cultural heritage.

Social and development impact bonds

Development Impact Bonds (DIBs) are results-based financing instruments that facilitate public–private partnership arrangements between donors and the private and non-profit sector to deliver specific development objectives related to the environment. Social Impact Bonds (SIBs) are similar, but the risk is borne by the government rather than the donors for social development objectives. They typically require the engagement of three key players including the investors, service providers or the implementation agencies and outcome funders. The initial investors would provide the seed capital for investment, while the outcome funders reward the investors with the initial capital plus a return on investment, if successful.

The difference between impact bonds and traditional bonds is the return on investment. In a traditional bond, the return is fixed with specified rates of return and maturity for repayment. However, impact bonds are only payable or redeemable when the desired objective has been achieved.

Social and development bonds incentivise risk in areas which investors would not typically consider, using a pay for performance mechanism based on development outcomes. For example, in 2019, the World Bank, UN Women and Small Industries Development Bank of India (SIDBI) joined forces with leading wealth managers and corporates to launch a women's livelihood social impact designed to help rural women in some of India's poorest states in the development of their own enterprises. Almost ten years from when the first SIB was issued in 2010, approximately US$431 million in financing has been mobilised across 25 countries for social interventions around education, health poverty and the environment (Carè and De Lisa, 2019). For Blue Economy considerations, these models present several opportunities for exploration around ocean renewable technology, coastal and marine management and conservation, sustainable livelihoods and education and skills training.

The complexities involved in designing social and development impact bonds have resulted in a relatively low uptake in most developed countries, especially the Caribbean. As such, high transaction costs are incurred in developing the instrument. The instruments also take time to develop quantifiable performance metrics (used to trigger payments to the initial funder), to bring the best combination of mix of partners together (capital investor(s);

218 *Justin Ram and Donna Kaidou-Jeffrey*

implementation partner(s); results monitoring evaluator; and outcome funder (s)) (CDB, 2018). Despite the complexities, the Caribbean can leverage the experience of other development partners such as the World Bank who recently issued a Sustainable Development Bond[6] to raise awareness, develop capacity and seek a regional approach to a Blue-Economy-related bond issue.

Debt swaps for ocean conservation

Debt for nature swaps typically mobilise private resources in exchange for high-interest-bearing sovereign debt for which national authorities commit to conservation efforts related to climate change and environmental protection. There are typically three parties to the transaction whereby the creditor(s) agrees to sell all or part of the outstanding debt to a third party (typically a conservation organisation) at a price lower than the face value. It is also possible to have a bilateral swap which is negotiated between the creditor and debtor government in exchange for conservation activities in the debtor country. In either case, the motivation is driven by conservation activities. The world's first climate adaptation debt conversion was completed in 2016 whereby finance was mobilised for the conservation of Seychelles' Exclusive Economic Zone and climate adaptation. This arrangement led to an increase in Seychelles' marine protected waters from less than 1% to more than 30%.

Swapping debt for ocean conservation is one area in which highly indebted Caribbean countries could develop a win–win solution to reducing debt levels and preserving the marine ecosystems. A debt for Blue Economy swap for Caribbean countries with high debt levels would generate significant savings through lower debt servicing costs which could be used for conservation-related investments. However, the circumstances around debt in the Caribbean vary by country. In instances where the stock of domestic debt is higher than external debt, a debt swap may not be feasible as typically debt swaps are applied to long-term external debt. Retiring external debt, however, has an additional benefit where savings from debt repayment (in the form of spending on conservation activities) are in local currency and hence create additional economic impacts compared to the foreign currency payments which would have been due on that portion of external debt. Similarly, in the case of multilateral debt, whereby most Caribbean countries access funding from the Caribbean Development Bank, World Bank and Inter-American Development bank, debt swaps may not be feasible. However, the proposal from the Commonwealth Secretariat for a multilateral debt swap for mitigation and/or adaptation for the Caribbean may be an avenue for also incorporating Blue Economy considerations. For the few countries which hold market-issued or bilateral debt, a swap for ocean conservation may be more feasible.

Typically, debt swaps are complex and require proper design in the context of national priorities and circumstances, government and stakeholder buy-in and long-term commitment, negotiations, partnerships, implementation and monitoring capacity. As such, executing a debt swap for one country may take several years to execute. While a few mechanisms may be dealt with at the regional level in terms of public education, training and capacity enhancement, other areas of developing a debt swap may become cumbersome at the regional level. However, this does not negate the need for a joint approach to negotiating debt reductions in light of the risks and vulnerabilities that climate change pose to the Caribbean, particularly small states. The Economic Commission for Latin America and the Caribbean (ECLAC) has commenced a Debt for Climate Adaptation Swap Initiative which could set the stage for Blue Economy considerations. Similarly, the World Bank's debt for nature financing facility could be leveraged.

Conservation Trust Funds

Conservation Trust Funds mobilise resources from various sources including donors, national governments and private sector to provide sustainable finance for conservation activities. Trust funds use diverse financing mechanisms, manage and invest financial assets. Resources are disbursed in the form of grants to support programmes and projects through various entities. Trust funds can also be used to fund Blue Economy activities. The World Bank in 2018 established "PROBLUE", a Multi-Donor Trust Fund (MDTF) to finance activities related to the oceans and forms part of the Bank's Blue Economy strategy. Other examples include the Mesoamerican Reef Fund (MAR Fund), established in 2014 to protect the reef eco-region between four countries (Thiele & Gerber, 2017). Within the Caribbean, trust funds related to the environment or the Blue Economy are not entirely new. Belize established the Protected Areas Conservation Trust (PACT) in 1996 to strengthen biodiversity conservation and natural resource management. Similarly, Grenada has established a local trust fund, the Grenada Sustainable Development Trust Fund (GSDTF) that will seek to finance conservation priorities which are expected to be defined under the potential debt for nature swap being developed with TNC. At the regional level, the Caribbean Biodiversity Fund (CBF) was established in 2012 for the purposes of financing conservation and sustainable development in the Caribbean region.

Innovative domestic resource mobilisation

Domestic Resource Mobilisation (DRM) combined with other resources could demonstrate the commitment of authorities to Blue Economy development and ocean conservation and thereby attract or complement funds from other sources. Domestic resources however, could also support blended interventions using development and market finance using innovative strategies for risk and benefit sharing.

220 *Justin Ram and Donna Kaidou-Jeffrey*

Blue levy

In the Caribbean, opportunities for raising taxes are limited, particularly as they concern tourism-related taxes and fees. Many countries impose different levies that are targeted towards environment protection in the form of environmental or tourist enhancement levies or taxes. These are applied in different ways at different rates on importation, consumption (accommodation and service) or travel. The British Virgin Islands for example, imposed an Environmental and Tourism Levy of US$10 to be paid on arrival at all ports of entry. Integrating Blue Economy considerations into fiscal policy formulation has potential for larger economic and sustainable development gains. For instance, there may be opportunities to shift the tax burden in a revenue-neutral manner to enhance welfare gains from the environment. However, a comprehensive analysis of the burden of taxes will have to be conducted before domestic taxes can be raised for Blue Economy investments. A well-designed blue tax or levy, whether mandatory or voluntary, based on targeted ocean-based activities could be directed towards investments in the Blue Economy. Any instrument which is designed must be transparent, and use of the funds should be guided by clearly defined criteria and investments related to national or regional development. The extraction, cruise and shipping industries are potential areas for blue levies which could be directed towards the expansion of economic infrastructure, as well as building greater resilience to climate change adaptation and mitigation and conservation of the ocean economy.

Insurance and the Blue Economy

The insurance sector is critical to the sustainable development of the Caribbean given the extreme vulnerability to the impacts of climate change. The role of risk pooling and risk transfer has become more important for the Caribbean as the occurrence and intensity of natural disasters increase. For the Caribbean, given that Blue Economy investments are relatively under-developed, the level of risk may be higher from an investment perspective. Insurance can bridge the gap by providing a means to transfer the risks associated with investments in Blue Economy activities. Insurance geared towards the Blue Economy or the oceans could stir new business models around managing risk and reducing economic impact on related activities. Marine insurance, which is well developed in the Caribbean, can be explored for developing insurance products tailored to the Blue Economy. Over time, the insurance sector has started to branch into unmet niches of the Blue Economy using parametric insurance. Parametric insurance is a form of ex-ante disaster financing which make payments based on the intensity of an event and the amount of loss calculated in a pre-agreed model based on the level of the hazard and impact. Parametric insurance differs from traditional indemnity settlements in that it does not require an on-the-ground assessment

Financing the Blue Economy 221

of individual losses, but rather depends on a triggering mechanism, that is, a predefined methodology based on variables that are exogenous to both the individual policyholder and the insurer. For example, the Caribbean Oceans and Aquaculture Sustainability Facility (COAST) is a parametric insurance facility developed jointly by the Caribbean Catastrophe Risk Insurance Facility – Segregated Portfolio Company (CCRIF-SPC), the United States Department of State, the World Bank, TNC and the Food and Agriculture Organisation. COAST targets the fisheries sector specifically and is geared towards addressing the impacts of natural hazards on food security and livelihoods of those working in the fisheries sector of the Caribbean. This policy was first issued in July 2019 for Grenada and Saint Lucia. The Caribbean would benefit from drawing lessons learnt from these examples and scaling up insurance for other Blue Economy areas.

Caribbean Blue Economy financing facility

A Caribbean Blue Economy financing facility may help address some of the challenges which are anticipated if Blue Economy investment financing is to be scaled up. The Blue Natural Capital Financing Facility, supported by the Government of the Grand Duchy of Luxembourg and managed by the International Union for Conservation of Nature (IUCN) is an example of such a facility. At the regional level a financing facility would serve to build technical capacity in developing and structuring financial instruments which are aligned with the objectives of the Blue Economy. This will include market research, scoping and valuation studies to inform investment in the Blue Economy. The facility would work to leverage and align existing resources more efficiently to Blue Economy activities. This will include bringing together development partners, as well as private funders. It is anticipated that the agency would act on behalf of national and regional governments to issue financing instruments tailored for initiatives around the Blue Economy. Further, the agency will seek to build capacity to help implement those projects for which financing has been raised and monitor the results and effectiveness.

Perhaps, the largest untapped potential resource for the Caribbean rests with climate finance. In order to tap into these existing resources, a new approach will be needed in designing projects and programmes that seek to benefit from climate finance. Climate change, through the impacts on the oceans, is already closely aligned with the Blue Economy. Hence a Blue Economy perspective may help to unlock some of the potential financing around climate change from an adaptation and mitigation perspective. On the investments side, building resilience to climate change also contributes to long-term sustainable development and growth, particularly protecting livelihoods. Additional benefits may accrue in terms of lower outlays on insurance and may signal lower risk to potential investors over time.

Strategies which can assist the Caribbean Blue Economy Financing Facility to test some of the innovative finance instruments and proposals include

222 *Justin Ram and Donna Kaidou-Jeffrey*

innovation networks, accelerators and incubators which could leverage technologies and communities of practice, as well as global practices to develop the Blue Economy. This includes bringing small groups together (youth groups or practitioners) from across the region to develop solutions to identified issues. For instance, the Caribbean Science Foundation uses various platforms to engage and educate aspiring engineers and scientists across the region. Similarly, Ten Habitat, a start-up ecosystem, has mushroomed across the region, where potential entrepreneurs are supported and funded using a range of practical tools including networking and mentorship.

Caribbean Blue Economy innovation network

A regional collaboration that brings together scientific and industry leaders to advance the Caribbean Blue Economy will be important. This will help foster a participatory approach and engagement of wider stakeholders. Innovation networks will leverage a broader and more diverse skills set based on training and experience. This approach would help in developing the broader vision but also widen the areas of focus across many sectors related to the Blue Economy. This will help with the establishment of clusters related to the technology and availability of resources. Based on a survey of ten ocean economy innovation networks, the OECD found that these networks generally had positive impacts within and beyond the ocean economy, improved cross-sector synergies, access to research facilities and specialised knowledge and dedicated support for start-ups. Some of the challenges identified included coordination between organisations given varying mandates, as well as finding a balance between research and innovation (OECD, 2019).

Caribbean Blue Economy incubator and accelerator

Incubators and accelerators targeting the Blue Economy could help with business start-ups and innovations. These will help provide an environment which facilitates the testing of business models, relationship building and access to finance. This is akin to the concept of sandboxes which have been proposed in the financial innovation sector. Such a facility will enable start-ups to focus on growth, before they can be scaled into full businesses. Typically, start-ups are matched with partners who have similar needs. The IDB Blue Tech challenge of 2018 sought business models across the Caribbean that integrated new technology or solutions for long-term sustainability of the ocean economy.

Along with the Blue Economy incubator and accelerator, governments should be encouraged to develop junior and micro stock exchanges as a means to boost equity finance for entrepreneurs engaged in Blue Economy projects and initiatives. A junior stock exchange targeting small enterprises will enable entities to access capital based on specifically tailored regulatory frameworks and requirements which they are able to meet. The ability to exit

Financing the Blue Economy 223

via the stock exchange might seem contradictory to the need to encourage private sector finance, however, the ability to exit the initial investment is the best incentive for private equity to enter the Blue Economy market. Many new businesses require capital to propel them to the next level of profitability. Private equity investors could be encouraged to invest in Blue Economy projects, if junior and micro stock exchanges are developed to help access private finance, thereby giving investors an avenue to exit their initial investment. Jamaica's junior stock exchange established in 2009 is an example which can be replicated across the region.

Blue tokens

Financial technology (Fintech) refers to the use of new technology by companies, business owners and consumers to improve the management and access of their financial operations and processes. It involves the use of specialised software and algorithms on a range of devices including computers and smartphones. For example, online banking or a digital wallet which allows customers access to their financial resources from their smart device is an example of the increased use of Fintech over the last decade and expansion into areas such as insurance and investing. Fintech has enabled faster transactions and improved compliance and has also allowed investors to raise financing on the open market with much less friction. Blue tokens, an initiative being proposed here, could use block chain technology or another technology to raise money for Blue Economy projects with development and financial returns. The government, regulator or private issuer could set an amount that they would like to raise, e.g. US$10 million with an initial fixed coupon. The initial price of each token could then be set at say, US$10, and one million tokens issued on a secure digital blue token platform. Any investor with a smart device and who has gone through rigorous identification checks (KYC and AML checks) can then buy tokens and either hold to maturity or trade on the secure blue token platform. The Blue Economy credit rating agency (alluded to before) could also rate the issuance (initially and later annually) for development outcomes and financial viability, thereby giving investors maximum information to assist with their investment decision. Blue tokens, if developed well, could democratise investments, allowing almost anyone to invest in Blue Economy initiatives and giving all stakeholders, including citizens and residents in Caribbean states, a real stake in the Blue Economy. Thus blue tokens give potentially all citizens an opportunity to invest in the new narrative and future of these nations as BODS rather than the conventional notion of SIDS.

Conclusion

Caribbean countries are heavily indebted, due to their many vulnerabilities which span economic, social and environmental considerations. Ocean space

224 *Justin Ram and Donna Kaidou-Jeffrey*

around many of them accounts for up to 80 times their total economic zone. The Blue Economy seeks to develop this ocean space for the mutual benefit and sustainable development of these Caribbean SIDS. The narrative is now to move away from considering Caribbean nations merely as SIDS but rather as BODS. This will require funding. However, public finance is constrained and so new innovative financing modalities will have to be examined; finance that will seek to crowd in as much private capital as possible. In fact, private capital will have to take the lead. Therefore in this chapter we have attempted to provide ideas about what type of financing modalities the Caribbean should consider as it contemplates sustainable use of its vast ocean resources. Blended finance, debt swaps, blue bonds and impact bonds are some of the initiatives they have explored. Finance for Blue Economy entrepreneurs is also important and so development of the region's equity markets, in particular the junior and micro stock exchanges will be critical to encourage private equity to invest in new ventures. Finally, we believe that the growth of financial technology should not be ignored, since it provides a way to democratise investments in the Blue Economy and bring greater efficiencies to investment including investment for the Blue Economy. We have therefore put forward the idea of a blue token which if designed and properly regulated could provide a platform that can raise funds from any person with a smart device and allow for the buying, selling and trading of these tokens. The capital raised from these tokens will be invested in Blue Economy projects with specific development outcomes and viable financial returns which would pay the specified coupon in tokens. However, for Blue Economy financing to truly come to fruition, a few prerequisites could help accelerate the Blue Economy agenda. These include the establishment of a regional working group or agency, valuation and scoping studies, development of a project pipeline as well as a Blue Economy credit rating agency. The credit rating agency would rate Blue Economy projects on development outcomes, overall risk and financial viability. Investors would then have maximum information from a trusted independent source. The Blue Economy credit rating would provide investors with some comfort and could spur private investment into the Caribbean Blue Economy.

Notes

1 Convergence is the global network for blended finance which generates blended finance data, intelligence and deal flow to increase private sector investment in developing countries.
2 Finance which is granted on more favourable or attractive terms or conditions than what prevails on the market.
3 The financing instrument should make a greater contribution than what is available or exists in the market but, should not crowd out the private sector.
4 Disclosure policies including accountability for blended concessional finance, while tailored to different stakeholders, must balance dual objectives of confidentiality but also uphold standards related to ethics, reporting and transparency.

Financing the Blue Economy 225

5 Bond pays a coupon of 0.375% and maturity of five years.
6 The World Bank (International Bank for Reconstruction and Development) launched a Sustainable Development Bond in the amount of EUR10 million for a ten-year period to raise awareness of the critical role that water and ocean resources play in development around the world.

References

Acevedo, S. *et al.* 2013. *Caribbean Small States: Challenges of High Debt and Low Growth*, Washington, DC: International Monetary Fund.

Alleyne, T., Otker, I., Ramakrishnan, U. & Srinivasan, K. 2018. *Unleashing Growth and Strengthening Resilience in the Caribbean*. Washington, DC: International Monetary Fund.

Andersen, W. *et al.* 2019. *Blended Finance Evaluation: Governance and Methodological Challenges*, OECD Development Co-operation Working Papers. Paris: OECD.

Carè, R. & De Lisa, R. 2019. Social impact bonds for a sustainable welfare state: The role of enabling actors. *Sustainability*, 11 (10), 2884.

CDB. 2017. *Implementation: Delivering Results to Transform Caribbean Society*, Bridgetown: Caribbean Development Bank.

CDB. 2018. *Financing the Blue Economy: A Caribbean Development Opportunity*, Bridgetown: Caribbean Development Bank.

ECLAC. 2018. *Resilience and Capital Flows in the Caribbean*, Washington DC: Economic Commission for Latin America and the Caribbean.

Kathuria, S. et al. 2005. *A Time to Choose: Caribbean Development in the 21st Century*, Washington DC:World Bank.

McLean, S. & Charles, D. 2018. *Caribbean Development Report: A Perusal of Public Debt in the Caribbean and its Impact on Economic Growth*. ECLAC Studies and Perspectives Series – The Caribbean, Volume 70. Available at: http://caribbean.cepal.org/content/ca ribbean-development-report-perusal-public-debt-caribbean-and-its-impact-economic-gro wth.

OECD. 2018. *Making Blended Finance Work for Sustainable Development Goals*. Paris: OECD Publishing.

OECD. 2019. *Rethinking Innovation for a Sustainable Ocean Economy*. Paris: OECD Publishing.

Otker, I. & Srinivasan, K. 2018. Bracing for the storm: For the Caribbean, building resilience is a matter of survival. *Finance & Development*, March, 55 (1): 49–51.

Ram, J., Cotton, J., Frederick, R. & Elliott, W. 2019. *A Multidimensional Vulnerability Index for the Caribbean: Measuring Vulnerability: A Multidimentional Vulnerability Index for the Caribbean*. Bridgetown: Caribbean Development Bank.

Roth, N., Thiel, T. & Unger, M. V. 2019. *Blue Bonds: Financing Resilience of Coastal Ecosystems*. Geneva: Blue Natural Capital Financing Facility.

Thiele, T. & Gerber, L. R. 2017. Innovative financing for the high seas. *Aquatic Conservation: Marine and Freshwater Ecosystems*, 27 (S1): 89–99.

Wright, A., Grenade, K. & Scott-Joseph, A. 2017. *Fiscal Rules: Toward a New Paradigm for Fiscal Sustainability in Small States*. IDB Working Paper Series, Volume 8208.

18 Limits and opportunities in supporting the Blue Economy

A diplomat's view

Sir Ronald Sanders

Introduction

Undoubtedly, developing untapped resources in the Blue Economy would increase the economic capacity of Caribbean countries, particularly small island developing states (SIDS), beyond their small land masses by extending their Exclusive Economic Zones (EEZs) up to 200 nautical miles. Blue Economy activity is already taking place especially in tourism, transportation and fisheries. But for most of the Caribbean, any opportunities that exist for growing into new blue-growth areas, such as marine biotechnology, deep seabed mining, oil and gas production and ocean renewable energy, are unexploited and are likely to remain so in the absence of access to adequate financial support. Even the existing sectors of activity – tourism and fisheries – are not uniform in their contribution to the Gross Domestic Product (GDP) of many Caribbean countries. Cruise ship tourism has not delivered on the capital investment by the majority of governments and experts have argued for a modulated emphasis on the industry. This chapter discusses the potential and constraints for developing the Blue Economy as well as the practical areas for accessing and attracting greater levels of funding to convert potential into reality.

Unlocking the potential for the Blue Economy

The existing literature on the potential of the Blue Economy assumes the presence of growth sectors. However, Caribbean countries have not sufficiently and effectively mapped the areas within their maritime boundaries to determine what exists. Therefore, a first step for each of them or, better still, all of them is to undertake such a mapping exercise. The process is expensive and would be best undertaken by regional states collectively. However, to date, Caribbean governments, including the 15-nation treaty group, the Caribbean Community (CARICOM), have not adopted a collective approach to the Blue Economy, whereas the much larger and richer countries of the European Union (EU) have done so.[1]

Limits and opportunities 227

While a Meeting of the Ministerial Council of the Caribbean Regional Fisheries Mechanism (CRFM) – an organ of CARICOM – was held in June 2019 with the Blue Economy as part of its agenda, it made no real attempt to formulate a comprehensive plan by which the potential and opportunities of the Blue Economy could be harnessed.[2] In any event, the key to unlocking the potential of the Blue Economy, once the EEZs have been mapped, is access to affordable long-term financing. Therein lies the difficulty for all Caribbean countries. Several factors militate against regional governments accessing money on terms that would allow them to take advantage of opportunities in the Blue Economy.

Disqualification from concessional financing

Caribbean governments are restricted from accessing concessional financing by international financial institutions and donor governments on the sole criterion of high per capita income. The one exception to this attitude by donors is the Government of the Peoples Republic of China which has made soft loans and grants available to regional countries with which it has diplomatic relations.[3] The Prime Minister of Antigua and Barbuda, Gaston Browne, has noted that "the World Bank, a developmental lending agency, cannot even match the lending rates, being provided by China". He stated that China provides loans, for up to 20 years at 2% interest with a five-year moratorium, adding that "not even the World Bank, as a developmental institution, (provides) that type of concessional funding" (Pride, 2019).

Little Official Development Assistance

Apart from access to concessional financing, Official Development Assistance (ODA) to the Caribbean has declined consistently, falling from 0.72% of global ODA to 0.52% in 2016.[4] Significantly, more than 50% of the total aid to the Caribbean goes to Haiti, a least developed country, with the balance shared among at least 16 countries.

High debt to GDP ratios

The region is also plagued by high debt, incurred, in most cases, because of the effect of climate change which has produced more frequent and intense hurricanes since 1995 than in previous years. The cost of reconstruction and building resilience after repeated disasters, with little access to concessional financing, has led these countries to borrow on the international commercial market, escalating their debt to GDP ratios, in some cases to unsustainable levels.[5] Repayment of this high debt has severely restricted the funds left to governments for running day-to-day operations of their countries and gravely limited their capacity to invest in capital projects, or to raise financing through the issuance of new debt instruments, including bonds. Therefore,

228 *Sir Ronald Sanders*

governments themselves are restrained from investing in new sectors of the Blue Economy.

Threats to participation in global trade and financial system

De-risking and the withdrawal of correspondent banking relations from Caribbean financial institutions by banks in the US and Europe threaten to cut off the Caribbean from the global trading and financial system. The phenomenon of de-risking was introduced after regulatory pressure in the US and Europe on the provision of correspondent banking relationships (CBRs) to banks in developing countries. This regulatory pressure arose from the several blacklists produced since 1996 by the Organisation for Economic Cooperation and Development (OECD) and its sister organisation, the Financial Action Task Force (FATF) as well as the European Commission and agencies of the US government.

However, correspondent banking is a longstanding system of bank-to-bank trusted relationships that enables a wide range of commercial and trade activity. It facilitates the engagement of developing countries, such as those in the Caribbean, in cross-border activity through this network of banking linkages. Without these links, the Caribbean would be unable to participate in the global trading and banking system since it would be unable to: (a) pay for goods and services it imports or for those that it exports; (b) receive remittances from its diaspora; (c) repatriate profits to foreign investors; and (d) borrow or repay money in the international system.

Presently, the withdrawal of CBRs from the Caribbean has reached near crisis proportions with most banks in the region reduced to only one correspondent bank. In July 2016, as Managing Director of the World Bank, Christine Lagarde warned that the world should care about the problem "because affected countries often are very vulnerable – they include small island economies and countries in conflict. These are countries with minimal access to financial services in the best of circumstances" (Lagarde, 2016). Despite many IMF and World Bank studies and public statements by Caribbean Heads of Government in which they declared their abhorrence of lists "which convey the erroneous perception of the Caribbean as high risk and so targeted for the de-risking strategies of global banks" (CARICOM, 2019), the problem of the loss of CBRs continues, hanging like the sword of Damocles over the region.

The difficulties of private sector financing

Attracting private sector financing in new and untried areas is an extremely difficult undertaking. Even EU countries have encountered this problem, cautioning that: "In most cases, finding private finance is not an easy task. It requires patience and compelling arguments to convince private investors and/ or lenders that they are considering a good investment opportunity".[6]

Limits and opportunities 229

Traditionally, private investors in the Caribbean require tax holidays for 15 years with a waiver of duties on goods imported for projects. The IMF has repeatedly warned that "the benefits of tax incentives in terms of increased foreign direct investment (FDI) appear to have been limited",[7] because governments have to forgo decades of tax revenues in return for low-skilled jobs provided by foreign firms. This situation persists in known, profitable land-based projects in the region, largely because, instead of settling regional agreements on guidelines and standards for tax and other concessions, governments operate beggar-thy-neighbour policies in relation to all situations in which they compete with each other for investment. Thus, it can be assumed that hefty tax concessions will be demanded by any private investor in the Blue Economy. If governments acquiesce, the resulting inequalities between foreign investors and local communities will worsen public dissatisfaction that already exists throughout the Caribbean in relation to land-based projects.

The forbidding experience of cruise ship tourism

One sector of the Blue Economy in which the Caribbean has decades of experience is the cruise ship industry. The experience has not been inspiring and, on the available facts, the cruise industry could well become a casualty in the Blue Economy unless circumstances change. At the root of the issue is an overlord attitude of the Florida-based Cruise Ship Association (FCSA), an alliance of the cruise ship companies that ply the Caribbean, where 35.5% of global cruise tourism takes place. Allied to the problem is the beggar-thy-neighbour policies, employed by Caribbean governments when they compete for business and investment. Although, for more than two decades, the FCSA has dictated the passenger head tax and port charges that its member companies pay to individual governments, the governments have opted to accept lower revenues than to combine their forces to negotiate better terms with the alliance of cruise companies.

The cruise ship companies have not been above using their clout to continue to demand low port and other charges from governments. As an example, when in February 2019, Antigua and Barbuda's Prime Minister, Gaston Browne, publicly complained about the US$5 passenger head tax that Carnival Cruise Lines (the main partner in the FCSA) had been paying his government since 1993 despite the expenditure of hundreds of millions of dollars in tax payers' money to develop port facilities for cruise ships, the cruise line immediately withdrew all its calls to the island state.[8] It was the second time in 10 years that the cruise company had lowered the boom on Antigua and Barbuda when it asked for consultations on a higher passenger head tax. No other government joined the Antigua and Barbuda government in its complaint.

Experts have pointed to the exploitation of the region by the cruise ship companies which made estimated revenues of US$40 billion in 2016 from the Caribbean, but failed to contribute proportionately to the development of ports or the enhancement of the economies of the region.[9] The experts argue that

230 *Sir Ronald Sanders*

"land-based stayover tourism is far more valuable than cruise tourism" and "Governments should make cruise tourism only a small part of the tourism sector".[10]

Settling maritime boundaries

An issue that has not been considered in the existing literature on accessing finance for the Blue Economy is maritime boundary delimitation in the Caribbean. Investors are unlikely to put money into projects where disputes exist over sovereignty and rights in an area of investment. Although in the wider Caribbean, some maritime boundaries have been settled by agreements, most remain undetermined. Two have been settled by resort to arbitration under the United Nations Convention on the Law of the Sea (UNCLOS), after disputes. These are the Barbados/Trinidad and Tobago Boundary Arbitration of 2016[11] and the Guyana/Suriname Maritime Boundary Arbitration of 2017.[12] Both cases were related to resources in disputed maritime areas: fisheries in the Barbados/Trinidad case and oil and gas in the case of Guyana/Suriname. Indeed, in the latter case, force was used by the Suriname military to remove a Guyana-licensed oil rig and this caused the Tribunal to adjudicate on wider international law prohibiting the use of force.[13] Both these events underscore the necessity for clear and settled national boundaries between Caribbean states not only for maritime security and enforcement, but also for establishing the correct basis for developing and financing Blue Economy projects.

Climate change as a restraint on financing

A review of the literature on the Blue Economy does not reveal mention of climate change and its attendant global warming and sea-level rise as a constraint to accessing financing. Yet, it clearly is. In 2007, the Intergovernmental Panel on Climate Change (IPCC) concluded that climate change would impede the ability of many nations to achieve sustainable development by mid-century. More particularly, the panel concluded that:

> Small Island Developing States (SIDS) have characteristics which make them particularly vulnerable to the effects of climate change, sea-level rise (SLR) and extreme events, including: relative isolation, small land masses, concentrations of population and infrastructure in coastal areas, limited economic base and dependency on natural resources, combined with limited financial, technical and institutional capacity for adaptation.
> (IPCC, 2007)

Significantly, Caribbean SIDS contribute less than 1% to global greenhouse gas emissions; yet they are now among the worst victims as the 2017 hurricane season proved when at least seven countries were impacted severely. The population of Barbuda became the first "climate refugees" in the Caribbean when they were all evacuated to Antigua in the wake of Barbuda's complete destruction. Two years later, in 2019, Barbuda, which suffered damage estimated by the World Bank at more than US$200 million, had been still only partially reconstructed. Promises of assistance at a United Nations Development Programme (UNDP) pledging conference yielded little, and most of the burden fell to the already cash-strapped government of Antigua and Barbuda which could not afford to borrow any more money on commercial terms, having done so for more than a decade.

These threats and constraints faced by the Caribbean region were summed-up in a statement, made to Caribbean Heads of Government in July 2019, by the United Nations Secretary-General, António Guterres. While his statement was not specifically about financing the Blue Economy, it underscores the serious difficulties the region faces economically. He said:

> As climate-related natural disasters grow in frequency and severity, the risks to families and to development overall will only intensify. The Caribbean experience makes abundantly clear that we must urgently reduce global emissions and work collectively to ensure that global temperature rise does not go beyond 1.5 degrees above pre-industrial levels.

Tellingly, he added:

> Small Island Developing States face a range of economic constraints. The small size of their domestic markets and their limited capacity to participate in global markets, hinder them from generating economies of scale. Their heavy dependence on imports, particularly of energy and food, make (sic) them highly vulnerable to price fluctuations and other external shocks. And their very high levels of national debt constrain their ability to effectively address high and persistent levels of poverty and inequality. These challenges are further complicated by the difficulties (that) SIDS face in mobilizing development finance on affordable and appropriate terms.[14]

It should be evident that, as long as climate change persists and sea-levels rise, Caribbean countries will experience repeated damage and greater challenges in securing financing.

All of this underscores the relevance of the conclusion, reached in a global context, but nonetheless relevant to the Caribbean, that: "Traditional sources of financing projects have proven inadequate. Innovative and robust financing models must be adopted for a sustainable Blue Economy".[15]

Raising finance for the Blue Economy: The experience so far

Caribbean states have had some success in accessing relatively small sums of money from environment and development agencies for projects. However,

232 Sir Ronald Sanders

these projects tinker at the edges of developing a Blue Economy and a description of them are worth noting. Among the agencies are: the Global Environmental Facility, the UNDP, the World Bank Group and the Food and Agriculture Organisation. The projects, funded by these institutions, have focussed on marine ecosystem degradation, sustainable fisheries aquaculture and conservation of coastal and ocean habitats. But, as one expert put it: "Collectively, current financing is – and will remain – insufficient for the Blue Economy to represent a serious transformation pathway for small states" (Rustomjee, 2016, 2).

A number of intergovernmental financial institutions have shown interest in the Blue Economy. But this interest has not gone much beyond commissioning and publishing papers and holding seminars. Certainly, no significant pocket of money has been provided from which governments or the private sector could call for investment. For example, in September 2019, the Inter-American Development Bank, in collaboration with others, launched a project to "identify firms and organizations looking to pilot and scale up business models that use cutting edge technologies to contribute to the sustainable management of oceans, marine ecosystems and coastal resources" in 14 target Caribbean countries. However, grants ranged only between US$150,000 and US$500,000, and loans are "within a range of US$500,000 to US$2,000,000", of which the borrowing entity would be expected to contribute at least 50% of the project budget (IDB, 2019).

For its part, in September 2018, the World Bank Group announced the creation of PROBLUE, a multi-donor trust fund to "support healthy and productive oceans by tackling marine pollution, managing fisheries and fostering the sustainable growth of coastal economies" (World Bank, 2018). PROBLUE is part of the World Bank's overall oceans programme, which in 2018 was reported to amount "to around US$4.1 billion with a further US $1.5 billion in the pipeline". Significantly, this fund is open to many countries, including all of Africa and the Pacific, rendering it insignificant in relation to the individual needs of states. Caribbean countries, already burdened with heavy debt, would be hard pressed to borrow from this fund whose emphasis is on non-revenue producing projects.

The Caribbean Development Bank (CDB) has also been active in publishing papers and organising seminars designed to create awareness of the potential of the Blue Economy among its borrowing member countries. The bank has issued a very useful publication entitled "Financing the Blue Economy: A Caribbean Development Opportunity". It sets out the economic context and rationale for the Blue Economy in the Caribbean as well as the challenges that the region faces. The publication states the view that in the Caribbean, "the Blue Economy has not been formally recognised as an important economic driver" (Caribbean Development Bank, 2018, 27). This view might not be entirely correct. Caribbean Heads of Government and Finance Ministers have attended and participated in seminars organised by the World Bank in Washington, DC during joint meetings of the Bank and

Limits and opportunities 233

the IMF. They are sufficiently sensitised about the potential of the Blue Economy, but as one Prime Minister remarked at one of the seminars, "That's the blue, but where's the green?" ("Green" is a slang term for US paper dollars.)

Against the background of the grave constraints that Caribbean countries face, and that have been described earlier in this chapter, the CDB's publication details many useful theoretical and conceptual ideas about how Caribbean countries might finance the Blue Economy, including issuing blue bonds, diaspora financing, debt swaps, blended financing and contingency recoverable grants. But the Bank itself has no money to fund the development of the Blue Economy. However, it makes the compelling point that:

> Investing in Blue Economy-related activities and sectors requires developing innovative and robust financing models. It may also require a reconsideration of the rules on concessional finance to make a more strategic link between climate change, environmental sustainability and green and Blue Economy innovations.
>
> (Caribbean Development Bank, 2018, 86)

This argument has been consistently made by Caribbean governments at the UN and at IMF/World Bank meetings. So far, it has produced no meaningful response from the governments of the world's richest nations that control the global financial institutions. In this regard, the 2018 Global Sustainable Blue Economy Conference probably got it right when the participants declared: "Traditional sources of financing projects have proven inadequate. Innovative and robust financing models must be adopted for a sustainable economy".[16] Thus far, their declaration, too, has become a refrain, blowing in the wind.

Conclusion

The Blue Economy, undoubtedly, has potential for allowing Caribbean countries to unlock new sectors such as marine biotechnology, deep seabed mining and ocean renewable energy. But, at the bottom line, access to adequate and affordable financing is vital to converting potential into reality. That financing does not exist in the public intergovernmental financial institutions on the scale and terms that are necessary. Until it is, Caribbean governments, beset with myriad urgent economic and financial issues, are unlikely to make new projects in the Blue Economy a priority anytime soon.

Notes

1 For a brief summary of the activity, jobs and revenues from the Blue Economy in the European Union, see European Commission (2015).
2 See press release issued by the Meeting (CRFM, 2019).
3 For instance, the People's Republic of China has loaned the government of Antigua and Barbuda and its Port Authority $100 million with a repayment period of 20 years, including a five-year moratorium on payments, at 2% interest for the

234 *Sir Ronald Sanders*

reconstruction and modernisation of the country's main cargo port, confirmed in an interview by the author with Darwin Telemaque, Director of Ports on 5 August 2019; see also Oswald (2019).

4 See Caribbean Development Bank (2018).
5 Ibid., p. 61.
6 The European Union and neighbours (2018), p. 22.
7 See, for instance, Sosa (2006).
8 For a full discussion, see Walker (2019).
9 See CREST (2017) and MacLellan (2019).
10 CREST, op. cit., p. 18.
11 See Permanent Court of Arbitration (2016).
12 See Permanent Court of Arbitration (2017).
13 For a full discussion of this case, see Ramphal (2008).
14 See full statement (United Nations Secretary-General, 2019).
15 See IISD (2018).
16 Op. Cit., Note 19.

References

Caribbean Development Bank. 2018. *Financing the Blue Economy: A Caribbean Development Opportunity.* Bridgetown, Barbados: The Caribbean Development Bank (CDB). Available at: http://www.caribbeanhotelandtourism.com/wp-content/uploads/2018/09/CDB-Financing-the-Blue-Economy-A-Caribbean-Development-Opportunity-2018.pdf.

CARICOM. 2019. Communique of the 40th Meeting of the Caribbean Community Heads of Government in July 2019. Available at: https://www.caricom.org/media-center/communications/communiques/communiqu-issued-at-the-conclusion-of-the-fortieth-regular-meeting-of-the-conference-of-heads-of-government-of-the-caribbean-community-gros-islet-saint-lucia-3-5-july-2019.

CREST. 2017. Lesson learned from 50 years of cruise ship tourism in the Caribbean. 27 November. Available at: https://www.galvestonparkboard.org/DocumentCenter/View/1308/Cruise-Tourism-in-the-Carribean.

CRFM. 2019. Fisheries Ministers underscore need for urgent response to Sargassum scourge and IUU fishing, 18 June. Available at: http://www.crfm.net/index.php?option=com_k2&view=item&id=635:fisheries-ministers-underscore-need-for-urgent-response-to-sargassum-scourge-and-iuu-fishing&Itemid=179 (last accessed 5 August 2019).

European Commission. 2015. The Blue Economy of the European Union. Available at: https://ec.europa.eu/maritimeaffairs/sites/maritimeaffairs/files/docs/publications/poster-blue-growth-2015_en.pdf(last accessed 4 August 2019).

Inter-American Development Bank. 2019. IDB launches Blue Tech Challenge with up to US$2M in funding for Blue Economy proposals. Available at: https://www.iadb.org/en/idb-launches-blue-tech-challenge-us2m-funding-blue-economy-proposals.

Intergovernmental Panel on Climate Change (IPCC). 2007. *Climate Change 2007: Impacts, Adaptation and Vulnerability.* Contribution of Working Group II to the Fourth Assessment Report of the Intergovernmental Panel on Climate Change, M. L. Parry, O.F. Canziani, J.P. Palutikof, P.J. van der Linden and C.E. Hanson (Eds). Cambridge: Cambridge University Press, pp. 7–22.

International Institute for Sustainable Development (IISD). 2018. The Sustainable Blue Economy Conference Bulletin 26–28 November 2018. *Sustainable Blue*

Economy Bulletin, Vol. 208 No. 31. Available at: https://enb.iisd.org/oceans/blue economy/2018/html/enbplus208num31e.html (last accessed 5 August 2019).

Lagarde, C. 2016. 'Relations in Banking – Making it Work for Everyone', speech at the New York Federal Reserve, 18 July. Available at: https://www.imf.org/en/News/Articles/2016/07/15/13/45/SP071816-Relations-in-Banking-Making-It-Work-For-Everyone.

MacLellan, R. 2019. A call for Caribbean governments to tax cruise sector more and tax air passengers less, *eTurboNews*, 6 July. Available at: https://www.eturbonews.com/257439/a-call-for-caribbean-governments-to-tax-cruise-sector-more-and-tax-air-passengers-less/ (last accessed 4 August, 2019).

Oswald, R. 2019. Caribbean Islands becoming hot spots for Chinese investment, *Roll Call*, 25 March. Available at: https://www.rollcall.com/news/congress/caribbean-islands-becoming-hot-spots-for-chinese-investment (last accessed 5 August 2019).

Permanent Court of Arbitration. 2016. Press Release, The Hague, April. Available at: https://pcacases.com/web/sendAttach/1114 (last accessed 4 August, 2019).

Permanent Court of Arbitration. 2017. *Guyana v. Suriname.* Case Report, The Hague, September. Available at: https://pca-cpa.org/en/cases/9/ (last accessed 4 August, 2019).

Pride. 2019. Antigua Prime Minister backs China's aid packages to the Caribbean, *Pride –Canada's Daily African Canadian Caribbean Magazine*, 17 April. Available at: http://pridenews.ca/2019/04/17/antigua-prime-minister-backs-chinas-aid-packages-caribbean/.

Ramphal, S. 2008. *Triumph for UNCLOS: The Guyana-Suriname Maritime Arbitration, a Compilation & Commentary.* London and Hertfordshire: Hansib.

Rustomjee, C. 2016. *Financing the Blue Economy in Small States*, CIGI Policy Brief, No. 78, May. Available at: https://www.cigionline.org/sites/default/files/pb_no78_web.pdf.

Sosa, S. 2006. *Tax Incentives and Foreign Investment in the Eastern Caribbean.* IMF Working Paper WP/06/23, January. Available at: https://www.imf.org/en/search#q=reduce%20tax%20concessions%20in%20Caribbean&sort=relevancy (last accessed 4 August 2019).

The European Union and neighbours. 2018. Section 3.6. Case B: mainly privately funded projects/programmes, in *Facilitating Application Procedures for Blue Economy Project Funding: Accessing Blue Economy Finance, a Step-by-Step Approach for Practitioners.* Handbook, Version 1, August, pp. 22–25.

United Nations Secretary-General. 2019. UN Secretary-General's remarks at 40th meeting of CARICOM [as delivered], 3 July. Available at: https://www.un.org/sg/en/content/sg/statement/2019-07-03/un-secretary-generals-remarks-40th-meeting-of-caricom-delivered (last accessed 4 August 2019).

Walker, J. 2019. Carnival drops Antigua like a hot potato, again, *Cruise Law News*, 12 March. Available at: https://www.cruiselawnews.com/2019/03/articles/caribbean-islands/carnival-drops-antigua-like-a-hot-potato-again/ (last accessed 4 August 2019).

World Bank. 2018. PROBLUE: The World Bank's Blue Economy Program. Available at: https://www.worldbank.org/en/programs/problue.

19 The Blue Economy in the Wider Caribbean
Opportunities, limitations and considerations

Peter Clegg, Robin Mahon, Patrick McConney and Hazel A. Oxenford

Introduction

In the preceding chapters, planners and practitioners alike would have found a wealth of conceptual and technical information that is critical for understanding and developing Blue Economies in the Wider Caribbean Region (WCR). Many cases focused on the English-speaking smaller island countries in which issues and approaches are now being actively addressed in efforts to boost the Blue Economy. In addition to many useful details there are some key messages, which if ignored, could seriously impact the potential benefits from Blue Economic development in this region. In this brief concluding chapter, we will revisit and summarise these key messages in the hope that readers will be encouraged to explore them further and be guided by them in future thinking and practice. As the WCR moves to embrace Blue Economic growth, it must take care not to forget the cultural and spiritual connection of Caribbean societies with the sea and stewardship. Whatever form Blue Economies take, this connection should be unassailable.

The development of Blue Economies will require recognising the value of all marine ecosystem services; and appreciation of the current health of critical marine habitats and fishery resources. It will also need to incorporate the projections of continued climate change and variability. Political decision-makers must actively guide urgently needed improvements in ocean policy, planning and the coherence of institutional arrangements for more adaptive implementation of the Blue Economy agenda. For example, combining land and marine spatial planning, and incorporating knowledge mobilisation across public and private sectors and civil society, are crucial.

Growth of marine-based tourism, already a mainstay of many economies, especially vulnerable small islands, will need to mitigate and manage climate change as well as other global risks. These include economic shocks and acts of terrorism that significantly impact the travel industry, and public health issues, as recently demonstrated by cruise ship tourism being associated with the coronavirus pandemic. Growth in the fishery sector will require

The Blue Economy in the Wider Caribbean   237

rehabilitating habitats and rebuilding some stocks to meet their harvest potential while investing more in developing value-added products. Aquaculture will require value chain analysis to ensure sustainability of critical coastal and marine ecosystems, with a consideration of issues such as preventing environmental damage, producing products that can compete with others on the global market, and ensuring the availability of affordable financing and technical support to build knowledge capacity. Expansion of port facilities to accommodate cruise ship traffic and container transhipment will bring opportunities as well as pose challenges to small islands. Development of marine-based renewable energy sectors is being pursued by several countries requiring innovative technology and funding mechanisms. Expanding marine oil and gas industries is inevitable, with major new finds in the Guyana–Suriname Basin, but raises concerns about the fit into a responsible Blue Economy. Extracting deep seabed minerals and genetic resources are areas for exploration in a Blue Economy, although the challenges of obtaining benefit shares from such resources remains an issue for Small Island Developing States (SIDS). The way ahead is uncertain, but the outlook is positive. Blue Economic development is not new to the WCR, but this is a good time to review progress and move ahead on the basis of lessons learned by heeding broad key messages.

Marine ecosystem health is fundamental

The first key message is that coastal and marine ecosystem health is fundamental as the foundation of the Blue Economy, and will require much better collaboration among different economic sectors and stakeholders to improve environmental stewardship (Chapter 4). Unless ecosystem degradation can be halted and reversed, the ecosystem services that support existing ocean-based economic activities and that could support new economic activities will be lost. New activities must also be developed in ways that do not contribute to ecosystem degradation; within the context of an ecosystem approach. Halting and reversing ecosystem degradation and resource overexploitation has been an issue in the WCR for the past several decades. Laissez-faire approaches to development and resource use have consistently trumped ecosystem protection (Chapter 4). Several changes in modus operandi are needed. First is substantially reducing land- and marine-based sources (LBS and MBS) of pollution, with the former being the most significant. Addressing LBS takes us in the direction of reducing direct polluting inputs by setting and enforcing limits, as well as instituting the "polluter pays principle". It also takes us in the direction of a watershed or "ridge to reef" approach for indirect LBS such as fertilisers, pesticides and agricultural and domestic wastewater (Chapter 16; Pallero Flores et al., 2017). For most SIDS this approach encompasses the entire country. Overall, there is the need to upscale understanding of and action on the connection between land use practices and the sea. It is also necessary to halt and reverse resource overexploitation by eliminating

238 *Peter Clegg et al.*

overfishing and destructive fishing practices, especially in vulnerable reef associated ecosystems. However, few countries have the capacity to manage coastal fisheries, or even coastal tourism which is often a major source of environmental damage. New approaches such as marine spatial planning (MSP), can help, but ultimately, it will be about the political will to make people change their behaviour (Chapter 10).

Equitability and social justice

The second key message concerns equitability and social justice. Uptake of new opportunities may produce significant benefits, but will require significant investment in technology and expertise (Chapters 13, 14 & 15). These new opportunities also come with significant risks. Unless well managed they can contribute to further ecosystem degradation and loss of benefits. The large investments required for many of the new ocean opportunities also mean that they are susceptible to benefiting primarily the wealthy and possibly even contributing to poverty and other forms of social injustice (Bennett et al., 2019). Already, in small-scale fisheries for example, the spectre of further marginalisation of people and privatisation of the assets on which their livelihoods depend is the main image being projected (Chapters 3 & 10; Cohen et al., 2019). Similar concerns exist for other sectors such as vertically integrated and all-inclusive hotels displacing smaller-scale and community-based tourism (Chapters 3 & 11). Therefore, Blue Economic development in the WCR must include explicit pro-poor policies that promote equitable opportunities and social justice. Failure do so will likely result in opportunities for the wealthy and large (mostly foreign-owned) corporations while leaving (primarily local) small and medium entrepreneurs behind. This will increase the already large inequalities between the rich and the poor (Chapter 3; Bennett et al., 2019). While national growth statistics may appear good, human well-being indicators will not. Ultimately, this will backfire as the social environments that emerge will not be attractive to investment. Programmes that provide support for small and medium-sized enterprises (SMEs) and build capacity of local entrepreneurs will be needed; as also noted for Blue Economy development in Southeast Asia (Whisnant and Ross, 2019). Similarly, programmes that facilitate partnership of local and national enterprises with external investors may be needed to bring essential investment and technical inputs to SMEs without overwhelming them or stifling well-grounded innovation and entrepreneurship.

Effective governance

A third key message that emerges across the chapters is the importance of good and effective governance for orderly and equitable Blue Economic development to take place. This includes local level governance of coastal and marine areas for productive fisheries and tourism, perhaps by exploring community-based management or other innovative approaches (Chapters 6 & 10). It also includes attention to national-level arrangements that enable and provide context for local level governance, as well as connection to the regional level (Chapter 8; Gonzales et al., 2019). Finally, it requires attention to, and support for the sub-regional and regional initiatives that are currently struggling to mainstream ocean governance (Chapter 9). At all levels, strengthening governance architecture, processes and policy implementation to meet certain fundamental principles is required (see WWF, 2018; EU/ WWF/WRI/EIB, 2018). Inclusivity, efficiency, transparency and account-ability are among the key considerations that must be applied to enable sus-tainable Blue Economic development. Business as usual will not be enough.

Capital investment is required to realise much of the new potential identi-fied by several authors, such as renewable energy, fisheries post-harvest, eco-tourism and ports (Chapters 10, 11, 13, 15, 16, 17 & 18). Investors will want to see good governance in place to minimise investment risk; for example, general rule of law, capacity for enforcement, enabling infrastructure, spatial planning with clear zoning and property rights. Transparency and streamlined administrative processes that facilitate investment are also likely to be key. Underlying all of this are stable national governments as also noted for Southeast Asia (Whisnant and Ross, 2019). European Union reports that indicate MSP may already be having a positive impact on investment are encouraging (European Commission, 2019). It is heartening to note that many WCR countries already appreciate the importance of MSP (e.g. OECS, 2019). However, there are significant barriers to attracting greater levels of finance, for example due to high debt to GDP ratios, the region's relatively high level of per-capita income, and de-risking and the withdrawal of corre-spondent banking relations from Caribbean financial institutions by North American and European banks (Chapters 17 & 18).

Good governance includes systems to monitor and report on progress with Blue Economy development (e.g. European Commission, 2019). Without appropriate sets of indicators supported by regular and reliable data and information, evaluating Blue Economy development success and responding to emerging threats and opportunities will be difficult. To address the ecosys-tem health message, monitoring should include natural capital and ecosystem services accounting at national and regional levels (Chapter 7; European Commission, 2019). There is the need to think beyond conventional indica-tors that focus primarily on economic metrics and include indicators that measure stakeholder engagement, social justice and human well-being in ocean-related sectors (Mahon et al., 2017).

Uncertainty and climate change

Mainstreaming climate change (here including climate variability) is essential for Blue Economic development (Chapter 5). However, climate is not the only source of uncertainty and risk to be managed, especially for the SIDS of the

240 *Peter Clegg et al.*

region with highly open economies that are extremely dependent on global tourism and trade. Even when global climate models and their projections are downscaled, there remains a high level of uncertainty in the likely outcomes and impacts (Chapter 5). Where mitigation options are limited, there must be more attention on adaptation. Blue Economy approaches hence need to be designed from the start as systems that embrace learning and adaptation rather than relying on prediction and control. An example is the recent "surprise" of massive sargassum seaweed influxes that may either be a threat or an opportunity depending on the readiness and orientation of Blue Economic development (Chapter 4). The scales of ecosystems and marine governance systems need to be better matched. Mismatches will result in institutional surprises perhaps as much as, or more than, ecosystem uncertainty. The multi-level initiatives at the scale of the Caribbean, North Brazil Shelf and Gulf of Mexico Large Marine Ecosystems (Chapter 9) can go far to support Blue Economies and address several sources of social-ecological system uncertainty.

Science-based development

Technical capacity across the range of sciences required for successful Blue Economy development is often weak in the countries of the WCR. By science we mean the full range of bio-geophysical and social science inputs that are essential for planning, implementing, monitoring (progress and impacts) and evaluating Blue Economy initiatives. Without increased attention to the science needs of the many components of Blue Economy development, both old and new, progress is likely to be poorly advised and haphazard. The advent of the Intergovernmental Oceanographic Commission (IOC) Decade of Ocean Science in 2021 (van Hoof et al., 2019) provides a timely opportunity for the WCR to engage the global science community. Note also that science based-development is not just about having good scientists, it is about converting their outputs to information that is usable in decision-making and in creating pathways for the uptake of that information in practice. Interestingly, the intergovernmental conclusions and recommendations of the Third Meeting of the Forum of the Countries of Latin America and the Caribbean on Sustainable Development (ECLAC, 2019) does not mention Blue Economy or the ocean. This brings home the need to promote Blue Economy awareness and inclusion in policy-making and advice in the WCR.

Closing thoughts

Many of the potential benefits of Blue Economy development involve taking better care of economic activities already occurring in coastal and marine ecosystems and adding value where appropriate. Others involve new and emerging technologies such as ocean energy, deep-sea mining and marine genetic resources that are said to hold great potential. It is crucial to have a realistic understanding of the time-frames associated with taking advantage of

The Blue Economy in the Wider Caribbean   241

these opportunities. Developing them will require long-term investment in infrastructure and human technological capacity if WCR countries are to partner successfully with external governments and corporations, and get a fair share of the benefits. Some recommend that external experts be engaged at the prefeasibility level to manage expectations and fully evaluate risks and the probability of success (Whisnant and Ross, 2019).

The WCR is part of a multilevel interconnected global system. Blue Economic growth is being pursued worldwide. International agencies such as the World Bank, Inter-American Development Bank, Asian Development Bank, the Global Environment Facility, the UN Development Programme and big international NGOs are already well into programmatic approaches that can drive regional and national development agendas. It is the responsibility of WCR countries and regional bodies to ensure that these agendas are consistent with and support national and regional agendas rather than driving them in inappropriate directions. The same applies to global corporate entities whose investment the WCR needs, but not at any cost. Consideration must be given to how to maintain an appropriate balance and linkage between blue and green economies that value land-based assets, marine assets and Caribbean people and culture. State and non-state actors will need to be sensitive to global perspectives and proactive in creating a suitable Caribbean intersectoral reality that values nature and recognises power asymmetries in the region (Chapter 3; Voyer et al., 2018). Thinking and planning ahead will allow WCR countries to develop their individual and collective approaches so as to attract and take advantage of what is available in a coordinated comprehensive way rather than ad hoc and piecemeal. It is our hope that this book can contribute to such a coordinated comprehensive approach so that Blue Economic development in the WCR delivers all that is anticipated.

References

Bennett, N. J., Cisneros-Montemayor, A. M., Blythe, J. *et al.* 2019. Towards a sustainable and equitable blue economy. *Nature Sustainability*, 2, November: 991–993.

Cohen, P., Allison, E. H., Andrew, N. L. *et al.* 2019. Securing a just space for small-scale fisheries in the blue economy. *Frontiers in Marine Science*, 6. Available at: http s://www.frontiersin.org/articles/10.3389/fmars.2019.00171/full.

ECLAC. 2019. *Intergovernmentally Agreed Conclusions and Recommendations of the Third Meeting of the Forum of the Countries of Latin America and the Caribbean on Sustainable Development*. Economic Commission of Latin America and the Caribbean, Santiago, Chile, LC/FDS.3/4 ECLAC/RFSD/2019/1, 26 April, 10 pp.

EU/WWF/WRI/EIB. 2018. *Declaration of the Sustainable Blue Economy Finance Principles*. European Commission, World Wildlife Fund, World Resources Institute, European Investment Bank, 2 pp. Available at: http://d2ouvy59p0dg6k.cloudfront. net/downloads/sbefp_declaration___6_aug_2018.pdf.

European Commission. 2019. *The EU Blue Economy Report*. 2019. Publications Office of the European Union, Luxembourg, 205 pp. Available at: https://prod5.assets-cdn. io/event/3769/assets/8442090163-fc038d4d6f.pdf.

Gonzales, A. T., Kelley, E. and Bernad, S. R. Q. 2019. A review of intergovernmental collaboration in ecosystem-based governance of the large marine ecosystems of East Asia. *Deep-Sea Research*, Part II, 163: 108–119.

Mahon, R., Fanning, L. and McConney, P. 2017. Assessing governance performance in transboundary water systems. *Environmental Development*. 24: 146–155. http://dx.doi.org/10.1016/j.envdev.2017.06.008.

OECS Commission. 2019. *Process Framework Report: Coastal and Marine Spatial Plans and Training*. OECS, Castries, St. Lucia, 115 pp.

Pallero Flores, C., Barragán Muñoz, J. M. and García Scherer, M. E. 2017. Management of transboundary estuaries in Latin America and the Caribbean. *Marine Policy*, 76: 63–70.

van Hoof, L., Fabi, G. and Johansen, V. *et al.* 2019. Food from the ocean: Towards a research agenda for sustainable use of our oceans' natural resources. *Marine Policy*, 105: 44–51.

Voyer, M., Quirk, G., McIlgorm, A. and Azmi, K. 2018. Shades of blue: What do competing interpretations of the Blue Economy mean for oceans governance? *Journal of Environmental Policy & Planning*, 20: 595–616.

Whisnant, R. and Ross, S.A. 2019. *Enabling Blue Economy Investment for Sustainable Development in the Seas of East Asia: Lessons on Engaging the Private Sector for Partnership and Investment*. Partnerships in Environmental Management for the Seas of East Asia (PEMSEA), Quezon City, Philippines, 118 pp.

WWF. 2018. *Principles for a Sustainable Blue Economy*. World Wildlife Fund Briefing, Washington, DC, 6 pp. Available at: http://d2ouvy59p0dg6k.cloudfront.net/downloads/wwf_marine_briefing_principles_blue_economy.pdf.

Index

Page numbers in *italics* and **bold** indicate Figures and Tables, respectively.

abyssopelagic communities 36
agricultural nutrients 198–199
air pollution 148
Antigua 133, 233–234n3
aquaculture: development opportunities 123; ecosystem value 37; global growth in 25; inequality and 24–25; production levels 202–203; sustainable expansion 123; value chain analysis 237; *see also* fisheries
Areas Beyond National Jurisdiction (ABNJ) 17
Association of Caribbean States (ACS) 10, 106, 107–108, 115–116n2

Bahamas 17, 133, 136, 161
ballast water management 149–150
Barbados: blue economy policies 10; Coastal Zone Management Unit 67; coastline management 138; government ministry for blue economy 143; green economy scoping study 9; ICZM planning 66–67, **69**; Ministry of Maritime Affairs and the Blue Economy 94; oil and gas industry 17; Public Sector Smart Energy Programme 162; renewable energy programmes 162; ridge to reef projects 139–140; sea defences at Holetown *68*; sea level rise 66–67; tourism 67
Barbuda 133, 231, 233–234n3
bathypelagic communities 36
Belize 67–71, *70*, 219
Beneficiary Pays Principle (BPP) 86, 132
biodegradable materials 206

Biodiversity Beyond National Jurisdiction (BBNJ) 18, 32, 191–192
biogas 205
blended finance 214–215, 224n1
blue bonds 216–217
blue carbon 57
blue economy: activities, industries and growth drivers **144**; as a buzzword 1; CDB definition of 143; countries promoting concept of 1; cross-cutting issues shaping 11–14; development trends 32; economic plans 21–22; financing (*See* financing the blue economy); good governance principle 29–30; government intervention in 79–81; implementation of 14; investment in 5–6, 213–223; justice principle 28–29; key sectors influencing 14–18; managing coastal and ocean resources 13; misapplication of 22; policies 4–5, 10–11; principles 4, 26–31; private-public partnerships 153; qualifying as 207; resilience principle 30–31; response measures **58–59**; strategy 143–144; as sustainable ocean economy 3–4; United Nations and 3–4; unlocking potential for 226–227; well-being principle 27; World Bank and 3–4, 196; *see also* ocean economy
blue economy initiatives: coastal and marine activities as 101; economic opportunities and 21; environmental sustainability and 23; fisheries and 125; governance arrangements and 31–32, 92; investment in 223; national inter-sectoral coordination

244 *Index*

mechanisms (NICs) 96–97; science-based development 240; seabed mining and 25–26

blue levy 220

Blue Natural Capital Financing Facility 221

blue tokens 223, 224

bonds 216–218

British Virgin Islands 220, 227, 229

brown economy 23 *see also* blue economy, green economy

business development, holistic approach to 27

capital stock, baseline economic values for 82–83

Caribbean: as biodiversity hot spot 191; debt to GDP ratios *211*, 227–228; economic challenges in 78–79; economic sectors of 9; governance of 26

Caribbean Biodiversity Fund (CBF) 219

Caribbean Blue Economy financing facility 221–222

Caribbean Community (CARICOM) 9–11, 94, 106, 115–116n2, 166, 192 *see also* Caribbean Regional Fisheries Mechanism (CRFM)

Caribbean Development Bank 10, 16, 143, 206, 232–233

Caribbean Energy Security Initiative 17

Caribbean Green Economic Conferences (CGEC) 9

Caribbean Hotel Energy Efficiency and Renewables initiative 17

Caribbean Natural Resources Institute (CANARI) 9, 27

Caribbean Oceans and Aquaculture Sustainability Facility (COAST) 221

Caribbean Regional Fisheries Mechanism (CRFM) 11, 54

Caribbean Regional Oceanscape Project (CROP) 10–11, 98

Caribbean Sea Commission 108

Caribbean Sea Initiative 107

Caribbean Shipping Association (CSA) 146–147

Caribbean Sustainable Energy Roadmap and Strategy (C-SERS) 157–158

CARIMET Forum 166

Cartagena Convention 13, 44–45, 105–106, 147, 196

Cayman Islands 162

Central American Integration System (SICA) 11, 115–116n2

China 233–234n3

Clarion-Clipperton Zone (CCZ) 182

climate adaptation debt conversion 218

climate change: adaptation strategies 56–58; alternative livelihoods and 56–57; cost of doing nothing 206–207; economic cost of 49; as financing restraint 230–231; fisheries sector and 53–54; hurricanes and 136; living resources impacted by 50–51, **52**; mainstreaming 239–240; marine climate variables 49, **50**; marine ecosystems and 43–44; non-living resources impacted by 51–56; ocean acidification 12; pre-existing vulnerabilities 30; renewable energy sector and 55–56; response measures 57; sargassum seaweed 12; sea surface temperatures and 12, 43; shipping sector and 54–55; tourism and 53, 135–136

climate finance 221

climate proofing sectors 30–31

climate refugees 231

climate variability *see* climate change

CLME Initiative 109

CLME Project: ACS/CSC interactions and 113; direction for 110; LME Governance Framework 110–112; Strategic Action Programme 108, 111–112, 125–126

coastal and marine ecosystems *see* marine ecosystems in the WCR

coastal and marine planning, island systems approach to 13–14

coastal tourism *see* tourism

coastal zone management 56

coastal zone management planning (CZMP) 63–65, 66–71, 138 *see also* integrated coastal zone management (ICZM)

Common Heritage of Mankind (CHM) principle 183, 190–191

common property 80

Commonwealth Blue Charter 185

communication 88

community-based organisations (CBOs) 72–73, **74**

concessional financing 212, 214–215, 227

conservation: Blue Economy trade-offs 81–82; correcting market failures 85;

cost-benefits of 83–85; fiscal policies 85–87
conservation trust funds 219
convergence 224n1
coral disease 42
coral reef ecosystems 38, 43–45, 51, 83, 199, 201–202, 237–238
Corporation for the Sustainable Development of the Archipelago of San Andres, Providencia and Santa Catalina (CORALINA) 73
correspondent banking 228
Costa Rica 10
Covid-19 pandemic 172, 175
cruise tourism: ballast water management 149–150; as casualty in blue economy 229–230; growth of 16, 133–134, 143; port infrastructure and 145–146, 150–151, 229–230
Cuba 170–171

debt finance 211–212
debt for ocean conservation 218–219
deep-sea mineral resources 17–18; demand for 182; economic implications 183; International Seabed Authority 183, 184; investments in 189–190; opportunities for 183–186; risks 189–190; volatile prices of 189; see also polymetallic nodules
deep-sea mining (DSM): CHM principle and 190–191; Commonwealth Blue Charter 185; costs associated with 185; developing states' disadvantage 184–185; in Jamaica 186; pollution from 200–201; polymetallic nodules 184–185; sponsoring state's role in 187–189
deep water drilling 17
deoxygenation 199
development aid 212
development bonds 216–217
development finance 213–215
development impact bonds 217–218
disaster financing 220–221
dive tourism 53
domestic resource mobilisation 219
domestic wastewater 197–198, 205–206
Dominican Republic 135, 139

Eastern Caribbean Regional Ocean Policy (ECROP) 108
Ecologically or Biologically Significant Marine Areas (EBSAs) 36

Economic Commission for Latin America and the Caribbean (ECLAC) 219
economic development: resilience principle and 30–31; risks to 24–25
economic valuation: benefits and measures of **84**; communication and 88; defined 79, 82; of goods and services 12–13; public sector revenues and 86–87; spatial representation of 88–89; value estimates 88
ecosystem-based management 105–106, 109
ecosystems: human wellbeing and 79, 82; measurement and mapping of 78–79; measuring services 82; see also coral reef ecosystems, mangrove ecosystems, marine ecosystems in the WCR
ecotourism 135
energy sector: electricity generation 161; electricity tariffs 156; as fossil-fuel centred 156; see also oil and gas in the Caribbean, renewable energy
energy security 16, 156
energy transition 176
environmental degradation 80–81, 83–85
environmental NGOs 95
environmental sustainability 23–24, 31, 81, 135, 146–150
environmental taxes 86
equitability and social justice 238
eutrophication 51, 199
exclusive economic zones (EEZs) 17–18, 26, 37, 105, 119, 183, 226
ExxonMobil 17, 171, 173

financing the blue economy: access to 231–233; blended finance 214–215, 224n1; blue bonds 216–217; blue tokens 223, 224; challenges to 210–213; climate change as restraint on 230–231; concessional financing 212, 214–215, 227; conservation trust funds 219; debt for nature swaps 218–219; debt to GDP ratios 227; development aid 212–213; development impact bonds 217–218; disaster financing 220–221; domestic resource mobilisation 219; financing mechanisms 153; incubator and accelerator 222–223; innovation networks 222; innovative instruments and mechanisms 213; levies 220;

246 Index

private sector 228–229; public debt 211

fisherfolk 15, 21–23, 28–29, 72, 95, 120, 125–127

fisheries 15; annual production 120; in a blue economy 124–127; climate change and 30–31, 53–54, 121; communities dependent on 120–121; diverse fleets 119–120; ecosystem value 37; enhancing values of 125; equitability and social justice 238; export/import policies 124; future focus of 124–127; governance of 122; growth of 236–237; illegal, unreported, unregulated (IUU) fishing 122–123; importance of 119; institutionalising management of 56; as niche tourism 127; open access 118–119, 122; over-exploitation 122; parametric insurance for 221; production potential 121–122; seafood consumption 202; small-scale fisheries 29, 95; as social safety net 118, 121; sustaining improvement 125–126; threats and challenges for 121–123; value chains 123–124, 126–127; waste reduction 127; *see also* aquaculture

Fisheries Advisory Committees (FACs) 96

Fisheries and Aquaculture Organisation for Central America (OSPESCA) 122

floating power platforms (FPP) 161

Florida-based Cruise Ship Association (FCSA) 229

French Guiana 173

gender equality 99

global energy system 175 *see also* energy sector

Global Maritime Energy Efficiency Partnerships Project (GloMEEP Project) 149

Global Maritime Technology Network (GMN) project 149

global mineral demand *see* deep-sea mineral resources

global warming 43, 148 *see also* climate change

good governance: capital investment and 239; community-based management 238–239; examples of 137; importance of 238–239; marine spatial planning 239; risks to 26

good governance principles 29–30, 97–98, *98*, 99

governance *see* good governance

green bond market 216

green economy 9, 22, 196 *see also* blue economy, ocean economy

greenhouse gas emissions 134, 148–149

Grenada 10, 132

Grenada Sustainable Development Trust Fund (GSDTF) 219, 231

Guyana 172, 173–174, 178

Guyana-Venezuela border dispute 178

Harmful Algal Blooms (HAB) 203

harvest/post-harvest sectors 54

heritage tourism 135

Honduras 10

human wellbeing 79–80, 82, 87

hurricanes 53, 136

hydrocarbons 169, 171, 174

hypoxia 199, 203

ICZM Planning Framework 65

illegal, unreported, unregulated (IUU) fishing 122–123

indigenous fisherfolk 120

industrial effluents 41–42

insurance sector 220–221

integrated coastal zone management (ICZM): Barbados 66–67; in the Blue Economy 71–75; co-management approach to 72–73; community-based organisations (CBOs) 72–73; defined 66; evaluating success of 65; governance arrangements 72–75; implementation stage 65; initiation stage 64; as intersectoral endeavor 72; marine spatial planning 71–72; monitoring stage 65; need for 63–64; regional initiatives for 66; structure of 64–65; *see also* coastal zone management planning (CZMP)

Inter-American Development Bank (IDB) 232

Intergovernmental Oceanographic Commission (IOC) 64, 240

Interim Coordination Mechanism (ICM) 109

International Coastal Clean-up 199

International Convention for the Control and Management of Ships' Ballast Water and Sediments BWM Convention 149

Index 247

International Convention for the Prevention of Pollution from Ships (MARPOL) 147
International Convention on the Law of the Sea Convention (UNCLOS) 184–185
International Maritime Organisation (IMO) 147–150
International Seabed Authority (ISA) 183, 184
International Seabed Disputes Chamber 188–189
Isla de Aves (Bird Island) 177

Jamaica: deep-sea mining 186; deep water drilling 17; exports 131; green economy scoping study 9; marine protected areas of 81–82; mass tourism 135; New World Group 132
justice principle 28–29

Laborie Development Foundation 28, 228
land-based pollution 13, 35, 197–200
Land-based Sources and Activities (LBS) Protocol 196
Large Marine Ecosystem (LME) Governance Framework 99, 110–112
Law of the Sea Convention (LOSC) 176–177
levies 220
Liquefied Natural Gas (LNG) 152
Local Green-Blue Enterprise (LGE) Radar 27
Loran-Manatee natural gas field 179–180

mangrove ecosystems 38, 42, 45, 51, 83
marine-based tourism 236–237
marine climate variables 49, **50**
marine ecosystems in the WCR: anthropogenic stressors 41–44; climate impacts on 43–44, 50–56; coral reefs 38; diversity 36–37; economic benefits of 83; ecosystem services provided by **39–40**; endangered species 45; environmental sustainability and 23–24; habitat restoration 45; health trends 38, 237–238; mangrove forests 38, 42; physical destruction 42–43; reversing degradation of 237–238; seagrass 38, 51; value 37–38
marine pollution 13, 41–42, 201–203, 205
marine protected areas (MPAs) 44–45

marine renewable energy *see* renewable energy
marine resources 56
marine spatial planning 71–72, 126, 239
maritime border disputes 178–179, 230
maritime economy *see* blue economy
maritime industries 28, 150
maritime transportation 146
maritime zones 139–140, 177
MesoAmerican Barrier Reef 36, 70
mesopelagic communities 36
Mexico 10
micro-, small and medium enterprises (MSMEs) 21–22, 31–32
microplastics 51, 199–200 *see also* plastic waste
minerals *see* deep-sea mineral resources
mining and extraction industries 25, 216

national income accounting 87
national inter-sectoral coordination mechanisms (NICs) 72, 92–93, 95–98, 100–101
natural assets 79, 82–83, 87
nature-based micro-enterprises 31 *see also* micro-, small and medium enterprises (MSMEs)
New International Economic Order (NIEO) 183–184
New World Group 132
niche tourism 127
non-climatic stresses 56
Nordic Investment Bank 216
nutrient pollution 41

ocean acidification 12
ocean-based mining/extraction industries 25
ocean economy: defined 1–4; economic value of 144–145; financing of 3; gross revenues 145; industries 2; OECD definition of 2; as precursor to blue economy 1; size of 2, **3**; *see also* blue economy, green economy
Ocean Energy Forum (OEF) 163
ocean eutrophication 12
Ocean Governance and Fisheries (OGF) 98
ocean governance committees (OGCs) 96
ocean grabbing 95
ocean thermal energy 160–165
ocean thermal energy conversion (OTEC) 161

248 *Index*

Official Development Assistance (ODA) 212, 227
offshore mining 200–201
offshore oil and gas industry 17
off-shore wind energy 159–160, 165
oil and gas in the Caribbean 17; frontier provinces of 171; future of 174–176; geopolitical realities of 177–180; history of 170–171; hydrocarbon potential 171; Loran-Manatee natural gas field 179–180; maritime border disputes 178–180; petrochemical sector 170; polluting activities of 200–201; risks of 177–180; shift from onshore to offshore 176–177; state of 171–172; subsea petroleum development 176–177; volatile nature of 172
open access 118–119, 122
Organisation for Economic Co-operation and Development (OECD) 2, 5, 214–215, 222, 228
Organisation of Eastern Caribbean States (OECS) 10–11, 22, 72, 106–109, 112–113, 115–116n2, 143
OTEC International 161–162
over-harvesting 42

parametric insurance 190, 220–221
Partners for Inclusive Green Economy 26–27
peak oil 169
pelagic communities 36
People Managing Oceans 29
PetroCaribe 16, 156
plastic waste 42, 51, 195, 199–200, 203–204 *see also* solid waste, waste management
Polluter Pays Principle (PPP) 86
pollution: agricultural nutrients 198–199; air 148; bacterial loads 42; costs associated with 80–81; of cruise ships 134; economic impact of 196, 197; land-based 13, 35, 197–200; marine 41–42, 201–203; ocean-based 147–148, 200–201; of offshore mining 200–201; polluter pays principle 237; population growth and 195; urban wastewater 197–198; *see also* plastic waste, solid waste
polymetallic nodules 183–184 *see also* deep-sea mineral resources
poverty alleviation 22–25, 124, 191
private-public partnerships 153
private sector financing 228–229

PROBLUE (World Bank) 219, 232–233
Protected Areas Conservation Trust (PACT) 219
public debt 211, 224
public goods 80
public-private partnerships 153
Puerto Rico 133

recreational fishers 119, 120
recycling 203–204, 205–206
regional fisheries management organisations (RFMOs) 122, 125–126
regional ocean governance: challenges to 114; fragmentation of 104; framework 110–112; lessons learned 113–115; promotion of 106; supporting aspects 113–114; *see also* CLME Project
renewable energy 16–17; biogas 205; case study 165; challenges to 167; climate change and 55–56; environmental impact 165; floating power platforms 161; growth of 237; knowledge sharing on 166; land-based 158; marine-based 158, 237; ocean thermal energy 160–165; off-shore wind energy 159–160, 165; policy development 157–158, 167; sea water air conditioning 163–164; technology solutions 158–159; tidal energy 162–163; from waste 205; wave energy 163, 164–165
resilience principle 30–31
ridge to reef projects 139–140
Rystad Energy 173

sargassum seaweed 12, 51, 203
science-based development 240
seabed mining 9, 25, 237
seagrass ecosystems 38, 51
sea level rise 43, 44, 54–55, 66–67
sea surface temperatures 12, 43
sea water air conditioning (SWAC) 163–164
sediments 41
Seychelles 216
ship-based pollution 13
shipping and transport 16; ballast water management 149–150; capacity-building investments 152; climate variations and 54–55; container port throughput 145; environmental sustainability 146–150; greenhouse gas emissions 148–149; maritime pollution 147–148; port infrastructure and

150–151; regional gateway container demand 145; sustainability of 153; waste disposal 147–148, 200; *see also* cruise tourism
small island development states (SIDS): interdependencies of 93; transitioning to Blue Economy 93–94, 101–102
small-scale fisheries 29, 95
social development risks 24–25
solid waste 41, 42, 51, 199–200 *see also* plastic waste, waste management
Specially Protected Areas and Wildlife (SPAW) Protocol *see* Cartagena Convention
sport fishing 139
subsea petroleum development 176–177
subsistence fishers 119
Suriname 170–171, 172, 174
Sustainable Blue Economy Conference 10
sustainable ocean economy *see* blue economy, ocean economy

The Nature Conservancy (TNC) 216–217
tidal energy 162–163
Toucan Trail 135
tourism 9, 15–16; accommodations sector 202; Barbados 67; blue economy and 136–137, 140; challenges to 53; climate extremes impacting 53; coral reefs and 201–202; Covid-19 pandemic and 175; cruise ship visitations 16, 133–134; development of 131–133; economic value of 133; ecotourism 135; environmental threats 135–136; fisheries value chains and 123; GDP contribution 133; governance framework 137; gross revenues 37, 201; growth of 236–237; heritage tourism 135; hurricane season 53; importance of 134–135; inequality in 24; international air travel 132–133; leveraging economic opportunities 138–139; marine-based 236–237; marine energy development and 157; marine pollution and 201–202; recreational fishing 120; reliance on marine ecosystems 37; sea level rise and 136; small-scale businesses 138–139; sport fishing 139
transboundary governance: approach to 109; weakness in 105–106
transboundary linkages 100–101

travel and tourism *see* tourism
Treaty of Basseterre 108
Trinidad and Tobago: exports 131; hydrocarbons economy of 174; natural gas economy of 170, 174; as oil producer 170, 172; tourism economy of 133
trust funds 219
Tullow Oil 172, 173

UNDESA 94
UN Economic Commission for Latin America and the Caribbean (ECLAC) 145
UN Environment Caribbean Environment Programme 10
United Nations 3, 105
United Nations Environment (UNE) 64
United Nations General Assembly 107
up-cycling marine litter 205
urban wastewater 197–198, 205–206

value chains 123–124, 237
Venezuela 16, 156, 177, 178–179

waste disposal 13, 147–148
waste management: biodegradable materials 206; challenges to 203–206, **204**; circular economy for 203–204; nutrient recovery 205–206; up-cycling 205
wastewater 197–198, 205–206
Waters, Neil 135
wave energy 163, 164–165
well-being principle 27 *see also* human wellbeing
Western Central Atlantic Fishery Commission (WECAFC) 122
Wider Caribbean region (WCR): biodiversity of 11–12; biogeographic regions if 119–120; coastal population 37; ecosystem-based management 105–106, 109; ecosystem diversity 35–37; ecosystem health 38; ecosystem value 37–38; fisheries and 15; garbage discharge requirements 148; geography of 35–36; geopolitical complexity of 105; heterogeneity of 36–37; intergovernmental arrangements 108; natural assets 37–38; ocean governance cluster *107*; policy coordination mechanism 114; regional

250 *Index*

governance framework 110–112, *112*; regional ocean governance 104, 106; regional political integration organisations 115–116n2; transboundary issues affecting 105–106; *see also* marine ecosystems in the WCR

wind energy 159–160

wind power 149

wind turbines 159

women: gender equality for 99; maritime industries and 28; post-harvest activities 120

World Bank 3, 94, 219, 232–233

World Tourism Organisation (UNWTO) 152

World Travel and Tourism Council (WTTC) 133

Zaedyus well 173